MASSACHUSETTS

AND

RHODE ISLAND

TRAIL GUIDE

7th edition

Also available from AMC Books

MASSACHUSETTS

AND

RHODE ISLAND

TRAIL GUIDE

7th edition

APPALACHIAN MOUNTAIN CLUB BOOKS
BOSTON, MASSACHUSETTS

Cover photograph: *Bash-Bish Falls* by Daniel Stone, AMC Boston Chapter Outdoor Photography Committee.

Distributed by The Globe Pequot Press, Inc. Old Saybrook, CT

Library of Congress Cataloging-in-Publication Data

Massachusetts and Rhode Island trail guide. — 7th ed.
    p.   cm.
    Revised ed. of: AMC Massachusetts and Rhode Island trail guide. 6th ed. c1989.
    ISBN 1-878239-39-2
    1. Hiking—Massachusetts—Guidebooks. 2. Hiking—Rhode Island—Guidebooks. 3. Trails—Massachusetts—Guidebooks. 4. Trails—Rhode Island—Guidebooks. 5. Massachusetts— Guidebooks. 6. Rhode Island—Guidebooks. I. Appalachian Mountain Club. II. Title: AMC Massachusetts and Rhode Island trail guide.
GV199.42M47   1995
917.44—dc20   95-7959
                                                            CIP

The paper used in this publication meets the minimum requirements of the American National Standard for Information Sciences—Permanence of Paper for Printed Library Materials, ANSI Z39.48–1984.∞

Due to changes in conditions, use of the information in this book is at the sole risk of the user.

Printed on recycled paper using soy-based inks.

Printed in the United States of America.

10 9 8 7 6 5 4 3   98 99

Contents

Introduction

Ask some hikers from southern New England for their favorite trails, and most likely you'll hear about the White Mountains of New Hampshire, or perhaps Vermont's Green Mountains or Maine's mighty Katahdin. Too often overlooked are the abundant hiking opportunities in their own backyard.

While southern New England trails may lack the high elevations of their northern counterparts, they do not lack scenic beauty. Lakes and waterfalls, cliff-top vistas, forests and bogs, old stone walls and cellar holes, are all to be seen here. Whether you're looking for a short day hike or a chance to test out your new tent on a weekend outing, there is a surprising variety of trails to try in southern New England.

If you live in Massachusetts or Rhode Island, local trails provide a convenient alternative to lengthy car trips. Within an hour's drive of Boston, Worcester, or Providence, there's an interesting hike that you've never done. And don't worry about having to give up peace and quiet. You'll probably find that most of the trails in this book are less crowded than your favorite White Mountain footpath.

Hiking in southern New England is also significantly less hazardous than hiking in northern New England. Here the areas are generally less remote, and the differences in latitude and elevation combine to make the weather much less severe. As a result, the hiking trails of this region are ideal for families with young children, and for novice hikers seeking an opportunity to learn and practice backcountry skills.

As with so many other natural resources, it is also important that we not take these hiking trails for granted. As a result of development and suburban sprawl, many trails described in previous editions of this guide no longer exist or cannot be easily accessed. As open space disappears, so do our opportunities for healthy outdoor recreation.

ABOUT THIS BOOK

This book provides comprehensive coverage of the nine major trail systems in the Massachusetts/Rhode Island area:

Appalachian Trail—Perhaps the nation's most famous footpath, the AT travels over 2,000 mi. between Springer Mt. in Georgia and Katahdin in Maine. Eighty-five miles are located in Massachusetts, running north and south through the Berkshires. It reaches many of the highest summits in the region, including Mt. Greylock, the highest point in Massachusetts.

South Taconic trails—The 16-mile South Taconic Trail and a network of connecting trails provide access to the southern end of the Taconic Range in the southwest corner of Massachusetts. These trails extend into New York and Connecticut.

North Taconic trails—The northern end of the Taconic Range, straddling the Massachusetts–New York border, has a network of more than 100 miles of hiking trails, including the 21-mile Taconic Skyline Trail and the 29-mile Taconic Crest Trail.

Metacomet–Monadnock Trail—This 98-mile trail follows the ridges bordering the Connecticut River Valley, including the exceptionally scenic Holyoke Range and Mt. Tom. It begins on the Connecticut state line (where it connects with the Metacomet Trail) and ends on the summit of Mt. Monadnock in southern New Hampshire (where it connects with the Monadnock–Sunapee Greenway Trail to Mt. Sunapee).

Midstate Trail—The 92-mile Midstate Trail runs north and south across Massachusetts through the woodlands, open fields, and isolated hills of Worcester County. It traverses Mt. Wachusett, the highest peak in eastern Massachusetts. At its northern terminus in Ashburnham, just south of the New Hampshire border, it connects with the Wapack Trail leading into New Hampshire.

Warner Trail—The 30-mile Warner Trail stretches from Canton, Massachusetts, just south of Boston, through the woodlands of Norfolk County to Diamond Hill State Park in Rhode Island.

Blue Hills Reservation—Close by Boston's skyscrapers is the MDC's Blue Hills Reservation. An extensive network of hiking trails, bridle paths, and woods roads connects hills, ponds, rock quarries, and other scenic attractions.

Arcadia Management Area—Located just a short drive southwest of Providence, the Arcadia Management Area includes Rhode Island's largest network of hiking trails. This system connects with the Narragansett Trail system in Connecticut, making even longer hikes possible.

Bay Circuit Trail—The region's newest trail system is still under development. When completed, the Bay Circuit Trail will extend in a 200-mile arc around the Boston metropolitan area, from Newbury and Ipswich on the north shore to Duxbury and Kingston on the south shore.

For each of these trail systems, this book describes the main trail as well as the principal side trails and connecting trails.

In addition to these major trail systems, this guide also includes descriptions of many other significant trails throughout the region. Although these other trails stand apart from the major trail networks, and thus may be of less interest to the overnight backpacker, they still offer excellent choices for interesting day hikes.

Some of the trails described in this book are suitable for cross-country skiing during winter, but others are not. Where a trail is not specifically maintained for skiing, skiers should not rely on a hiking guidebook description to determine its suitability. Rather, they should hike the trail before snow falls with an eye toward grades, overhead clearances (which can be a problem if there is significant snowfall), and the amount of brush on the footpath (which can be a problem if there is little snow cover).

Some of these trails also provide excellent mountain biking opportunities. Mountain bikers must observe local restrictions. Where biking is permitted, riders should take care to avoid colliding with hikers, and suspend biking during wet weather in areas where trail erosion is a problem.

At the back of this book, a directory lists various organizations that can provide more detailed information about these hiking trails, including changes that have occurred since the book's publication.

In addition to the trails described in this book, there are many other, smaller trails in parks and reservations of interest to the outdoor enthusiast. These are more apt to be considered nature walks than hikes, and generally these trails are well marked and easy to follow. There are many fine books devoted to these shorter trails, among them *Nature Walks in Eastern Massachusetts, Country Walks Near Boston,* and *Short Nature Walks on Cape Cod and the Vineyard.* We have not attempted to duplicate their efforts in this volume.

A final note: The trails that we use and enjoy are only in part the product of government agencies and public nonprofit organizations; there is ultimately no "they" responsible for providing the hiking public with a variety of interesting, convenient, well-maintained trails. Small groups care for many of the trails. Funds for trail work are scarce, and unless hikers contribute both time and money to trail maintenance, the diversity of trails available to the public is almost certain to decline. Every hiker can make some contribution to the improvement of the trails, if nothing more than pushing a fallen branch off the trail rather than walking around it. These trails belong to us, and without our participation in their care they will languish. Many of the organizations mentioned in this book, including the AMC, will welcome you as a volunteer.

ABBREVIATIONS

The following abbreviations are used for the major trail maintenance organizations in this region:

AMC	Appalachian Mountain Club
ATC	Appalachian Trail Conference
BCAMC	Berkshire Chapter, Appalachian Mountain Club
FOW	Friends of the Wapack
LHA	Laurel Hill Association
MaDEM	Massachusetts Department of Environmental Management
MAS	Massachusetts Audubon Society
MDC	Metropolitan District Commission
NCAMC	Narragansett Chapter, Appalachian Mountain Club
NETC	New England Trail Conference
PAOC	Phillips Academy Outing Club
RIDEM	Rhode Island Department of Environmental Management
SEAMC	Southeastern Massachusetts Chapter, Appalachian Mountain Club
THC	Taconic Hiking Club (Troy, NY)
TR	The Trustees of Reservations
WOC	Williams Outing Club

AMC MASSACHUSETTS AND RHODE ISLAND TRAIL GUIDE COMMITTEE

Editor
Jeff Wulfson

Assistant Editors
Cindee Campisano
William R. (Russ) Whitney

Mary Kingsley
Rolf Larson
Bruce Dunham
Ellen Pippenger
Pat Boland
Patrick Fletcher
Harold Sharff
Dennis Skillman

Cartographers
Pat Dunlavey
Robert Halloran

The editors wish to thank the many members of the AMC's Berkshire, Worcester, Boston, Southeast Mass., and Narragansett chapters who volunteered hundreds of hours of time to field check the trail descriptions for this edition. Thanks also to AMC Books Editor and Publisher Gordon Hardy; Production Manager Carol Tyler; Publishing Assistant Carrie Loats; and Greylock Visitor Center staff Tim Loveridge and Dennis Regan.

SECTION 1
Preparing for Your Hike

Hiking is a sport of self-reliance. A hiker assumes complete responsibility for his or her well-being in the backcountry. Part of the challenge of hiking is gaining the knowledge and experience needed to complete a trek safely even in the face of changing or unexpected conditions.

This section discusses briefly the most important elements in preparing for a hike. Numerous books devoted exclusively to hiking skills provide more detailed information, but written texts can never substitute for in-the-field experience.

TRIP PLANNING

Use the trail descriptions in this book to select a trail whose length and difficulty match both your skills and the time available for your hike. When hiking with a group, base the level of difficulty on the abilities of the least experienced member of the group.

In many areas you can combine two or more trails to provide an interesting loop walk. On other hikes, it will be necessary to return via the same trail. If you are planning a car shuttle to allow an end-to-end hike, allow extra time for driving and finding both trailheads.

The hiking times shown in this guidebook are estimates of the time an average hiker will require under normal weather conditions. Your hiking speed may be faster or slower. After you have done a few hikes and compared your hiking times to those listed in the book, you will get a sense for the necessary correction factor. Carrying a heavy pack or traveling in a large group will generally require additional time. If you decide to hike a steep trail in the opposite direction to the guidebook description, you will also need to adjust your time estimate.

Plan to start your hike as early in the day as possible. Know what time sunset will be, and start early enough to allow for a return while there is still plenty of daylight. *Remember that dusk and darkness come quickly in the woods.* Hiking after dark, even with flashlights (which frequently fail), makes finding trails more difficult and crossing streams hazardous. For longer hikes in more remote areas, it is also important to let someone know your route and when you expect to be back.

With appropriate clothing, you can hike all of the trails in this book safely and comfortably during the spring, summer, and fall. For spring hikes, be alert to the possibility of difficult brook crossings due to the runoff from melting snow. Winter hiking, with the additional hazards of snow and extreme cold, requires special skills and preparation. Under such conditions, novice hikers should always hike with more experienced trekkers.

Another seasonal hazard is the fall hunting season. If you are planning a hike during hunting season, try to select trails through those parks and reservations where hunting is prohibited. Where hunting is permitted, wear hunter's orange clothing or a bright red hat, vest, or coat.

Obtaining the latest weather forecast for the area is another essential element of trip preparation. Keeping in mind the vagaries of New England weather ("if you don't like the weather, wait a minute"), prepare for the worst possible conditions. During your hike, constantly re-assess the weather forecast by observing clouds and wind, and be prepared to change the itinerary as necessary.

WHAT TO TAKE

Here is a typical list of useful day-hiking gear for southern New England:

Sweater or jacket	Light plastic tarp
Rain gear	Guidebook
Wool hat	Compass
Mittens	Map
Extra socks	Whistle
Snacks	Waterproof matches

Water	Trash bag
First-aid kit	Personal medications
Pocket knife	Insect repellent
Flashlight	Sunglasses
Cord	Sunscreen

Make adjustments to this list based on the trail to be hiked and the expected weather. A short hike on a well-travelled trail on a clear July day will obviously have different needs from a long hike in a remote area on an overcast November day.

For groups hiking on longer day trips in remote areas, one sleeping bag can provide an additional element of safety, as it can be used to keep an injured hiker warm while awaiting assistance.

On all but the warmest days, dress in layers, so that you can remove clothing as needed due to exertion and warming temperatures. The top layer should be wind and water resistant to protect against inclement weather.

Avoid cotton clothing on all serious hikes because it loses all insulating value when wet. Even in dry weather, cotton clothing can become quickly saturated with perspiration, which at the least is uncomfortable and at the worst can lead to hypothermia in cooler conditions. Wool and polypropylene are probably the two most popular fabrics for hiking clothes.

For all but the shortest hikes, hiking boots are much preferred over sneakers or walking shoes, as they provide better traction and ankle support and help to reduce foot fatigue. Both leather and synthetic boots are available. Leather boots must be properly broken in before being worn on an extended hike. For younger children, hiking boots are not always practical due to financial considerations. If it is necessary for children to hike in sneakers, choose shorter trails with smoother footing.

FOLLOWING A TRAIL

Getting lost is probably the novice hiker's single greatest fear. Basic navigational skills are not difficult to learn, and with them even the beginning hiker should have the confidence to complete a hike successfully. But to be a true expert requires not only learned skills but also a "woods sense" that can only be acquired through experience.

Most of the time a trail can be followed simply by alert observation. Look for worn footing or footprints, evidence of trail maintenance (such as water bars or sawn logs), or gaps in the undergrowth. But keep in mind that many of the trails described in this book are not heavily traveled or regularly maintained, so the pathway may not always be obvious. At unmarked junctions, it helps to know the general direction in which the trail should be heading.

Blazes, typically geometric shapes painted on trees, are used to mark some trails. In some cases, the blaze might be a metal cut-out attached to a tree or a mark painted on the rocks underfoot. If you have been following a well-blazed trail and the blazes suddenly stop or change color, you might have taken a wrong turn. Pay particular attention to a double blaze mark, which indicates a sudden change in trail direction.

Trail descriptions in a guidebook are an important source of information, but don't assume that they are infallible. Trails may be re-routed, abandoned, or closed by landowners; signs may be stolen or fall from their posts; bridges can get washed away; storms may cause blowdowns or landslides, which can obliterate a trail for an entire hiking season or longer. Trail guides are an aid to planning, not a substitute for careful observation and good judgment.

Maps are another important navigational tool, but as with trail guide descriptions, they cannot be relied upon blindly. They are especially useful in trip planning and in visualizing the overall "lay of the land." Be prepared to find discrepancies between a trail's plotted location and its actual location. This book includes trail maps for some of the major hiking areas in the region. The back of the book lists sources for obtaining maps for other areas.

A compass, and knowledge of how to use it, are important complements to trail maps. The best compass for hiking is the protractor type: a circular, liquid-filled compass that turns on a rectangular, clear plastic base. Excellent compasses of this type, with leaflets that give ample instructions for their use, are available for less than $10. Novice hikers in the woods sometimes forget which is the north end of the compass needle. It is therefore helpful to scratch a reminder somewhere on the case. Compass directions in the text and on the maps give true north rather than magnetic north. In Massachusetts and Rhode Island the compass will point about 13 degrees west of true north.

One common source of confusion in trail navigation arises from crossings of other trails and streams. Because most of this region was settled at one time, many small paths and woods roads cross most hiking trails. Many of these are not documented in trail descriptions and on maps. Conversely, intersecting paths that are mentioned may become so overgrown as to be missed entirely. A brook crossing might be deemed too small to be mentioned in the trail guide. At the same time, a documented watercourse might happen to be dry and therefore go unnoticed by the hiker.

The careful hiker will use all sources of information—visual observation, guidebook descriptions, and maps—to chart progress. Try at all times to have at least a general sense of your location, which can be confirmed or corrected when reaching major, unmistakable landmarks such as bridges, signed trail junctions, or summits.

Even the most experienced hiker will occasionally lose a trail. This is not necessarily a serious matter, even in remote areas. First, stop. Go back over your route slowly, marking it clearly, until you pick up a sure indication of the trail. The point of your first mistake will usually be evident then. If, after a careful and deliberate search, you are still unable to find the trail, your course of action will depend on whether you are on a mountain. If you are on a mountain, you can usually reach a road in a few hours or less simply by going downhill until you reach a brook or stream and then following it downward. If you are in comparatively level woodland, you can take a compass bearing and follow it until you reach a road. If you know your general position on the map, your selection of the direction to travel will be easier.

When traveling with a group on a hard-to-follow trail, each hiker should stay within sight of the next person. If the group becomes too spread out, it is almost inevitable that at least one person will take a wrong turn. In no event should slower hikers be allowed to lag behind. If you do become separated from your group, do not wander. Stay in one place and signal your location from time to time by three blasts on a whistle or three loud shouts.

BACKCOUNTRY SAFETY

Safe hiking means knowing how to avoid dangerous situations as well as being prepared to deal with problems when they do occur. Basic first-aid training is an essential part of that preparation.

Falls and injuries. The remoteness of the backcountry makes any injury a potentially serious matter. Be alert to places where the footing might be poor, especially on steep or wet sections of trail. In autumn, wet leaves are a particular hazard. Remember that carrying a heavy pack can affect your balance. Do not try rock climbing without proper training and equipment.

In case of serious injury, apply first aid and keep the injured hiker warm and comfortable. Then take a minute to assess the situation before going for help. Backcountry evacuation is usually measured in hours, not minutes, so don't rush. Write down your location, the condition of the injured person, and any other pertinent facts. At least one person should stay with the injured hiker while two others go for help. (For this reason, it is safest to hike in the backcountry in groups of four or more.)

Insects and ticks. Black flies and mosquitoes are as much a part of New England woodlands as maple trees, and are more a nuisance than a hazard. Various commercial preparations are available which may or may not have any useful repelling effect. Bee stings are a significant concern for any hiker who is allergic to them; be sure to carry appropriate medication. Lyme disease is spread by deer ticks, which can be found anywhere in the region but are most prevelent in coastal areas. Minimize your exposure by wearing long-sleeved shirts and long pants tucked into your socks, and use insect repellent on the clothing. Lyme disease is treated easily but can become extremely serious if not treated; symptoms include fever, chills, and circular rashes.

Brook crossings. Rivers and brooks are often crossed without bridges, and it is usually possible to jump from rock to rock; a hiking staff or stick is a great aid to balance. Use caution; serious accidents have resulted from hikers (particularly solo hikers) falling on slippery rocks and suffering an injury that rendered them unconscious, causing them to drown in relatively shallow streams. If you need to wade across (which is often the safer course), wear your boots. Note that crossings that may only be a nuisance in summer may be a serious obstacle in cold weather, when your feet and boots must be kept dry. Higher waters, which can turn innocuous brooks into virtually uncrossable torrents, occur in the spring as snow melts, or after heavy rainstorms, particularly in the fall when trees drop their leaves and take up less water. Avoid trails with potentially dangerous stream crossings during these high-water periods. If you are cut off from a road by a swollen stream, it is better to make a long detour. Rushing currents can make wading extremely hazardous. Flood waters may subside within a few hours, especially in small brooks. It is particularly important not to camp on the far side of a brook from your exit point if the crossing is difficult and heavy rain is predicted.

Drinking water. The pleasure of quaffing a cup of water fresh from a pure mountain spring is one of the traditional attractions of the mountains. Unfortunately, the presence of cysts of the intestinal parasite *giardia lamblia* in water sources throughout the region is probably pervasive. It is impossible to be completely sure whether a given source is safe, no matter how clear the water or remote the location. The symptoms of *giardiasis* are severe intestinal distress and diarrhea, but such discomforts can have many other causes, making the disease difficult to diagnose accurately. The safest course for day hikers is to carry their own water, allowing 2 quarts per person for a full-day hike, more in hot weather. If it is necessary to use sources in the woods, it must be treated. The traditional methods of boiling or treating water with iodine are effective but somewhat inconvenient. A popular choice today is one of the newer, light-weight filtering units, which produce tasty, safe drinking water. Although somewhat expensive, these filters are durable and easy to use.

HIKING ETHICS

Every hiker has an obligation to respect and care for the outdoor environment, so that it may be enjoyed by all who follow. As you hike, try to adhere to these rules of the outdoors:

- Carry out everything you carry in. Go a step further: carry out any litter that you find.

- Don't pick the flowers and avoid gathering wood. Even dead trees have their place in the ecosystem and should be left undisturbed.

- Stay on the trail, and try to avoid muddy places where foot traffic can cause erosion.

- Bury human waste at least 200 feet from the trail and any water sources. The careless disposal of human waste is probably the principal cause of the spread of *giardiasis*.

- Do not light a campfire unless it is an emergency. If you are using a backpacking stove, do not leave it unattended.

- If you wish to listen to music, wear headphones. But it's much more interesting to listen to the sounds of the forest. Preserve the forest sounds for others to enjoy.

- The propriety of bringing pets (especially dogs) on hikes is the subject of much debate. But everyone can agree that pets should never be allowed to be a nuisance to other hikers.

- On overnight trips, travel in small groups and practice low-impact camping. Use established campsites if available; if not, camp well away from trails and streams and avoid using sites that have been used previously by campers.

Many trails described in this book lie on private property and exist only with the consent of the landowners. Hikers must respect the rights of these owners and observe all the customary rules of courtesy if the privilege of trail walking on private property is to continue. In particular, do not bend or break fences; leave gates open or closed, as you found them; and respect no trespassing signs. Never camp on private land without permission.

SECTION 2
Natural History of Southern New England

The face of the land in southern New England has changed dramatically over time. The region has experienced the rise of colossal mountain ranges, submergence under seas, the roar of ancient volcanoes, and the slow, relentless scouring of advancing ice-age glaciers. The evolution of life has followed these changes, painting ever-changing scenes on the geologic canvas.

Human history spans only a small fraction of earth history, yet we have been able to exert an impact upon the land that rivals nature's great forces. It is only recently that we have begun to understand our place in the earth's delicate environmental balance.

GEOLOGY

Within the rocks of southern New England lie clues to more than half a billion years of earth history. For much of the last 200 million years, New England has been relatively quiet from a geologic perspective. During this time period there have been no volcanoes or mountain-building events, and few earthquakes. Instead, erosional forces have dominated in shaping the land. Prior to this period of erosion, the geologic record tells of major mountain-building events, earthquakes and uplift, and volcanic activity. Great mountain ranges, rivaling today's Himalayas, were once present here.

Current understanding of geologic history is based upon the theory of plate tectonics. The earth's crust is composed of many mobile plates of two basic varieties, continental and oceanic crust. Land masses are typically formed from the less-dense continental crust; the oceans are underlain by more-dense oceanic crust. These plates move on a weak and somewhat plastic layer located just beneath the earth's crust. As the plates move slowly over geologic time, collisions occur in mountain-building events called orogenies. Elsewhere plates are split apart; this is known as rifting.

9

Evidence of past orogenic and rifting events can be seen in the rocks of New England.

The first major event that can be interpreted from the rocks of southern New England is known as the Taconic orogeny. The Berkshire Hills are remnants of the great mountain range created by this event. What is today New England was once largely over-lain by an ocean known as the Iapetus. Land that now forms the Adirondack Mountains and Hudson Highlands bounded its western shore more than 500 million years ago. Sediments from the land were deposited into the Iapetus and eventually formed the rocks now found in the Berkshires. Trilobites, small aquatic arthropods related to modern lobsters, insects, and spiders, were abundant dur-ing the time in which these rocks were formed.

Between 500 and 440 million years ago, the Iapetus Ocean began to close as plates that now form parts of Europe approached the proto-North American continent. As the tectonic plates were compressed, the sedimentary rocks beneath the Iapetus were folded and crumpled upward to form a great mountain range known as the Taconics. These mountains may have been more than 10,000 feet high. Within the mountains, heat and pressure transformed the sed-imentary rocks into metamorphic rocks. These are the rocks we see in the Berkshires today.

Between 440 and 410 million years ago, a period of erosion reduced the lofty Taconic Mountains down to sea level, and oceans once again covered much of New England. Closure of the Iapetus continued, and several small land masses were added to the North-east approximately 400 million years ago. One of these masses, known as Avalonia, can be traced today from southeastern Con-necticut and Rhode Island, through southeastern Massachusetts, northward through parts of coastal Maine and Newfoundland. Sim-ilar rocks and fossils appear in the Carolinas and parts of England and Wales, but nowhere else in the world. All of these areas are thought to be part of the original Avalonian land mass, which is classified by geologists as a suspect terrane. No one is quite sure where it came from!

Around 380 million years ago, a major collision of two continents occurred as the northern Iapetus closed. The protocontinents
of North America and Northern Europe collided, resulting in the
Acadian orogeny. Avalonia and other small land masses crumpled
between the two continents, and a majestic mountain range formed.
Many of New England's granites were formed as compressed rocks
miles beneath the surface melted under extreme heat and pressure.
The granites we see today are mere roots of the tremendous mountains formed during the Acadian orogeny.

At the time of the Acadian orogeny, many fish swam in the
seas, and plants covered much of the land. Animals such as insects
and amphibians began to evolve terrestrial lifestyles. From approximately 360 to 290 million years ago swamplands covered much of
present day North America. As swampland plants died and
decayed, organic material accumulated and was buried. Over time,
these materials were transformed into coal. Deposits of coal from
this time period include the extensive coal beds of Pennsylvania.
Isolated locations in southeastern Massachusetts and Rhode Island
also contain coal.

The Alleghenian orogeny began approximately 290 million
years ago and was the most recent mountain-building event to
affect New England. The Acadian orogeny had brought together
North America, Greenland, Europe, and Asia into one land mass
called Laurasia. Similarly Africa, South America, Australia, and
Antarctica had formed the supercontinent Gondwana, which collided with Laurasia from the south during the Alleghenian orogeny.
A continuous, towering mountain range ran from New England to
Texas during this period, marking the boundary of the former continents. When Siberia collided with Europe during the latter part of
the orogeny, all of the earth's land masses joined to form one
supercontinent called Pangea. This orogeny had a greater impact in
the southern Appalachians than in New England, but the rocks of
Massachusetts and Rhode Island show evidence of folding and volcanic activity from this period.

Sediments were deposited into the Narrangansett Basin located
in Rhode Island and southeastern Massachusetts, and into localized

areas near Boston, at the end of the Alleghenian orogeny. Sediments carried down from the towering mountains in the west into lowland swamps were buried, and eventually formed the rocks that we see in these areas today. Iycophyte trees, giant horsetails, ferns, and primitive conifers (cordaites) dominated the swamps. During this same time period, reptiles and seed-bearing plants evolved. But 245 million years ago a mass extinction occurred, eliminating nearly half of all animal and plant species. The cause of this extinction, which marked the end of the Paleozoic Era, is still a mystery.

During the Triassic and Jurassic periods of the Mesozoic Era (245 to 145 million years ago) the supercontinent Pangea began to break up and the Atlantic Ocean began to emerge. A mechanism called rifting separated the continents; the actual rift zone that formed lies in the center of the Atlantic Ocean and is still active. Evidence of a failed rift zone appears in the rocks of the Connecticut River Valley.

As a rift zone forms, tension pulls the rocks apart, causing faulting, and volcanic activity brings molten rock to the surface from deep within the earth. The basalt cliffs of Mt. Tom and the Holyoke Range are spectacular examples of these lava flows.

The characteristic red sedimentary rocks of the Connecticut Valley are interbedded between the lava flows. These rocks contain iron, and their red color indicates that they were deposited in dry desertlike conditions. These sediments contain dinosaur footprints and other fossils that can be observed at many locations along the Connecticut River.

After the catastrophic episodes of volcanic activity and faulting during the Triassic and Jurassic periods, New England entered a period of relative quiescence dominated by erosional forces. The lack of significant tectonic activity continues today. The towering mountains of early times were eroded to a relatively flat plain. More resistant rocks formed the highlands we know today. Mt. Greylock and Wachusett Mountain are examples of these erosional remnants.

During the Cretaceous Period (145 to 65 million years ago), mammals, birds, and flowering plants, including grasses, evolved.

Dinosaurs still dominated the earth. Sixty-five million years ago, at the end of the Cretaceous Period and the Mesozoic Era, mass extinctions again occurred. Some scientists believe that these extinctions were caused by a meteorite impact that temporarily altered world climate.

The last major geologic event to shape the landscape of southern New England began approximately 3 million years ago, during a time of global climate change. World-wide temperatures dropped, initiating the growth of glaciers that have advanced and retreated eighteen to twenty times since then. In New England, the last and greatest glacial advance began 70,000 years ago, reached its greatest extent approximately 20,000 years ago, and ended approximately 10,000 years ago. At the glaciers' peak advance, 5 million square miles of ice covered Canada, much of the northeast, and parts of the plains and northwest. So much of the earth's water was locked up in the glaciers that sea level in northern Europe and North America was at least 350 feet below present levels. Species were displaced southward or became extinct.

Glaciers scoured the landscape, smoothing and rounding mountains and valleys, creating hills and depressions, and depositing piles of unsorted rock and soil debris known as till. Existing valleys were widened by the glaciers and became U-shaped. Meltwater streams and lakes contained glacial outwash, another type of glacially deposited soil. Evidence of the glaciers' advance and retreat can be seen throughout New England.

Rocks fell from the downslope side of hills and mountains as the glaciers overrode them. This can be seen in the asymmetrical profile of bedrock hills. Many hills and mountains in New England have gradual, smooth sides facing north-northwest and steep rugged sides to the south-southeast.

Scouring of the bedrock left linear marks—called striations—throughout New England. Striations formed as the glaciers dragged rocks trapped beneath tons of ice over the bedrock surface. In some areas, the ice overlying New England may have been as much as one mile thick. Striations are indicators of the localized flow direction of the ice.

Boulders left behind as the glaciers melted and receded are known as glacial erratics. It is important to realize that glaciers advanced as the weight of additional ice and snow pushed them downhill and southward. They retreated by merely melting away as the climate began to warm. Some erratics traveled hundreds of miles carried by the glaciers. These boulders are common throughout New England. Well-known examples include Plymouth Rock; Cradle Rock in Barre, Massachusetts; Doane Rock near Eastham on Cape Cod; and the boulder fields of Cape Ann.

Other evidence of glacial activity includes eskers, drumlins, moraines, and kettles. Eskers are long, sinuous hills or ridges, formed as streams flowed through tunnels beneath the glacial ice and deposited gravel and cobbles. Eskers are common in much of eastern and central New England, but rare in Connecticut and Rhode Island. In the Boston area, you can see esker deposits in the Auburndale section of Newton, to the east of the Charles River near the intersection of the Massachusetts Turnpike and Route 128.

As the glaciers overrode the countryside they deposited streamlined, oblong hills of till known as drumlins. These hills are common in Massachusetts; notable examples include Bunker Hill, Breed's Hill, Dorchester Heights, and many of the Boston Harbor islands. Generally, drumlins are aligned in the same direction (often northwest to southeast) and indicate the local direction of ice flow.

Moraines are piles of boulders and debris deposited at a glacier's edge. Terminal moraines mark the furthest extent of glaciation. Southeastern New England provides classic examples of terminal moraines. The glaciers' furthest extent is marked by an undulating line of moraine deposits running east to west through Nantucket, Martha's Vineyard, and Long Island. From this line, an unbroken sheet of ice extended 2,000 miles northward. As the glaciers retreated they stopped temporarily, forming a second line located farther north through Cape Cod, the south side of Buzzard's Bay, and westward through southwestern Rhode Island. The Mid-Cape Highway (US 6) follows the crest of the Sandwich Moraine from Sagamore to Dennis.

As the ice receded, moraines often functioned as dams, and temporary lakes formed. One of the largest in New England was Lake Hitchcock, which lasted several thousand years. Lake Hitchcock filled the Connecticut River Valley from Middletown, Connecticut, northward well into Vermont and New Hampshire. The Connecticut River Valley was first widened into the characteristic U-shape of a glaciated valley as the glaciers advanced, and then was partially filled by sediments deposited in glacial Lake Hitchcock.

Beyond the glacier's edge stretched the outwash plain where streams of water carried finer-grained materials from the melting ice. Often, large chunks of ice would break off as the glacier retreated and become buried in the outwash. As these isolated chunks melted they formed holes called kettles. Today kettles typically remain as ponds or bogs. They are particularly common on Cape Cod and in southeastern Massachusetts. One well-known example is Thoreau's Walden Pond in Concord, Massachusetts.

As the glaciers melted and receded, sea levels rose and modern shorelines formed. New England has once again entered a geologically quiet period dominated by erosional forces.

POST-GLACIAL FORESTS

The development of today's temperate forest in New England spanned thousands of years after the retreat of glacial ice. Species that were displaced southward migrated back to the north at different rates depending on their adaptability to the changing climate.

Pollen evidence indicates that tundra plants were the first to return. These species include low-growing grasses, sedges, willows, alders, dwarf birches, flowering herbs, mosses, and lichens. Some of these plants still exist on New England's highest mountain tops, including the Presidentials and Katahdin.

Approximately 12,500 years ago, larger trees of the Boreal Forest began to displace the tundra species. Conifers, primarily spruce and pine, dominated, but cold-tolerant deciduous trees, such as alders, birches, poplars, and arctic willows, were also present. As more diverse plant species returned, herbivores were again able to survive here and life began to diversify. Grazing animals such as bison, elk, and moose entered the region, and birds, bears, and numerous small mammals returned. The first clear evidence of human habitation by Paleo-Indians is from this time.

A dramatic change occurred approximately 9,500 years ago, as the climate grew significantly warmer. Spruce gave way to the deciduous hardwoods and the pines of the temperate forest. A great variety of food-rich species including beeches, hickories, oaks, pines, and hemlocks began to thrive. The diversity of plant and animal life increased and human populations continued to grow.

By 6,000 years ago, most of the species found today in New England were present. The climate was warmer and drier, temperate deciduous forests covered the land, and seasonal migration patterns for fish and birds were generally established.

CIVILIZATION AND ITS IMPACT

The Archaic Period of North American civilization lasted from 9,000 to 3,000 years ago. During this time period the indigenous people of the region relied on the choice hunting and gathering areas along the shores of New England's estuaries. The Woodland Period marked the final 3,000 years of civilization prior to colonization by the Europeans. During this period there was great diversification among native cultures. People established semi-permanent villages and developed both pottery and agriculture. They used fire to clear the fields, and cultivated corn, beans, squash, and gourds. They gathered roots, herbs, berries, and nuts. During this period the post-glacial coastlines stabilized, and shellfish beds became another food resource.

Woodland Indians were the first to encounter the Europeans as they reached the eastern shores of North America. Europeans were first drawn to the Grand Banks fisheries in the early sixteenth century. Then came the fur traders, who had devastating effects on the native populations. Native American lifestyles had developed over 12,000 years to take advantage of the cycle of seasons and the diversity of plants and animals in the different climates, terrains, and forest types of the region. The arrival of the Europeans brought a shift from seasonal hunting and fishing to trapping and trading.

Although the indigenous peoples had cleared some land for planting, the European colonists greatly accelerated the agricultural process. When agriculture reached its peak in the mid-nineteenth century, approximately 23 million acres (slightly more than half) of New England's land area had been cleared.

By the late 1800s, demographics began to shift as the Industrial Revolution attracted more people to the cities and towns. In 1840, less than one-fifth of New England's population resided in towns; by 1880, more than half of the population lived in towns and cities of 2,500 or more people. Slowly, fields and pastures were abandoned and the forests began to recover. Yet even today, only small pockets of old-growth forest remain in New England. It will take hundreds of years for the previously cleared forests to reach full maturity again, and in some areas, like the moorland of Nantucket, the forest has not yet returned.

Clearing of the forests resulted in the destruction of habitat. It is now known that the extinction of the passenger pigeon resulted largely from the clearing of beech trees for farming. As forest habitat shrank and human populations grew, the numbers of larger predators such as wolves, bears, and wildcats, which require large ranges, dwindled.

The settlers altered the landscape not only by clearing trees, but also by introducing nonnative species of plants, animals, and disease. Although the introduced species included cultivated plants and domesticated animals which provided some benefit to the people of New England, the unintentional introduction of diseases such as typhoid fever, diptheria, measles, tuberculosis, and chicken pox devastated indigenous populations. Until the early 1900s, the American Chestnut was a dominant species in southern New England; an exotic fungal blight all but eradicated this species which now survives only as a small understory tree or shrub. A more recent introduction is the gypsy moth which seriously threatens the White Oak.

The latest chapter is still being written, as the pressures of suburban sprawl and unregulated development in the second half of the twentieth century have caused the loss of much forest land and open space throughout the region. At the same time, more than a century of industrial and post-industrial pollution has also taken its toll on the health of the region's natural resources.

TODAY'S FOREST LANDS

The forests of eastern North America can be roughly divided into three major areas. The dividing lines are determined by the region's three major climatic factors—latitude, altitude, and proximity to the ocean. Canada contains the pure, coniferous Boreal Forest. The Mixed Deciduous Forest is located in the south, extending as far north as south central and southeastern Massachusetts. The Transition Forest is in between, covering northern New England as well as the highlands of western and north central Massachusetts.

The Transition Forest, like the Boreal Forest to the north, has numerous lakes and bogs. This forest is sometimes referred to as the White Pine–Hemlock–Northern Hardwood Forest. The most common conifers are the eastern white pine and the eastern hemlock; other conifers include the eastern aborvitae and a variety of spruce species. Deciduous trees are also abundant in the Transition Forest, including beech and a variety of birch and maple species. This forest is the northern range limit for hickories, most oaks, and the American beech. The red maple is the most common tree east of the Mississippi, and is well known for its spectacular fall colors. The sugar maple is also common in the Transition Forest. Paper birch, yellow birch, and American basswood are also common. Roots of the basswood (and sometimes spruce) were used by the Eastern Abenaki as sewing twine for birch bark canoes. Fruit trees—apple, cherry, pear, and plum—are somewhat less common.

Common understory trees found in the Transition Forest include the mountain maple, the striped maple, the American mountain ash, and the hop hornbeam. Bushes and shrubs grow beneath the understory. Two of the most common types of shrubs are witch hazel and a variety of viburnums. Highbush blueberries thrive in swamps and moist woodlands; lowbush blueberries are found in bogs, especially in alpine zones. Shadbush, a member of the rose family often found in wetlands, produces white flowers early in spring when anadromous fish like the alewife and shad (herring) run. Ferns and clubmosses are common. A small sampling of the herbaceous plants of this region includes starflower, milkworts, wood lily, twinflower, baneberry, violets, trillium, and clematis.

The Transition Forest is home to a wide variety of animal species. Mammals include the white-tailed deer, moose, black bear, gray wolf, beaver, fox, raccoon, opossum, porcupine, mink, muskrat, fisher, squirrel, and numerous small rodents. There are more than a dozen species of raptors including eagles, owls, and hawks. Songbirds and grouse, sparrows and waterfowl, all inhabit these forests. Diverse insects can be found in the soil, on the vegetation, and in the air and waters of this region.

Moving southward, there is a gradual transition through central and southern Massachusetts from the Transition Forest to the Mixed Deciduous or Oak–Hickory Forest. This forest type predominates in eastern Massachusetts and Rhode Island. Its major tree species are oaks, hickories, and ashes. Until the early 1900s chestnut trees were also common, but as previously mentioned, these have been largely eradicated by an exotic fungal blight. Other common deciduous trees include beech, maple, and yellow poplar. Conifers are less common in the Mixed Deciduous Forest than in the Transition Forest. Pines and hemlocks are the most common evergreen species.

Understory trees include dogwoods, mountain laurel, American holly, striped maple, hop hornbeam, and magnolias. Shrubs such as spicebush, witch hazel, pawpaw, wild hydrangea, mountain pepperbush, and Hercules' club, grow beneath these. Hundreds of species of wildflowers exist in the Mixed Deciduous Forest including trout lily, lady's slipper, bloodroot, wood poppy, larkspur, phacelia, spring beauty, trillium, violets, and mints. Ferns and clubmosses are also abundant here.

The Mixed Deciduous Forest zone is also marked by extensive wetlands, both coastal and inland. Some notable examples are the Ipswich River Wildlife Sanctuary, with its extensive estuary and salt marshes; Belle Island Marsh, a salt marsh just north of Boston; and Ponkapoag Pond in the Blue Hills, with its quaking sphagnum bog.

Many of the same animal species occur in both the Transition Forest and the Mixed Deciduous Forest. Fewer large mammals, such as bear, deer, and moose, are found in the Mixed Deciduous Forest of southern New England. Human populations are generally more dense here. Birds and smaller mammals are abundant, and many species of amphibians, including frogs and salamanders, are found in the Mixed Deciduous Forest.

The Sand Plain Community is marked by a very different type of forest, the Scrub Oak–Pitch Pine Forest. The south shore of Cape Cod, the islands to the south, and the coast of Rhode Island are dominated by extensive dune fields, barrier beaches, sand spits, and salt marshes. These contrast the rugged, rocky shores found in northern New England. Although the Sand Plain Community is primarily a coastal environment, it also exists inland in areas of southeastern Massachusetts and northern Rhode Island.

Although this region has the mildest climate in New England, poor soils provide a substrate for only the hardiest plant species. Forested areas are dominated by scrub forest of oak and pitch pine. Pitch pine has a deep root system, which allows it to obtain water from the dry, sandy soils and stand up to the strong winds of the Cape and the islands. Trees of the sand plain forests are also adapted to survive frequent fires; the pitch pine has excellent post-fire, stump-sprouting ability. Bear oak occurs as a shrub or small tree and is the most common oak across much of Cape Cod. Post oak reaches its northern range limit on the Cape and is present here as a smaller tree than in the heart of its range farther south. American holly is an understory tree on the sand plain that reaches the northern limit of its range in Quincy, Massachusetts. Other trees of this community include the dwarf chestnut oak, the black oak, scarlet oak, and the white oak. In localized areas, the soil is better and a wider variety of trees is present, including species of birch, sassafras, maple, locust, and beech.

Huckleberry, lowbush blueberry, sheep laurel, and wintergreen are all shrubs found in the sand plains. Bearberry is one of the most common shrubs on Cape Cod. Sweet fern, inkberry, and broom crowberry are also found here. One of the more unusual plants found in the southern New England sand plain community is the prickly pear cactus, the only cactus found in the east.

Scotch heath and heather—introduced by settlers—now dominate Nantucket's moorlands. This area was cleared of its natural forest for use as pasture land. When the pastures were abandoned, the poor soils failed to support reforestation, and the heath and heather, well adapted to the difficult environment, spread.

Wet areas in the sand plain regions generally support bogs in which a variety of heaths thrive. Cranberry bogs are abundant in southeastern Massachusetts and on the Cape, and produce the region's chief agricultural crop. The largest and best cranberries are harvested from the American cranberry which is found only in North America. A variety of other wetland communities are present in the sand plain region. Cape Cod National Seashore, which is known for its magnificent sand dunes and beaches, also encompasses salt marshes, heath swamps, red maple swamps, and an American white cedar swamp.

The Sand Plain Community is home to diverse groups of wildlife. White-tailed deer, raccoon, beaver, skunk, fox, and small mammals inhabit the forests. The many types of wetlands provide habitats for waterfowl, amphibians, insects, fish, turtles, and snakes. The beaches and marshes are home to a wide variety of seabirds, including a number of threatened and endangered species.

Massachusetts and Rhode Island comprise a region of diverse flora and fauna, a varied landscape of many ecological communities. From the mountains of the Berkshire region to the sands of

Cape Cod, the trails of Massachusetts and Rhode Island offer opportunities to experience the region's diversity. This introduction to the natural history of southern New England provides only a brief overview of the forces that have shaped the land and influenced its inhabitants. The back of this book lists some of the many excellent field guides and reference books that can provide more detailed information on these topics.

SECTION 3
The Berkshires

The Appalachian mountains pass through Berkshire County, the westernmost section of Massachusetts. The Berkshires, as the area is popularly known, consist of extensive woodlands and hills, with the highest mountain peaks of southern New England. The Connecticut River watershed lies to the east, and to the west, the Hudson River. Recreational and cultural attractions abound, making the area a popular vacation destination for travelers from both the Boston and New York metropolitan areas.

The Berkshires are comprised of three major ridges, all running generally north and south. The Taconic Range lies west of the Housatonic and Green rivers, overlapping the New York State border. The Hoosac Range is located to the east. The Mt. Greylock Range, capped by Mt. Greylock—the highest point in Massachusetts—runs between the northern parts of these two ridges.

Maps are available from various sources for the areas described in this section; see the appendix for further information. Also refer to the Greylock and Southwestern Massachusetts trail maps included with this guide.

APPALACHIAN TRAIL (BCAMC)

Ninety miles of the 2,158-mi. Appalachian Trail (AT) are located in Berkshire County. The trail enters Massachusetts from Connecticut near Sages Ravine, passes over Mt. Race, Mt. Everett, and Mt. Bushnell, and then across the Housatonic Valley. Passing over June Mtn., the trail climbs steeply to East Mtn. State Forest and descends to MA 23. After skirting Benedict Pond in Beartown State Forest, it ascends to the headwaters of Swan Brook and descends through Tyringham Valley. Beyond Tyringham, the trail touches Upper Goose Pond, crosses the Massachusetts Turnpike (I-90) at Greenwater Pond, and enters October Mtn. State Forest, where it leads over Becket Mtn. and Bald Top. After climbing Warner Hill, the trail runs through continuous woods, except for the towns of Dalton and Cheshire, ascends Saddle Ball Mtn. and Mt. Greylock, passes over Mt. Fitch and Mt. Williams, and again descends. After crossing Hoosac Valley at Greylock, a suburb of North Adams, the AT reaches the Vermont line, where it continues north as both the AT and the Long Trail.

For day hikers, the AT serves as an access route to a number of Berkshire summits. It can be entered at numerous highway crossings, usually marked with signs. (*Caution:* Always park cars well off the highway.) Through hikers should consult volume 3 of the Appalachian Trail Conference's trail guide series, *Appalachian Trail Guide to Massachusetts–Connecticut.* A number of shelters are located on or near the trail, generally one-day's hike apart. Off-trail accommodations are within easy reach.

The Berkshire Chapter of the Appalachian Mountain Club maintains the Appalachian Trail in Massachusetts. Hikers interested in participating in these maintenance efforts are always welcome; contact the AMC for more information.

White rectangular paint blazes, 2 in. by 6 in., indicate the trail route; double blazes warn of abrupt changes in direction. Most side trails are blue-blazed. The exact trail routing is always subject to change, as a result of ongoing efforts to run the trail through protected corridors and to avoid paved road sections. Relocations are always well marked in the field.

Appalachian Trail: Massachusetts–Connecticut Line to Jug End Rd.

The southern end of the Massachusetts section of the AT is not directly accessible by car. The closest access point is where East St. in the town of Mt. Washington crosses the Connecticut state line. Just south of the state line, a woods road (Northwest Rd.) leads east for about 0.7 mi. to the AT.

The trail crosses into Massachusetts and descends into scenic Sages Ravine. The trail follows the south side of the brook, passing a designated campsite on the left (across the brook) located entirely on state-owned land. At 1 mi. north of the state line, the trail turns sharply left and begins a gradual ascent up the ridge leading to Mt. Everett. Before crossing Bear Rock Stream (a path on the right leads a short distance to a falls and a designated campsite with an outhouse), the trail continues north through an open hemlock grove in a gradual ascent of the ridge.

After emerging from the woods, the trail reaches the south end of open cliffs, which offer outstanding views in a sweep from northeast to southeast. The trail follows the cliff edge rather closely for 0.3 mi. and passes a large cairn on the left. It reaches the summit of Race Mtn. (2365 ft.) and begins a descent to the saddle between Race Mtn. and Mt. Everett. It soon intersects with the blue-blazed Race Brook Trail on the right in the saddle between Race Mtn. and Mt. Everett. (The Race Brook Trail leads 0.5 mi. to the top edge of Race Brook cascade, where five falls combine to make a stunning cascade of several hundred feet. *Caution:* The descent is very steep. MA 41 is 0.8 mi. beyond. Trailhead parking is available where the trail meets MA 41.) The AT turns left and begins to ascend the south slope of Mt. Everett. This ascent is rocky and fairly steep. Use caution in wet conditions.

The fire tower on the summit of Mt. Everett (2602 ft.), no longer in service, is closed to the public. The summit offers extensive views in all directions: Monument Mtn. and Mt. Greylock to the north, and East Mtn., Warner Mtn., and the Housatonic Valley to the east. To the south are Race Mtn. and Bear Mtn., while to the west are Mt. Frissell, Alander Mtn., Mt. Darby, and, in the distance, the Catskills.

At the base of the fire tower, the AT turns sharply right and begins to descend. The trail enters an abandoned road formerly used to service the tower. After about 50 yd., the AT leaves the road, continues straight ahead down an embankment, and enters the woods. (At this point, the old service road turns sharply right. About 100 yd. away is a poorly maintained stone shelter and parking area. Camping is not permitted at the shelter, which leaks during a heavy rain.) The trail continues down past a register box and enters onto a gravel road. The trail turns left and about 100 ft. along crosses the road and enters the woods on the right.

Continuing the descent, the trail enters Guilder Pond Picnic Area (2042 ft.) with a pond close by (accessible by car from East St.). The trail turns sharply right at the picnic area past some outhouses. A side trail that circles Guilder Pond soon enters from the left. The trail descends a short pitch, crosses a brook, and turns left. A side trail to Glen Brook Shelter exits on the right. The AT then begins a gentle descent along the east slope of Mt. Undine (2203 ft.) and turns sharply left. (At this point, the blue-blazed Elbow Trail intersects from the right. The Elbow Trail leads 1.5 mi. southeast to Berkshire School and MA 41.) Soon the AT begins a gradual ascent to reach the summit of Mt. Bushnell (1834 ft.). The trail crosses two intermediate peaks and reaches Jug End summit at the north end of the ridge, where there is a spectacular view. After a gradual descent from Jug End summit, the AT reaches a crest of rock outcrops with extensive open views to the northwest and southeast. Mt. Greylock is clearly visible to the north. The trail turns sharply right and shortly begins a steep descent over rock ledges. Use caution when the trail is wet. The descent moderates a little as the trail approaches Jug End Rd.

Appalachian Trail: Massachusetts–Connecticut Line to Jug End Rd.

Distances from the Massachusetts–Connecticut Line
    to Sages Ravine and campsite: 0.7 mi. (20 min.)
    to Bear Rock Falls and campsite: 1.4 mi. (1 hr.)
    to Race Brook Trail: 4.2 mi. (2 hr. 50 min.)
    to summit of Mt. Everett: 4.9 mi. (3 hr. 45 min.)
    to Glen Brook Shelter: 6 mi. (4 hr. 45 min.)
    to Elbow Trail: 6.7 mi. (5 hr. 15 min.)
    to summit of Jug End: 8.4 mi. (6 hr.)
    to Jug End Rd.: 9.5 mi. (7 hr. 10 min.)

Appalachian Trail: Jug End Rd. to US 7

To reach the trailhead, from the junction of MA 41 and MA 23 take MA 41 south to Jug End Rd. on the right. The trail crosses Jug End

Rd. at a small roadside turnout. At 0.1 mi. south, a spring is piped to the roadside, and the trail soon crosses a stone wall in the middle of a mature white-pine forest. Upon reaching an open pasture, the trail crosses another stone wall and traverses 100 yd. of wet pasture before coming to MA 41. At 1.1 mi. the trail passes along a fenced pasture and crosses a farm brook. A gradual ascent brings the trail along a woods road atop a ridge. It crosses a series of bog bridges at 1.6 mi. on the way to higher ground and another ridge. The trail drops off this hemlock ridge to the east and follows an old, wet, grassy road through the next swamp. At 2.4 mi. another series of bog bridges leads the trail to South Egremont Rd. The trail goes south on South Egremont Rd., passing over Hubbard Brook. The trail goes south on South Egremont Rd., passing over Hubbard Brook. At 3.0 mi. is an historic marker indicating the last battle of Shays' Rebellion of 1787. Turn left onto a grassy farm road just past the stone monument and into open fields. Cut across fields to the woods and follow along the edge of the fields to the right with excellent views of Mt. Everett to the southwest. At 3.5 mi. leave fields and cross the small hill. Descending the hill, turn right onto a woods road at 3.8 mi. Follow the road to open fields and continue straight ahead along edge of field, eventually curving to the left and cross West Sheffield Road at 4.2 mi. The trail follows the edge of a swamp, crosses it on a long set of bog bridges and at 4.7 mi. crosses railroad tracks. Descend the embankment and cross the field to Rte. 7 at 4.8 mi. (*Note:* This section of the trail may be relocated to avoid the portion on South Egremont Rd.)

Appalachian Trail: Jug End Rd. to US 7
Distances from Jug End Rd.
>   *to* MA 41: 0.9 mi. (20 min.)
>   *to* US 7: 4.8 mi. (2 hr.)

Appalachian Trail: US 7 to MA 23
The trail crosses Rte. 7 about 3 mi. south of Great Barrington. (Parking is not allowed on Rte. 7) Leaving the east side of the highway, the trail follows a grassy farm road which soon curves right past a small pond and over a stream on a bridge at 0.2 mi. The trail imme-

diately enters a field and goes left to the Housatonic River where it takes a right and continues along the bank through a series of fields. At 0.9 mi. the trail takes a left on Kellog Rd., crosses the Housatonic, and at 1.0 mi. reenters the woods on the north side of the road. At 1.1 mi. the trail enters a field and turns right along the edge until it curves along and follows Kellog Rd. to its intersection with Boardman St. at 1.3 mi. It enters the woods across from Boardman St. and reaches height-of-land. At 2.4 mi. the trail bears right onto an old woods road and continues 250 ft. after crossing a brook. Homes Rd. intersects at 2.8 mi., and the trail bears left diagonally across the road for 100 ft. and then turns right into the woods. The trail turns left onto an old woods road, ascends a ridge, and soon takes a sharp right at the end of the relocation onto the old trail. At 3.7 mi. it crosses a deep cleft in a glacial boulder (there is a spring at the bottom of the cleft) and descends sharply around a split glacial boulder. The trail begins a moderate-to-steep ascent at 3.9 mi. to attain the top of a ridge. For the next 0.4 mi. several exposed ledges afford fine views to the south and west. The Catskills are clearly visible, and the Taconic Range, with Mt. Everett (2602 ft.) dominating, lies west across the Housatonic Valley.

The trail passes a small spring in a gully at 4.2 mi. and soon reaches a large boulder at the south end of East Mtn. This exposed location offers more good views, especially to the south. The AT makes a sharp turn left, passes an obscure woods road leading left, and begins to cross undulating terrain, never getting far from the rim of a steep slope on the right. At 6.4 mi. is the short side trail to Tom Leonard Shelter. The trail then descends ledges with views into Ice Gulch and crosses Lake Buel Rd. at 7.5 mi. After crossing numerous horse trails and Shore Camp Rd., a broken dam across the outlet of Lake Buel Swamp is crossed at 8.1 mi. Rte. 23 is rached at 8.4 mi.

Appalachian Trail: US 7 to MA 23

Distances from US 7

> *to* Boardman St.: 1.3 mi. (30 min.)
> *to* Holmes Rd.: 2.8 mi. (1 hr. 30 min)
> *to* Tom Leonard Shelter: 6.4 mi. (4 hr.)

to Rte. 23: 8.4 mi. (5 hr. 30 min.)

Appalachian Trail: MA 23 to Tyringham

To reach the trailhead, from Monterey go 5 mi. south on Rte. 23, or take Exit 2 from the Massachusetts Turnpike and drive 5 mi. south on US 20 to MA 23.

From MA 23 on the Monterey–Great Barrington line the trail crosses an open field, then leaves the gullied road for higher ground to the west. At 0.5 mi. the new trail joins the old trail and drops toward an intermittent stream gully. After climbing an old hillside pasture, the trail descends gradually to a red maple swamp at 1 mi. On bog bridges and stepping stones, the trail arrives at Blue Hill Rd. A steep boulder-field ascent brings the trail to the top of a cliff with potential views of East Mtn. State Forest. Soon the trail goes by an old circular charcoal pit and then along a ridge to the junction with the old trail. At 1.7 mi. the trail leaves the woods road, turning left onto a cut trail and soon crossing a paved service road. The trail crosses the stream outlet at the south end of Benedict Pond, then turns left (side trail to privy and phone). At 2.2 mi. it crosses a bridge and turns right onto a wide trail. With terraced ledges on the right, it begins a sharp ascent to a formation known as The Ledges and turns sharp right to cross the outlet of a beaver dam.

The trail follows the edge of The Ledges offering fine views of East Mtn., Warner Mtn., Mt. Everett, and the distant Catskills. It soon turns left away from the ridge and begins a moderate to sharp descent. After crossing a series of brooks and a woods road, the trail begins an ascent. A good spring is located at 3.3 mi. on the right, and 150 ft. farther along on the right a side path leads to Mt. Wilcox South Shelter, located 200 ft. uphill from the trail. (There is a spring off the side path to the shelter.) The trail continues sharply uphill and after a steady climb reaches a fieldlike plateau with good views south at 4 mi. At 4.5 mi. the trail crosses the outlet to a beaver pond, following the east shore of the pond, then turns sharply right to join the old trail. At 5.1 mi. the trail reaches a brook; Mt. Wilcox North Shelter is located 70 ft. to the left. The brook is an uncertain source of water during the dry season.

Here the trail turns sharp left onto a relocated section and descends steadily off the ridge to the north. At 5.8 mi. the trail crosses Beartown Mtn. Rd. (dirt) as it passes through some swampy areas, then ascends a white-pine ridge. A steep zig-zag descent down the north side, crossing Fernside Rd. (dirt), leads to a gas pipeline crossing at 9.5 mi. The trail follows Hop Brook for a short distance, then crosses a barbed-wire fence onto the Tyringham Cobble Reservation (TR). The trail slabs around the south side of Cobble Hill; at 10.7 mi. a side trail leads left to the summit. Descending from Cobble Hill, Jerusalem Rd. is crossed at 11 mi. In a hemlock grove at 11.3 mi. the trail crosses Braided Brooks, and shortly thereafter it crosses a pipeline right-of-way. The trail follows fences and hedgerows around a wet field and crosses Hop Brook at 10.7 mi., soon reaching Main Rd. in Tyringham.

Appalachian Trail: MA 23 to Tyringham
Distances from MA 23
to Benedict Pond: 2 mi. (1 hr.)
to The Ledges: 2.6 mi. (1 hr. 20 min.)
to Mt. Wilcox South Shelter and outhouse: 3.3 mi. (2 hr.)
to Mt. Wilcox North Shelter: 5.1 mi. (3 hr. 30 min.)
to Tyringham: 12.1 mi. (7 hr.)

Appalachian Trail: Tyringham to US 20 (Jacob's Ladder Highway)

The trail begins on US 20, 5 mi. east of Lee. From Main Rd. in Tyringham 0.9 mi. east of the town center, the trail climbs over a knoll and an old field plateau. At 1.9 mi. it descends steeply over cobbles to unpaved Webster Rd. At 2.2 mi. it crosses an inlet to Knee Deep Pond. After going through a hemlock grove and some girdled timber stand improvements, the trail passes a short side trail at 3.4 mi. (The side trail leads 0.1 mi. to a spring.) At 4.3 mi. the trail enters Goose Pond Rd., where there is room to park three or four cars. The road continues 3 mi. east to MA 8.

The trail passes by a stone wall, with a house visible on the right, and soon crosses a small brook. The trail parallels another stone wall with abundant ferns and ground pine, leading to a marsh and pond on the right. The trail enters a hemlock forest, crosses a log bridge over the outlet of a pond, then ascends slightly through a deciduous forest. It ascends over some big rocks and at 5.4 mi. passes the Upper Goose Pond sign and starts to descend very steeply. The trail levels off and bears right around the east end of Upper Goose Pond, which is now visible. Just beyond, at 5.9 mi., there is a spring near the trail. This is designated a "Natural Area," and no fires are permitted. (A caretaker is on duty.) The trail bears left at a double blaze (do not walk straight up the hill) and crosses the inlet to Upper Goose Pond at 6.2 mi. The trail passes an old chimney and Mohhekennuck plaque at 6.7 mi.

At 7 mi. the trail turns sharply right at the junction with a side trail to Upper Goose Pond cabin and campsite (0.5 mi. farther along the side trail). At 8.2 mi. the AT crosses the Massachusetts Turnpike (I-90) on a foot bridge and at 8.6 mi. intersects US 20. Lee is 5 mi. west. Exit 2 of the Massachusetts Turnpike (I-90) is located in Lee, with bus connections to Boston and Pittsfield just beyond. Cars may be parked on US 20, 0.3 mi. west of the trail crossing.

Appalachian Trail: Tyringham to US 20 (Jacobs Ladder Highway)

Distances from Tyringham

    to trailhead on Goose Pond Rd.: 4.2 mi. (1 hr. 50 min.)

    to side trail to Upper Goose Pond camping area and cabin: 7 mi. (3 hr. 30 min.)

    to US 20: 8.6 mi. (5 hr. 15 min.)

Appalachian Trail: US 20 to Pittsfield Rd.

The trailhead is located on US 20, 5 mi. east of exit 2 of the Massachusetts Turnpike and the town of Lee. Starting on the north side of US 20, the trail passes under a high-tension line at 0.2 mi. The trail levels off, turns right, and ascends gently. At 0.7 mi. it crosses paved Tyne Rd. (leading right 3.5 mi. to Becket on MA 8 and left 0.9 mi. to US 20). The trail reaches the summit of Becket Mtn. (2180 ft.) at 1.3 mi., where a register box is nailed to a tree. Several concrete footings indicate that a tower stood here at one time. After about 0.5 mi. there are views to the south of the hills around Goose

Pond, and at 2.3 mi. the trail reaches the overgrown summit of Walling Mtn. (2220 ft.). The descent is over a rocky trail. At 2.8 mi. on a relocated section of the trail on the west side of Finerty Pond, the trail soon takes a sharp left next to the pond. After skirting the pond on stepping stones, the trail turns north away from the pond.

At 3.8 mi. the trail crosses a logging road and joins the old trail. At 4.4 mi. the trail passes a fast-moving brook on the right. It then intersects unpaved County Rd. at 5.4 mi., which is passable by automobile and provides space for parking. (A right turn leads 5 mi. to Becket on MA 8.) The trail turns right and then left into the woods. It then begins a steep ascent up a gullied trail to the overgrown summit of Bald Top Mtn. (2040 ft.) at 5.6 mi. The trail soon crosses a motorcycle trail, and at 6.9 mi. it crosses an underground cable right-of-way. After crossing a small brook, there is a short side trail to the left for October Mountain Lean-to.

Cross the abandoned West Branch Rd. at 7.9 mi. (Right leads 0.6 mi. to Pittsfield Rd. and old Washington Town Hall.) From here to Pittsfield Rd. the trail is mostly level. At 9.3 mi. the trail intersects an unpaved service road for the Pittsfield Water Company and turns right. A short distance along is Pittsfield Rd. (paved). Pittsfield is 8 mi. north. Cars can be parked along this road.

Appalachian Trail: US 20 to Pittsfield Rd.

Distances from US 20

  to Tyne Rd.: 0.7 mi. (30 min.)
  to summit of Becket Mtn.: 1.3 mi. (1 hr.)
  to summit of Walling Mtn.: 2.3 mi. (1 hr. 30 min.)
  to Finerty Pond: 2.8 mi. (1 hr. 45 min.)
  to County Rd.: 5.4 mi. (3 hr. 30 min.)
  to summit of Bald Top Mtn.: 5.6 mi. (3 hr. 40 min.)
  to October Mtn. lean-to: 7.8 mi. (5 hr.)
  to Pittsfield Rd.: 9.4 mi. (6 hr. 15 min.)

Appalachian Trail: Pittsfield Rd. to Dalton

The trail begins on Pittsfield Rd., 5 mi. from Becket and 8 mi. from Pittsfield. The trail continues from Pittsfield Rd. to unpaved Beech Rd. and immediately turns left into the woods. It crosses a small stream at 0.6 mi., then at 1.6 mi. passes over a stone wall to cross a bridge over a stream at 2.1 mi. After ascending beside an overhanging 30-ft. cliff, the trail turns sharply left on top of the ridge. At 3 mi. it crosses Blotz Rd. (Left leads 6 mi. to Pittsfield; right leads 1.3 mi. to MA 8.) The trail continues to the top of Warner Hill (2050 ft.) at 3.9 mi., with views to the west and north including Mt. Greylock, then turns sharply left. The actual summit is marked by a cairn a few feet off the trail to the right. The trail then descends through a beautiful area of ferns, then crosses telephone lines at 4.8 mi., after which it might become muddy. At 6.5 mi. it crosses under high-tension lines, where there is a good view to the west. A short distance along, a side trail to the Kay Wood Shelter intersects. At 6.9 mi., the trail crosses Grange Hall Rd. and then follows a stream, crossing it once before slabbing steeply to the summit of Day Mt. at 7.7 mi. Descend along a mossy ledge followed by a more gradual descent through open woods to railroad tracks at 9.0 mi. Use caution on these active tracks. Proceed down the Depot St. extention, cross Housatonic St. and continue down Depot. St. to the intersection with Rte. 8 at 9.4 mi. Turn left onto Rte. 8 and at 9.6 mi. reach the juntion of Rts. 8 and 9.

Appalachian Trail: Pittsfield Rd. to Dalton

Distances from Pittsfield Rd.

> *to* Blotz Rd.: 3 mi. (1 hr. 30 min.)
> *to* summit of Warner Hill: 3.9 mi. (2 hr.)
> *to* Grange Hall Rd.: 7 mi. (4 hr.)
> *to* MA 8/MA 9 (Dalton): 9.6 mi. (6 hr.)

Appalachian Trail: Dalton to Cheshire

Cross Rte. 9 and leave the highway onto a cul-de-sac of High St. Follow High St. west and at 0.9 mi. cross Park Ave. onto Gulf Rd. At 1.0 mi. turn right into the woods. The trail ascends ridges as it follows along the Dalton–Lanesboro line and at 4.3 mi. passes under a powerline. At 4.7 mi. there is a side trail to the Crystal Mountain Camping area with an outhouse. The trail arrives at a hemlock grove with good views of the west side of Gore Pond. At 5.6 mi. it passes over the outlet of Gore Pond and ascends to an overgrown summit pasture. After crossing numerous old logging roads, the trail skirts the Dalton–Cheshire granite boundary. It passes a USGS bronze marker on Cheshire South Cobble at 7.5 mi. A short distance along, the trail intersects with a side trail to North Cobble with a dramatic view of Mt. Greylock. It then turns right at a private driveway that becomes Furnace Hill Rd. At the bottom of the hill, turn left toward the center of Cheshire, cross the Hoosic River and railroad tracks and, at 8.8 mi. turn right onto School St., across from the post office. On the corner there is a replica of the giant press used to make the famous "Cheshire Cheese" in the early 1800s. Turn left just past the senior citizens center on to the grassy path leading to open fields and cross Rte. 8 at 9.3 mi.

Appalachian Trail: Dalton to Cheshire

Distances from MA 8/MA 9 (Dalton)
>   *to* Gulf Rd.: 1.0 mi. (30 min.)
>   *to* Gore Pond: 5.6 mi. (2 hr.)
>   *to* side trail to North Cobble: 7.6 mi. (2 hr. 45 min.)
>   *to* Furnace Hill Rd.: 8.4 mi. (3 hr. 30 min.)
>   *to* MA 8 (Cheshire): 9.3 mi. (4 hr.)

Appalachian Trail: Cheshire to MA 2 (North Adams)

From Rte. 8 the trail ascends an eroded farm road to open fields with views of Cheshire. It soon enters the woods an at 0.6 mi. crosses a stile over barbed wire into a hay field. Outlook Ave. is crossed at 0.8 mi. just north of the interesting rock formation called "Reynolds Rock." The trail enters a field beside a stone wall and hedgerow and soon crosses a powerline. After traversing a hillside with cliffs the trail turns right (north) by a gullied brook, ascends steeply, and reaches a hemlock ridge with a precipitous drop to Kitchen Brook Valley in the west. The trail leaves the breezy hemlock ridge, following some high ground between two swamps, and comes to a brook flowing east at the bottom of a rock-strewn gully. A gradual descent brings the trail to the Mt. Greylock State Reservation boundary in the midst of a red spruce grove. At 3.5 mi. the trail crosses unpaved Old Adams Rd.

Leaving the red spruce grove, the trail weaves between some huge boulders and arrives at the bottom of a steep, short pitch of stone steps. After passing a view to the south, a side trail at 4.4 mi. leads 0.2 mi. to the Mark Noepel Shelter where water, tent sites, and an outhouse are available. The trail gradually ascends to the the balsams on the summit of Saddle Ball Mt. at 5.0 mi. and the intersection with the Jones Nose trail. (There are excellent views to the south within 0.3 mi. and the Jones Nose day-use parking lot on Rockwell Rd. within 1.0 mi.) The trail then veers east, bypassing a large balsam swamp, and comes to a small view to the east from a knoll on Saddle Ball Ridge.

Just before reaching the topmost hairpin curve on Rockwell Rd., the trail crosses a sphagnum moss bog. The trail intersects two side trails (the Cheshire Harbor Trail leads 6 mi. east to Adams, and the Hopper Trail leads 1.1 mi. west to a campground) as it crosses the road at 7.2 mi. It then crosses the junction of Notch Rd., Summit Rd., and Rockwell Rd. after skirting the south side of the old water supply pond. (The Gould Trail leaves this intesection to the east and descends steeply for 1.0 mi. to Peck's Brook Shelter and Falls.) Leaving the stunted spruce and fir woods, the trail emerges into the open by a television tower. The summit of Mt. Greylock (3491 ft.), the highest point in Massachusetts. Bascom Lodge, also on the summit, provides meals and lodging. It is managed by the AMC.

After turning north from the tower toward the end of a parking lot, the trail drops sharply and crosses Summit Rd. before leveling off on the ridge line, where two side ski trails go off to the east (right). The trail passes an unusual outcrop of milky quartz, coming to the rounded, tree-covered top of Mt. Fitch (3110 ft.). Ascending steadily, the trail passes blue blazes and a granite marker (indicating the western boundary of North Adams watershed property) before arriving at a register on top of Mt. Williams (2951 ft.) at 10.0 mi.

The trail crosses Notch Rd. at 10.9 mi. on a level spot near a day-use parking lot. After passing through the spruce forest called Wilbur Clearing, the trail bears right and the Money Brook Trail bears left (0.3 mi. to the Wilbur Clearing lean-to and intermittent water supply). Fires are allowed here. Leaving the red spruce grove, the trail ascends steeply over ledges to an awesome view of Williamstown and the Taconic Range. The Mt. Prospect Trail leaves south 2.0 mi. to its junction with the Money Brook Trail in the Hopper. Descending steeply through northern hardwoods, the jagged tread moderates as the trail crosses a logging road near the northern boundary of Mt. Greylock State Reservation. At 13.1 mi., after passing through a spruce plantation and over a bridge, the trail reaches Pattison Rd. The trail descends through the woods past the North Adams Water Treatment Plant to the Phelps Ave. extension. It then goes left downhill, crosses Catherine St. and continues on Phelps Ave. untill it reaches Rte. 2 at 14.0 mi.

Appalachian Trail: Cheshire to MA 2 (North Adams)

Distances from MA 8 (Cheshire)

>   *to* Outlook Ave.: 0.8 mi. (30 min.)
>   *to* Old Adams Rd.: 3.5 mi. (2 hr.)
>   *to* side trail to Mark Noepel Shelter and outhouse: 4.4 mi. (2 hr. 45 min.)
>   *to* Saddle Ball Mt. and side trail to Jones Nose: 5.0 mi. (3 hr.)
>   *to* junction of Hopper Trail and Cheshire Harbor Trail: 7.0 mi. (3 hr. 45 min.)
>   *to* summit of Mt. Greylock: 7.6 mi. (4 hr. 15 min.)
>   *to* summit of Mt. Williams: 10.0 mi. (5 hr. 15 min.)
>   *to* Notch Rd.: 10.9 mi. (5 hr. 40 min.)
>   *to* Money Brook Trail (lean-to): 11.0 mi. (6 hr.)
>   *to* Mt. Prospect Trail: 11.2 mi. (6 hr. 20 min.)
>   *to* Pattison Rd.: 13.1 mi. (7 hr. 45 min.)
>   *to* Rte. 2 (North Adams): 14.0 mi. (8 hr. 30 min.)

Appalachian Trail: MA 2 (North Adams) to the Massachusetts–Vermont Line

North Adams offers gas stations, fast-food outlets, and an all-night supermarket just 0.7 mi. east of the MA 2 trailhead. On the north side of MA 2, by the traffic light, an elaborate steel-and-concrete footbridge passes over the B&M Railroad and the Hoosic River to

Massachusetts Ave., where the trail turns right (east). Just before Sherman Brook goes under Massachusetts Ave., the trail leaves the paved road and turns north along the west side of Sherman Brook for 50 yd. on a gravel driveway. At 0.4 mi. it passes over two well-built footbridges and then runs along an old spillway that releases water from a dam. A high-voltage powerline crosses the trail at 0.6 mi. The trail climbs steadily through separate hemlock groves for the next 0.4 mi. and joins a logging road for a short distance. After passing Pete's Spring, a side trail at 1.7 mi. leads left to Sherman Brook Campsite and outhouse. The trail ascends a long, gradual ridge covered with laurel patches. At 2.4 mi. the trail turns sharply toward the west and heads steeply uphill through a jumble of granite, marble, and quartz.

After a couple of steep, narrow switchbacks, the trail climbs to the top of an eastern-facing bluff overlooking the Hoosac Range. On a wide section of East Mtn. ridge, the trail passes around the north side of a fragile mossy pond and arrives at an area of quartzite cobbles at 2.7 mi. A short distance across the cobbles at 2.8 mi. is the intersection of the Pine Cobble Trail (blue rectangles). (A sign at the junction of the two trails says it is 1.3 mi. to the Massachusetts–Vermont line and 2.7 mi. to MA 2.) About 100 ft. south on the Pine Cobble Trail is the marble top of East Mtn. and a panoramic view. A dip in the ridge shows an old logging road at 3.1 mi. as the trail goes up through azaleas, sheep laurel, and pink lady's slippers. Out of the woods again, the trail comes to Eph's Lookout at 3.3 mi. Off the trail to the east about 0.3 mi. is Bear Swamp and Brook in Clarksburg State Forest. The trail rises sharply for 0.1 mi. to the Massachusetts–Vermont line and the Long Trail register. There, a Long Trail Historic and Mileage sign reads: "Seth Warner Shelter, 3.1 mi.; jeep road, 2.6 mi." This is the end of the Massachusetts section. The trail continues into Vermont, where it is maintained by the Green Mountain Club. (See the *Guide to the Appalachian Trail in New Hampshire and Vermont,* published by the Appalachian Trail Conference.)

Appalachian Trail: MA 2 (North Adams) to the
Massachusetts–Vermont Line

Distances from MA 2 (North Adams)
   to Sherman Brook campsite: 1.7 mi. (1 hr.)
   to Pine Cobble Trail: 2.8 mi. (1 hr. 30 min.)
   to Eph's Lookout: 3.3 mi. (1 hr. 50 min.)
   to Massachusetts–Vermont line: 4.1 mi. (2 hr. 20 min.)

MT. EVERETT

Mt. Everett (2602 ft.) ranks second, next to Mt. Greylock, in impor-
tance among the Berkshire Hills, although it is far from being the
second highest peak. Called The Dome by old-timers, it is located
in the town of Mt. Washington in the southwestern corner of the
county. Its prominent crown is covered by stunted pitch pines and
topped by a fire tower, no longer open to the public. From the summit, distant peaks are visible in all directions. Mt. Greylock, 40 mi.
away in the north, is visible on clear days. Bear Mtn. in Connecticut
stands on the eastern side of the range to the south.

The upper region of the mountain and picturesque Guilder Pond
at an elevation of 2042 ft. form the 1,100-acre Mt. Everett State
Reservation, where camping, swimming, and fishing are prohibited. A narrow but well-maintained gravel road ends at two parking
and picnic areas a short hiking distance from the summit. Another
picnic area (no water) is located near the pond, and a red-blazed
path circling the pond begins here. Flowering azaleas and laurel
are abundant in early summer. The road (closed after dusk and during the winter) is accessible from Egremont, MA or Copake Falls,
NY by following the brown state-park signs.

Elbow Trail (Berkshire School)

To reach the blue-blazed Elbow Trail, take MA 41 3.5 mi. south
from its intersection with MA 23 in South Egremont. The paved
access road to Berkshire School exits right (west) from MA 41 and
continues onto the school grounds; take the first right off it, then
turn left off this to pass between large Memorial Hall on the left

and Stanley Hall on the right. Bear right, traveling uphill past a house and onto a dirt road (200 yd.). Park behind the gymnasium.

Ascend the well-worn Elbow Trail to reach the Appalachian Trail 1.5 mi. north of Mt. Everett. Turn left onto the AT to eventually reach the summit of Mt. Everett. To the right 0.5 mi. is the summit of Mt. Bushnell (1834 ft.) on the northern end of the Mt. Everett ridge.

Elbow Trail (Berkshire School)

Distances from Berkshire School parking area
>   *to* Appalachian Trail: 1.2 mi. (1 hr.)
>   *to* summit of Mt. Everett (via Appalachian Trail): 2.7 mi. (2 hr. 20 min.)

Appalachian Trail (BCAMC)

See Appalachian Trail: Sages Ravine to Jug End Rd. for a complete description.

Race Brook Trail (BCAMC)

This public access trail to the Appalachian Trail is marked with blue blazes and ascends steeply along Race Brook with views of five falls, one nearly 100 ft. high. It starts from a parking area on the west side of MA 41, approximately 50 yd. north of the Salisbury Rd. intersection. Parking is available on a turnout on the west side of MA 41. The trail reaches the Appalachian Trail 0.8 mi. south of Mt. Everett. This is a steep climb and rather spectacular, especially when there is a heavy volume of water flowing over the falls in the spring. To the right on the Appalachian Trail is the summit of Mt. Everett. To the left 1.1 mi. on the AT is the summit of Mt. Race (2365 ft.), near the southern end of the Mt. Everett ridge, from which there are fine views from the open top and the cliffs on the south side.

Race Brook Trail (BCAMC)

Distances from MA 41
>   *to* Appalachian Trail: 1.5 mi. (1 hr. 20 min.)
>   *to* summit of Mt. Everett: 2.5 mi. (2 hr. 10 min.)

MT. WASHINGTON STATE FOREST AND THE SOUTH TACONIC TRAIL

In the extreme southwestern corner of Massachusetts is an extensive trail network through the southern Taconic range. Most of the trails are on protected public land: the 3,300-acre Mt. Washington State Forest, and the adjoining Bash-Bish Falls State Forest and the Taconic State Parks of New York and Connecticut. Principal summits include Mt. Frissell (2453 ft.) and Alander Mtn. (2239 ft.). Just to the east of the state forest are Mt. Ashley (2390 ft.) and Mt. Plantain (2088 ft.). Bash-Bish Falls, one of the finest cascades in the Berkshires, is another well-known landmark.

Reach the area via Mt. Washington Rd., which leaves the village of Egremont near the junction of MA 23 and MA 41. Mt. Washington Rd. becomes West St. in the town of Mt. Washington, and passes the forest headquarters, where trail information is available. Overnight campers must register at the headquarters. Refer to the Southwestern Massachusetts map included with this guide.

South Taconic Trail

The South Taconic Trail (white blazed) extends 15.7 mi. in a north-south direction along the western escarpment or range of the prominent Southern Taconic Highland, which is located in the tri-state area of Massachusetts, New York, and Connecticut. For the most part, the trail lies within Taconic State Park (NY) and Mt. Washington State Forest (MA). It parallels the Appalachian Trail, which follows the eastern side of the highland. Its highest point is Brace Mtn. in New York (2311 ft.). There are many marked access trails, including some that link with the AT, providing hikers with extended circuit- or loop-hiking opportunities. The trail is well maintained by volunteers from the Berkshire chapter of the Appalachian Mountain Club, members of the Mid-Hudson Chapter of the Adirondack Mountain Club, the NY/NJ Trail Conference, and the Sierra Club.

The trail follows a highly scenic route with extensive open views, notably from South Brace Mtn. and Brace Mtn., with 0.75 mi. of almost continuous open crest on Alander Mtn., Prospect Hill, and Mt. Fray by the Catamount Ski Area. The views west over New York's Harlem Valley to the Catskills are outstanding. They sweep over the Southern Taconic Highland and extend to the Shawangunk Mtns. and the Hudson Highlands (NY) on the southwest and to Mt. Greylock (MA) on the north. An especially steep bypass section of the trail passes by spectacular Bash-Bish Gorge and Falls (MA). A public campground is located at the Taconic State Park's Copake Falls Area, a little northwest of the lower Bash-Bish Falls parking area on NY 344, where the trail passes.

The trail's southern terminus is located at Rudd Pond Farms off Rudd Pond Rd. in New York's Harlem Valley north of Millerton, and its northern end is at the Catamount Ski Area on MA 23 in Egremont, MA, where the latter crosses the Taconic Range just east of the New York–Massachusetts line. Through hikers wishing to traverse the trail can do so in a weekend. The state forest cabin at Alander Mtn. is located at the approximate halfway point on the trail. It is open free of charge on a first come, first served, basis and can accommodate six persons.

South Taconic Trail: Southern Section (Rudd Pond Farms to NY 344)

To reach the southern end of the trail, drive 5.5 mi. north on NY 22 from the traffic light at Millerton. Take a right onto White House Crossing Rd. and follow it to the end. Turn left on Rudd Pond Rd. for 0.3 mi., then right (east) onto Deer Run Rd. into Rudd Pond Farms, a residential development. Take a left onto Quarry Hill Rd. and follow it about 0.5 mi. to the east side of the development, where there is a small parking area at the edge of the woods. Look for the Taconic State Park sign about 75 ft. east of the road.

From the parking area at an elevation of 950 ft., the South Taconic Trail travels east along the edge of field, enters the woods, and starts to ascend the western escarpment of the Southern Taconic Highland. A steep, rough section begins at 0.4 mi. The trail passes a high waterfall and ascends cliffs along switchbacks, with open views to the west. Near the top of the steep section, there is a good view of Harlem Valley. A short distance beyond this, the trail takes a sharp left. (Here is the start of a 0.3-mi., red-blazed side trail leading to a fine viewpoint on Negro Hill looking to the west and north over Harlem Valley.)

The South Taconic Trail proceeds north on the escarpment with more views to the west, then climbs South Brace Mtn. with views to the south. At 1.4 mi. the trail turns left at a junction with a blue-blazed trail of uncertain maintenance, which leads right (south). (**Update** August 1995: at the Connecticut border this trail enters private land; the owners do not permit passage, so there is no access to Riga Lake from the trail.) About 70 yd. along, the trail reaches an open area on South Brace Mtn. affording an excellent view south over the Riga Plateau section of the highland, featuring Riga Lake and South Pond beyond it. The trail crosses the open area, with the summit of South Brace Mtn. (2304 ft.) just to the right. It descends moderately to a saddle, then it ascends along the attractive open crest of Brace Mtn. to its summit (2311 ft.) at 1.9 mi. The summit is marked by a large pile of stones that has given Brace Mtn. the local name of Monument Mtn. Splendid views overlook Bear Mtn. (CT) to the east and Mt. Frissell (MA) to the northeast. (This is the trail's highest point.)

The trail descends north on a woods road to a junction at 2.2 mi. with the Brace Mtn. Trail, a woods road that leads right (south-east) 1.6 mi. to Mt. Washington Rd. in Connecticut, 2 mi. north of the dam at South Pond. (You can reach the Appalachian Trail on the east via side trails from this road.) The South Taconic Trail continues north for 200 yd. to another junction, where it exits left from the woods road at the same place the Mt. Frissell Trail exits right. (Note: The red-blazed Mt. Frissell Trail, 2.2 mi. long with fine views, goes east to the tristate boundary marker—the highest point in Connecticut, which is on Mt. Frissell's south slope—to the summit of Mt. Frissell [2435 ft.] [MA], and then to the summit of Rounds Mtn. [CT], ending on Mt. Washington Rd. at the Massachusetts–Connecticut line.)

The South Taconic Trail proceeds from the Mt. Frissell Trail junction along an open crest with fine views and enters Massachusetts from New York. The trail regains the woods road and continues north on a route previously called the State Line Trail. At 3.1 mi. a blue-blazed side trail proceeds right (northeast) to the Ashley Hill Trail, which connects with the Mt. Washington State Forest headquarters on the north and the Mt. Frissell Trail and the Brace Mtn. Trail on the south. At 4.5 mi. the Robert Brook Trail exits left. (The red-blazed Robert Brook Trail descends along the ravine of Robert Brook in New York and ends 1.1 mi. later at the Alander Brook Trail near Undermountain Rd. off NY 22.)

The South Taconic Trail continues north, and at 5 mi., where it curves left to descend, the Alander Loop Trail forks right. (This blue-blazed trail, more than 1 mi. long with fine views, climbs roughly north up to and along the height-of-land to the eastern summit of Alander Mtn. [2240 ft.]. It then leads a short distance west over an intervening knob, through a notch, and past a shelter to rejoin the South Taconic Trail on the western summit of Alander Mtn.) The Alander Loop Trail is a quicker route to Alander Mtn. and the shelter. From the junction with the Alander Loop Trail, the South Taconic Trail descends into New York from Massachusetts, crosses a bridge over Alander Brook, and 60 yd. beyond, at 5.2 mi., it climbs steeply right from the woods road. (The blue-blazed Alander Brook Trail, which is 1.5 mi. long, continues straight ahead on a woods road, descending south along the ravine of Alander Brook and making left turns at junctions, crossing Alander Brook and proceeding on level terrain to Undermountain Rd. in Harlem Valley, NY.)

From the woods road, the South Taconic Trail climbs gradually, then steeply up the southwestern shoulder of Alander Mtn., reaching an open crest at 5.7 mi. The trail reenters Massachusetts at a boundary marker and goes northeast, ascending along the open shoulder with fine views. The trail reaches the western summit of Alander Mtn. (2240 ft.) at 6 mi., where the foundation of a former fire tower is located.

(A few yards beyond, the blue-blazed Alander Loop Trail leads right, descending into a small notch, where it bears right at the junction. Here another blue trail, the Alander Mtn. Trail, goes straight ahead past a state forest cabin, descends northeast and east, passing the primitive camping area of Mt. Washington State Forest on the right, and ends at the state forest headquarters at the junction of West and East streets in the town of Mt. Washington.)

The South Taconic Trail goes north along the remainder of Alander's open crest, a splendidly scenic section. To the east is the rural town of Mt. Washington, with Mt. Everett (2602 ft.), on the eastern escarpment, the dominant feature. At 6.4 mi. the trail descends into woods and continues north along the ridge. At 6.8 mi. there is a view of a beautiful secluded valley to the west, with Mt. Washburn beyond. At 7.9 mi. the trail reaches a high point on the northern section of a ridge (Bash-Bish Mtn.) and descends to a lookout point. Cedar Mtn., across Bash-Bish Gorge, is visible to the north. From here, the trail descends steeply to a short, level stretch where, at 8.2 mi., the blue-blazed Bash-Bish Gorge Trail goes right, while the main trail goes left.

Entering New York from Massachusetts, the trail turns left (south) where a short spur trail continues west to a rock outcrop with beautiful views down the valley of Bash-Bish Brook and beyond to the village of Copake Falls, NY. From here, the trail descends with turns to the unpaved road of Taconic State Park along a brook and near a shower house on the right. The trail turns left off the road, crosses a bridge over Bash-Bish Brook, and comes out near the lower Bash-Bish parking area on the right. Here the northern section of the South Taconic Trail begins.

South Taconic Trail: Southern Section (Rudd Pond Farms to NY 344)

Distances from Rudd Pond Farms

   to summit of South Brace Mtn.: 1.7 mi. (1 hr. 15 min.)
   to summit of Brace Mtn.: 1.9 mi. (1 hr. 30 min.)
   to Brace Mtn. Trail: 2.2 mi. (1 hr. 40 min.)
   to Mt. Frissell Trail: 2.4 mi. (1 hr. 50 min.)
   to side trail to Mt. Washington State Forest headquarters: 3.1 mi. (2 hr. 20 min.)
   to Robert Brook Trail: 4.5 mi. (3 hr. 15 min.)
   to Alander Loop Trail: 5 mi. (3 hr. 30 min.)
   to Alander Brook Trail: 5.3 mi. (3 hr. 45 min.)

to western summit of Alander Mtn. and cabin: 6 mi. (4 hr. 30 min.)

to Bash-Bish Gorge Trail: 8.2 mi. (6 hr. 15 min.)

to lower Bash-Bish parking area: 9.7 mi. (7 hr. 30 min.)

South Taconic Trail: Northern Section (NY 344 to MA 23)

From the entrance to the lower Bash-Bish parking area, at an elevation of 725 ft., the trail crosses NY 344. It leads up the west side of Cedar Brook after crossing a small stone bridge, turns right onto a woods road for a short distance, and soon makes a steep turn to the right through a red pine forest. At 0.5 mi. a small clearing offers limited views. The trail ascends moderately on a woods road, passing two side trails on the left. At 0.9 mi. the yellow-blazed Grey Birch Trail exits to the left, leading southwest to the Copake Falls Area of New York's Taconic State Park.

The South Taconic Trail turns right; state park markers of another trail are visible along with the white blazes of the South Taconic Trail. Leveling off, the trail descends gradually into Cedar Brook Ravine. You can hear the sound of running water to the right. At 1.4 mi. the trail turns left at its junction with the blue-blazed Cedar Brook Trail, then ascends moderately to the open summit area at 1.8 mi., where a narrow side trail with red markers leads left (west) a short distance to Sunset Rock. The elevation here is 1788 ft.

The trail continues northeast on a wide path through thick scrub growth. Here it has yellow state-park markers in addition to its white blazes. At 2.2 mi. the trail takes a sharp left off the wide path and leads to Sunset Rock Rd., 50 yd. west of the Massachusetts–New York line in New York State. (This unpaved road runs eastward into Mt. Washington, MA, as part of West St. and westward, descending steeply, into North Mountain Rd. in Harlem Valley, NY. It is closed in the winter.)

The trail crosses the dirt road and at 2.4 mi. turns right onto a footpath that crosses a brook by an old springhouse. It climbs Prospect Hill northeast through dense scrub oak and mountain laurel and at 2.7 mi. reaches the open summit area (1919 ft.) with good views. It turns left at the Massachusetts–New York boundary monument and reaches an open ledge with outstanding views north, west, and south; the views of Harlem Valley and the town of Hillsdale, NY, are especially lovely.

The trail enters Massachusetts, descends Prospect Hill gradually with a good view north at 3 mi., and follows the lower crest. It enters New York and at 3.7 mi. reaches an open section along the edge of an escarpment, with pleasant views of a valley to the southwest. The trail continues to Mt. Fray and parallels its crest. At 4.1 mi. it turns right and climbs a short distance to the crest, with a fine view from an open area. It then goes north along the broad summit area of Mt. Fray (1900 ft.), where open areas in the scrub growth offer distant views, including Mt. Greylock to the northeast. From here on, the trail is on the privately owned land of the Catamount Ski Area.

At 4.3 mi. the trail turns right onto Ridge Run, the first ski trail encountered, which descends east along the ridge just below and to the right of the ski-lift apparatus on the summit. (A short distance to the left, or west, is an area with splendid views, including the two upper chair-lift terminals of the ski area.) The trail follows Ridge Run east (downhill) for 1 mi., reentering Massachusetts. Near the end, it climbs right a few yards to a pleasant view of Jug End valley and ridge. At the end of Ridge Run, at the top of the ski slope, is a view of the ski area.

The trail then climbs steeply east for a short stretch and continues along a wooded crest, turning north and descending. It enters a driveway at 5.7 mi., descends it (with a shortcut at the curve), enters another dirt road coming in from the left, and finally turns left for 65 yd. to reach MA 23, where it crosses the height-of-land. This is the northern terminus of the South Taconic Trail at 6 mi. (15.7 mi. from its southern end). (Note: If you lose the trail at this point, simply follow any ski run down to the base lodge. MA 23 is a short distance away on the ski-area access road.)

A parking area is located on the south side of MA 23; 150 yd. to the left (west) of MA 23 is Hillsdale, NY, and to the east is South Egremont, MA. Overnight and day parking is allowed in the ski-area parking lot. Hikers should ask permission to park at the ski-area office. Be advised that the parking lot is locked at dusk and vehicles not removed by then must remain overnight.

South Taconic Trail: Northern Section (NY 344 to MA 23)
Distances from NY 344

    to Grey Birch Trail: 0.9 mi. (40 min.)
    to Cedar Brook Trail: 1.4 mi. (1 hr.)
    to Sunset Rock: 1.9 mi. (1 hr. 15 min.)
    to Sunset Rock Rd.: 2.2 mi. (1 hr. 25 min.)
    to summit of Prospect Hill: 2.7 mi. (1 hr. 45 min.)
    to summit of Mt. Fray: 3.7 mi. (2 hr. 30 min.)
    to Ridge Run ski trail: 4.3 mi. (2 hr. 45. min.)
    to MA 23: 6 mi. (3 hr. 45 min.)

Mt. Frissell Trail (from the west)

Mt. Frissell (2453 ft.) stands on the Southern Taconic Highland, its summit being in Massachusetts and the highest point of Connecticut lying on its southern slope at the Massachusetts–Connecticut line. The scenic Mt. Frissell Trail, lying in three states and marked with red-painted blazes, travels over the mountain. It extends 2.2 mi. from the South Taconic Trail on the west to the Mt. Washington Rd. at the Massachusetts–Connecticut line on the east.

To reach the western end of the Mt. Frissell Trail, at its junction with the South Taconic Trail 0.3 mi. north of the summit of Brace Mtn., you can hike the scenic southern section of the South Taconic Trail in New York, starting at the Rudd Pond Farms vacation home development. (This development is located on the east side of Rudd Pond Rd. about 5 mi. north of Millerton, NY. See the description under South Taconic Trail: Southern Section.) The trail follows the edge of a field eastward, enters the woods, and ascends steeply up the western escarpment of the highland, running north along the escarpment. It climbs South Brace Mtn. (2304 ft.), descends a modest notch, and climbs Brace Mtn. (2311 ft.). The South Taconic Trail then continues north past the junction with the Mt. Frissell Trail at 2.3 mi. The distance from Rudd Pond Farms to the trailhead via the South Taconic Trail is 2.4 mi. (1 hr. 50 min.).

To reach the junction of the South Taconic and Mt. Frissell trails from Connecticut, you can hike along the Brace Mtn. woods road, which goes westward from the unpaved Mt. Washington Rd. 2 mi. south of the Massachusetts–Connecticut line. This road connects with the village of Salisbury, CT, to the southeast. The unblazed woods road climbs part of the way up Brace Mtn. and meets the South Taconic Trail. Take a right on this trail and follow it along the crest for 200 yd. to the junction with the red-blazed Mt. Frissell Trail. The distance from Mt. Washington Rd. in Connecticut to the trailhead is 2 mi. (1 hr. 15 min.).

At 0.3 mi. from the junction with the South Taconic Trail, the Mt. Frissell Trail crosses the broad Ashley Hill Brook Trail and shortly arrives at the point where Massachusetts, New York, and Connecticut meet. (A granite boundary marker lists only Massachusetts and New York.) The trail continues east through thick mountain laurel and scrub oak along the Massachusetts–Connecticut line, climbing Mt. Frissell, to the highest point in Connecticut (2380 ft., not the summit), which is marked by a cairn and pipe. About 30 yd. along, the trail turns north onto an open slope with a splendid view of the highland and ascends to the summit of Mt. Frissell (MA), marked by a trail register maintained by the New Haven Hiking Club.

Mt. Frissell Trail (from the west)
Distances from the South Taconic Trail
   to tristate point: 0.4 mi. (20 min.)
   to highest point in Connecticut: 0.8 mi. (35 min.)
   to summit of Mt. Frissell: 0.9 mi. (50 min.)

Mt. Frissell Trail (from the east)
Start at Mt. Washington Rd. (called East St. in the town of Mt. Washington, MA) on the Massachusetts–Connecticut line on the Southern Taconic Highland. Hike northwest on a woods road from Mt. Washington Rd. in Massachusetts. At 0.1 mi. the trail turns left and follows a narrow path through dense growth, going into Connecticut and then heading west to climb very steeply up Round Mtn. The trail reaches Round Mtn.'s broad, open summit (2296 ft.)

at 0.7 mi., then descends northwest, reentering Massachusetts and reaching a notch where a side path descends right to a shallow pond (dry in the summer). The trail ascends Mt. Frissell very steeply, with a fine view from the eastern ledges of the summit area. At 1.2 mi. the trail reaches the highest point in the woods, marked by a trail register and stone pile.

Mt. Frissell Trail (from the east)

Distances from Mt. Washington Rd.

   to summit of Round Mtn.: 0.7 mi. (45 min.)

   to summit of Mt. Frissell: 1.2 mi. (1 hr. 15 mi.).

Alander Brook Trail

To reach the trailhead, located in the area of Boston Corners in New York's Harlem Valley, take NY 344 to NY 22 in Copake Falls. Follow NY 22 south about 4 mi. to unpaved Under Mountain Rd. Drive on this road 0.8 mi. to the blue-blazed Alander Brook Trail, which exits left as a woods road. Park at the trailhead.

The trail goes north past the intersection of the red-blazed Robert Brook Trail, which exits right (east). At 0.75 mi. the trail crosses Alander Brook, turns right, and ascends through mountain laurel. It then turns right again onto another woods road. The trail ascends east and northeast along the deep, hemlock-clad ravine of Alander Brook to where the blue blazes end (this is the end of the Alander Brook Trail) and the white blazes of the South Taconic Trail begin.

To ascend Alander Mtn., turn left onto the South Taconic Trail, which climbs steeply north up the mountain. The South Taconic Trail continues on to the open crest of Alander's southwest shoulder, passing from New York into Massachusetts (boundary marker), and ascends northeast along the crest for 0.3 mi. to the western summit of Alander Mtn. The foundation of a former fire tower is located here. Proceeding north 0.25 mi. on the South Taconic Trail or east 0.33 mi. along Alander's open crest on the blue-blazed Alander Loop Trail affords commanding views of the highland in Massachusetts and New York's Harlem Valley, with Mt. Greylock and the Catskills in the distance.

Alander Brook Trail

Distances from Under Mountain Rd.
   to South Taconic Trail: 1.45 mi. (1 hr.)
   to western summit of Alander Mtn. via South Taconic Trail:
      2.25 mi. (2 hr.)

Robert Brook Trail

Hike north about 150 yd. from the trailhead of the Alander Brook Trail. The red-blazed Robert Brook Trail, a woods road, turns right and ascends rather steeply along the Robert Brook ravine. The trail reaches an 1898 New York–Massachusetts boundary monument and climbs north as a footpath along the state line to a second such monument. It continues north to the junction with the white-blazed South Taconic Trail, where the Robert Brook Trail ends.

Going left (north) on the South Taconic Trail, proceed to the intersection of the blue-blazed Alander Loop Trail at 0.5 mi. You can continue along the South Taconic Trail another 0.2 mi. to the upper end of the blue-blazed Alander Brook Trail, then follow the white-blazed South Taconic Trail up Alander Mtn. as described in the preceding section. Alternatively, you can ascend the blue-blazed Alander Loop Trail northeast into Massachusetts to a notch at the height-of-land, then follow the trail north along the crest as a narrow path through thick scrub growth, with good views over the highland from open areas, to the eastern summit of Alander Mtn. This has the same elevation as the western summit (2240 ft.) and has a nice view eastward over the highland in Massachusetts. The Alander Loop Trail continues a short distance west, climbing over a small intervening rise and descending into a final small notch in which a state forest cabin lies to the right. It then joins the white-blazed South Taconic Trail. From here it is a short climb to the western summit of Alander Mtn. along the South Taconic Trail.

Robert Brook Trail

Distances from Under Mountain Rd.
   to South Taconic Trail: 1.2 mi. (1 hr.)
   to Alander Loop Trail via South Taconic Trail: 1.7 mi. (1 hr. 20 min.)

> *to* eastern summit of Alander Mtn. via Alander Loop Trail: 2.6
> mi. (2 hr.)
> *to* western summit of Alander Mtn. via South Taconic Trail: 2.8
> mi. (2 hr. 10 min.)

Ashley Hill Trail

This blue-blazed trail leads to the heart of Mt. Washington State
Forest. The trail starts with the Alander Mtn. Trail at the trailhead
from the Mt. Washington State Forest parking area on East St. in
Mt. Washington, MA. It leads west across a field and into the forest and soon emerges into another field. The trail descends past a
ruined house on the right and crosses Lee Pond Brook on a wood-
en bridge. Following a woods road for about 0.25 mi., the Ashley
Hill Trail branches left at the intersection with the Alander Mtn.
Trail. Do not turn right on the Alander Mtn. Trail, which quickly
crosses a brook. The Ashley Hill Trail ascends gradually along a
woods road and always keeps Ashley Hill Brook to the right, never
crossing the brook. After about 2.5 mi. of easy climbing, the Ashley Hill Trail exits the woods road on the left and continues as a
less well-defined trail uphill at a slightly steeper grade. (A blue-
blazed side trail continues straight through this intersection, crosses Ashley Hill Brook, and ascends on a less well-defined path for
about 1 mi. to intersect with the white-blazed South Taconic Trail.)
The Ashley Hill Trail is well marked and generally follows another
woods road to the Massachusetts–New York line, where it intersects the red-blazed Mt. Frissell Trail (see the description of the
Mt. Frissell Trail from the west). Straight ahead, the Ashley Hill
Trail continues on a less well-defined trail a short distance through
laurel bushes to intersect with the Brace Mtn. Trail on the Connecticut–New York line just below the Taconic ridge and the
white-blazed South Taconic Trail. Take either the Mt. Frissell Trail
or the Brace Mountain Trail to the right a short distance to the
South Taconic Trail.

Ashley Hill Trail

Distances from Mt. Washington State Forest parking area (East St.)
> *to* side trail to Ashley Hill Brook: 2.1 mi. (1 hr. 30 min.)

to Mt. Frissell Trail: 3.4 mi. (2 hr. 10 min.)
to Brace Mtn. Trail: 3.5 mi. (2 hr. 15 min.)

Alander Mtn. Trail

Alander Mtn. (2240 ft.), with its twin summits, stands on the western escarpment of the Southern Taconic Highland. The blue-blazed trail starts at the Mt. Washington State Forest parking area on the west side of East St. in the town of Mt. Washington, MA. The trail proceeds west across a field and then through the woods. It descends through another field, crosses a brook by a vacant house (*do not* turn left on the woods road before the brook), and at 0.6 mi. intersects the blue-blazed Charcoal Pit Trail, which branches left. At 0.8 mi. the blue-blazed Ashley Hill Trail forks left. The Alander Mtn. Trail forks right, first descending to cross Ashley Hill Brook and then climbing westward. At 1.5 mi. a side trail ascends left to a primitive camping area of the state forest. The main trail continues west and southwest, ascending as it narrows, and reaches a state forest cabin in a small notch just below the summit of Alander Mtn. The cabin has wooden bunks and a wood stove, and backpackers can stay here overnight at no charge on a first-come, first-served basis. The nearest water supply is back down the Alander Mtn. Trail about 400 yd. A few yards beyond the cabin is the junction of the blue-blazed Alander Loop Trail on the left. The Alander Mtn. Trail joins the white-blazed South Taconic Trail a short distance up and to the west (right) on the summit of Alander Mtn.

Alander Mtn. Trail

Distances from Mt. Washington State Forest parking area (East St.)
to campground: 1.5 mi. (45 min.)
to cabin: 2.7 mi. (1 hr. 30 min.)
to western summit of Alander Mtn.: 2.8 mi. (1 hr. 35 min.)

Alander Loop Trail

This trail is a quicker, highly scenic alternate route to the South Taconic Trail around the east side of Alander Mtn. (Refer to South Taconic Trail: Southern Section for a description.)

Bash-Bish Falls Trail

The blue-blazed trail starts at the eastern end of the lower Bash-Bish parking area on NY 344, about 1 mi. east of Copake Falls, NY. It follows the broad footway east along the north side of Bash-Bish Brook, entering Bash-Bish Falls State Forest (MA) from Taconic State Park (NY). At 0.7 mi. the trail turns left and ascends steeply to the upper Bash-Bish parking lot. If you continue straight ahead a few yards on a broad path before making the ascent, you will find splendid Bash-Bish Falls, with the deep, narrow, twisting gorge of Bash-Bish Brook lying above it.

Bash-Bish Falls Trail

Distances from lower Bash-Bish parking area (NY 344)
>   *to* Bash-Bish Falls: 0.7 mi. (30 min.)
>   *to* upper Bash-Bish parking area: 1 mi. (50 min.)

Bash-Bish Gorge Trail

This trail connects Bash-Bish Falls with the South Taconic Trail. It was originally part of the South Taconic Trail until that trail was rerouted to avoid the crossing of Bash-Bish Brook.

From the upper Bash-Bish parking area on Falls Rd. in Massachusetts (a continuation of NY 344), the trail descends a state forest road on the right to Bash-Bish Brook and crosses it above the gorge. (*Caution:* Be prepared to wade across the stream, not easy in high water.) The trail ascends a very steep pitch by the fence above Bash-Bish Gorge, offering spectacular glimpses into the gorge with its cascading stream. At the crest of the fence line, on the high southwestern precipice of the gorge, the trail goes left to ascend southwest through an extensive hemlock forest. At 0.6 mi. the trail intersects the recently relocated South Taconic Trail (see South Taconic Trail: Southern Section). Turning left, the South Taconic Trail climbs steeply to the northern end of the upper crest of Bash-Bish Ridge, with a view of Cedar Mtn. across the gorge to the north. Turning right at the intersection, the South Taconic Trail descends to the camping area of Taconic State Park and the lower Bash-Bish parking area. This makes an excellent loop hike.

Bash-Bish Gorge Trail

Distances from Upper Bash-Bish Parking Area

   to South Taconic Trail: 0.6 mi. (30 min.)
   to Taconic State Park camping area (via South Taconic Trail):
      1.4 mi. (1 hr. 15 min.)
   to lower Bash-Bish parking area in Taconic State Park (via
      South Taconic Trail): 1.5 mi. (1 hr. 20 min.)
   to Upper Bash-Bish parking area: 2.4 mi. (2 hr. 10 min.)

TACONIC SKYLINE TRAIL

The Taconic Skyline Trail of western Massachusetts was originally
blazed by the CCC in the 1930s. Paralleling the Appalachian Trail
on the west, it starts from MA 41 in the town of Richmond and
goes in a generally northerly direction along the crest of the Taconic Range and its Brodie Mtn. continuation, ending at US 7 south of
the Brodie Mtn. Ski Area. About half of this 21-mile trail lies within Pittsfield State Forest, while the rest is on private land. The trail
largely utilizes the state forest-fire road and other woods roads,
although the trail is expected to be relocated off some sections of
the fire road in the future. A state forest camping area is located
near the trail's midpoint at Berry Pond, which is reachable by car.
This camping area makes a suitable overnight destination for
through-hikers.

   You can enjoy good viewpoints along the route from Richmond
Point, Tower Mtn., Berry Hill, and the upper ski slopes of Jiminy
Peak and Brodie Mtn. The other principal attractions are Berry
Hill's azalea fields and adjacent Berry Pond, the highest pond in
Massachusetts (2060 ft.). On the north the trail reaches its highest
point at the abandoned fire tower on Brodie Mtn. (2613 ft.). The
former route of the trail along Brodie Mtn. north of the fire tower
has been abandoned, but there are plans to attempt a 5-mi. extension over Brodie Ridge to the summit of Mt. Greylock. The trail
now descends southeast from the tower to US 7 just south of the
Brodie Mtn. Ski Area entrance and parking lot.

The Taconic Skyline Trail is marked with triangular white blazes. In the Pittsfield State Forest, the blazes are sometimes edged with blue. Outside the state forest, the trail is maintained by the Williams Outing Club (WOC). The Taconic Hiking Club of New York maintains most of the trail inside the forest.

Also included in this section are several side trails and access trails that connect with the Skyline Trail.

Taconic Skyline Trail: Southern Section (MA 41 to US 20)

The trail starts on private land on the west side of MA 41, just opposite the Richmond cemetery, where parking is available. This point is 0.4 mi. north of the junction of MA 41 and MA 295 (Canaan Rd.). At 1210 ft., it is the lowest point of the trail. The southern section of the trail ascends to both Richmond Point and Perry's Peak.

Starting on a logging road, the trail goes west 0.2 mi., turns right onto a woods road, and soon ascends northwest, with a brook and ravine on the right. At 0.8 mi. the trail turns left, changing from a footpath to another woods road. At 1.1 mi. a broad trail intersects from the left. The trail ascends to Richmond Point (1910 ft.) at 1.4 mi., an open area with outstanding views of the Berkshire landscape to the south.

The trail continues along a semi-open level section, turns right (north) at a trail junction, and ascends to Perry's Peak (2070 ft.) at 2 mi., bearing left at a junction of woods roads in the summit area. This used to be an open area, but a pine plantation has obscured the view.

The trail then descends northwest through a wet section, swings east through an open area, and turns sharply left at a trail junction at 2.7 mi. (watch for blazes). It continues north on the crest, remaining inside Bates Memorial State Park, which extends to US 20 and is administered as part of Pittsfield State Forest. The trail is narrow in places and passes through open areas with good views north. It descends through the woods, turns right, and reaches US 20 (Lebanon Mtn. Rd.) at 3.6 mi. Here the highway crosses the crest of the Taconic Range, linking Pittsfield, MA, on the east with New Lebanon and Albany, NY, on the west.

When hiking in the opposite direction, from US 20 south, start on the dirt road, turn right after a few yards (*do not* follow the woods road ascending straight ahead), and bear left at the next two junctions.

Taconic Skyline Trail: Southern Section (MA 41 to US 20)
Distances from MA 41
   to Richmond Point: 1.4 mi. (45 min.)
   to Perry's Peak: 2 mi. (1 hr. 10 min.)
   to US 20: 3.6 mi. (2 hr. 15 min.)

Taconic Skyline Trail: Middle Section (US 20 to Brodie Mtn. Rd.)

For most of this section along the crest of the Taconic Range, the trail travels the length of Pittsfield State Forest for 9.5 mi. to Potter Mtn. Rd. In the state forest, except for several sections where it is a footpath, the trail follows an unimproved jeep or fire road, much of which is rutted and has large mud puddles in wet weather. The fire road has many ups and downs, with orange snowmobile markers (or orange blazes) supplementing the white hiking-trail blazes in places. North of the state forest this section goes over Jiminy Peak and bypasses Widow White's Peak.

From the north side of US 20 (1500 ft.), with a spacious parking area on the left, the trail ascends the eroded fire road roughly northward, reaching a 1,900-ft. level stretch. With various minor ups and downs, the trail passes Cranberry Pond at 1.2 mi. on the right, with informal campsites nearby, and the edge of Twin Ponds at 1.5 mi. on the right. After crossing the Twin Ponds outlet, the trail leaves the ridge, skirting it on the western side. (*Note:* The trail might be relocated over this ridge in the future. Watch for blazes after Twin Ponds.) The trail passes a junction at 1.9 mi., where it crosses a small stream. The trail to the right offers routes down to West St. in Pittsfield or back to US 20 across from the Hancock Shaker Museum. From the junction the trail ascends briefly to a small open area offering limited views to the west. It passes through a tall Norway spruce stand, descends, and crosses Lebanon Springs Rd. in a notch at 3.1 mi. (This is a rough, narrow dirt road, not recommended for auto travel. It descends southeast to the end of West St., west of Pittsfield; in the opposite direction it descends west to Lebanon Springs, NY.)

At 3.8 mi. the trail crosses a telephone line right-of-way. (You can ascend the right-of-way to the right—southeast—for 0.2 mi. to the crest of the ridge, where there are fine views in either direction. Turning left—north—onto a woods road leads to the wooded sum-mit of Smith Mtn., 2170 ft., with its impressive stands of azaleas. The woods road continues west back to the Skyline Trail at a point 0.3 mi. north of the telephone-line crossing.)

Continuing north, the Skyline Trail intersects Tower Mtn. Rd. at 4.9 mi. (This is a woods road that descends northwest to Goodrich Hollow Rd. and NY 22 south of Stephentown, NY; in the other direction it becomes Brickhouse Mtn. Rd. and descends southeast to Cascade St. in Pittsfield, MA). The trail proceeds left on Tower Mtn. Rd. for a short distance and quickly turns right onto a narrow path that ascends Tower Mtn. It reaches the broad, open summit (2193 ft.) at 5.2 mi., where there are good views mostly to the west, with the Catskills of New York on the southwestern horizon.

The trail descends Tower Mtn. northeast on a narrow footpath and turns left at 5.4 mi. to proceed along a fire road, with Tilden Swamp and Tilden Pond lying off to the right (southeast). In anoth-er 0.3 mi. it turns left off the fire road and onto a footpath, continu-ing along the crest of a hill (2188 ft.). It then descends to Berry Pond Circuit Rd. at 6 mi. (This is a one-way paved road that ascends 1000 ft. to Berry Hill and Berry Pond from the state forest headquarters near Cascade St. on the southeast, then descends to complete the loop.)

The Skyline Trail crosses the paved road and passes Berry Pond on the right. State-forest picnic facilities and campsites are located near the pond. The trail follows the paved road for a short distance, passing over the Berry Pond outlet, and climbs along the road to an excellent view west of the adjacent valley. It soon reaches a park-ing area on the south slope of Berry Hill, with a broad panorama

over New York. It then follows a woods road north over Berry Hill
(2200 ft.) with its extensive fields of azaleas, a splendid spectacle
when the flowers are in bloom in early June.

The trail descends to rejoin paved Berry Pond Circuit Rd. for a
few yards, then exits left through a semi-open area with a pleasant
view. A recent relocation of the trail follows a footpath through the
woods north and east, regaining the fire road after passing over a
2280-ft. hill, where at 7.7 mi. the Colonial Trail exits right. The
Skyline Trail forks left on the fire road and ascends through shrub-
by growth to the flat, partly open summit of Poppy Mtn. (2311 ft.)
at 7.9 mi., which affords a distant view over intermittent growth.

The trail turns right and descends the fire road to Daniels
Brook. After crossing the brook, it turns left and passes the Daniels
Brook Trail and the Burgoyne Trail, which descend right to Potter
Mtn. Rd. It goes over the summit of Potter Mtn. (2157 ft.) and
descends to Potter Mtn. Rd. at 9.5 mi., leaving Pittsfield State Forest. (This is an unpaved road, drivable in summer, which crosses
the pass here in the Taconic Range at 1925 ft. and extends from
Hancock, MA, on the west to Balance Rock Rd. in Lanesboro,
MA, on the southeast.) Going right a short distance to the powerline, you have an open view east and southeast, including Pontoosuc Lake in Pittsfield and Lanesboro.

The Taconic Skyline Trail follows Potter Mtn. Rd. left in the
pass under the powerline for 200 yd. then exits right onto a woods
road. (Trail users should note that the section of the Taconic Skyline
Trail from Berry Pond to Potter Mtn. Rd. in Pittsfield State Forest is
also considered to be the final section of the Taconic Crest Trail by
the Taconic Hiking Club, which is the principal maintainer of this
trail. The Taconic Crest Trail, marked with white diamond-shaped
markers, goes from here down Potter Mtn. Rd. to Hancock, then it
climbs the Taconic Range north along the Massachusetts–New York
line for 29 mi. to North Pownal, VT. For a description see Taconic
Crest Trail: Rathbun Hollow, NY, to the Taconic Skyline Trail
[Pittsfield State Forest].)

The trail follows the woods road north to the summit of Jiminy
Peak (2392 ft.) at 10.3 mi. A short side hike to the left takes you to

the top of the ski area, which affords beautiful views north and west. The Skyline Trail soon forks right onto a ski run, following it northeast along the crest and descending with excellent views. (*Note:* The white blazes are difficult to find at times because they are located on the right side of the ski run in the treeline.) The trail turns right from the ski run at a point where the ski run takes a sharp left and begins a steep descent. The trail exits into the woods, becoming a footpath to pass northwest of Widow White's Peak. It passes through briar patches and becomes a woods road again, then descends north to Brodie Mtn. Rd. at 12.1 mi. on the height-of-land of the Taconic Range. This is a paved road connecting US 7 on the east with MA 43 on the west, where it crosses a gap in the range at 1640 ft. (In the future, the Skyline Trail may be relocated over the summit of Widow White's Peak from the summit of Jiminy Peak to avoid the ski trail.)

Taconic Skyline Trail: Middle Section (US 20 to Brodie Mtn. Rd.)
Distances from US 20

> *to* Cranberry Pond: 1.2 mi. (35 min.)
> *to* Twin Ponds: 1.5 mi. (45 min.)
> *to* Lebanon Springs Rd.: 3.1 mi. (1 hr. 25 min.)
> *to* Tower Mtn. Rd.: 4.9 mi. (2 hr. 10 min.)
> *to* summit of Tower Mtn.: 5.2 mi. (2 hr. 20 min.)
> *to* Berry Pond (picnic facilities and campsites): 6.1 mi. (3 hr.)
> *to* summit of Berry Hill: 6.3 mi. (3 hr. 10 min.)
> *to* summit of Poppy Mtn.: 7.9 mi. (4 hr.)
> *to* Daniels Brook Trail and Burgoyne Trail: 8.2 mi. (4 hr. 15 min.)
> *to* Jiminy Peak: 10.3 mi. (5 hr. 35 min.)
> *to* Brodie Mtn. Rd.: 12.1 mi. (6 hr. 45 min.)

Taconic Skyline Trail: Northern Section (Brodie Mtn. Rd. to US 7)

The trail in this section follows the crest of the southern two fifths of Brodie Mtn. to the abandoned fire tower, then descends southeast to US 7. Brodie Mtn. is a ridge lying between the Mt. Greylock Range on the east and the Taconic Range on the west, being a continuation of the Taconic Range south of it.

The trail starts on an abandoned jeep road off Brodie Mtn. Rd. and follows the road steeply to the southern end of Brodie Mtn. At 1.1 mi. the trail turns right onto a footpath. (The jeep road continues northwest to Sheeps Heaven Mtn. and the southern end of the Brodie Mtn. ridge.) The trail ascends north, passing through briar patches and running east of and below the ridge's highest point at 2621 ft. It follows the crest to the fire tower at 2.6 mi., which is the second highest point of the Brodie Mtn. ridge at 2613 ft. The tower is unsafe.

The trail turns right and descends southeast on a jeep road, past a woods road exiting right. There are good views to the east of the Mt. Greylock range from the upper end of the ski slopes. After a descent of 1170 ft., the Skyline Trail ends on US 7 at 4.5 mi., or 20.2 mi. from the southern end of the trail. The trailhead here is 0.5 mi. north of the US 7 junction with Brodie Mtn. Rd. and 0.3 mi. south of the southern entrance to Brodie Mtn. Ski Area. Hikers can park their cars at the edge of the jeep road a few yards in from the highway. (A 5-mi. extension of the Taconic Skyline Trail over the Brodie Mtn. ridge to the summit of Mt. Greylock via Rockwell Rd. on US 7 is possible in the near future.)

Taconic Skyline Trail: Northern Section (Brodie Mtn. Rd. to US 7)

Distances from Brodie Mtn. Rd.

to unmarked side trail to Sheeps Heaven Mtn.: 1.1 mi. (45 min.)

to fire tower on Brodie Mtn.: 2.6 mi. (1 hr. 15 min.)

to US 7: 4.5 mi. (2 hr. 30 min.)

Tower Mtn. Rd.

This rough road, not passable by car, provides access from New York to the Taconic Skyline Trail near the summit of Tower Mtn. (2193 ft.). To reach this road, proceed north 0.7 mi. from the Columbia–Rensselaer county line sign on NY 22 north of Lebanon Springs. Turn right onto Goodrich Hollow Rd., which is passable by car. Tower Mtn. Rd. starts on the right, 0.8 mi. from NY 22, where Goodrich Hollow Rd. makes a sharp turn left. Tower Mtn.

Rd. ascends through the forest to the Taconic Skyline Trail and the summit of Tower Mtn. There are good views, mostly west, from the open summit.

Tower Mtn. Rd.

Distances from Goodrich Hollow Rd.

  to Taconic Skyline Trail: 1.3 mi. (1 hr. 10 min.)

  to summit of Tower Mtn. (via Taconic Skyline Trail): 1.7 mi. (1 hr. 30 min.)

Brickhouse Mtn. Rd. (DEM)

This abandoned road, not passable by car beyond the last farm-house, provides access to Tower Mtn. and the Taconic Skyline Trail from Massachusetts. Follow the state forest signs from West St. in Pittsfield to the junction with Churchill St. Turn right onto Churchill St. Take the first left (west) onto Cascade St. and continue past the dead-end sign. Brickhouse Mtn. Rd. ascends through the woods past a wide fire road on the right. The Taconic Skyline Trail enters from the left and continues to the summit of Tower Mtn.

Brickhouse Mtn. Rd.

Distances from Cascade St. (Pittsfield)

  to Taconic Skyline Trail: 2 mi. (1 hr. 20 min.)

  to summit of Tower Mtn. (via Taconic Skyline Trail): 2.3 mi. (1 hr. 40 min.)

Hawthorne Trail (DEM)

This narrow trail leads over forested Pine Mtn. (2220 ft.) to Tilden Pond, from which you can reach Tower Mtn. and Berry Pond. The trail starts at the Pittsfield State Forest ski lodge. Crossing the foot-bridge in front of the lodge, it bears right after 500 ft. and again at 0.3 mi. The trail ascends along the right (east) side of a brook and turns right at the first trail junction (left leads 0.25 mi. to the top of the Ghost and Shadow ski trails). It continues past a stone boundary marker on Pine Mtn. and descends to Tilden Pond. At the trail junction, left leads to Tower Mtn. via a fire road and right leads to Tilden Pond Dam and to Berry Pond via the same fire road.

Hawthorne Trail

Distances from Pittsfield State Forest ski lodge
>   *to* first trail junction: 0.9 mi. (50 min.)
>   *to* Pine Mtn.: 1.4 mi. (1 hr. 15 min.)
>   *to* Tilden Pond junction: 2 mi. (1 hr. 35 min.)
>   *to* summit of Tower Mtn. (via fire road and Taconic Skyline Trail): 2.7 mi. (2 hr. 10 min.)
>   *to* Berry Pond (via fire road and Taconic Skyline Trail): 3 mi. (2 hr. 20 min.)

Parker Brook Trail (DEM)

This trail starts in back of the comfort station at the Parker Brook Campground in Pittsfield State Forest. At 500 ft. a cross-country ski trail exits left over a bridge to the Hawthorne Trail (0.3 mi.). At 0.2 mi. the Parker Brook Trail crosses a brook and continues ascending through the forest or along woods roads to the fire road at Tilden Pond dam. Follow the road left to the Hawthorne Trail, Pine Mt., and Tower Mt., right to Berry Pond.

Parker Brook Trail

Distance from Parker Brook Campground comfort station
>   *to* Tilden Pond: 1.3 mi. (1 hr. 10 min.)

Turner Trail (DEM)

This woods road, between the two branches of Berry Pond Circuit Rd., provides the shortest footpath to Berry Pond (2060 ft.) as well as access to Berry Hill (2200 ft.). Berry Pond is the southern terminus of the Taconic Crest Trail, which coincides with the Taconic Skyline Trail from Berry Pond on the south to Potter Mtn. Rd. on the north. Berry Hill, with fine views west toward the Catskills and Adirondacks, is traversed by the Taconic Skyline Trail.

To reach the Turner Trail, drive to the comfort station at Parker Brook Campground. Just beyond, a small road on the right leads to the start of the wide trail on the left. It passes a cross-country ski trail and bears left at the fork. A short side trail on the left leads to Berry Pond. The Turner Trail continues through azalea and berry fields to follow the auto road uphill a short distance, to Berry Hill on the left.

Turner Trail

Distances from Parker Brook Campground comfort station
   to side trail to Berry Pond: 1.5 mi. (1 hr. 5 min.)
   to auto road: 1.7 mi. (1 hr. 15 min.)
   to Berry Hill: 1.8 mi. (1 hr. 20 min.)

Lulu Brook Trail (DEM)

This narrow, sometimes obscure, footpath parallels Lulu Brook. It
starts at the Lulu Cascade Picnic Area on the right of the auto road
just before the stone bridge. The trail clings to the steep side of the
brook and ends at the fire road. (The wide Honwee Circuit Trail,
described below, and its northern extension parallel the Lulu Brook
Trail from end to end.) At the junction with the fire road, left leads to
Berry Pond Circuit Rd. near a large "Berry House" sign. You can
follow this road and the Taconic Skyline Trail to the summit of
Berry Hill.

Lulu Brook Trail

Distances from Lulu Cascade Picnic Area
   to fire road: 1.6 mi. (1 hr. 15 min.)
   to Taconic Skyline Trail (via fire road): 1.9 mi. (1 hr. 25 min.)
   to summit of Berry Hill (via Taconic Skyline Trail): 2 mi. (1 hr.
      30 min.)

Honwee Circuit Trail (DEM)

This trail, with a connecting trail from the north, passes over the
wooded summit of Honwee Mtn. (2313 ft.). The trail starts 120 ft.
beyond a small rustic building opposite the Lulu Cascade Picnic
Area on the right side of the auto road (the Lulu Brook Trail is 150
ft. farther along). It ascends gradually on a gravel road and passes
a dead-end service road on the right. At 0.9 mi. it turns right uphill.
(The road straight ahead passes a wide side trail on the right in 0.4
mi. and reaches the fire road in 0.7 mi. The side trail branches left
to the Colonial Trail at 0.5 mi. and right to the Honwee Circuit
Trail at 0.4 mi.) Near the summit, if you turn 180 degrees, you will
see the Colonial Trail on the left. The trail passes over the flat sum-

mit and descends to the Lulu Cascade Picnic Area, 200 ft. south of the starting point.

Honwee Circuit Trail

Distances from Lulu Cascade Picnic Area

   to right turn: 0.9 mi. (35 min.)

   to summit of Honwee Mtn. and connection to Colonial Trail: 1.5 mi. (1 hr. 20 min.)

   to Lulu Cascade Picnic Area (loop): 3 mi. (2 hr. 5 min.)

Colonial Trail (DEM)

The Colonial Trail (formerly Churchill Brook Trail), along with the Burgoyne and Daniels Brook trails, connects Potter Mtn. Rd. with the Taconic Skyline Trail and the Taconic Crest Trail. To reach Potter Mtn. Rd., take US 7 0.6 mi. north from the Lanesboro town line at Pontoosuc Lake. Blue Hill Rd. exits left (west) from US 7. Follow it to Balance Rock Rd. Take Balance Rock Rd. to the junction with Potter Mtn. Rd. at 2 mi. on the right. Potter Mtn. Rd. is rough but passable by car, except in the winter. It is also accessible from MA 43 in Hancock on the other side of the Taconic Range.

From the start of Potter Mtn. Rd. drive 0.8 mi. to a small parking area south of Daniels Brook, where the Colonial Trail and Daniels Brook Trail begin at the brook (avoid the wide woods road on the left). At 850 ft. the orange-blazed Colonial Trail bears left; the blue-blazed Daniels Brook Trail leads right. The Colonial Trail crosses Churchill Brook, passes a connecting trail to the Honwee Circuit Trail on the left, and reaches the Taconic Skyline Trail 0.5 mi. north of Berry Pond Circuit Rd.

Colonial Trail

Distances from Daniels Brook

   to Churchill Brook: 1.2 mi. (55 min.)

   to Taconic Skyline Trail: 1.9 mi. (1 hr. 20 min.)

Daniels Brook Trail

This narrow, blue-blazed trail follows the west side of Daniels Brook. The trail starts in concert with the Colonial Trail and then bears right at 850 ft. At 0.3 mi. a bridge over a rocky chasm leads to a small camping area. From the junction of the Daniels Brook Trail with the Taconic Skyline Trail at 1.4 mi., it is 0.8 mi. south to the Colonial Trail and 0.1 mi. north to the Burgoyne Trail.

Daniels Brook Trail

Distances from Daniels Brook
>   *to* chasm: 0.3 mi. (20 min.)
>   *to* Taconic Skyline Trail: 1.4 mi. (1 hr. 10 min.)

Burgoyne Trail (DEM)

This orange-blazed trail, also known as the Smoke Trail, starts on Potter Mtn. Rd. 0.3 mi. north of Daniels Brook. At 0.2 mi. a cutoff to the Colonial Trail exits on the left. The Taconic Skyline Trail intersects at 1.3 mi.

Burgoyne Trail

Distances from Potter Mtn. Rd.
>   *to* cutoff to Colonial Trail: 0.2 mi. (10 min.)
>   *to* Taconic Skyline Trail: 1.3 mi. (1 hr. 5 min.)

Balance Rock Trail (DEM)

This white-blazed trail is located in Balance Rock State Park in Lanesboro. The park entrance is on Balance Rock Rd. past the intersection with Potter Mtn. Rd. (see Colonial Trail description). The trail begins at Balance Rock, a group of Ice Age boulders, located near the parking area. It starts as a wide woods road on the left of Balance Rock. It proceeds straight ahead through a turn-around, crosses a brook, and bears right at a fork (left leads to Potter Mtn. Rd.). The trail intersects Potter Mtn. Rd. and the Taconic Skyline Trail at 2.3 mi.

Balance Rock Trail

Distances from Balance Rock
>   *to* turnaround: 0.3 mi. (10 min.)
>   *to* fork: 1.5 mi. (50 min.)
>   *to* Potter Mtn. Rd. and Taconic Skyline Trail: 2.3 mi. (1 hr. 35 min.)

TACONIC CREST TRAIL (THC)

The white-blazed Taconic Crest Trail runs for 35 mi. in a north-south direction along the ridge of the Taconic Range on the Massachu-setts–New York border from Prosser Hollow in the town of Peters-burg, NY to Rte. 20 in the town of Hancock, MA. The trail elevation varies from 1000 ft. at Prosser Hollow to 2798 ft. on the summit of Berlin Mtn. The cumulative ascent along the trail in a south-north direction is 6700 ft. The trail's average elevation exceeds 2200 ft. The Taconic Range is covered by hardwoods with open meadows on some of the higher elevations. These open areas afford fine views of the Green Mtns., the Catskills, and the Adirondacks.

The trail was established and is maintained by the Taconic Hik-ing Club (THC) of Troy, NY. It is marked by white, diamond-shaped markers and supplemental white blazes. Access trails are designated by similar blue markers. Because this is a ridge trail, water sources close to the trail are infrequent. The following descriptions are in sections, each a day's hike apart. Access trails are described after the final section. While access trails other than those mentioned here exist, they have been omitted from this guide because they lie on private property and are not maintained by the THC. These trails, which are always the fastest way down the ridge to civilization, should be used only in case of emergency.

The trail runs in large part over private property with the gener-ous consent of the landowners. Hikers should respect signs posting property adjacent to the main trail and the access trails and take special care with fires.

Also included in this section are several side trails and access trails that connect with the Taconic Crest Trail.

Taconic Crest Trail: Prosser Hollow, NY to Petersburg Pass (NY 2)

The northern terminus of the Taconic Crest Trail is located on Prosser Hollow Road which is to the east of Rte. 22 between the towns of North Petersburg and Petersburg, NY. The trail rises steeply to the ridge and turns south, reaching a sharp drop-off to the east. From this point the racetrack at Green Mtn. Park is visible. Continuing south, at 4.5 mi. a side trail to the left (marked "S.H.") enters from North Pownal and leads to Snow Hole, a deep cleft that generally contains snow year-round.

From Snow Hole the trail continues south through hardwoods, emerging into a number of clearings on the western side of the ridge that look out over the valley. Visible are NY 2 to Petersburg, NY, the abandoned ski area at Petersburg Pass, and Mt. Greylock to the southeast. About 1 mi. after the clearings the red-blazed Birch Brook Trail descends left to the Hopkins Memorial Forest. In another 0.75 mi. the blue-blazed R.R.R. Brooks Trail exits left. The Taconic Crest Trail eventually emerges in a clearing and descends to meet NY 2 at 7.4 mi. Parking is available here.

Taconic Crest Trail: Prosser Hollow, NY, to Petersburg Pass (NY 2)

Distances from Prosser Hollow Rd.

to top of the ridge: 1.8 mi. (1 hr.)

to side trail from North Pownal to Snow Hole: 4.5 mi. (2 hr. 50 min.)

to Birch Brook Trail: 5.5 mi. (3 hr. 30 min.)

to R.R.R. Brooks Trail: 6.9 mi. (4 hr. 30 min.)

to Petersburg Pass (NY 2): 7.4 mi. (4 hr. 50 min.)

Taconic Crest Trail: Petersburg Pass (NY 2) to Southeast Hollow, New York

The parking lot is located 4.0 mi. from the intersection of MA 2 and US 7 in Williamstown. From the west end of the parking lot, follow a level road past an abandoned quarrying site along the hillside. The trail soon descends then rises steeply on old woods roads to a junction that leads left to the summit of Mt. Raimer and views from the abandoned ski slopes. Stay to the right, following white markers on a heavily rutted woods road that winds along the wooded ridge. The trail turns right at a fork and descends into an open meadow above Berlin Pass, which offers extensive views.

Descending to the pass, the trail intersects the old Albany–Boston Post Road (also known as the Berlin Pass Trail; description with access trails). To the west it is 1.4 mi. to Greene Hollow and

4.5 mi. to Berlin, NY. To the east it is 0.8 mi. to Bee Hill Rd., which goes to Williamstown, MA. You can find water down the post road to the east. Bottle gentians are common here.

Crossing the Post Road and ascending the woods road south, the trail reaches the summit of Berlin Mtn. (2798 ft.) at 2.67 mi. From the summit, the highest point on the trail, there are fine views in all directions. Especially prominent is Mt. Greylock to the east. The blue-blazed Berlin Mtn. Trail and the old Williams College Ski Trail exit left (east) from the summit remains of an old fire tower. These trails lead to the abandoned Williams College Ski Area parking lot and Berlin Rd., respectively. Follow the blue-and-orange blazes of the Berlin Mtn. Trail (on the right, about 50 yd. below the summit) if you wish to descend on this trail.

From Berlin Mtn., the Taconic Crest Trail descends to the southeast through a dense spruce grove, continuing through an open, predominantly hardwood, forest. (About 0.3 mi. southeast of the main summit in New York is a smaller, unnamed peak which is the second highest summit in Massachusetts). At a saddle 2 mi. from the summit, a small but reliable spring is located 90 yd. down the hill to the west. At 5.2 mi. the trail reaches the saddle at the head of Southeast Hollow, where it intersects an old dirt road. To the right (west) is the Southeast Hollow Trail (description with access trails), which leads 1.7 mi. to Southeast Hollow Rd. and 5 mi. to Berlin, NY. To the left (east) it is 2 mi. via the unmarked Mills Hollow Trail to Oblong Rd. near MA 43 in Hancock, MA.

Wild ginger is found near the junction with the Southeast Hollow Trail. Water is found about 0.7 mi. down this access trail. A few yards south of the junction is a stone monument marking the New York–Massachusetts border.

Taconic Crest Trail: Petersburg Pass (NY 2) to Southeast Hollow, New York

Distances from Petersburg Pass (NY 2)

> *to* Albany–Boston Post Road (Berlin Pass Trail): 1.9 mi. (1 hr. 15 min.)
>
> *to* summit of Berlin Mtn.: 2.7 mi. (1 hr. 50 min.)
>
> *to* Southeast Hollow: 5.2 mi. (3 hr. 30 min.)

Taconic Crest Trail: Southeast Hollow, New York, to Bentley Hollow, MA

The Taconic Crest Trail proceeds south from the junction with the Southeast Hollow Trail and in a few yards turns sharply left at the stone monument marking the New York–Massachusetts border. After a short distance it bears right and climbs steeply to a small open space, then descends to a small meadow affording fine views to the southeast. Reentering the woods, the trail descends a long ridge. Passing over several knobs to Bentley Hollow, it meets the blue-blazed Bentley Hollow Trail (description with access trails) on the left at 3 mi.

Taconic Crest Trail: Southeast Hollow, NY, to Bentley Hollow, MA

Distances from Southeast Hollow Trail
    to meadow with views: 1.9 mi. (1 hr. 10 min.)
    to Bentley Hollow: 3 mi. (2 hr. 15 min.)

Taconic Crest Trail: Bentley Hollow, MA, to Rathburn Hollow, NY

The Taconic Crest Trail proceeds south from the junction with the Bentley Hollow Trail, soon beginning a long ascent. At 0.5 mi. is a metal state-line marker and at 1 mi. a stone state-line monument. You can find water in the next low place, where the Taconic Crest Trail joins a snowmobile trail.

The trail now wanders over the several summits of Misery Mtn. The topography is confusing here because the summits are elongated at right angles to the general trend of the range, and care must be taken to keep on the white-marked trail. After crossing the main peak (2611 feet) of Misery Mtn., the trail veers south through hardwoods and across several knobs. It exits off the jeep trail that was the old Taconic Crest Trail (watch for blazes) and comes out on the last summit in an open meadow covered by hackle bush. (You can continue on the unmarked jeep trail for 1 mi. to rejoin the Taconic Crest Trail. This offers a faster but less scenic route.) From the last summit the trail descends steeply to the junction with the Rathburn Hollow Trail.

Taconic Crest Trail: Bentley Hollow, MA, to Rathburn Hollow, NY

Distances from Bentley Hollow Trail

    to main peak of Misery Mtn.: 1.9 mi. (1 hr. 15 min.)

    to jeep trail: 3.2 mi. (2 hr.)

    to meadow on last summit: 3.5 mi. (2 hr. 15 min.)

    to Rathburn Hollow Trail: 3.9 mi. (2 hr. 35 min.)

Taconic Crest Trail: Rathburn Hollow, NY, to Rte. 20, Hancock, MA

The Taconic Crest Trail crosses a small stream immediately south of the Rathburn Hollow Trail and ascends through hardwoods along the left (east) side of the ridge. Nearing the summit, the trail bears to the right side of the ridge and climbs, emerging at the top of an open meadow known as Bill's Lunch, where there is a small grove of evergreens. There are good views of the Taconic Valley from here.

For the next 0.75 mi. the trail descends steeply through the meadow, enters the woods, and follows a small stream. It then turns westward downhill through mixed hardwoods and evergreens. After crossing a stream, it crosses a snowmobile trail and begins a long ascent to the open summit of Rounds Mtn. (2257 ft.) at 2.5 mi.

At Rounds Mtn. the trail turns left for about 100 yd. on a well-used dirt road, then turns sharp left into the woods. The unmarked Rounds Mtn. Trail continues straight ahead. (*Caution:* Due to an absence of trees, neither of the two trail junctions with this dirt road is well marked.)

The trail now descends steadily, steeply in spots, finally meeting a well-used woods road at about 3.2 mi. Crossing the road, the trail makes a gradual ascent through a birch grove, turns sharp right, and descends steeply to Madden Rd., meeting old MA 43 at 4.7 mi. in the village of Hancock, MA. From here the trail follows roads a short distance through the village to MA 43. Crossing MA 43, the trail follows Potter Mtn. Rd. for 1.5 mi. to the height-of-land in Pittsfield State Forest. The white-blazed Taconic Skyline Trail exits left (north) just before the powerline crossing. Continuing under the powerlines, the Taconic Crest Trail parallels the Taconic Skyline Trail and coninues south to Berry Pond. After skirting the west side of Berry Pond on a road, the trail reenters the woods, crosses the open summit of Tower Mt. (views to the south and west) and follows the forested ridge to the parking area on Rte. 20, 6.0 mi. west of Pittsfield, MA.

Taconic Crest Trail: Rathburn Hollow, NY, to Rte. 20, Hancock, MA

Distances from Rathburn Hollow Trail
    to Bill's Lunch: 1.1 mi. (35 min.)
    to summit of Rounds Mtn.: 2.5 mi. (1 hr. 15 min.)
    to woods road: 3.2 mi. (1 hr. 50 min.)
    to old MA 43 (Hancock): 4.7 mi. (2 hr. 30 min.)
    to Potter Mtn. Rd.: 4.9 mi. (2 hr. 40 min.)
    to Taconic Skyline Trail: 6.2 mi. (3 hr. 10 min.)
    to Berry Pond: 10.5 mi. (5 hr. 30 min.)
    to Rte. 20: 15.5 mi. (7 hr. 30 min.)

Birch Brook Trail (WOC)

This access trail to the Taconic Crest Trail begins in the Hopkins Memorial Forest of Williams College in Williamstown, MA. To get to the forest, go west on Main St. in Williamstown to US 7 north for 0.4 mi.; bear left on Bulkley St. and continue 1 mi. to Northwest Hill Rd. The Birch Brook Trail is 1.4 mi. along Northwest Hill Rd.

On the left side of the road are two circular turnouts. From the first turnout the trail ascends gently and then descends, making a sharp bend to the left. It continues to the north branch of Birch Brook at 0.9 mi., bearing right along the north side of the brook. The trail climbs to the west, parallel to the brook. A loop trail exits right at 1 mi. The trail gradually moves away from the brook, and the loop trail reenters from the right at 1.3 mi. The trail then turns left and ascends to the last stream crossing at 1.4 mi. A mile-long steep climb through deciduous forest (crossing the Massachusetts–New York line at 2 mi.) ends at the junction with the white-blazed Taconic Crest Trail.

Birch Brook Trail

Distances from Northwest Hill Rd.

   to Birch Brook: 0.9 mi. (35 min.)

   to Taconic Crest Trail: 2.7 mi. (1 hr. 50 min.)

Berlin Pass Trail (WOC)

To reach the north end of this blue-blazed trail at Berlin Pass by car, start 3 mi. southwest of Williamstown at the junction of US 7 and MA 2. Take MA 2 uphill (west) for 0.5 mi. and turn left onto Torrey Woods Rd., which meets Bee Hill Rd., continue west on Bee Hill Rd. to the abandoned Williams College Ski Area parking lot. Park on the right (north) side of the lot and take the path to the dirt road just ahead. (*Do not* take the trail blocked by a vandalized gate.)

   This trail, once a section of the Boston–Albany Post Road, leads uphill 0.8 mi. to the Taconic ridge at Berlin Pass (2220 ft.), where it intersects the Taconic Crest Trail. Following the Crest Trail to the left (south), it is 1.2 mi. to the summit of Berlin Mtn. (The remains of an old charcoal kiln are located off the trail 100 ft. to the right, 0.5 mi. beyond the pass.) The old post road crosses the pass and descends the west slope of the Taconic Range to Berlin, NY. Following the Crest Trail to the right (north) at the junction leads across scenic open meadows to an abandoned ski area and NY 2 in Petersburg Pass.

Berlin Pass Trail

Distances from Williams College Ski Area parking lot

   to Berlin Pass (Taconic Crest Trail): 0.8 mi. (1 hr.)

   to summit of Berlin Mtn. (via Taconic Crest Trail south): 2 mi.
      (1 hr. 30 min.)

   to NY 2 in Petersburg Pass (via Taconic Crest Trail north): 2.7
      mi. (2 hr. 15 min.)

Berlin Mountain Trail (WOC)

This blue-blazed trail was originally constructed in 1933 by members of the Williams Outing Club. It was relocated around its original trailhead at Haskin Farm in 1980. To reach the trailhead by car, follow the instructions under the Berlin Pass Trail. The trail begins on Bee Hill Rd., 1.1 mi. from the junction of Bee Hill Rd. and Torrey Woods Rd. The parking lot, located on the left side of the road a short distance past some residences and Haskin Farm, can accommodate two or three cars.

From the parking area, the trail enters the woods, quickly turning left along a woods road. At 0.25 mi. the trail turns right and descends to Hemlock Brook at 0.3 mi. After crossing the brook, it joins another woods road, turning left along it and then right up a steep gully. At 0.7 mi. the trail levels off and then descends to an abandoned campsite at 1 mi. It turns sharp right, crosses a stream, and turns right again onto another woods road. At 1.25 mi. the trail leaves the woods road and begins a steep ascent to a ridge at 1.5 mi. (Do not take the orange-blazed side trail on the left. This leads downhill to a seminary off Oblong Rd. in Williamstown, MA.) It follows the ridge to the summit of Berlin Mtn. at 2.5 mi.

Berlin Mountain Trail

Distances from Bee Hill Rd.

　　to Hemlock Brook: 0.3 mi. (15 min.)
　　to ridge: 1.5 mi. (1 hr.)
　　to summit of Berlin Mtn.: 2.5 mi. (1 hr. 50 min.)

R.R.R. Brooks Trail (WOC)

Paralleling MA 2, this blue-blazed trail is a direct route from Williamstown to Petersburg Pass through the 930-acre Taconic Trail State Park. From the junction of MA 2 and US 7 in Williamstown, go south on US 7 0.8 mi. to graveled Bee Hill Rd. on the right. Ascend to a reservoir and dam.

The trail starts on the left end of the dam, turns right into the woods, clings to the side of Flora Glen, and gradually meets a stream. It ascends through pines and forks right (left leads to Bee Hill, 1428 ft.). At 0.75 mi. the trail comes out on the southeast end of a field and continues across the field on a barely noticeable footpath until the narrow field opens up on both sides. The trail is often wet and waist high with weeds. It goes diagonally left across the field and toward the treeline straight ahead. (When MA 2 becomes visible, keep it in sight but do not hike toward it, heading instead for the opposite treeline.) The trail bears left along a dirt road after entering the treeline and becomes more visible just before the dirt road meets the highway. The trail follows the woods road that parallels the highway for 0.5 mi. It eventually ascends the ridge past a scenic clearing, enters the woods, and soon meets the white-blazed Taconic Crest Trail at Petersburg Pass.

R.R.R. Brooks Trail

Distance from dam on Bee Hill Rd.
   to Taconic Crest Trail (at Petersburg Pass): 3.3 mi. (2 hr. 30 min.)

Southeast Hollow Trail (THC)

The trail begins off Southeast Hollow Rd., which intersects NY 22 at the southern boundary of Berlin, NY. Follow Southeast Hollow Rd., bearing right at all junctions, to a bridge marked "narrow," 3.3 mi. from NY 22. The access trail begins from the left side of the road, about 15 ft. past the narrow bridge. The trail follows an old road to the top of the ridge. At first it parallels a small stream, then turns right and gets steeper before meeting the white-blazed Taconic Crest Trail at 1.7 mi. on the top of the ridge.

(*Note:* Parking is limited, as Southeast Hollow Rd. is quite narrow at the start of the access trail. Space for about four cars is available at the top of the hill, about 200 yd. west of the narrow bridge. Do not park blocking the trail because it is used as a jeep road.)

Southeast Hollow Trail

Distance from Southeast Hollow Rd.
   to Taconic Crest Trail: 1.7 mi. (1 hr.)

Bentley Hollow Trail (THC)

The blue-blazed trail starts on MA 43 4.5 mi. north of Brodie Mtn. Rd. (the turnoff to the Jiminy Peak Ski Area) and 0.3 mi. north of the Hancock Tire and Machine Co. You can park on the Roberts property south of the house with permission.

The trail passes between two meadows and soon enters the woods, climbing steadily on a tote road until it reaches the Taconic

Crest Trail. There are springs on the left side of the trail about 500 ft. below the Taconic Crest Trail. Camping is allowed here.

Bentley Hollow Trail

Distance from MA 43
   to Taconic Crest Trail: 1.2 mi. (45 min.)

Rathburn Hollow Trail

The trailhead is located on Rathburn Hollow Rd. To get there, follow MA 43 1.25 mi. north of Brodie Mtn. Rd. (the turnoff to the Jiminy Peak Ski Area). About 100 yd. south of a grade school on the opposite side of MA 43 is Rathburn Hollow Rd. Turn left onto Rathburn Hollow Rd. and continue 1.5 mi. to a parking area, located just before the road turns sharply left to cross a brook.

   Crossing the brook on a bridge, the trail goes uphill along the road, passing to the right of and behind the brown house. About 100 ft. past the house the trail turns right into the woods, where the blue blazes begin. The trail ascends gradually, becoming steeper and finally leveling off when it meets the Taconic Crest Trail at 0.8 mi. Do not drink from the brook until above the brown house. (Note: Local usage favors the spelling "*Rathbun*" rather than "*Rathburn*," which is used on the USGS maps. Local road signs will probably read "*Rathbun*.")

Rathburn Hollow Trail

Distance from Rathburn Hollow Rd.
   to Taconic Crest Trail: 0.8 mi. (45 min.)

Rounds Mtn. Trail

The trailhead is located on Rounds Mtn. Rd., which exits MA 43 at the Millhof Lodge 1.1 mi. east of NY 22. The road sign for Rounds Mtn. Rd. is about 100 ft. from MA 43. Follow Rounds Mtn. Rd. 1 mi. to a stable and house trailer. Parking is available in a meadow beside a modern home a short distance past the trailer. Park so that your car is not blocking the trail, which is used as a jeep road. The blue-blazed trail follows the jeep road, climbing steadily to the crest of Rounds Mtn. Due to an absence of trees, the junction with the Taconic Crest Trail is not well marked and care is necessary, both in locating the white blazes of the Crest Trail and in identifying which section leads south to Hancock, MA, and which leads north to Rathburn Hollow.

Rounds Mtn. Trail

Distance from Rounds Mtn. Rd.
   to Taconic Crest Trail: 1 mi. (50 min.)

MT. GREYLOCK

In the northwest corner of Massachusetts is the state's highest summit, 3491-ft. Mt. Greylock. Running slightly more than 11 mi. in length from north to south, the Greylock range is bordered on the west by the Taconic range and on the east by the Hoosac range. To the north lies the Hoosic River valley, beyond which lie the Green Mountains of Vermont. The area encompasses parts of six towns: Adams, North Adams, Williamstown, New Ashford, Lanesborough, and Cheshire.

The principal summits of the main ridge, from south to north, include Rounds Rock (2581 ft.), the three peaks of Saddle Ball Mtn. (3238, 3228, and 3222 ft., respectively), Mt. Greylock, Mt. Fitch (3110 ft.), and Mt. Williams (2951 ft.) On a spur ridge leading east from the summit are the twin peaks of Ragged Mtn. (2528 and 2451 ft.). On the northwest side of the summit is a deep glacial ravine known as the Hopper. Mt. Prospect (2690 ft.) is the high point of the spur ridge on the far side of the Hopper.

An extensive trail network offers a variety of hikes ranging from easy to strenuous. Many of the trails have outstanding viewpoints over the surrounding countryside. The broad, open summit offers panoramic views extending over three states. Principal landmarks at the summit include Bascom Lodge, a radio tower, and a 180-ft. high granite war memorial.

Efforts to preserve the Mt. Greylock area began during the late 1800s, in a reaction to the devastation caused by logging, mining, and other nineteenth century industrial activities. Today, over 12,000 acres are protected as part of the Mass. Department of Environmental Management's Mt. Greylock State Reservation.

The summit and several trailheads can be reached via two paved roads extending through the reservation—Rockwell Rd. from the south and Notch Rd. from the north. To reach Rockwell Rd. from Lanesborough center, head north on US 7, bear right onto North Main St., take the first right at Greylock Rd. (also called Quarry Rd.), and the first left onto Rockwell Rd. Notch Rd. begins on Main St. (MA 2) in North Adams, just east of the middle bridge over the Hoosic River. The two roads meet just below the summit and run together for the last half mile to the summit. Total distance to the summit via either road is about 9 mi. Neither road is plowed in winter.

The Mt. Greylock Visitor Center, operated by the AMC in cooperation with DEM, is located near the lower end of Rockwell Rd. in Lanesborough. The AMC also operates Bascom Lodge at the summit, where meals and lodging are available between May and October (reservations required; tel. 413-443-0011). Trail information is available at both the visitor center and Bascom Lodge. Sperry Campground, on the west slope of the mountain at elevation 2400 ft., has facilities for individual and group camping. The campground is located on Sperry Rd. (dirt; passable by car), which leads north off Rockwell Rd. about 3 mi. below the summit. There are also several shelters and lean-tos on the trails which are available for backpackers on a first-come, first-served basis.

Refer to the Mt. Greylock map included with this trail guide.

Appalachian Trail

The Appalachian Trail (AT) traverses Mt. Greylock, following the crest of the ridge for most of its route. Road access is at Main St. (MA 2) in North Adams, the Greylock summit road, and Outlook Ave. in Cheshire. For a description of the trail route, see Appalachian Trail: Cheshire to MA 2 (North Adams).

Roaring Brook Trail

This trail is the shortest route to Mt. Greylock from the west. It is located 1 mi. off US 7, 4 mi. north of the Springs Restaurant and Motel in New Ashford and 1.5 mi. south of the junction of US 7 and MA 43 in South Williamstown. At sign turn onto a narrow gravel road, passable to cars, and continue to a parking place at 0.5 mi. On foot, bear left at the fork and follow the brook along a rough road. Cross the brook three times and continue to the junction with the Stony Ledge Ski Trail on the left (sign) at 0.5 mi. (30 min.). This is the beginning of the trail. The trail bears right and ascends steeply through birch and spruce woods. At a footbridge crossing Roaring Brook the trail crosses the Deer Hill Trail and the Circular Trail. At 1.5 mi. it bears left over a second bridge to Sperry Campground and Sperry Rd. From here the Hopper Trail leads to the summit of Mt. Greylock.

Roaring Brook Trail

Distance from Stony Ledge Ski Trail

> *to* summit of Mt. Greylock (via Hopper Trail): 4.4 mi. (3 hr. 20 min.)

Deer Hill Trail

This trail starts from the Roaring Brook Trail (see the previous description) just southwest of Sperry Campground. It descends steeply to the cascades on the left, following rock steps in places. After the falls, it continues to descend steeply until crossing a bridge over the stream. It then climbs past a lean-to, turns left (northeast), and slabs the side of the ridge. It crosses Sperry Rd. at 1.75 mi. and continues northeast, ending at the Hopper Trail.

Deer Hill Trail

Distances from Roaring Brook Trail

> *to* lean-to: 0.5 mi. (25 min.)
>
> *to* Sperry Rd.: 1.3 mi. (1 hr. 10 min.)
>
> *to* Hopper Trail: 1.7 mi. (1 hr. 20 min.)

Circular Trail

This trail, about 0.6 mi. long, leaves the south side of the Roaring Brook Trail at the first footbridge (see the description of the Roaring Brook Trail). It forms a loop that returns to the Roaring Brook Trail just before the latter reaches Sperry Rd.

Stony Ledge Trail

This trail, originally cleared as a ski trail, is a good circuit route to Stony Ledge. To reach the trailhead, follow the directions to the start of the Roaring Brook Trail. Bear left at the Stony Ledge Trail, continuing through overgrown fields and over stone walls to a woods road. At the end of the road, turn right onto a steep section and proceed past the lean-to to the outlook at Stony Ledge, where the trail meets the northern end of Sperry Rd. Sperry Campground is 0.5 mi. down Sperry Rd.

Stony Ledge Trail

Distances from Roaring Brook Trail
   to Stony Ledge: 2.6 mi. (2 hr. 5 min.)
   to Sperry Campground: 3.5 mi. (2 hr. 35 min.)

Hopper Trail

To reach the start of the trail, turn off MA 43 onto Hopper Rd. 2.5 mi. south of Williamstown at an abandoned gate of the former Mt. Hope Farm (Sweets Corner). Continue on Hopper Rd. about 1 mi., turn left, and in 0.5 mi. park off road on the left near the information kiosk. The trail begins beyond the gate then bears right at the junction with the Money Brook Trail. It passes through fields and ascends steeply through the woods to a level area of Sperry Campground. The trail bears left onto Sperry Rd., then leaves the road to the left at a parking area at the beginning of the March Cataract Trail. Shortly the trail turns sharp left onto an old carriage road as the Deer Hill Trail enters from the right. The Hopper Trail passes the Overlook Trail on the left and the hairpin turn of Rockwell Rd. on the right. The trail then ascends steeply to a junction with Rockwell Rd., the Cheshire Harbor Trail, and the Appalachian Trail. Turn left (north) on the Appalachian Trail to reach the summit of Mt. Greylock.

Hopper Trail

Distances from farm gate
   to Money Brook Trail: 0.2 mi. (5 min.)
   to Sperry Campground: 2.2 mi. (2 hr.)

to Appalachian Trail: 3.5 mi. (3 hr.)
to summit of Mt. Greylock (via Appalachian Trail): 4 mi. (3 hr. 25 min.)

March Cataract Trail

This short trail, steep in places, leads northeast from a parking area on Sperry Rd. to the scenic March Cataract Falls on Bacon Brook. (The Hopper Trail leaves Sperry Rd. at the same location, heading southeast.)

March Cataract Trail

Distance from Sperry Rd.
to March Cataract Falls: 0.8 mi. (45 min.)

Overlook Trail

The Overlook Trail connects Rockwell Rd. south of the summit with Notch Rd. north of the summit, and offers several good outlooks into the Hopper. It begins on the north side of the Hopper Trail, about 100 yd. before the latter reaches the hairpin turn on Rockwell Rd. Heading north and then east, the Overlook Trail follows the contour around the summit ridge, passing viewpoints to the northwest. At 1.2 mi. the trail crosses Notch Rd. and heads south on an old carriage road, climbing to a junction with the Appalachian Trail near the radio tower.

Overlook Trail

Distance from Hopper Trail
to Notch Rd.: 1.2 mi. (45 min.)
to Appalachian Trail: 1.6 mi. (1 hr. 10 min.)

Robinson's Point Trail

Beginning on Notch Rd. 0.1 mi. below (north of) the Overlook Trail crossing, this short but very steep trail leads down to a fine viewpoint of the Hopper and Mt. Prospect. Across the road from the trail entrance and slightly south is a blazed cutoff to the Appalachian Trail.

Robinson's Point Trail

Distance from Notch Rd.
    to view of the Hopper: 0.1 mi. (10 min.)

Money Brook Trail

This blue-blazed trail, in connection with the Appalachian Trail from the north, provides access to Mt. Williams and Mt. Greylock and can be used for a circuit trip. It is especially attractive in the spring because of the number and variety of wildflowers that grow along it. To reach the trail, go to the beginning of the Hopper Trail. At the trail junction (0.2 mi.) the Money Brook Trail bears left, passes through a camping area, and crosses Money Brook twice. Turning now to the north, the trail crosses two tributaries and then the main brook again, as the blue-blazed Mt. Prospect Trail exits to the left. The Money Brook Trail follows along the west bank of the brook for some distance, then crosses another tributary and passes a side trail on the right that leads 0.1 mi. to cascades. The main trail ascends steeply, reaching a plateau and a side trail to Notch Rd. on the right. It then passes a lean-to on the left and 0.2 mi. beyond reaches the Appalachian Trail near Wilbur Clearing and its junction with Notch Rd. 0.3 mi. farther east.

Money Brook Trail

Distances from Hopper Trail
    to Mt. Prospect Trail: 1.5 mi. (55 min.)
    to side trail to cascades: 2.4 mi. (1 hr. 35 min.)
    to lean-to: 3.1 mi. (2 hr. 5 min.)
    to Appalachian Trail: 3.3 mi. (2 hr. 15 min.)
    to Notch Rd. via Appalachian Trail: 3.6 mi. (2 hr. 30 min.)

Mt. Prospect Trail

Mt. Prospect (2690 ft.) is a wooded ridge on the northwest side of the Greylock range. To reach the start of the Mt. Prospect Trail, follow the Hopper Trail and Money Brook Trail for 1.7 mi. Turn left onto the blue-blazed Mt. Prospect Trail, which ascends steeply to the summit, continuing to a junction with the Appalachian Trail.

Mt. Prospect Trail

Distances from Money Brook Trail
>*to* summit of Mt. Prospect: 1 mi. (1 hr. 10 min.)
>*to* Appalachian Trail: 2 mi. (1 hr. 40 min.)

Bellows Pipe Trail

The trail begins on the south side of Notch Rd., where the road takes a sharp right turn before it enters the reservation from North Adams. Heading south, the trail starts out on a dirt access road for Notch Reservoir, then starts to climb, crossing numerous small brooks. The climb becomes steeper. At 2.2 mi., the trail enters a red spruce and red pine grove in the saddle between Mt. Greylock and Ragged Mtn. A few hundred yards beyond, after crossing a deep ravine, the trail turns sharply right (northwest) at a junction; the woods road straight ahead from the junction leads to Greylock Glen.

The Bellows Pipe Trail resumes its climb, passing a shelter on the right at 2.7 mi. and turning southwest for a level stretch. At 3.2 mi., the trail again turns northwest onto a woods road, ascending the ridge in a series of switchbacks. At the fourth switchback, the trail turns northwest off the woods road, which continues south to the Thunderbolt Trail. At 3.7 mi. the Bellows Pipe Trail ends at the Appalachian Trail. The summit of Mt. Greylock is about 0.5 mi. to the left.

Bellows Pipe Trail

Distances from Notch Rd.
>*to* shelter: 2.7 mi. (1 hr. 50 min.)
>*to* Appalachian Trail: 3.7 mi. (2 hr. 50 min.)
>*to* Mt. Greylock summit (via A.T.): 4.2 mi. (3 hr. 10 min.)

Thunderbolt Trail

One of the steepest trails on the mountain, the Thunderbolt was constructed by the CCC in 1934 as a championship ski trail. From the summit of Mt. Greylock, it drops 2260 vertical ft. on its 2 mile descent of the mountain. The trail was named after the roller coaster at Revere Beach near Boston because each was an unforgettable ride.

The Thunderbolt is accessed via the Appalachian Trail from the summit of Mt. Greylock, 0.4 mi. north of the summit parking area. The trail goes very steeply off the ridge on the wide, overgrown ski trail, crossing numerous woods roads on the lower reaches until reaching Thiel Rd. at 1.6 mi.

From the McKinley Monument in Adams, follow Maple St. to West Rd. Turn left and in 0.4 mi. turn right onto Gould Rd. and climb past orchards. Continue straight at the junction on Thiel Rd. The trail begins on the right just before the road ends.

Thunderbolt Trail

Distance from Thiel Rd.
>   *to* summit of Mt. Greylock: 2 mi. (2 hr. 5 min.)

Cheshire Harbor Trail

This trail is blazed with a white-paint ball over an orange-paint ball. To reach the trail, follow MA 8 to the McKinley Monument in Adams center. Maple St. exits right (west) at the monument. Follow Maple St. to West Rd. Turn left (south) onto West Rd., cross Pecks Brook, and take an immediate right onto West Mtn. Rd. Continue to the end of the road, where parking is available at the trailhead.

The trail zigzags steeply up to the junction with Old Adams Rd., an old stage road, which joins from the right. In a short distance the Cheshire Harbor Trail leaves the Old Adams Rd. to the right (northwest). (Left on the Old Adams Rd. leads 3 mi. to Jones Nose on Rockwell Rd.) Climbing less steeply for a stretch, a side trail leaves to the right and joins the Gould Trail near Peck's Brook Shelter and Falls. Resuming a steep climb, the trail reaches Rockwell Rd. at its junction with the Appalachian Trail, opposite the start of the Hopper Trail to the west. Turn right onto the Appalachian Trail to the summit of Mt. Greylock.

Cheshire Harbor Trail

Distances from West Mtn. Rd. (Adams)
>   *to* Old Adams Rd.: 1 mi. (40 min.)
>   *to* side trail to Peck's Falls: 1.5 mi. (1 hr. 10 min.)
>   *to* Rockwell Rd. (via Old Adams Rd.): 2.6 mi. (2 hr. 50 min.)

to summit of Mt. Greylock (via Appalchian Trail): 3.5 mi. (3 hr. 20 min.)

CCC Dynamite Trail

This connector trail leaves the Jones Nose Trail 0.3 mi. from the Jones Nose parking area. It proceeds north to Rockwell Rd. in 1.3 mi. with little change in grade. On the way it passes the site where CCC crews building the Rockwell Rd. during the 1930s stored their explosive dynamite. At Rockwell Rd. the trail meets Sperry Rd. into Sperry Campground.

CCC Dynamite Trail

Distances from Jones Nose parking area
   to CCC Dynamite Trail via Jones Nose Trail: 0.3 mi. (20 min.)
   to Rockwell Rd. (at Sperry Rd.): 1.3 mi. (45 min.)

Jones Nose Trail

This trail offers fine views as it climbs to the boreal forest on the summit of Saddle Ball Mt. The trail begins at the Jones Nose parking area on Rockwell Rd., and heads north through open fields with wide views to the east and west. The trail climbs steeply into the woods and levels out at the junction with the CCC Dynamite Trail at 0.3 mi. It again ascends steeply to a short side trail leading west with fantastic views from a rocky ledge. The trail becomes steeper, passes through balsam firs, and reaches the summit of Saddle Ball Mt. (3238 ft.) at 1.0 mi. from the parking area. The summit of Mt. Greylock is 2.6 mi. north via the Appalachian Trail.

Jones Nose Trail

Distances from Jones Nose parking area
   to CCC Dynamite Trail: 0.3 mi. (20 min.)
   to Saddle Ball Mt. and Appalachian Trail: 1.0 mi. (45 min.)

Rounds Rock Trail

This loop trail leaves the west side of Rockwell Rd., 0.7 mi. south of the Jones Nose parking area. Park off the road in one of the nearby pull-offs. The trail gradually ascends through mature woods to open ledges and a profusion of blueberry bushes. A short side trail leads to a cliff with outstanding views to the south. After passing a second outlook the trail reenters the woods and curves back northwesterly to Rockwell Rd. Turning right along the road for 200 yd. completes the loop.

PLEASANT VALLEY WILDLIFE SANCTUARY (MAS)

This 730-acre wildlife sanctuary, maintained by the Massachusetts Audubon Society, is located on the east slope of Lenox Mtn. in the town of Lenox. From the intersection of US 7 and US 20, drive north 3 mi. to West Dugway Rd. on the left. Follow West Dugway Rd. west to the sanctuary entrance on West Mountain Rd. Trail information is available at the small museum, open during the summer.

Trail of the Ledges (MAS)

This path, also known as the Fire Tower Trail, leads to the fire tower at the top of Lenox Mtn. (2124 ft.), which provides a fine panorama in all directions. There is also a communications tower on the summit.

The trail is blue-blazed outbound and yellow-blazed inbound. Reach the trail by following the Nature Trail 0.2 mi. west from the sanctuary's Trailside Museum to the north side of Pike's Pond. The trail ascends past the junction with the Laurel Trail at a lookout called Farviews. It continues past another lookout on the right at 0.75 mi. and reaches the summit just west of the fire tower. (*Note:* Use caution when descending the ledges.)

Trail of the Ledges

Distances from Pike's Pond
  to Laurel Trail: 0.5 mi. (20 min.)
  to lookout: 0.75 mi. (45 min.)
  to summit of Lenox Mtn.: 1.25 mi. (1 hr.)

Overbrook Trail (MAS)

An alternate route to the summit, this trail is the preferred route for descent. To reach the trail, follow the Bluebird Lane Trail north from the Trailside Museum. This trail passes the Alexander Trail and crosses a brook after entering the woods. Continue onto the Beaver Lodge Trail, then turn left onto the Hemlock Gorge Trail, following it to Old Wood Rd., exiting left. At the major trail junction (0.6 mi. from the museum) the Overbrook Trail goes straight ahead, crosses a brook several times, and reaches the summit west of the fire tower.

Overbrook Trail

Distance from Old Wood Rd.
    to summit of Lenox Mtn.: 0.7 mi. (40 min.)

Lenox Mtn. Trail

This trail ascends Lenox Mtn. from the north, passing over Yokun Seat, an open peak on the north end of the ridge with fine views. The trailhead is at the Bousquet Ski Area on Tamarack Rd. in Pittsfield. Begin by following the Grand Slalom Ski Trail, which begins to the left of the chair lift. Near the top of the trail, enter the Easy Rider Ski Trail, which curves right under the chair lift and then bends left to the summit of the ski area (1772 ft.). At this bend, cross over the snowmaking pipes onto an overgrown trail that leads to an opening in the woods. This is where the Lenox Mtn. Trail starts (marked with yellow paint), 0.7 mi. from the chair lift. It ascends along a woods road to Mahanna Cobble, continuing past open meadows and bridle trails on the ridge. The trail turns left and ascends to the open summit of Yokun Seat, where a level trail leads to the fire tower.

Lenox Mtn. Trail

Distances from base of Bousquet Ski Area chair lift
    to Mahanna Cobble: 1.1 mi. (45 min.)
    to Yokun Seat: 2.4 mi. (1 hr. 40 min.)
    to fire tower on summit of Lenox Mtn.: 3.2 mi. (2 hr.)

MONROE STATE FOREST

Monroe State Forest in the towns of Florida and Monroe covers some 4,321 acres in the northern part of the Hoosac range. A 9-mi. trail system provides an interesting circuit, and it is possible to make shorter circuits by using unpaved Raycroft Rd., which connects the trails. Little maintenance of the trails has been done in recent years, but the footway is fairly obvious and easy to follow. The trails are marked sporadically with blue paint; signs are usually missing. Elevations range from almost 1000 ft. to 2730 ft. on Spruce Mtn. Trail information is available at the Bear Swamp Visitors Center on River Road.

To reach the visitor center and eastern trailhead from MA 2, turn north at the Mohawk Bridge (1.7 mi. west of Charlemont) on Zoar/Rowe Rd. Continue 2.4 mi. to a T-intersection. Turn left onto River Rd., crossing the Florida Bridge at 1 mi. from the junction, and continue on River Rd. through the village of Hoosac Tunnel. Pass the railroad tunnel on the left at 4.5 mi. The Bear Swamp Visitors Center is on the right at 7.6 mi. The trail parking area is on the left at 8.5 mi., just before the Monroe–Florida line.

All of the other principal trailheads are located on unpaved Raycroft Rd. (also called South Rd.). It is most easily reached by turning north off MA 2 on Tilda Hill Rd. in Florida, 0.8 mi. west of Whitcomb Summit. Continue north 1.5 mi., then east, always on a paved road. Entering the town of Monroe, the name changes to Main Rd. At 4.1 mi., pass a forestry camp on the left; 0.2 mi. beyond the camp, Raycroft Rd. exits right at the Monroe State Forest sign. (Straight ahead on Main Rd. leads to Monroe Bridge in 3.45 mi.) Raycroft Rd. leads almost immediately to the upper end of the Dunbar Brook Trail on the left. The northern end of the Spruce Mtn. Trail is on the right at 0.2 mi., Raycroft Extension Rd. is on the left at 1.4 mi., the Raycroft Trail is on the left at 1.6 mi., and the southern end of Spruce Mtn. Trail is on the right at 2.2 mi., directly across from the Raycroft Lookout Trail. (Beyond this point Raycroft Rd. leads into Florida under the name of Monroe Rd., but is difficult or impassable for vehicles without four-wheel-drive.)

Raycroft Trail

The Raycroft Trail and the Dunbar Brook Trail coincide for the first 0.7 mi., beginning at the trail parking area on River Rd. The trails follow a southward path uphill, then turn right into the woods. They proceed almost due west, paralleling and a little above a stream. At 0.5 mi. there is a small camping area on the right, and at 0.7 mi. the trails divide. The Dunbar Brook Trail branches right and crosses the stream; the Raycroft Trail continues northwest a short distance, then switchbacks to the southeast and climbs, steeply at times, up the ridge.

Just before reaching the crest, the trail passes a shelter on the right (sleeps five). From this point the trail broadens into a woods road, proceeds west then south, and emerges on unpaved Raycroft Extension Rd. (rough, but passable by car). The trail turns right and follows the road 0.45 mi. Almost opposite a large boulder on the right, the trail leaves the road, bears left onto a grassy woods road, and in 0.1 mi. bears left again on a second woods road. After passing a shelter on the right, it descends moderately for 100 yd., then makes a sharp right uphill. (*Note:* Watch carefully for this important turn.) It soon crosses under transmission lines and continues moderately uphill, reaching unpaved Raycroft Rd. 0.25 mi. farther along. (On the descent, the trail leaves the east side of the road opposite a stone boundary marker and almost immediately bears right. Watch carefully for this turn.)

To reach the Raycroft Lookout Trail and the southern end of the Spruce Mtn. Trail, turn left (south) on Raycroft Rd.; turn right (north) to reach the northern end of the Spruce Mtn. Trail and the upper terminus of the Dunbar Brook Trail.

Raycroft Trail

Distances from parking area on River Road
 to Raycroft Extension Rd.: 1.5 mi. (1 hr.)
 to Raycroft Rd.: 2.5 mi. (1 hr. 20 min.)

Raycroft Lookout Trail (DEM)

This trail leads to Raycroft Lookout (2067 ft.), also known as Hunt Hill. A stone "balcony" built by the CCC near the summit affords an outstanding view of the Deerfield River Gorge.

The clearly-defined trail begins at the end of a gravel road that branches southeast from Raycroft Rd. at the height-of-land, directly opposite the south terminus of the Spruce Mtn. Trail. Cars can be parked 0.2 mi. down the gravel road in a clearing under the transmission lines. The trail begins as a woods road at the far end of the clearing, then enters hemlocks and becomes a footpath, continuing gradually downhill and running generally southeast about 0.3 mi. The trail ends at the stone balcony on Hunt Hill overlooking the Deerfield River Gorge.

Raycroft Lookout Trail

Distance from Raycroft Rd.
  to lookout on Hunt Hill: 0.5 mi. (15 min.)

Dunbar Brook Trail

This trail follows a stream most of the way and is especially attractive in high-water seasons; upstream are attractive cascades. The trail branches right (north) from the Raycroft Trail at 0.7 mi. from the parking area on River Rd., crosses the stream on a bridge, then goes up the north bank about 0.1 mi., passing three small camping areas. Leaving the stream, it climbs moderately to the northwest and crosses two tributaries on bridges. After the second bridge, it reaches the Dunbar shelter (sleeps five), passes behind the shelter (avoid the obvious path along the stream leading to a small overflow tent area), and climbs to the northwest. The trail crosses under transmission lines, then descends to and remains near the river for some distance.

Atop a small rise about 0.9 mi. from the shelter, the trail turns sharp right and goes uphill. (*Note:* This is an important turn; look carefully for blue and yellow paint on a tree.) The path straight ahead follows the stream closely, offering an alternate scenic route, albeit an increasingly rough and obscure one, to Raycroft Rd. The Dunbar Brook Trail climbs steeply, zigzagging among large boulders. After passing almost under one of the largest, it turns sharp left (an obscure turn on the descent) and soon reaches the top of the hill, continuing almost on the level on an old woods road. About 0.3 mi. from the boulder field the trail branches left and continues downhill. (The right fork leads shortly to paved Main Rd. 100 ft. east of its junction with Raycroft Rd.) After descending some worn wooden steps, the trail bears right, paralleling the river, crosses a small stream, passes an old foundation on the right, and ends just north of the bridge on Raycroft Rd. (*Note:* On the descent, look for the blue and yellow paint on trees along the road; the beginning of the trail might be obscure, as there are many unofficial paths along the stream.)

To reach the Spruce Mtn. Trail, turn left onto Raycroft Rd. and continue 0.2 mi. across a bridge and past a small parking area on the left. The Spruce Mtn. Trail begins on the right.

Dunbar Brook Trail
Distances from parking area on River Road
>   *to* Dunbar shelter: 1.1 mi. (30 min.)
>   *to* Raycroft Rd.: 2.8 mi. (1 hr. 30 min.)

Spruce Mtn. Trail

Spruce Mtn. (2730 ft.), the highest point in Monroe State Forest, is reached by a clearly defined, blue-blazed trail that begins and ends on Raycroft Rd. The northern terminus is located on the west side of Raycroft Rd. 0.2 mi. south of the upper end of the Dunbar Brook Trail, near some large boulders and just before the road turns right and proceeds uphill. (The entry might be obscure.) The trail climbs moderately southwest and in about 0.5 mi. reaches a ledgy opening with views east. From this point the route soon turns west and proceeds almost on the level for some distance. (*Note:* This section might be wet and overgrown, so careful attention is necessary.) Turning south again, the trail merges with and follows an overgrown woods road gradually uphill, emerging on the summit in 1.5 mi. (*Note:* In the reverse direction, watch carefully for the obscure right turn off the woods road.) The summit itself is wooded, but a rocky clearing reached by a short path on the right offers good views to the west and south.

Leaving the summit in an easterly direction, the trail passes a third vista (views to the south), then descends southeast along the crest of the ridge through open hardwoods. About 1 mi. from the third viewpoint the trail passes under transmission lines, then ends on Raycroft Rd. Left on Raycroft Rd. leads in 0.6 mi. to the upper end of the Raycroft Trail on the right and in 2.1 mi. to the beginning of the Spruce Mtn. Trail.

In reverse, the trail leaves Raycroft Rd. at the height-of-land directly opposite the gravel road at the start of the Raycroft Lookout Trail. The entry is unmarked but obvious.

Spruce Mtn. Trail

Distances from Raycroft Rd. (northern terminus)
to summit of Spruce Mtn.: 1.5 mi. (50 min.)
to Raycroft Rd. (southern terminus): 3.1 mi. (1 hr. 30 min.)
to Raycroft Rd. (northern terminus via Raycroft Rd.: 5.2 mi. (2 hr. 30 min.)

SAVOY MTN. STATE FOREST

The only prominent peaks in this 10,500-acre state forest are Spruce Hill and Borden Mtn., but scenic trails to North Pond, the three Balanced Rocks, and Tannery Falls are worth exploring. The roads to points of interest in the state forest are well marked, and extensive camping facilities are available.

Borden Mtn. (2576 ft.), the highest elevation in Savoy Mtn. State Forest, has a wooded summit, with a steel fire tower (closed to the public). The summit can be reached via the Kamick Rd. Trail (see below), or by an abandoned service road which leaves the south side of Adams Rd., 0.6 mi. east of Savoy Center.

Busby Trail (DEM)

This blue-blazed trail provides access to Spruce Hill (2566 ft.), also known as Mt. Busby. Spruce Hill is a rocky mountaintop on the western edge of the Hoosac range, with a splendid view across the Hoosic River Valley to Mt. Greylock and the southern end of the Green Mtns.

The trail begins on Shaft Rd. off MA 2, 2 mi. west of the Whitcomb Summit lookout tower. Access to Shaft Rd. also can be gained from MA 2 0.6 mi. east of the lookout tower. From this point proceed southeast on Shaft Rd. past an intersection on the left at 0.5 mi. and another on the right at 1.5 mi. At 2.1 mi. bear right along Shaft Rd. and continue for 0.9 mi. to a bend in the road just past the state forest headquarters building. Parking is available

on a wide turnout. A trail exits west on a wide path that was the
Florida–Adams Rd. About 30 ft. beyond is the start of the Busby
Trail on the right. The trail crosses two transmission lines. The
grass-grown trail ascends past a spring on the right (sometimes
dry) and two old cellar holes before its final steep ascent to the
summit.

Busby Trail

Distances from Shaft Rd.
   to spring: 0.9 mi. (35 min.)
   to summit of Spruce Hill: 1.3 mi. (1 hr.)

Old Florida Rd.

This trail is an abandoned county right-of-way known locally as
Old Florida Rd. It connects the Busby Trail trailhead near the parking area in Savoy Mtn. State Forest with E. Hoosac St. in the town
of Adams., and has a total ascent of 1300 ft. It is best to ask directions to E. Hoosac St. at the Adams public library on MA 8 since
the street is not well marked. Proceed on E. Hoosac St. past a large
mill on the right and over a sluiceway. Continue past the intersection with East Rd. at 1 mi. The road begins to climb steeply, reaching a hairpin turn at 1.75 mi. You will find the trailhead on the left
at the turn. Parking is available on the right side of the road above
the hairpin turn at several turnouts.

Old Florida Rd. immediately begins a gradual climb, passing two
woods roads that enter from the right within the first mile. At 1.9 mi.
the trail ascends some ledges and soon begins a gradual descent past
a wet area. It becomes deeply eroded in places, resembling a gully.
(Hikers might want to detour to the right of the trail for a few hundred yards.) Leveling off, the trail proceeds straight past an intersection on the left. At 2.7 mi. it enters an open area to pass along the
west side of a swamp. On the other side of the swamp, the trail passes under a powerline, enters the woods, and doubles back under the
powerline following it 0.25 mi. to a paved road at 4.1 mi. Just before
the trail ends on the paved road, the blue-blazed Busby Trail exits
left. (See the description of the Busby Trail.)

Old Florida Rd.

Distance from E. Hoosac St.
   to Busby Trail and paved road: 4.1 mi. (2 hr.)

Kamick Rd. Trail (DEM)

This trail follows an old woods road that connects Bannis Rd. and the service road to the fire tower on Border Mtn. From MA 116 in Savoy, turn east onto narrow Haskins Rd. (passable by car) opposite the church. At 0.6 mi. turn left onto unmarked Bannis Rd., a very rough jeep road. After passing over the height-of-land twice, you will see an old woods road on the left. This is the Kamick Rd. Trail. The trail continues 1.5 mi. to the service road, which leads in 0.3 mi. to the Borden Mtn. fire tower on the summit.

Kamick Rd. Trail

Distances from Bannis Rd.
   to service road: 1.5 mi. (50 min.)
   to summit of Borden Mtn.: 1.8 mi. (1 hr. 5 min.)

NOTCHVIEW RESERVATION (TR)

This property of The Trustees of Reservations consists of nearly 3,000 acres of forests and open fields in Windsor at an elevation above 2000 ft. It is located on MA 9, 1 mi. east of the white church in Windsor and 3.6 mi. west of the Cummington town line. Turn north off MA 9 at the Notchview sign, bear right (east), and enter the first driveway on the left (north). The parking area is marked. Trail information is available at the reservation visitor center. The trail system includes several short trails with descriptive names, longer trails that permit circuit hikes beginning and ending at the parking area, and an interesting trail along Steep Bank Brook, which ends in the picnic area of neighboring Windsor State Forest on River Rd. All trails are well maintained and marked with yellow blazes.

Judges Hill Trail (TR)

From the Notchview parking area, the trail travels north between the fences into spruce woods. When the path through the woods

emerges onto a wide, grassy lane, the trail turns left and crosses
Shaw Rd. about 100 ft. along. (Old USGS maps show Shaw Rd. as
High St.) It continues directly across Shaw Rd. onto an old road.
After crossing a small stream, the trail starts gradually uphill and
soon bears left at a fork in two woods roads. Then it climbs more
steeply to the summit of Judges Hill (2297 ft.). On the summit sits
the remains of a lunch shelter with a rock slab "table" inside. The
trail continues north past the foundation through a predominantly
beech forest, and downhill to Bates Rd. It turns right (southeast)
onto Bates Rd., passes the beginning of the Steep Bank Brook Trail
on the left in about 300 ft., and continues to the junction with Shaw
Rd. The trail turns sharp right (west) onto Shaw Rd. (a few feet to
the left on Shaw Rd. is one end of the Bumpus Trail) and follows
Shaw Rd. west back to the trail crossing. You can turn left (south)
and retrace your way back to the parking area or turn right onto the
Ant Hill Loop a short distance beyond for variation.

Judges Hill Trail

Distance from Notchview parking area
   to Notchview parking area (loop): *est.* 6 mi. (3 hr.)

Steep Bank Brook Trail (TR)

This trail begins at Bates Rd., approximately 1.5 mi. east of MA
8A. It can also be reached by following the Judges Hill Trail from
the Notchview parking area (about a 1-hr. walk to the trail).

   The trail enters the woods on the north side of Bates Rd. about
300 ft. east of the junction with the Judges Hill Trail. It goes over
the stone wall and proceeds through the woods, following a small
stream most of the way until the stream flows into a larger brook.
The trail then crosses an old road near the remains of a rotted
bridge. The path continues to follow the larger brook downstream
until the brook is joined by another of about the same size. Now
the brook is larger with a steeper bank, and the trail continues
along it, crossing small streams that run into it and crossing and
recrossing the brook as it separates and joins again to go around
islands of rocks and trees. After many crossings, the trail goes up

the right (south) bank of the brook, follows it for a short distance, then turns left (east) onto an old road. It goes downhill through hemlock woods and ends in the Windsor State Forest picnic area directly behind the rest rooms. A sign here reads "Steep Bank Brook Trail to Judges Hill Trail."

Steep Bank Brook Trail
Distance from Bates Rd.
   to Windsor Forest picnic area: 1.2 mi. (1 hr.)

Circuit Trail (TR)
From the Notchview parking area, go north between the fences into spruce woods. At the "Circuit Trail" sign, you can take either direction, but to follow this trail description, go right (southeast). The trail follows a path and then a road through the spruces, passing the Whitestone Trail on the left and a private area on the right. It emerges at the edge of a small field and turns left onto a dirt road with a farm building on the right. It then passes the Quill Tree Trail and the Mushroom Trail on the left and emerges in a large field, turning sharp left. (The Bumpus Trail begins in the field at this point.) The Circuit Trail passes the other ends of the Whitestone Trail, the Quill Tree Trail, and the Mushroom Trail on the left. At the junction with the Judges Hill Trail, turn left to return to the parking area.

Circuit Trail
Distance from Notchview parking area
   to Notchview parking area (loop): 1 mi. (1 hr.)

Bumpus Trail (TR)
From the Notchview parking area, go north between the fences into the spruce woods. Take the Circuit Trail to the right to a large field with a "Bumpus Trail" sign. There is a good view of the mountains as the Bumpus Trail follows the edge of the field. It then reenters the woods (predominantly maple and beech) on an old road. The trail turns left into an open grassy area and continues straight ahead. It descends and crosses a stone wall, eventually crossing a brook on a plank bridge and turning left along it, then

right uphill on an old woods road to reach Shaw Rd. very close to its junction with Bates Rd. From here the Judges Hill Trail goes left (west) on Shaw Rd. and uphill (north) on Bates Rd.

Bumpus Trail

Distance from Circuit Trail
   to Bates Rd. (Judges Hill Trail): 1.1 mi. (1 hr.)

MONUMENT MTN. RESERVATION (TR)

Monument Mtn. is an isolated mountain range located on the eastern side of the Housatonic River in the towns of Stockbridge and Great Barrington. Its prominent feature is the rocky crest of Squaw Peak (1642 ft.), which affords spectacular views in all directions. Inscription Rock is on the northern summit, and farther south is Profile Rock. When viewed from the south in the early morning light, the cliffs form the contours of a large Indian head. A freestanding pinnacle on the eastern side is known as Devil's Pulpit. This and the cliffs on the eastern side of Squaw Peak provide many routes for rock climbers. The terrain is not especially difficult, but caution is advisable because of loose rocks and the occasional rattlesnake.

Parking is available at a picnic area located at the base of Squaw Peak on US 7, 2.5 mi. south of Stockbridge and 3 mi. north of the junction with MA 23 in Great Barrington. A trail map is displayed at the northern end of the parking area.

Indian Monument Trail (TR)

Follow US 7 south 0.3 mi. from the Monument Mtn. Reservation picnic area to the beginning of the trail on the right, opposite a macadam road to a gravel pit. The trail enters the woods, where a sign points right to Indian Monument (a legendary pile of rocks about 100 yd. off the trail). It makes a sharp right and continues in a northerly direction past several junctions with woods roads. (Always select the trail on the right.) The trail steepens slightly and at approximately 1 mi. from the highway turns right from the woods road onto a narrow footpath. The white-blazed Hickey Trail enters on the left and leads right a few hundred feet to the summit.

Indian Monument Trail

Distance from US 7
   to summit of Squaw Peak (via Hickey Trail): 1.3 mi. (1 hr.)

Hickey Trail (TR)

This trail leaves the Monument Mtn. Reservation picnic area on US 7 in a northerly direction and is marked by round white blazes. (It can also be reached from another parking area on US 7 north of the picnic grounds.) The trail passes a well and a stone wall on the left, climbs steeply to a col north of Squaw Peak, and bears left at the junction with the Indian Monument Trail. The trail then continues to the summit at 0.8 mi.

Hickey Trail

Distance from Monument Mtn. Reservation picnic area
   to summit of Squaw Peak: 0.8 mi. (45 min.)

Three-Mile Hill Trail

Three-Mile Hill is a wooded ridge extending south from the Monument Mtn. range. To reach the northern end of this trail, drive 0.3 mi. south of the Monument Mtn. Reservation picnic area on US 7 to a macadam road on the left. Follow this road east 0.2 mi. to the first gravel pit on the left; park here. The white-blazed trail starts on the right side of the road under a barbed-wire fence. It follows old woods roads for its entire length and is well marked.

At 1.5 mi. it crosses a gravel road from US 7 in Great Barrington at Muddy Brook Rd. At approximately 2 mi. it passes a spectacular rock ledge 100 ft. to the left. The top of the ledge affords a good view of Mt. Wilcox and Beartown State Forest. The trail descends and at 3 mi. reaches MA 23 just east of the Butternut Basin Ski Area. Frequent azalea patches along the trail make an early June trip rewarding. Later in the month laurel decorates the entire length of the trail.

Three-Mile Hill Trail

Distances from gravel pit off US 7
  to gravel road: 1.5 mi (50 min.)
  to ledges: 2 mi (1 hr. 10 min.)
  to MA 23: 3 mi. (1 hr. 40 min)

BEARTOWN STATE FOREST

This highland region lies mostly in the towns of Great Barrington and Monterey. It is bordered on the west by the valley of the Konkapot and Muddy brooks, on the north by the Housatonic River, and on the east by the Tyringham Valley. Most of the highland is part of the 10,555-acre Beartown State Forest, with headquarters on Blue Hill Rd. in Monterey. This is the third-largest state forest in Massachusetts and remains largely undeveloped. The Appalachian Trail traverses it.

The highland includes several wooded peaks of around 1900 ft. with no trails to any of the summits. Laura Tower and the Alcott Trail lookout afford good views. The Laurel Hill Association (LHA) of Stockbridge maintains a trail system in this area. Literature is available at the Stockbridge Library.

Laura Tower Trail (LHA)

A steel tower on this 1465-ft. hill provides a fine view of the Catskills in the west, Mt. Greylock in the north, and the October Mtn. State Forest in the east. The blue-and-yellow-blazed trail leaves the parking space at the end of Park St. 500 ft. from its junction with US 7, just north of the Housatonic River Bridge in Stockbridge. It crosses the Memorial Bridge and railroad tracks and ascends 0.3 mi. to the Ice Glen Trail on the right (blue markers). It continues left, following the yellow markers to a small footbridge.

At the fork the trail bears right uphill, passing a springhouse on the right. Two alternate trails zigzag approximately 0.8 mi. to the wooded summit and the sturdy steel tower. Another trail, blazed with red markers, continues over the crest in an easterly direction to the Beartown State Forest in South Lee. At 1.8 mi. the Laura Tower Trail passes a lean-to (no water) on top of the abandoned Beartown Ski Area and several ski trails on the left. It proceeds east on a wide path for 0.3 mi. Just before the trail narrows to a woods road (the road leads to the base of the ski area), the trail turns sharply right onto a white-blazed trail that leads to Burgoyne Pass at 2.3 mi.

Laura Tower Trail

Distances from Memorial Bridge
    to Ice Glen Trail: 0.3 mi (15 min.)
    to Laura Tower: 0.8 mi. (45 min.)
    to lean-to: 1.8 mi. (1 hr. 20 min.)
    to Burgoyne Pass (via white-blazed trail): 2.3 mi. (1 hr. 35 min.)

Ice Glen Trail (LHA)

To find the start of this trail, follow the Laura Tower Trail 0.3 mi. to the split with the blue-marked Ice Glen Trail. This trail leads to Ice Glen, a short, steep-sided gulf with high boulders on the bottom and towering white pines and hemlocks. You may see deposits of ice under the rocks far into the summer.

Ice Glen Trail

Distance from Laura Tower Trail
    to Ice Glen: 0.3 mi. (15 min.)

Burgoyne Pass (DEM in part)

This abandoned woods road connects Beartown Rd. in South Lee with Ice Glen Rd. in Stockbridge. It provides an alternate return route for a walk over the Laura Tower Trail. You can reach the eastern end of the pass by ascending the path located 0.5 mi. from the junction of Willow St. and Beartown Rd. in South Lee. Look for the white blazes near a watering trough. At about 600 ft. the blazed trail to Laura Tower exits on the right. The overgrown Wildcat Cross-Country Ski Trail exits left beyond a small reservoir and the trail continues west over a col in a narrow valley. Descending through dense growth, it follows the white blazes across a brook to Ice Glen Rd. To the right (north) Ice Glen Rd. leads to US 7 just south of the railroad overpass in Stockbridge. To the left (south) Ice Glen Rd. connects with the Alcott Trail.

Burgoyne Pass

Distances from Beartown Rd.
> *to* trail to Laura Tower: 600 ft. (5 min.)
> *to* col: 0.5 mi. (20 min.)
> *to* Ice Glen Rd.: 1.8 mi. (1 hr.)

Alcott Trail (DEM in part)

This trail affords access to a scenic outlook on the western side of the Beartown Mtn. range. To get to the Alcott Trail, take Monument Valley Rd. 0.5 mi. from its junction with US 7 near the Monument Mtn. Regional High School. Follow Alcott St. (dry-weather road) 0.8 mi. to a parking space ahead of the bridge over the second branch of Konkapot Brook. Follow the woods road leading to Ice Glen Rd., marked with white paint balls. Watch for rectangular paint blazes 0.2 mi. along and turn right uphill onto Alcott Trail, continuing uphill to the lookout (1250 ft.), which offers a good view from Monument Mtn. to Mt. Greylock.

Alcott Trail

Distance from Ice Glen Rd.
> *to* lookout: 0.5 mi. (25 min.)

Wildcat Trail (DEM)

The southern end of this trail is on Beartown Rd., 1 mi. north of the Benedict Pond bathhouse. It ascends a wide, grassy woods road (well marked with orange blazes) and forks left at 2 mi. (The orange-blazed side trail on the right leads 0.3 mi. to the site of a former CCC camp on Beartown Rd. There are two stone fireplaces here, but camping is not permitted except by special permission of the Benedict Pond camping supervisor.) Wildcat Trail proceeds through the woods with slight changes in elevation to the junction with a blue-blazed trail on the left, which leads to an unfinished connection with the Alcott Trail. It descends to Beartown Rd. at the bridge near the entrance to Beartown State Forest.

Wildcat Trail

Distances from Beartown Rd.

    to side trail to CCC camp: 2 mi. (1 hr.)

    to blue-blazed trail: 3 mi. (2 hr.)

    to Beartown Rd.: 3.5 mi. (2 hr. 15 min.)

SECTION 4
Pioneer Valley and Environs

For the purposes of this guidebook, this section of Massachusetts includes the part of the state between Worcester County on the east and Berkshire County on the west. It is composed of Hampden, Hampshire, and Franklin counties, generally forming the Massachusetts watershed of the Connecticut River and its principal tributaries, the Millers, Deerfield, Chicopee, and Westfield rivers.

This is an area of natural beauty and historic interest. From the fertile valley of the Connecticut River rise sturdy hills, mostly wooded but many with rocky summits or open ledges, the sources of clear, tumbling brooks. Heavily traveled Indian trails once crisscrossed the region, and some of the bloodiest battles of the Indian wars were fought here. At one time or another elegant summit houses or hotels, accessible by carriage roads or inclined railways, graced the tops of Mt. Tom, Mt. Nonotuck, Mt. Holyoke, Mt. Toby, and Mt. Sugarloaf.

METACOMET–MONADNOCK TRAIL

The Metacomet–Monadnock Trail in Massachusetts, 98 mi. long, is a continuation of the Metacomet Trail in Connecticut. Commencing at the Connecticut–Massachusetts state line near the Southwick–Agawam town line, it runs north along the traprock ridge that borders the Connecticut River Valley on the west, passing over Provin Mountain, East Mountain, and the Mt. Tom range. Leaping the Connecticut River at Mt. Tom Junction, the trail proceeds east over the Holyoke Range, including Mt. Norwottuck and Long Mountain, then north along the hills that line the eastern edge of the Connecticut River Valley. Turning east in the Bald Hills of Northfield to the summit of Mt. Grace in the town of Warwick, it continues to the Massachusetts–New Hampshire state line. From there, an additional 20-mi. section of trail brings the hiker to the summit of Mt. Monadnock in New Hampshire. There it joins with the 51-mi. Monadnock–Sunapee Greenway Trail to the summit of Mt. Sunapee.

The trail has shelters and other established campsites along its route. At suitable intervals it crosses paved highways and other roads passable by car and can be easily traversed in successive one-day or half-day trips. The description below is divided into sections that each take about one day to hike. White rectangular blazes mark the route. Double blazes (one above the other) indicate abrupt changes in direction or turns in the trail. White plastic triangles are often used at road crossings and trail junctions.

The Metacomet–Monadnock Trail was originally laid out by Professor Walter M. Banfield of the University of Massachusetts. It is maintained by the AMC's Berkshire Chapter (BCAMC), with the aid of other local groups and individuals belonging to the Metacomet–Monadnock Trail Conference. The trail's existence is a tribute to the cooperation of numerous state forest and park organizations, town conservation and water departments, nonprofit organizations, wildlife sanctuaries, and the many private landowners whose generosity allows hikers to use this special resource.

For more information, write to: BCAMC Trails Committee; P.O. Box 369; Amherst, MA 01004. A published guidebook with maps is available.

Metacomet–Monadnock Trail: Massachusetts–Connecticut Line (Rising Corner, CT) to MA 57

From the intersection of Stone St. and Barry St. in Rising Corner, CT, the trail runs left up South Longyard Rd. After 0.2 mi., the trail leaves the road sharply to the right and enters an open field, following a fence. Walk along the edge of the field in a counter-clockwise direction, staying to the right. After circumnavigating the field, the trail drops down right (east) to a wet, swampy area with bog bridges. After crossing the bridge over a stream, a logging road leaves left. The trail proceeds steeply up the side of the Provin Mtn. ridge. At 0.8 mi., the trail reaches the ridgetop, bears left in the woods, and continues north to cross a gas line at 1.4 mi. There are limited views here to the west. Just beyond and about 150 ft. left of the trail is a spring. The trail continues north on an old logging road, turns east, crosses a small brook, and with abrupt turns reaches a crossroad at 1.8 mi. It then turns left, following a dirt road past the Agawam Bowman Archery Range and eventually enters a private driveway just before reaching MA 57 at 2.4 mi.

Metacomet–Monadnock Trail: Massachusetts–Connecticut Line (Rising Corner, CT) to MA 57

Distance from intersection of N. Stone St. and Barry St. (Rising Corner) to MA 57: 2.4 mi. (1 hr. 35 min.)

Metacomet–Monadnock Trail: MA 57 to US 20

This section of the trail follows the ridge of Provin Mtn., mostly along the western rim. The trail begins on MA 57, entering a wide driveway on the right leading to a locked iron gate. The Lane Quarry sign reads "No Trespassing," but permission has been granted to use this right-of-way. Do not block the gate or the private driveway on the right with cars. The trail goes straight ahead and soon bears right, then left, with the quarry excavation on the right. (*Caution:* The excavation area is dangerous due to loose and rotten rocks.) The trail now enters the woods and turns sharply right, and climbs moderately along the bottom of a talus slope to reach the top of the ridge at 0.6 mi.

Turning left at an intersection, the trail passes a stone town line marker at 1.5 mi. At 1.9 mi. it passes an observation tower and WWLP-TV (visitors and picnickers are welcome). Just beyond the television station the trail turns left off the paved road and goes downhill. It bears right, now proceeding north, and descends along the ridge.

With little ups and downs the trail continues along this ridge, passing near to and just above the hairpin turn on the access road for an underground reservoir. The trail descends below the ridgeline on the west side and continues to a large, open field on a grassy trail at 3.3 mi. Follow along the edge of the field at the base of the rock slope to the right for about 300 yd. Enter the woods and proceed to a chain-link fence at 3.6 mi., following it uphill steeply to the right, through hemlocks, to the ridge. Descend along the ridge on a wide path to a town line boundary marker. Turning left, the trail descends steeply and reaches a powerline at 3.9 mi. Turn left on the powerline access road, staying under the lines, and in 30 yd. turn right into the woods of Robinson State Park, where the trail soon joins MA 187 near a utility shed at 4.3 mi., just above the Westfield River.

Because the river cannot be forded safely, through hikers must make a long detour to the left (west) on MA 187 to the US 20 bridge at 5 mi. From the bridge, follow US 20 back east to the traffic light across from the Big Y Shopping Center (6.7 mi.), where the trail resumes.

Metacomet–Monadnock Trail: MA 57 to US 20

Distances from MA 57

   to observation tower and WWLP-TV: 1.9 mi. (1 hr. 20 min.)
   to Westfield River: 2.4 mi. (1 hr. 50 min.)
   to bridge on US 20: 5 mi. (3 hr. 15 min.)
   to resumption of trail on US 20: 6.7 mi. (4 hr.)

Metacomet–Monadnock Trail: US 20 to Bush Notch

From the traffic light at the shopping center on US 20, turn left at the light under the railroad overpass and left again onto Sykes Ave. Proceed 0.2 mi. to a gravel road with a Pioneer Valley Sportsman's Club sign on the left. Here the trail turns sharply left, past a large rock barrier onto an ORV trail leading uphill. After passing a sand and gravel pit on the left, turn sharply right at an intersection and proceed on level footing through a reclamation area of young red pines. Proceeding along the rim of this sandy plateau and bearing left, the trail shortly reaches the gravel road to the Pioneer Valley Sportsman's Club. The trail turns left onto this road and proceeds to the club's parking lot at 1 mi. It continues north past a gate on a woods road through hardwood forest sprinkled with white birches.

At 1.8 mi. the trail turns left and ascends, crossing a powerline and continuing to the top of the ridge. It soon enters a hemlock grove with the Lane Quarry on the western horizon. (*Caution:* Trespassing is prohibited because this is a blasting area.) The trail passes through another hemlock grove and descends, crossing a brook at 2.5 mi. It continues north, ascending the ridge once again, and at 2.7 mi. it descends into a forest of stately hemlock trees and oaks with many fallen chestnut trees, relics of the chestnut blight that swept across New England in the early 1900s.

The trail now turns northeast under a powerline at 3 mi. and slowly descends, passing through a long stretch of hemlock mixed forest. It crosses an east-west tote road diagonally, a small brook, and another east-west woods road. The trail now bears left uphill, continues along a little ridge, and descends. After turning left, it continues up a shallow gully, climbing steeply. It then bears right a bit to the top of the ridge's shoulder and winds along, always on about the same contour, reaching a logging road and then descending. It soon leaves the road bearing left and climbing, but remaining parallel to the top of the main ridge.

At 4.3 mi., the trail turns left and proceeds up and along the side of a small ridge. It continues up and over the main ridge and descends toward the Massachusetts Turnpike. The trail turns left near the turnpike fence, following the fence to its end. The trail then descends and continues to the quarry access road. It crosses the road to a railroad underpass, turns right through the underpass, and then turns left onto Old Holyoke Rd. at Bush Notch.

Metacomet–Monadnock Trail: US 20 to Bush Notch

Distances from Riverbend Shopping Center (US 20)

   to Pioneer Valley Sportsman's Club parking lot: 1 mi. (40 min.)

   to Bush Notch: 4.9 mi. (2 hr. 50 min.)

Metacomet–Monadnock Trail: Bush Notch to US 202 (Hugh McLean Reservoir)

From Bush Notch northward, the trail climbs to the crest of East Mtn. and follows its ridge. It proceeds entirely in the solitude of seemingly remote woodlands. Alternately, it searches out a spectacular viewpoint from the western edge of the escarpment and meanders along old mossy woods roads to the lovely shores of the Hugh McLean Reservoir.

The trail goes right and down Old Holyoke Rd. in Bush Notch, continues about 50 yd., and exits left opposite a small, swampy pond. It climbs very steeply up the end of the ridge and bears right uphill, with the ridge crest above on the left. It passes a fine outlook on the edge of the traprock cliff, then ascends sharply to the ridge top just beyond an iron pipe town-line post. The trail now descends gradually to the left. At 0.3 mi. it crosses a tote road and climbs the eastern side of the East Mtn. ridge. The trail turns right near the top and follows several jeep roads north, continuing past an abandoned beacon tower at 0.5 mi. and another beacon at 1 mi. There are excellent views south and west. Soon the trail turns left, follows briefly along the ledges on the western end of the ridge, and turns right to proceed down the center of the descending north slope.

At 2 mi. the trail ascends the southern end of Snake Pond Mtn., reaches its bare ledge crest, continues along the narrow rocky ridge, and descends to join an old woods road at 2.7 mi. It proceeds east down the well-worn road, descending left for 100 yd., and leaves the woods road to the right on steep, loose footing. The trail ascends to a summit (some views) at 2.9 mi. Descending from the summit, the trail comes out at a woods road at 3.2 mi., crossing the road to the right and leaving it abruptly to the left. The trail now follows a narrower footpath on the ridge, crossing a buried telephone cable and then descending gradually to a woods road. Follow the road left and soon bear right and descend to MA 202, where limited parking is available.

Metacomet–Monadnock Trail: Bush Notch to US 202 (Hugh McLean Reservoir)

Distances from Bush Notch

   to Snake Pond Mtn.: 2 mi. (1 hr. 30 min.)

   to US 202: 4 mi. (3 hr.)

Metacomet–Monadnock Trail: US 202 to MA 141 (Easthampton Rd.)

This very scenic section of the trail runs along the wooded crest of the northern spur of East Mtn., from whose abrupt traprock ledges a succession of fine views of the valley unfold. It follows old logging roads up the south slope of the mountain and similar woods roads north of East Mtn. to Mt. Tom.

From US 202, the trail follows a little ridge, then turns sharply right down to old US 202. It crosses this road diagonally onto a trail to an old dirt road, which is the old Westfield–Holyoke street-car right-of-way. The trail turns right onto this right-of-way and soon leaves it to the left onto an old woods road. It bears left at a fork in the road and continues northwest. The trail begins to ascend the talus slope, continues north along the ridge about 100 yd., then turns abruptly west away from the steep eastern face. It crosses the top of the ridge and at 1.6 mi. crosses a bare rocky ledge on the southern end of the ridge, with views of the Hugh McLean Reservoir and Hampden Ponds.

The trail now runs north along the western rim of this ridge through hardwoods and some hemlock. The trail crosses a little steep-sided hillock, turns away from the western edge of this ridge, and at 2.1 mi. crosses a narrow rock ledge with views south, west, and north. From here the top of the East Mtn. beacon tower appears above the treetops to the north. After crossing this ledge and descending into the woods, the trail winds around north and east to a junction at 2.4 mi. with a service road that goes up the mountain to an abandoned beacon. It passes under the tower of the beacon at 2.5 mi., continues north, and passes a huge rock at 2.6 mi. The trail turns abruptly left and continues southwest down a draw with many fallen chestnut poles. At the end of the descent, the trail turns right and climbs to the top of a rock escarpment. There are splendid views westward all along the rim of these cliffs to 3.2 mi., at which point the trail leaves the rim. It descends a steep talus slope to the north and turns right (east) at 3.4 mi. onto the Cherry St. extension, a paved town road.

The trail exits left off Cherry St. at about 3.7 mi. at the edge of a swamp at the boundary of the Holyoke Revolver Club. It proceeds north on bog bridges, then turns abruptly left (west) and climbs steeply to the crest of a small ridge, which it follows along the rim of cliffs overlooking the western countryside. At 4.1 mi. the trail leaves the ledges, turning back into the woods. After crossing a pipeline, the trail continues north through a hemlock mixed forest into a gray birch stand and proceeds onto a woods road. It turns left (west) at 4.6 mi. onto another woods road, beyond which are fields and a house to the north. At 4.8 mi. the trail turns south onto paved Southampton Rd.

The trail soon makes a 160-degree right turn off the paved road onto a sandy lane running north into the woods. It bears right at the intersection with another woods road that was once the route of an old stagecoach line to Northampton. The trail continues north on this road, then turns right at the fork. After descending, the trail bears left at another fork, then passes under a row of huge sugar maples on the site of an abandoned farm. The trail emerges onto a road pull-off (commonly used by hikers to park cars) beside MA 141 (Easthampton Rd.) at 6 mi.

Metacomet–Monadnock Trail: US 202 to MA 141 (Easthampton Rd.)

Distances from US 202
 to Holyoke Revolver Club: 3.7 mi. (2 hr.)
 to Southampton Rd.: 4.8 mi. (3 hr.)
 to MA 141: 6 mi. (4 hr. 15 min.)

Metacomet–Monadnock Trail: MA 141 to MA 47

This is one of the more spectacular sections of the trail in Massachusetts. It rides the skyline near the rim of steep talus slides and the cliffs of Mt. Tom and Whiting Peak, then passes through the hemlock glens of the Mt. Tom reservation center. It climbs over Goat Peak and Mt. Nonotuck, whose north slope it descends on an old carriage road under an arch of stately hemlocks.

Leaving MA 141 (Easthampton Rd.), the trail turns east onto a mossy woods road, which it follows north. At 0.3 mi. the trail leaves this road and climbs steeply to the top of Mt. Tom and the site of the old Mt. Tom Hotel, now occupied by a radio and television transmission station, at 0.7 mi. The trail continues north along the edge of the cliffs to the west, offering a succession of panoramic views of the countryside to the south, west, and north.

At about 2 mi. the trail meets and coincides for a few feet with the orange-blazed D. O'C Trail. (The upper branch of this trail leads right 0.2 mi. to the tote road of the Mt. Tom Ski Area; the lower branch leads right 1.1 mi. to the Quarry Trail.) At 2.7 mi., after a steep descent from Whiting Peak, partly on stone steps, the trail passes the woodsheds and shop area of the Mt. Tom State Reservation. The northern terminus of the Quarry Trail (orange blazes) is at this point. (It leads to the Mt. Tom Ski Area at 1.1 mi.) The Metacomet–Monadnock Trail continues north through hemlock groves and a picnic area, reaching paved Smith's Ferry Rd. at 3 mi. It exits right onto the road for 70 yd., then turns left into the woods opposite the Mt. Tom Reservation Museum. The trail continues north, soon leading up a low ridge clad with hemlocks. At 3.2 mi. the trail turns right and goes steeply uphill, then bears left, following the northern edge of the escarpment.

Widening views herald the summit clearing of Goat Peak at 3.4 mi. The trail crosses the clearing, with the summit observation tower on the right, then reenters the woods, following a zigzag course downhill through mountain laurel and mixed hardwoods. It crosses paved Goat Peak Rd. at 3.6 mi. and continues through the woods to the blue-blazed Beau Bridge Trail at 3.8 mi., which exits right (0.7 mi. to Hampden Field). Within a few yards the orange-blazed Tea Bag Trail also branches right (0.9 mi. to lower Bray Lake and Smith's Ferry Rd.). The Metacomet–Monadnock Trail continues north reaching Dry Knoll at 4.2 mi., which overlooks the oxbow and floodplain of the Connecticut River.

Descending and proceeding northeast, the trail intersects a paved road at 4.4 mi. (To reach the summit of Mt. Nonotuck, whose northern ledges provide wide views of the countryside, turn right onto the road and continue to a parking lot. From there follow a well-worn path to the ledges, where you will find the ruins of an old hotel, Eyre House.) The Metacomet–Monadnock Trail turns left onto the paved road, then right in about 50 yd. down the bank onto an old carriage road leading to Eyre House on the summit of Mt. Nonotuck.

The trail descends on the carriage road under a continuous arch of giant hemlocks, past a woods road entering left at 4.8 mi. On a sweeping curve at 4.9 mi., the trail, still descending, turns left onto another carriage road, which descends the mountain on a long, gentle grade. The trail follows the carriage road past two side roads coming down off the hill on the left and turns right at a fork in the carriage road, reaching a clearing and a powerline at 5 mi. It turns right onto a path under the powerline and continues to Underwood St. The trail turns left onto Underwood St. and follows it a short distance to East St. It turns right onto East St. and soon passes under the I-91 overpass to reach US 5 at the Mt. Tom Junction at 5.6 mi. The trail follows blazed telephone poles on a grassy section next to an electric-transformer yard adjacent to US 5. The trail leads to the state boat ramp on the Connecticut River Oxbow.

(*Note:* There is no public service by which hikers can cross the river here, but you can usually obtain a free boat ride from this heavily used ramp. Hikers should ask to be let off on the sandy beach between the two powerline crossings just upstream from a private camping area referred to as tent city.)

From the opposite bank, the white blazes lead a short distance to a large open field, where the trail follows the blazed powerline right-of-way to MA 47 on the Hadley–South Hadley line. The old Hockanum Cemetery is located at the intersection of MA 47 and the dirt entrance road into Skinner State Park (Mt. Holyoke) on the town line.

Metacomet–Monadnock Trail: MA 141 to MA 47

Distances from MA 141

    to summit of Mt. Tom: 0.7 mi. (45 min.)
    to D. O'C Trail: *est.* 2 mi. (1 hr. 15 min.)
    to Mt. Tom Reservation woodsheds and shop: 2.7 mi. (2 hr.)
    to Quarry Trail: 2.7 mi. (2 hr.)
    to Smith's Ferry Rd.: 3 mi. (2 hr. 10 min.)
    to Goat Peak: 3.4 mi. (2 hr. 25 min.)
    to Beau Bridge Trail and Tea Bag Trail: 3.8 mi. (2 hr. 35 min.)
    to Dry Knoll: 4.2 mi. (2 hr. 50 min.)
    to paved road to Eyre House: 4.4 mi. (3 hr.)
    to carriage road: 4.9 mi. (3 hr. 30 min.)
    to US 5: 5.6 mi. (4 hr.)

to Connecticut River boat ramp: 6 mi. (4 hr. 15 min.)

to MA 47 (Hockanum Cemetery) across Connecticut River: 6.6 mi. (5 hr. 15 min.)

Metacomet–Monadnock Trail: MA 47 (Hockanum Cemetery) to MA 116

The 2-mile section of this trail from Hockanum Cemetery to Taylor Notch is one of the most interesting and rewarding because of the succession of broad horizon views of the Connecticut River and its lovely valley farmlands. The restored Mt. Holyoke Summit House, (accessible by car) with its beautiful picnic grounds, is located at the center. There are only a few lookout points from Taylor Notch to Granby Notch. This section of the trail is ever rising and falling over the endless succession of minor hills that make up the range. It is forested, wild, and quite unspoiled.

From MA 47 the trail turns left onto the entrance road to Skinner State Park across from the Hockanum Cemetery. It proceeds about 100 ft., then turns right up a driveway (no cars allowed). About 80 ft. east on this driveway the trail turns left (north) and ascends up a traprock ledge. At 0.15 mi. it turns right, then descends east along the retaining bank of a pond. At the eastern end of the pond, the trail turns left (north) uphill through hemlocks and passes under high-tension lines. It proceeds briefly along the ledge, then turns northeast into the woods. After descending into a hemlock dell, the trail turns right (east) and continues south through a narrow defile. It turns east again and goes uphill, reaching a bare ledge at 0.6 mi. with good views of the Connecticut River to the south. The trail continues north up a bare rock slope, descends into another hemlock dell, bears north up a grade on rock ledges, and reaches the top of a narrow rock ridge at 0.9 mi. It then descends a talus slope to the western rim of traprock cliffs overlooking the river and valley.

Turning east and then north, the trail climbs a ledge farther back in the woods, reaching a junction with a blue-blazed trail entering from the west at 1.1 mi. The merged trails climb higher on the rising ridge, heading east and then north. The trail crosses a rock wall and bears left, descending on an old road northward. At 1.5 mi. it intersects the Halfway Trail which descends left to the tollgate in the park. The Metacomet–Monadnock Trail follows this broad trail right, ascending to the summit house.

At 1.6 mi. the Mt. Holyoke Summit House affords superb views of surrounding country. The trail passes around the rear of the house and continues east through the picnic area. At 1.7 mi. the trail descends abruptly east from the end of the picnic area and along broad switchbacks reaches Taylor Notch Rd. at 1.9 mi., crossing the road to the Mountain House. (This road leads back 1.5 mi. to Hockanum Cemetery at the southern entrance to the park.) The trail now climbs steeply east to a rocky ledge at 2.1 mi. along the eastern rim of Taylor Notch. It continues to the top of one hill (858 ft.) at 3.1 mi., with good views north, and to the top of a second hill (919 ft.) at 3.5 mi. At 4.5 mi. the trail passes an abandoned beacon on the crest of Mt. Hitchcock. (Mt. Monadnock in New Hampshire is visible from this tower on a clear day.) At 5.4 mi. it reaches the crest of Bare Mtn. (899 ft.), with superb views of the countryside north, east, south, and west. The trail bears right and descends by easy gradients and many stone steps on a switchback route to MA 116 opposite the Holyoke State Park Visitors Center at 6.3 mi.

Metacomet–Monadnock Trail: MA 47 (Hockanum Cemetery) to MA 116

Distances from MA 47 (Hockanum Cemetery)
   to Halfway Trail: 1.5 mi. (1 hr. 15 min.)
   to Mt. Holyoke Summit House: 1.6 mi. (1 hr. 20 min.)
   to Taylor Notch Rd.: 1.9 mi. (1 hr. 45 min.)
   to beacon tower on Mt. Hitchcock: 4.5 mi. (3 hr. 30 min.)
   to Bare Mtn.: 5.4 mi. (4 hr. 15 min.)
   to MA 116: 6.3 mi. (5 hr.)

Metacomet–Monadnock Trail: MA 116 to Harris Rd.

This is a very popular section of the trail because of the commanding heights of Mt. Norwottuck and Long Mtn. and the overhanging ledges of Mt. Norwottuck, the so-called horse caves of revolutionary days. This ridge trail in unbroken forested terrain runs entirely through hardwood forests and hemlock coves, a region that is a delight to naturalists.

From MA 116, the trail proceeds across the Holyoke State Park Visitors Center parking area and up the driveway to the right of the building. It enters the woods, turns right, and descends to an old streetcar right-of-way. The trail turns right onto the right-of-way for 100 ft., then turns left onto a gravel road and left again, skirting the quarry on the right. The trail soon crosses a high-tension line and bears right (south) at 0.6 mi. to ascend the ridge. (The orange-blazed Robert Frost Trail goes straight ahead from this intersection.) At 1.3 mi. it reaches the summit of Mt. Norwottuck and an abandoned beacon. The trail continues southeast above the high cliff on the eastern edge of the ridge, then descends steeply to the left. At 1.5 mi. it reaches the horse caves, a series of overhanging ledges, climbs through a crevice descending to the bottom of the ledge (caves on the right), and proceeds gradually downhill to the saddle of Mt. Norwottuck and Rattlesnake Knob, where the Robert Frost Trail reenters from the left and the red-blazed Swamp Trail leaves to the right. (From here to Harris Rd. in Amherst, the Robert Frost Trail and M-M Trail coincide.) The M-M Trail continues east along the ridge, passing the yellow-blazed Ken Cuddeback Trail on the left, then turns sharply right (just before a scenic viewpoint) onto a steep descent on an old woods road. At 2 mi. the road goes right and the trail merges with another woods road, bears left, and soon enters a hemlock stand.

At 3.1 mi. the trail turns right, leaving the woods road at the Amherst–Granby line. It reaches a ridge crest (775 ft.) at 3.3 mi., with a good view of Mt. Norwottuck. The trail continues east-north-east along the ridge and descends into a little dell. It continues uphill, swinging to the right and reaching the ledge top at 3.6 mi., with a good view southeast. The trail proceeds east, then north, on this ridge, reaching a steep descent at 3.7 mi. to a small flat. At 3.8 mi. the trail turns right onto a woods road and follows it southeast, ascending. It leaves the road at 3.9 mi. bearing left, and ascends a steep, smooth-floored gully up Long Mtn. to cliff ledges with superb 180-degree views west. The trail turns left at an abandoned beacon at 4.1 mi., descending briefly, then continues along the ridge to another open ledge. The trail now bears right, descending into a hardwood forest, and then goes east on an old tote road. At 5.1 mi. the trail turns abruptly left (northeast) off the tote road, ascends a gentle slope through hardwood cover, crosses the top of a knob, then drops steeply. At 5.3 mi. it turns abruptly right (east), continuing through a hardwood forest to Harris Rd. at 5.4 mi.

Metacomet–Monadnock Trail: MA 116 to Harris Rd.
Distances from MA 116
>   *to* summit of Mt. Norwottuck: 1.3 mi. (1 hr.)
>   *to* horse caves: 1.5 mi. (1 hr. 20 min.)
>   *to* Robert Frost Trail: 1.7 mi. (1 hr. 30 min.)
>   *to* Ken Cuddeback Trail: 1.9 mi. (1 hr. 40 min.)
>   *to* Harris Rd. 5.4 mi. (4 hr. 15 min.)

Metacomet–Monadnock Trail: Harris Rd. to MA 9 (Holland Glen)

This is a very pleasant walk over a succession of low, forested hills with occasional glimpses of the Holyoke Range to the west and the Belchertown ponds to the east. Bay Rd. is the only break in the wilderness solitude.

From Harris Rd. the trail continues east on a sandy woods road. At 0.2 mi. the trail leaves the road to the right (while the Robert Frost Trail continues straight ahead) and continues east ascending a gentle slope through a hardwood forest and briefly following an old tote road northeast. At 0.3 mi. the trail turns abruptly southeast, ascending a steep hillside, and continues along the hilltops through a hardwood forest on rolling ground. At 0.5 mi. the trail ascends a short, steep slope to the crest of the ridge, then turns abruptly left (northeast) and continues along the ridge, crossing a powerline. At the eastern end of the ridge, the trail bears right down a steep bank, crosses a little flat, and climbs eastward to a grassy knoll at the southern end of an apple orchard, with a good view of Mt. Toby to the north. It then descends steeply to Bay Rd. at 1.1 mi. and turns right onto the road.

At 1.2 mi. the trail continues on Bay Rd. past its intersection with Wright St., then it turns sharply left at 1.2 mi. onto an old woods road, ascending into a hemlock mixed forest. At 1.5 mi. the trail reaches the top of a hill (517 ft.) then bears right, descending steeply. It merges with a sandy lane at 1.7 mi., follows the lane briefly north, then bears right at a fork. The trail ascends, traverses a low hill, and descends into a tall pine stand on a flat, crossing a stone wall and then a ditch at 1.9 mi. Soon ascending, it traverses a second low hill covered with mixed forest and descends through tall pines to a tote road that crosses a tiny stream at 2.2 mi. The trail follows the tote road east through a hardwood sapling stand with clumps of hemlocks, crosses the plateau at 2.6 mi. and abruptly turns south through a semimature hardwood forest. At 2.7 mi. it abruptly turns left at the southern edge of this plateau overlooking Metacomet Lake.

The trail turns sharply left at right angles to and away from the edge of the plateau and continues north to a junction with a woods road coming up from Federal St. just north of Arcadia Lake in Belchertown. After bearing right at the top of the ridge, the trail reaches a side trail to a ledge overlooking Holland Lake. It then turns left downhill through hardwoods. At 3.6 mi. it bears right onto a skid road, then turns right onto a path and descends about 100 ft. to Federal St. Turn left just before a private home, proceed on a level contour through a recently cut over area, descend steeply to Orchard St., cross it to the right, and quickly come to Federal St. at the gate of a sand pit. This area is not well blazed, so just continue straight ahead for 100 yd., then left into the woods to cross a steep banked stream. The trail continues over a brush knoll and descends to the Central Vermont Railroad tracks at 4 mi. It crosses the tracks, continues east briefly on the shoulder of the railroad bed, then turns left (north) into the woods. After crossing the stream, it ascends the bank of MA 9, across from the entrance to Holland Glen at 4.2 mi.

Metacomet–Monadnock Trail: Harris Rd. to MA 9 (Holland Glen)

Distances from Harris Rd.
   to apple orchard: 1 mi. (45 min.)
   to Bay Rd.: 1.1 mi. (55 min.)
   to side trail to ledge overlooking Holland Lake: 3.3 mi. (2 hr. 15 min.)
   to MA 9 (Holland Glen): 4.2 mi. (3 hr.)

Metacomet–Monadnock Trail: MA 9 (Holland Glen) to Mt. Lincoln

An interesting walk over ridges and along streams on footpaths and old town roads, this section of the trail is bordered on the west by sturdy stone walls and old cellar holes that mark the site of an old agrarian community, now overgrown by mixed forest. Holland Glen is a steep-sided ravine with a clear stream shaded by a mature hemlock stand, which has been preserved by the Belchertown Historical Society.

From MA 9, the trail continues east through the woods into Holland Glen. At 0.15 mi. it crosses a brook and follows its right bank into the ravine. The trail climbs the steep side of the ravine, exiting right from the stream, continuing amid mature hemlocks and passing a waterfall at 0.4 mi. at the top of the glen. The trail continues upstream on the right bank, crossing a tributary stream. It then turns abruptly left at 0.5 mi. across a brook (good water) onto a woods road, which is overgrown by hemlocks west of here. The trail ascends a moderate slope covered with hardwoods and at 0.8 mi. crosses a bare rock ledge, which affords a good view southwest in winter toward Long Mtn.

The trail reaches the top of the ridge at 1.4 mi., then descends to a left turn onto a woods road. It passes an old farm clearing, now in Johnson grass, at 1.6 mi. on the top of the plateau. At 2.6 mi. the trail turns left onto a woods road, soon crossing a brook and continuing north through a cut over a hardwood stand. At 3.1 mi. it crosses a stone wall on West Hill into young pine growth and proceeds north through stone-wall pasture fences, with cellar holes on the left. At 3.4 mi., the trail follows a woods road to the right for about 150 yd. to a trail junction. The trail turns left here, then quickly bears left at another junction, and continues downhill to a driveway and cabin at unpaved Gulf Rd. at 3.6 mi.

Continuing straight across the road into the woods, the trail proceeds north, then west, paralleling Gulf Rd. At 3.9 mi. it turns left, crosses a wet, grassy trail, and heads north up a sandy bank through a white pine forest. The trail passes near an open field on the right with abandoned cars on the left. This route is followed west along the woodline, bearing left at 4.3 mi. Turning right, the trail passes through young scrub oak, and at 4.5 mi. crosses Enfield Rd. and proceeds north through the Cadwell Memorial Forest (University of Massachusetts). The trail leaves the road at 4.8 mi. and bears right uphill through a scrub-oak hardwood stand. At 5 mi. it passes the observation and fire tower atop Mt. Lincoln (360-degree view), passing to the left of the maintenance shed.

Metacomet–Monadnock Trail: MA 9 (Holland Glen) to Mt. Lincoln

Distances from Holland Glen
>   *to* Gulf Rd.: 3.6 mi. (2 hr. 45 min.)
>   *to* Enfield Rd.: 4.5 mi. (3 hr. 20 min.)
>   *to* summit of Mt. Lincoln: 5 mi. (3 hr. 50 min.)

Metacomet–Monadnock Trail: Mt. Lincoln to N. Valley Rd.

A delightful walk in any season, this section of the trail descends the northwest slope of Mt. Lincoln beside a fast-falling brook in a narrow hemlock glen, passes through a pine and hemlock mixed forest to Amherst's Hill Reservoir, and continues downstream beside Amethyst Brook. From the confluence of Amethyst and Buffum brooks the trail continues upstream under a canopy of hemlocks and pines along a series of waterfalls to a footbridge over Buffum Brook beside N. Valley Rd. in Pelham.

From the summit of Mt. Lincoln the trail continues west down the service road. At 0.2 mi. it exits right into the woods and descends across a woods road at 0.4 mi. It continues downhill to the northwest, crossing the brook at 0.85 mi. The trail bears left onto a woods road, then almost immediately turns left to follow the north bank of the brook downhill. At 1.35 mi. it turns right onto a woods road at the base of a rocky glen, crosses the brook, and descends left. At 1.45 mi. it turns right onto another woods road, which soon crosses the brook. The trail then emerges in a brushy field beside Pelham–Amherst Rd. and continues north to this road at 1.6 mi.

After crossing Pelham–Amherst Rd. the trail bears left up a steep sandbank into pines on a plateau. It continues through a dense seedling pine grove, then slowly descends to the west through beautiful pines to an intersection with an old, grassy road at 1.9 mi. The trail turns right on the grassy road and then quickly left onto a trail leading west through mixed woods and then hemlocks. It descends gradually, then steeply, to a gravel road at 2.2 mi., and turns right, proceeding north for 50 yd. on the road and turning left across a chained entrance to a lane leading to the Amherst reservoir at 2.4 mi.

Descending to the waterside, the trail crosses the reservoir on a footbridge, then proceeds west along the south bank. About 100 ft. beyond the reservoir dam it turns sharply right, leaving the service road beside a streamlet. The trail soon reaches the brook bank which it now follows, crossing Amethyst Brook at 3 mi. The trail continues west along the north bank to the base of Buffam Falls at 3.1 mi. Here the trail turns right, ascending beside a series of cascades in Buffam Brook to a bridge on the left, which is crossed to North Valley Rd. at 3.3 mi. Parking is available on a road shoulder under powerlines to the left.

Metacomet-Monadnock Trail: Mt. Lincoln to N. Valley Rd.

Distances from summit of Mt. Lincoln

   to Pelham-Amherst Rd.: 1.6 mi. (1 hr. 10 min.)
   to Hill Reservoir spillway: 2.6 mi. (1 hr. 55 min.)
   to Buffum Brook: 3.1 mi. (2 hr. 20 min.)
   to N. Valley Rd.: 3.3 mi. (2 hr. 30 min.)

Metacomet–Monadnock Trail: N. Valley Rd. to Market Hill Rd.

This section of the trail exits left off N. Valley Rd. at a stone marker and proceeds up a dirt lane between two houses whose owners welcome hikers. The trail climbs over the bare ledges of Mt. Orient, then runs the length of this ridge through oak and white birch woods, eventually descending to an improvised bridge over Big Hearthstone Brook. From this point it swings south over the shoulder of Poverty Mtn. and, following a pleasant old woods road down the west slope, emerges in a beautiful mixed pine and hemlock forest on Pratt Corner Rd.

Turning north onto N. Valley Road, the trail continues to the next mailbox at 0.1 mi. The trail turns left onto the faint track of an old tote road, proceeding west across the mowing into the woods beyond. At 0.5 mi. the trail bears left at the first fork and continues around a bend, passing under a powerline. The tote road soon heads northwest to a junction with the Robert Frost Trail. (The M-M Trail and the Robert Frost Trail coincide from here to the Atkins Reservoir.) At 0.6 mi. the road crosses a little stream; here the trail turns right and proceeds north along the stream, leaving the stream at 0.8 mi. The trail bears right uphill and soon crosses a woods road. The trail climbs in a slow right swing up the southwest slope of Mt. Orient. At 1.3 mi. it leads on a hand-and-foot climb up the steep slope of the mountain and at 1.5 mi. reaches the southern end of the ridge.

From the crest of the ridge, the trail swings west and descends somewhat through hemlock woods to the western edge of the ridge, then leaves the ledges and bends back east and then north along the ridge crest. After traversing the ridge, the trail descends gradually and crosses a stone wall and continues downhill to cross Little Hearthstone Brook at 2.4 mi. It continues north over this tableland, then descends steeply on erosion-control water bars to an old gravel road.

Turning right on the road, the trail crosses Big Hearthstone Brook on a culvert, then turns quickly left into the woods. Continuing west, it slowly veers away from the brook on the left, and descends to a low point between Mt. Orient and Poverty Mtn. The trail soon crosses a bog bridge over a swampy area, proceeding southwest, amid mature white pines. At 3.2 mi. the trail bears left onto a woods road that ascends up and over a shoulder of Poverty Mtn. The trail follows the woods road downhill through tall pines and a hardwood forest, descends more steeply, then bears right (north) onto another tote road. From here the trail turns left, descending through a mature mixed forest. It then turns right, descending through hemlock woods. After crossing a streamlet, the trail turns left at 4.2 mi. onto Pratt Corner Rd. (A swimming hole is located upstream from the bridge on the left of Pratt Corner Rd.) Pass over the bridge and immediately turn right onto a wood road. Follow this road north to Atkins Reservoir onto unpaved Market Hill Rd. at 4.6 mi.

Metacomet–Monadnock Trail: N. Valley Rd. to Market Rd.

Distances from N. Valley Rd.

   to Little Hearthstone Brook: 2.4 mi. (2 hr.)
   to Market Hill Rd.: 4.6 mi. (3 hr. 15 min.)

Metacomet–Monadnock Trail: Market Hill Rd. to Shutesbury–Leverett Rd.

In forested country, mostly on old woods roads, the trail climbs over the January Hills, through forests of oak, white birch, and white pine saplings, to emerge on grassy fields on the Shutesbury–Leverett Rd. This section repeatedly intersects and runs along powerlines and affords panoramic views from the hilltops.

   Turn right on unpaved Market Hill Rd. Turn left at a cabled gate after 75 yd. and follow a wooded lane under a pine forest skirting the eastern shore of the reservoir on the left. Several unmarked side trails lead to the water's edge. Crossing a small streamlet at 0.4 mi., the trail turns right onto a woods road at 0.5 mi. Ascending gently, the trail bears right at a junction, crosses a small stream, and bears left uphill, as the road becomes a grassy lane. At 1 mi. it passes under two powerlines in quick succession. Turn left under the second powerline and continue uphill on its maintenance road to the height-of-land, then downhill to an underground cable right-of-way at 1.7 mi. Turn left onto the cable line and proceed to the woodline, where there is a narrow trail on the right. Follow this downhill, joining with another wood road, and at 2.8 mi. turn left on a narrow path and descend gradually to the steep bank of Roaring Brook at 3.2 mi. Cross the brook (fording necessary at high water) and turn right, following the brook upstream. Here the trail turns left, ascending steeply to the paved Shutesbury-Leverett Rd. at 3.5 mi.

Metacomet–Monadnock Trail: Market Hill Rd. to Shutesbury–Leverett Rd.

Distances from Market Hill Rd.

   to Roaring Brook: 3.2 mi. (2 hr.)
   to Shutesbury–Leverett Rd.: 3.5 mi. (2 hr. 15 min.)

Metacomet–Monadnock Trail: Shutesbury–Leverett Rd. to N. Leverett–Lake Wyola Rd.

This section is interesting from two perspectives: (1) the wilderness character of the terrain along the winding trail (actually an old town road, as its enduring stone culverts make clear) through hardwood forests, white birches and pure stands of hemlocks beside the area's streams; and (2) the historic character of the area, indicated by the miles of sturdy stone walls and many cellar holes that echo an early pastoral community that existed when the Indians still controlled the Connecticut River and its broad valley.

Cross the paved Shutesbury–Leverett Rd. to a gravel lane on the right and go north for some 300 yd., ascending. Pass near the clearing of a powerline on the right in 0.3 mi. at a log landing, then go left on a woods road that crosses a stream and soon turns right toward Brushy Mtn. At 0.8 mi., cross Mountain Brook, then turn right at a fork and begin the ascent. At 1.9 mi. the woods road begins climbing the shoulder of a mountain, passing through dense laurel. At 2 mi. the trail crosses a small stream in a delightful hemlock dell in the height-of-land west of Brushy Mtn., and at 2.6 mi. it begins a gradual descent to a woods road on the right at 2.9 mi., passing an old mill site on the left. Continuing to descend moderately and passing over two small streams, the trail joins a powerline on an eroded, wide lumber access road, where it bears left (NNW) and continues descending through a recently harvested area.

At 3.9 mi. the trail turns right at the junction with Rattlesnake Gutter Rd. Descending, it exits left onto a woods road through a mixed pine and hemlock forest. At 4.3 mi. the trail turns left onto a gravel road, passing charcoal beehive kilns. At 4.3 mi. it turns right and crosses the bridge over Saw Mill River. At 4.7 mi. it turns left onto paved N. Leverett–Lake Wyola Rd.

Metacomet–Monadnock Trail: Shutesbury–Leverett Rd. to N. Leverett–Lake Wyola Rd.

Distances from Shutesbury–Leverett Rd.

   to Rattlesnake Gutter Rd.: 3.9 mi. (2 hr. 35 min.)
   to Saw Mill River: 4.5 mi. (3 hr. 15 min.)
   to N. Leverett–Lake Wyola Rd.: 4.7 mi. (3 hr. 25 min.)

Metacomet–Monadnock Trail: N. Leverett–Lake Wyola Rd. to Farley

This section travels almost entirely over gravel roads, woods roads, and forest-service roads. From N. Leverett–Lake Wyola Rd. the trail ascends the north slope of the Saw Mill River valley along Williams Brook, gradually rises high on a shoulder of Dry Hill, then descends via Ruggles Pond, Lyons Brook, and forest service roads to Farley. Most of the section lies within the Wendell State Forest on the south slope of the Millers River Valley.

The trail turns right off N. Leverett–Lake Wyola Rd. onto gravel Richardson Rd. just after crossing Williams Brook. At 0.4 mi. it passes farm buildings on the left and continues uphill on a gravel road. At 0.9 mi. it passes the fields of an abandoned farm at the top of the slope, then turns west at 1.5 mi. at the dead-end intersection with an east-west gravel road. It crosses a bridge at 1.9 mi. and turns right at the crossroads. At 2.1 mi. it turns left onto a power-line service road at the bridge on the west side of the brook. The trail crosses the powerline clearing, bears left past a private camp, then bears right at a fork in the road. At 2.6 mi. it bears right at a second fork in the road, then passes a forest-service water hole and continues straight onto Burkhart Rd., a forest service road. This road rises high on the east slope of Dry Hill, then descends to the north. The trail turns left onto a gravel road at 4 mi. and continues to the intersection of Montague Rd. at 4.7 mi. It crosses Montague Rd. and continues northeast onto Ruggles Rd., following it to Ruggles Pond.

The foundation and clearing at 4.9 mi. mark the site of a CCC camp, now maintained by the forest service. Picnic tables, fireplaces, and swimming are available. (A parking fee is charged in season.) The trail turns left across the parking lot, then proceeds downhill about 200 yd. to an Adirondack shelter suitable for eight to ten persons. A fireplace, wood, and outhouse are available. A fine-walled spring is located a few yards farther down the trail. The trail continues downhill on an old tote road east of Lyons Brook. At 5.3 mi. it turns left to the east bank of the brook, then proceeds downstream to a crossing at 5.7 mi. at the brook's confluence with Lyons Brook. The trail soon turns right, leaving the brook and proceeding up the steep bank through laurel scrub. It crosses the brook at 5.9 mi. and turns north along the base of a ridge, turning right and ascending south on a forest service road.

At the junction with the dirt Jerusalem Rd. the trail takes a sharp right turn, going uphill on Jerusalem Rd. to a junction with a side trail in 150 yd. next to a small parking area. The trail turns left up this side trail to the ridge and then turns right (north) to follow the ridge line. On a narrow track, the trail continues over several wooded hills for about 1 mi. to the junction of two woods roads.

The trail follows woods roads as it drops down at the end of the ridge to an unpaved camp road. It turns left on the camp road a short distance to Davis Rd., then descends steeply to the right on Davis Rd. to Mormon Hollow Brook.

The trail continues right and downhill on a washed-out section of Davis Rd. and crosses Mormon Hollow Brook on a rustic bridge. After crossing the bridge, take a sharp left and follow the scenic brook bank. The trail passes some old dam structures and cellar holes to emerge on Mormon Hollow Rd. Go left on this blacktop road, then sharp right under the powerlines down to a meadow used for parking by local fishermen. The trail continues along Mormon Hollow Brook with its attractive cascades, pools and glades of mature hemlock. Crossing the brook three times (use caution), it finally picks up an old skid road on the north side and proceeds to the Millers River, passing just below the railroad bridge. Climb the steep railroad bank, cross the bridge, and descend to the river. (*Note:* During low water, it may be possible to ford the river on a gravel bar under the bridge.)

At the river, the trail heads east along the densely vegetated flood plain. At the end of the flood plain it rises steeply up onto the railroad embankment and follows the tracks for several hundred yards before descending again into the woods and the riverbank. (*Caution:* The railroad tracks are active.) The trail continues through woods parallel to the river before passing the foundations of a nineteenth-century knitting factory and piano works. The trail emerges on Farley Rd. next to the Farley Bridge at 9.8 mi.

Metacomet–Monadnock Trail: N. Leverett–Lake Wyola Rd. to Farley

Distances from N. Leverett–Lake Wyola Rd.

  to recreation area and Adirondack shelter at Ruggles Pond: *est.*
    4.8 mi. (3 hr. 10 min.)
  to Lyons Brook: 5.5 mi. (3 hr. 35 min.)
  to Farley: 9.8 mi. (5 hr. 15 min.)

Metacomet–Monadnock Trail: MA 2 (Farley) to Gulf Rd.

This section of the trail climbs steeply from Farley, at first in pastureland in the shadow of the high cliffs of Rattlesnake Mtn., then along the hemlock ravine of Briggs Brook. From here it proceeds northeast on the ridge and ledges of Hermit Mtn., rising high above Millers River, then abruptly turns north through the Irving State Forest to the bare ledges of Crag Mtn. in Northfield. This is one of the more interesting sections of the trail in Massachusetts.

Cross MA 2 to the right of the old Erving Cycle Shop (parking available here) and continue to Holmes St. Pass Wells St. on the left and continue to Briggs St. Turn left onto Briggs St., following it to the end. Enter the woods on a wide woods road, ascending gradually to a right turn across Briggs Brook on a primitive

footbridge. Turn left, climbing on the right side of the brook. At
0.6 mi. the trail crosses Briggs Brook a short distance above the lip
of some high falls, then turns upstream on the far side of the brook
into a hemlock ravine. At 0.8 mi. it passes a side trail to Rose
Ledge. (This Rose Ledge trail runs upstream beside Briggs Brook,
then west and south to the southern rim of Northfield Mtn., known
as the Rose Ledge. There are spectacular views of the Connecticut
River valley to the south and west from this ledge. This trail
intersects several hiking, snowshoe, and ski trails maintained by
Northeast Utilities Co. as the Northfield Mountain Recreational
Area. For maps and information, write to Recreation Supervisor,
RR 1, Box 377, Northfield, MA 01360.)

At this junction the Metacomet–Monadnock Trail turns right
(northeast) and crosses the brook. In a few yards, it turns right
again and climbs out on a rocky ledge. At 0.9 mi. it crosses a
woods road, continuing north and rising slightly while staying
close to the rim of the ridge, which falls away steeply from the trail
to the river. The Northeast Utilities pumped-storage reservoir is on
the left. At 1.4 mi. the trail turns right and proceeds east downhill
on a woods road to Packard Brook. At 1.7 mi. it intersects a tote
road coming up from Farley and turns left onto this road. The trail
leaves the road among hemlocks at 1.9 mi., bears right beyond a
big hemlock, then climbs upward on a ridge. At 1.8 mi. it traverses
ledges overlooking the Millers River and continues eastward from
ledge to ledge. The trail turns east 0.25 mi. east of the last ledge
and descends the ridge, crossing a dry brook bed at 2.9 mi.

The trail now turns sharp left (north) and continues ascending
moderately for 0.3 mi. on a north-northwest bearing through a
hardwood forest. The terrain levels off, and hemlocks soon become
the principal forest component. At 3.4 mi. the trail turns right (east)
onto a tote road, then as this road changes its bearing from east to
southeast, the trail turns left (north) at 3.2 mi. It turns east once
more at 4 mi. onto a second, much broader tote road but soon jogs
south from this broad road onto a narrower road, and within 80 ft.
the trail leaves the road, turning east. It climbs slightly, reaching a
high ledge at 4.2 mi. and shortly descends the ledges, bearing north

to more level terrain. It proceeds northeast through hardwoods with some pines to the junction with Mountain Rd. at 4.3 mi., just south of the padlocked gate on the west side of the road. This gate leads to Northfield Mtn. Reservoir, which is off-limits to hikers.

The trail continues north on Mountain Rd. to the Northfield–Erving line at 4.5 mi., where it turns right (east) onto an abandoned town road. After crossing a tiny streamlet, it continues east. At 4.7 mi., opposite a meadow, the trail turns left (north) into a gray birch and pine forest and soon crosses a small swampy stream. It continues north through pole stands of birch, maple, and pine, then begins climbing gently. It jogs left through pines, turns north, then descends slightly and crosses a little dell, turning west as it skirts the base of a rock outcrop. It soon turns north again through a break in the ledge and within 150 ft. turns right onto S. Mountain Rd. At the crest of the ridge (5.2 mi.) the trail turns left (north) onto a long gravel private driveway. Turn right before reaching the house and begin a short climb of a steep slope to the summit of Crag Mtn., where there are views east to Mt. Grace, east-northeast to Mt. Monadnock in New Hampshire, and south. At 6.3 mi. another ledge looks to the north and west. The trail continues north, and turns right to leave the woods road at 7 mi. At 7.1 mi. there are more ledges with open views of Mt. Grace and Mt. Monadnock. At 7.5 mi., on a northerly descending rock ledge, the trail leaves the ledge bearing right and then left, descending on a woods road which soon turns east next to a powerline and descends to Gulf Rd. in Northfield.

Metacomet–Monadnock Trail: MA 2 (Farley) to Crag Mtn.

Distances from MA 2

> *to* Rose Ledge side trail: 0.8 mi. (30 min.)
> *to* ledges overlooking Millers River: 2.2 mi. (1 hr. 15 min.)
> *to* Mountain Rd.: 4.3 mi. (2 hr. 15 min.)
> *to* southern summit of Crag Mtn.: 6.2 mi. (3 hr. 45 min.)
> *to* Gulf Rd.: 7.9 mi. (4 hr. 30 min.)

Metacomet–Monadnock Trail: Gulf Rd. to Mt. Grace

Passing across the tops of Northfield's Bald Hills, which are covered with hardwoods and some mixed forest, this section of the trail proceeds to the southern end of Mt. Grace. From there it climbs on the old Snowshoe Trail to the fire tower at the summit of Mt. Grace.

At 0.2 mi. the trail turns right off of Gulf Rd. under a power-line, then left onto a woods road before reaching the first pylon, proceeding northeast. At 0.5 mi. it turns left onto an old tote road, proceeding on the same contour north to a brook at 0.8 mi. The trail crosses the brook, proceeds on its north bank upstream for 100 ft., then turns left and goes another 100 yd. northeast. It bears left, climbing hills and soon reaching some rock outcrops. At 1.1 mi. it turns right from the ledge and continues through an open pine forest, soon ascending sharply through hardwoods to cross a powerline near the top of the Bald Hills. The trail continues east on bare rock, following several cairns to the eastern rim of the hill (1345 ft.). Mt. Grace looms ahead through the trees.

Here the trail turns left, descending through pine forests, then ascending. At 1.8 mi. it emerges on the eastern rim of a hardwood-covered ridge and proceeds north, soon descending. It crosses a boulder-strewn, fast-falling streamlet (mostly dry in summer) at 2.1 mi., then ascends through a mixed forest of hemlock. Skirting the east slope of the hill (1285 ft.), the trail descends rapidly to the junction with the woods road extension of Warwick's White Rd. at 2.4 mi. As you descend for 0.3 mi. from the Bald Hills on White Rd., look for a sign marking a sharp left into the woods. From here the trail winds through open hardwoods of a recently harvested area to join a snowmobile trail, where it turns left (NW) to join a major woods road at 2.9 mi. The trail proceeds right on this road (the historic Fifth Massachusetts Turnpike, dating from 1775), crossing a junction with the unpaved White Rd. at 3.4 mi., and proceeds east to a small clearing.

The trail crosses a brook on a culvert, then narrows to a woods road, ascending and crossing another woods road at 3.6 mi. after detouring around a new house. The trail continues east on snow-

mobile trails to connect with paved Northfield Rd. The trail parallels the highway and emerges near the junction of White Rd. and
Northfield Rd. The trail crosses the road, crosses a brook on a rustic bridge, and then climbs up to join the Round the Mountain Trail
in Mt. Grace St. Reservation at 5.1 mi.

Here you can either turn right at once (an unmarked shortcut) or,
for a more leisurely walk, continue left on Round the Mountain
Trail for about 0.2 mi., then turn right off the trail, ascending
steeply to the old Snowshoe Trail and turn sharply right onto this.
The trail proceeds to a cluster of seven oaks at 5.7 mi., turns sharply
left, and begins a steady ascent of the knife-edge of a ridge. Beneath
the hemlocks at the crest of the ridge are lookouts to the west.

The trail descends through the forest to a draw in a tall pine
grove at 6.1 mi., then climbs again amid pines and hemlocks past
more westward lookouts and a northward glimpse of the Mt. Grace
summit and fire tower. With a gradual descent the trail joins the
fire tower service road from Warwick village at 6.4 mi. and follows
this steep road to 6.6 mi., where it leaves the road to follow a telephone line. It soon rejoins the road and follows it to the summit of
Mt. Grace at 6.8 mi.

Metacomet–Monadnock Trail: Gulf Rd. to Mt. Grace

Distances from Crag Mtn.

   to White Rd: 2.4 mi. (2 hr.)

   to Northfield Rd.: 5 mi. (3 hr. 30 min.)

   to summit of Mt. Grace: 6.8 mi. (4 hr. 50 min.)

Metacomet–Monadnock Trail: Mt. Grace to MA 32

From the summit of Mt. Grace the trail descends to MA 78 along
the old Winchester Trail. After another 1 mi. eastward, the trail
passes just above attractive Highland Falls and enters a stretch of
unbroken woodland and, climbing up and down over an interesting
series of steplike ridges, reaches a high point just south of the
Massachusetts–New Hampshire line. From here the trail proceeds
roughly parallel to the line to the end of this section.

The trail runs along the summit of Mt. Grace, past the fire
tower on the left and a boulder with a plaque on the right, to begin

its northerly descent via a ski trail. It bears left onto the trail away from the service road and on its steep descent affords a glimpse of the ultimate goal, Mt. Monadnock. At 0.3 mi. the trail turns abruptly left off the ski trail to descend steeply past a spring (right) at 0.5. mi. Then it winds down more gently, on and off through old woods, to a junction with a tote road just below a large sawdust pile. This road descends through hemlocks to a level stretch at 1 mi., where it crosses a brook and passes an Adirondack shelter built in 1970 by DEM.

The trail continues down the road to a beautiful pool, then descends along the edge of the ravine. It bears right around a white pine grove, still on the road, then crosses Mirey Brook below a broken dam to reach MA 78 at 1.6 mi. (Turning right on MA 78 leads to Mt. Grace State Forest picnic area in 0.5 mi.) The trail crosses MA 78, climbs a steep bank, and at the top of a grassy knoll turns right through a corridor cut in thick pines. Emerging onto a faint path, it turns abruptly left at 1.7 mi., angles down to cross a brook, and 40 ft. east of the brook meets a woods road. The trail turns left onto the road, proceeds north 0.1 mi., bears right, and travels continuously through a white-pine forest, gradually ascending on an easterly bearing. The trail enters a pole stand of Scotch pine, turns sharply left (north), and presently emerges on Old Winchester Rd. (gravel). It crosses the road and in another 70 ft. bears right, ascending. At 1.9 mi. it turns left onto a woods road and soon descends to cross another woods road. Continuing northeast, it crosses Kidder Brook under a powerline at 2.1 mi. and bears left at a fork in the road beyond the bridge, ascending. There is a good lunch spot at 2.5 mi., with views west from the ledges a few yards from the trail under a powerline.

In a small clearing at 2.8 mi. the trail turns left, then right, and descends briefly. It then ascends again, past an interesting pothole swamp to the right, and leaves the road at 3.1 mi. to climb straight up the ridge. After a dip through a little dell, the trail climbs steeply to a second ridge at 3.4 mi., descends, and climbs again to the top of the ledges at 3.6 mi. Here the trail turns sharply left, descending along a boundary line, then climbs once more through many fallen hemlocks to an important right turn at 3.8 mi. The trail makes a steep descent into a gully and an equally sharp ascent over a rocky knoll, repeating this pattern twice within 0.5 mi., until at 4.3 mi. it emerges onto and turns left down an abandoned farm road. At 4.5 mi. the trail leaves this road to go straight uphill, and at 4.7 mi. it reaches Richmond Rd. (graded gravel) within sight of the Massachusetts–New Hampshire state line marker on the left, on the south slope of Whipple Hill.

The trail proceeds right (south) onto Richmond Rd. and turns left at 5 mi. onto a maintained gravel road. The maintenance ceases at the entrance to the last house. As the road and trail wind steeply down, there are views of Ball Hill ahead in the dormant season. The trail crosses the headwaters of Tully Brook at 5.1 mi. and continues past a cellar hole, then turns left onto another abandoned road at 5.3 mi. The trail goes up and over the shoulder of Ball Hill through hemlock woods, then descends past another cellar hole to a road entering right at 6.3 mi. Shortly, the road turns sharply left onto Parker Road and the trail goes straight up, down, and up again to reach the southern end of a rocky ridge. Ball Hill is visible to the west and White Hill is visible to the east across the valley. After crossing and then following the ridge to its northern end (where a glimpse of Mt. Monadnock is possible), the path descends in steep zigzags.

At 6.8 mi. the trail enters a clear-cut, proceeds to the brook, goes downstream briefly, then crosses and soon proceeds right along a logging road. Near a small open area at 6.9 mi. the trail turns left and proceeds up a steep slope on a logging road, which soon shrinks to a narrow footpath, still climbing southeast to a tote road. The trail turns right onto the road and follows it up and over the summit (1361 ft.) of White Hill. At the summit the trail goes left into an old timber cut, descends steeply, passes a slight rise at the foot of the hill, continues through a small clearing, and joins Bliss Rd. (graded gravel) at 7.6 mi. (limited parking available).

The trail crosses Bliss Rd. and its stone wall fence and proceeds generally east through interesting forest terrain. It soon crosses another stone wall, then another at 7.9 mi., at a blue-stake boundary of a former pasture. With still another stone wall on the left and descending slightly through hemlock hardwoods, the trail soon enters a red-pine pole plantation, bearing left over the needle carpet. It leaves the plantation at 8.1 mi., crosses a small hill, continues over a flat area, then ascends a hardwood slope with a tiny streamlet on the right (south) side. At 8.3 mi., now on a plateau, the trail enters a stand of large hemlocks with great boulders scattered over the undulating terrain. At 8.5 mi. it crosses an east-west stone wall about 80 ft. west of MA 32.

Although you might want to end your hike at MA 32, you can take a side trip to Falls Brook, which is less than 1 mi. farther along the trail. To do so, follow the trail right onto MA 32. The trail crosses the highway in about 50 ft., then follows along the more northerly of two dirt roads. The trail soon passes the entrance to Newton Cemetery, bearing right (east), then at 8.6 mi. bears right (south) at a fork onto a skid road. It continues south-southeast past a tote road that descends down a steep slope. At 8.8 mi. with two great, declining beech trees on the right, the trail descends into a brushy area. It enters a closed canopy of hardwoods, now steeply descending, and crosses a tiny stream, continuing parallel to the stream on its north bank. At 9 mi. the trail recrosses the stream and continues south. At about 100 ft. Falls Brook is visible to the east at the base of the glen. Still bearing south, the trail now descends to Falls Brook and continues along its bank.

The trail crosses the brook at 9.1 mi. on a boulder ford that is only 0.05 miles from the lip of the falls. (*Caution:* this can be a dangerous place for children.) In the interest of safety, follow a more interesting route and a spectacular approach to the falls by continuing uphill due east from the brook crossing and bearing right as you crest the slope. You will soon enter the well-used but unmarked trail to the falls. (This path leads from Falls Rd. about 0.3 mi. to the east. Falls Rd. south to this path is passable only by four-wheel-drive vehicles). The path leads 0.1 mi. to a high ledge overlooking the falls. It proceeds along the edge of the gorge, guarded by a steel cable fence, to the Metacomet–Monadnock Trail beside the brook.

From Falls Brook the trail heads generally northeast into New Hampshire, crossing Little Monadnock Mtn., passing through Troy, NH, and finally ascending to the summit of Mt. Monadnock (3165 ft.).

Metacomet–Monadnock Trail: Mt. Grace to MA 32

Distances from summit of Mt. Grace

    to brook crossing and Adirondack shelter: 1 mi. (30 min.)
    to MA 78: 1.6 mi. (45 min.)
    to Kidder Brook: 2.1 mi. (1 hr.)
    to Richmond Rd.: 4.7 mi. (2 hr. 20 min.)
    to Tully Brook: 5.1 mi. (2 hr. 45 min.)
    to Bliss Rd.: 7.6 mi. (3 hr. 50 min.)
    to MA 32: 8.5 mi. (4 hr. 15 min.)
    to Falls Brook: *est.* 9 mi. (4 hr. 30 min.)

ROBERT FROST TRAIL

The Robert Frost Trail starts at Holyoke Range State Park and runs 33 mi. north to Mt. Toby State Forest. It traverses several attractive peaks and hills with views across the Connecticut River Valley and passes through the 1,000-acre Lawrence Swamp and half a dozen other Amherst conservation areas. A detailed map of the trail is available from various outlets in the Amherst area. The trail is marked with rectangular orange blazes.

Robert Frost Trail: Southern Section (MA 116 to Pelham Rd.)

The trail leaves MA 116 near the Granby–Amherst line from behind the Notch Visitor Center, in concert with the Metacomet–Monadnock Trail. At 0.6 mi. the M–M Trail leaves to the right, while the Frost Trail continues east along the wooded north slopes of the Holyoke Range, eventually turning right to rejoin the M–M trail in the Mt. Norwottuck–Rattlesnake Knob col. The Frost Trail follows the white-blazed M–M Trail for the next 4 mi. over Long Mtn., descending to Harris Mtn. Rd. (5.1 mi.) and continuing east 1 mi. over the easternmost part of the Holyoke Range to Bay Rd., near Snow's Farm and Poultry Market Store. From there the trail leaves the Metacomet–Monadnock Trail and follows Warren Wright Rd., a narrow gravel lane that becomes paved at Orchard St. 1 mi. north. Across from Goodell Rd., the trail turns left (west) through a gate and follows a farm road along the edge of some cornfields, continuing into the wooded Lawrence Swamp.

The trail traverses the western side of the swamp on old woods roads, heading generally northwest past Town Well No. 4 at 8.3 mi. It turns left (west) across Hop Brook, then turns right (north) at 9 mi. onto a narrow trail that crosses several hundred feet of bog bridge through an old beaver swamp before crossing Baby Carriage Brook. At 9.3 mi. it turns right (north) (Baby Carriage Trail continues straight, leading in 0.4 mi. to S. East St.) and begins meandering through the rest of Lawrence Swamp to Station Rd. (10.3 mi.). The trail turns right (east) onto Station Rd. and continues across the Central Vermont Railroad tracks, turning left (north) onto an old road at 10.8 mi.

The trail turns right (east) to follow the southern edge of the last small field, then picks up a woods road and turns left into the Amherst Woods subdivision. The trail zigzags north through the development, following easements and short sections of road to Wildflower Drive. It turns left onto Wildflower Drive and in 0.1 mi. reenters the woods on the right. The trail continues north to Old Belchertown Rd. at 12.1 mi., where it turns left for 0.2 mi. to MA 9, 0.5 mi. west of the Amherst–Belchertown line. It follows MA 9 west for 200 ft., then turns right (northeast) near a chain-link fence and continues north past the Amherst landfill and into the Harkness Brook Conservation Area. At 13 mi. the trail turns left (east) onto Stony Hill Rd., continues past Gatehouse Rd., and turns left onto a woods path. At 14.5 mi. it reaches Ward St., heads north 200 yd., and crosses Pelham Rd. to the parking lot of the Amethyst Brook Conservation Area.

Robert Frost Trail: Southern Section

Distances from Notch Visitor Center

    to Metacomet–Monadnock Trail: 1.7 mi. (50 min.)
    to tower on summit of Long Mtn.: 3.9 mi. (2 hr.)
    to Harris Mtn. Rd.: 5.1 mi. (2 hr. 30 min.)

to Bay Rd.: 6.1 mi. (3 hr.)
to Orchard St.: 6.9 mi. (3 hr. 30 min.)
to Baby Carriage Trail: 9.3 mi. (4 hr. 25 min.)
to Station Rd.: 10.3 mi. (5 hr.)
to Old Belchertown Rd.: 12.1 mi. (6 hr.)
to MA 9: 12.3 mi. (6 hr. 10 min.)
to Stony Hill Rd.: 13 mi. (6 hr. 30 min.)
to Gatehouse Rd.: 13.2 mi. (6 hr. 40 min.)
to Ward St.: 14.5 mi. (7 hr.)
to Pelham Rd.: 14.6 mi. (7 hr. 15 min.)

Robert Frost Trail: Northern Section (Pelham Rd. to Mt. Toby and Reservation Rd.)

The trail heads north from the Amethyst Brook parking area, cross-es a field and a cable suspension bridge, then leads east along Amethyst Brook. A left (northeast) turn away from the brook at 0.5 mi. begins the ascent of Mt. Orient (957 ft.) to its ledges with impressive views west and south. The trail continues through the backwoods of the Pelham Hills north to Pratts Rd. (4.4 mi.). The trail turns left (west) onto Pratts Rd. and after 100 yd. it turns right (north), continuing to Market Hill Rd. at Atkins Reservoir, a good place to spot migrating waterfowl.

The trail turns left (west) onto unpaved Market Hill Rd. 400 yd. along the reservoir, then turns left (southwest) and continues over wooded Mt. Boreas, crosses Flat Hills Rd., and gradually descends to Market Hill Rd. The trail crosses to a short rise and a bluff overlooking Cushman Brook, descends to cross Bridge St., and follows Cushman Brook high above the cascades, across the Central Vermont Railroad, and down a steep drop to join the Kevin R. Flood Handicapped-Access Trail. It crosses Robert Fran-cis Bridge and at 7.2 mi. turns left (west) onto State St. for 100 ft., then turns right (north) along the edge of Puffer's Pond. It turns right again at a paved access road and immediately climbs left up a steep hill, past Pulpit Hill Rd., and across the wooded ledges of Pulpit Hill. At 8.3 mi. the trail enters the fields of the Eastman Brook Conservation Area and turns right at a pair of stiles. It then turns left and follows the railroad tracks 0.6 mi. to cross Juggler Meadow Rd. at 9.3 mi.

The trail continues north through wooded country west of the tracks, crosses to the east side of the tracks, and follows a series of rocky knolls to Depot Rd. at 10.2 mi. It turns left (west) onto Depot Rd. and follows it to MA 63. The trail turns left onto MA 63 and then right onto Bull Hill Rd. Just past the bridge over Long Plain Brook (11.8 mi.), a short distance before reaching the Leverett-Sunderland line, the trail turns right into the woods along the west bank of the brook.

After leaving the brook, the trail turns left to ascend on a woods road, then right at a saddle, and continues easterly to pick up a steep ridge, which it follows northwest to the wooded summit of Bull Hill at 12.3 mi. The trail continues on the ridge to the blue-blazed South Mountain Rd., an abandoned woods road. It turns right (east) onto the road and descends, crossing a stream and a north-south woods road at 13.6 mi. It continues northeast, crossing several more streams before it ascends steeply to a powerline crossing and a left turn onto yet another woods road. As the ascent becomes steeper, the Frost Bypass Trail leaves on the left. The main trail continues to a saddle where it turns left (north) to cross a broad plateau and drop again to an old cabin at 15.5 mi. A side trail leading east from the cabin ascends Roaring Mtn.

The main trail descends northwest to Roaring Brook, then turns left and follows a well-hiked old road south, finally winding back around to the north, passing the other end of the Frost Bypass Trail, and reaching the Mt. Toby fire tower at 16.7 mi. The descent is by a cleared powerline that strikes off to the northeast. A left at a saddle and another left off the powerline leads to a woods road near Cranberry Pond. The trail turns left here and continues to its end at Reservation Rd. in Sunderland (18.7 mi).

Robert Frost Trail: Northern Section

Distances from Pelham Rd.

   to summit of Mt. Orient: 1.9 mi. (1 hr.)
   to summit of Mt. Boreas: 6 mi. (3 hr.)
   to Puffer's Pond: 7.6 mi. (3 hr. 45 min.)

to Eastman Brook Conservation Area: 8.3 mi. (4 hr. 10 min.)
to Long Plain Brook: 11.8 mi. (6 hr.)
to summit of Bull Hill: 12.3 mi. (6 hr. 30 min.)
to Bypass Trail: 14.8 mi. (7 hr. 30 min.)
to Metawampe cabin: 15.5 mi. (8 hr.)
to Mt. Toby fire tower: 16.7 mi. (8 hr. 45 min.)
to Cranberry Pond: 18.4 mi. (9 hr. 15 min.)
to Reservation Rd.: 18.7 mi. (9 hr. 45 min.)

MT. TOM STATE RESERVATION

Mt. Tom State Reservation preserves an area of 1,800 acres, including that section of the traprock cliffs that lies between Easthampton and Holyoke just west of the Connecticut River commonly known as the Mt. Tom range. Within its boundaries are Mt. Nonotuck (882 ft.), Goat Peak (850 ft.), Whiting Peak (1015 ft.), Dead Top (1100 ft.), and Mt. Tom (1202 ft.). The summit of Mt. Tom, now occupied by television and radio transmission stations, was once the site of a fashionable hotel and summit house, reached by railway from Mountain Park to the east. The building burned about 1900, was rebuilt, and burned again in 1929; now only the foundation and promenade remain. Picnic areas, a trailside natural-history museum, scenic drives, and ice skating in season are the principal attractions of the reservation for the general public.

For the hiker, the Mt. Tom trail system consists of 20 mi. of marked and maintained trails. Trail maintenance is supervised by the Mt. Tom Citizens Advisory Committee. Blazed trails are marked by standard 2-by-4-inch paint blazes and normally have signs at both ends and at all junctions. Trail signs at roadheads are usually posted a short distance in from the road. (*Note:* On trail signs, the Metacomet–Monadnock Trail and Smith's Ferry Rd. are identified as "M–M Tr." and "Bray Rd." respectively.) About half the trails are suitable for cross-country skiing, of easy-to-moderate difficulty. Trail bikes and snowmobiles are not permitted on reservation trails. The Mt. Tom Ski Area, while outside the reservation proper, is operated throughout the year, offering an alpine slide, lifts, a snackbar, and a ski shop. Parts of several reservation trails extend onto ski area property.

The reservation headquarters (commonly known as the Stone House), museum, and surrounding picnic areas are accessible by paved Smith's Ferry Rd., which leaves US 5 about 2 mi. north of the access road to the Mt. Tom Ski Area, and by Christopher Clark Rd, which leaves MA 141 just north of the height-of-land. Smith's Ferry Rd. is plowed in the winter; Christopher Clark Rd. is plowed as far as the headquarters. Paved Reservation Rd. (0.8 mi. long) runs from Easthampton to the reservation center, which begins at a stone gateway on East St. just north of the intersection with Clark St. The road is barred to vehicles, but it is an easy access to the reservation center for walkers. Parking fees are charged in season.

Fires are permitted only in the fireplaces of the picnic areas. The pump at the Stone House is the only sure and safe source of drinking water during the summer months. Spring water is normally available at signed locations in Hamden Field (off Smith's Ferry Rd., across from the museum) and on the south side of Christopher Clark Rd., 0.3 mi. west of Stone House.

Trail information is available at the Stone House and, in season, at the museum. See the Mt. Tom/Holyoke map included with this book, and refer to the USGS Easthampton, Mt. Tom, and Mt. Holyoke quadrangles and a small portion of the USGS Springfield North quadrangle.

Metacomet–Monadnock Trail

This is perhaps the most scenic section of this long-distance hiking trail. For a complete description of this section, see Metacomet–Monadnock Trail: MA 141 to MA 47.

Beau Bridge Trail

This blue-blazed trail begins near the east side of Hamden Field. To get to the trailhead, follow Smith's Ferry Rd. 0.4 mi. from the Stone House past the museum and two parking areas, then turn left onto a paved dead-end road. The trail begins on the right just before the picnic area. (The trail sign is usually missing; look for blue-blazed trees.)

The trail proceeds northwest for about 100 yd. through open woods, then turns sharp right (the obvious path straight ahead is an unmarked route that leads to Goat Peak in 0.3 mi.) and descends to Cascade Creek. For the next 0.3 mi., the trail follows the creek downstream, repeatedly crossing and recrossing it on the bridges for which the trail was named. After the ninth bridge, the trail leaves the stream and turns uphill (north), soon merging with and following an old woods road 0.3 mi. to its junction with the Meta-comet–Monadnock Trail.

Beau Bridge Trail

Distances from Hamden Field (Smith's Ferry Rd.)
   to final crossing of Cascade Creek: 0.4 mi. (20 min.)
   to Metacomet-Monadnock Trail: 0.7 mi. (35 min.)

Beeline/Link Trail

This trail, like the Lost Boulder Trail, is not designed to have a visible footway, being merely a marked route through the woods. Marked with white blazes, it begins at a barway on the south side of Smith's Ferry Rd., 0.2 mi. above the Cascade Creek bridge. Leaving the road toward the south, the trail quickly bears left, then soon turns south again and ascends a steep slope. At 0.2 mi. it crosses the Kay-Bee Trail, reenters the woods, and at 0.3 mi. crosses the Keystone Trail. The Beeline/Link Trail now descends to a stream, crosses it, and ascends the opposite slope. After climbing a steep, rather unstable rocky embankment, it proceeds steadily southwest, first through thick hemlock woods and then through a more open hardwood forest. It terminates at the glacial erratic, which also marks the upper end of the Lost Boulder Trail.

Beeline/Link Trail

Distances from Smith's Ferry Rd.
   to Kay-Bee Trail: 0.2 mi. (10 min.)
   to Keystone Trail: 0.3 mi. (15 min.)
   to Lost Boulder Trail: 0.8 mi. (30 min.)

Bray Loop Trail

This trail offers an easy circuit of Bray Lake and its inlet valley, and it connects the lower termini of five other trails. From the southwest end of the main Lake Bray parking area, follow a paved path uphill past a barway to a small clearing. The Bray Loop Trail (yellow blazes) begins as a woods road at the upper edge of this clearing, which is also the lower end of the Kay-Bee Trail. It proceeds almost on the level for some distance, paralleling—and a little above—the western shore of the lake. At 0.1 mi. the Keystone Trail branches right, and the blue-blazed Inner Bridge Link branches left (leading 0.2 mi. across the inlet to the eastern arm of Bray Loop). The trail soon begins a gradual climb, crosses several seasonal streams, and shortly before it reaches its highest point, the white-blazed Lost Boulder Trail branches right.

The trail now descends at a moderate rate, crosses the inlet stream on a bridge, and at 0.9 mi. meets the lower end of the Bray Valley Trail. Crossing the low-lying and frequently wet valley floor, the trail ascends partway up the opposite ridge and turns northeast, passing the Knox Trail at 1.1 mi. and then gradually descending toward the lake. It reaches the other end of the Inner Bridge Link at 1.4 mi. and then continues almost at water level along the southeastern shore of the lake. This section is frequently very muddy. The trail ends on Smith's Ferry Rd., about 0.2 mi. below the Lake Bray parking area.

Bray Loop Trail

Distances from Lake Bray parking area

> *to* Keystone Trail and one end of the Inner Bridge Link: 0.1 mi. (5 min.)
>
> *to* Lost Boulder Trail: 0.6 mi. (15 min.)
>
> *to* Bray Valley Trail: 0.9 mi. (30 min.)
>
> *to* Knox Trail: 1.1 mi. (45 min.)
>
> *to* other end of the Inner Bridge Link: 1.4 mi. (1 hr.)
>
> *to* Smith's Ferry Rd.: 1.8 mi. (1 hr. 15 min.)

Bray Valley Trail

This short trail (red-blazed) links the southern end of the Bray Loop Trail with the Mt. Tom Ski Area. The first part is low-lying and usually quite wet. It leaves the Bray Loop Trail just beyond the upper bridge and runs generally southwest, crossing several minor streams. After about 0.3 mi. it veers more to the west and begins a gradual climb out of the valley, terminating in a rocky gully just below the boundary fence of the lowest ski slope. From this point, you can reach the Knox Trail by contouring the ski slope to the left about 0.2 mi.; the Knox Trail Extension is about 0.3 mi. to the right.

Bray Valley Trail

Distance from Bray Loop Trail
   to Mt. Tom Ski Area: 0.4 mi. (15 min.)

D. O'C Trail

This red-blazed trail connects the Quarry Trail with the Metacomet–Monadnock Trail atop the cliffs and then with an old tote road. It branches right (west) from the Quarry Trail about 0.3 mi. from the maintenance sheds, turns sharply left after about 100 yd., then climbs gradually by several switchbacks; some sections are wet seasonally. After 0.5 mi. the trail bears south-southwest through hardwoods, crosses several semiopen ledgy areas, then curves more to the west and meets the Metacomet–Monadnock Trail midway between Deadtop and the Quarry Trail. The D. O'C Trail and the Metacomet–Monadnock Trail coincide for several yards, then the D. O'C branches left (south) and proceeds more or less on the level for 0.2 mi. to end near the top of the tote road. Right leads in about 0.1 mi. to the upper station of the Mt. Tom ski lift; left leads in 0.4 mi. to the upper terminus of the Middle Loop Trail.

D.O'C Trail

Distance from Quarry Trail
   to Metacomet–Monadnock Trail: 0.9 mi. (45 min.)

Kay-Bee Trail

This blue-blazed woods road connects the Lake Bray area with the central part of the reservation and is an alternate to the longer but somewhat steeper Keystone Trail. It begins at the clearing above the Lake Bray parking area (see the description of the Bray Loop Trail) and immediately begins a steady climb westward, away from the lake. At 0.3 mi., just before a small rocky knoll on the right, the white-blazed Beeline/Link Trail cuts across, and the gradient soon eases. The final 0.3 mi. is almost level, and the trail ends at Keystone Junction, where it meets the Keystone Trail and the Keystone Trail Extension.

Kay-Bee Trail

Distances from Lake Bray parking area
   to Beeline/Link Trail: 0.3 mi. (15 min.)
   to Keystone Junction: 0.6 mi. (25 min.)

Keystone Trail

This was one of the original ski trails cleared in the reservation long before the advent of the private ski areas. The trail follows a woods road for much of its length; it is unblazed but is sparsely marked with red wooden "Keystone" signs. It begins as a path on the south side of Smith's Ferry Rd., opposite the second of the two upper parking areas, about 0.3 mi. from Stone House and just before the dead-end road to Hamden Field. At 0.1 mi. a blue-blazed link branches right (leading in 0.1 mi. to the Nature Trail), and the Keystone Trail veers southeast, ascending slightly until it emerges in a small opening known as Keystone Junction. Here the Kay-Bee Trail branches left, the Keystone Trail Extension branches right, and the Keystone Trail follows a woods road straight ahead, descending in wide-sweeping curves through hemlock and hardwood forests. It crosses the Beeline/Link Trail at 0.7 mi., and the descent steepens somewhat. Near the foot of the hill the trail reaches its lowest point, ascends slightly, and ends at the Bray Loop Trail. The Lake Bray parking areas are about 0.2 mi. to the left.

Keystone Trail

Distances from Smith's Ferry Rd.
   to Keystone Junction: 0.3 mi. (15 min.)
   to Beeline/Link Trail: 0.7 mi. (20 min.)
   to Bray Loop Trail: 1 mi. (30 min.)

Keystone Trail Extension

The red-blazed Keystone Extension begins at Keystone Junction, 0.3 mi. from the upper end of the Keystone Trail. Proceeding west, the trail crosses several ledgy areas, and at 0.3 mi. it descends from a rise and crosses a swampy section, which it negotiates on a series of bog bridges. At 0.4 mi., near the top of a second rise, a blue-blazed link branches right (leading in 0.1 mi. to the Nature Trail). Just over the rise, the trail makes a sharp left onto a relocation, descends, and circles around another swamp, then rejoins the original route, descending to the left. Reaching the valley floor at 0.7 mi., it turns right, proceeds on the level to a bridge, crosses the stream, and ends just beyond it at the Quarry Trail, opposite the lower terminus of the D. O'C. Trail.

Keystone Trail Extension

Distance from Keystone Junction (Keystone Trail)
  to Quarry Trail: 0.8 mi. (30 min.)

Knox Trail

This red-blazed trail connects the Bray Loop Trail with the I-91 overlook and the Mt. Tom Ski Area. It leaves the eastern branch of the Bray Loop Trail 0.7 mi. from Smith's Ferry Rd., climbs steeply to the top of the ridge, then bears right and follows the ridge mostly through hardwoods in a generally south-southwest direction. Descending slightly, the trail approaches within sight of the overlook but stays well above the guard fence. After paralleling the fence about 200 yd., the trail bears sharply right onto a woods road and follows it 0.5 mi. to terminate at the lowest parking area of the Mt. Tom Ski Area.

From this point, it is possible to reach both the Bray Valley Trail and the Knox Extension Trail. Remember, however, that the ski area is private property, and you should use both caution and courtesy. To reach the Bray Valley Trail, turn right and continue about 200 yd. to the end of the open area, passing a warming shelter on the right and paralleling the water pipe. Just before a second shed, descend right into scrub, bear left, and follow a narrow path for 100 ft. to a rocky ditch. Descend to the right for a few yards to the trailhead.

Knox Trail

Distances from Bray Loop Trail
> *to* I-91: 0.5 mi. (20 min.)
> *to* Mt. Tom Ski Area: 1 mi. (40 min.)

Knox Trail Extension

To reach the Knox Trail Extension from the lowest parking area of the Mt. Tom Ski Area, cross the open area in a northwest direction to a red-blazed telephone pole and ascend slightly on semiopen ledges (look for paint markings on the rocks). The Knox Trail Extension enters the woods above the open ledges and soon meets and turns right onto an old road. It follows the road about 0.2 mi., circling left around a rocky knoll, then crosses a stream bed and turns sharply right (west) uphill for about 100 yd. to its end at the Quarry Trail.

Knox Trail Extension

Distance from Mt. Tom Ski Area
> *to* Quarry Trail: 0.3 mi. (20 min.)

Lost Boulder Trail

Like the Beeline/Link Trail, this trail is designed not as a path but merely as a marked route through the woods. The white-blazed trail leaves the Bray Loop Trail 0.6 mi. from the Lake Bray parking area, ascends first through hemlocks, then zigzags upward through an open hardwood forest. At 0.3 mi. it makes a sharp left, reenters the hemlocks, and after 100 yd. bears right uphill, to terminate at a large glacial boulder. This is also the upper end of the Beeline/Link Trail.

Lost Boulder Trail

Distance from Bray Loop Trail
> *to* boulder and Beeline/Link Trail: 0.4 mi. (30 min.)

Middle Loop Trail

This red-blazed trail connects the Quarry Trail with the lower end of the old tote road in the ski area. Combined with the D. O'C.

Trail, it offers an interesting if undemanding circuit. The Middle Loop Trail branches right (west) from the Quarry Trail 0.7 mi. from the maintenance area, just before the height-of-land. The trail climbs gradually, and just after topping a low ridge, it divides. The main route descends and curves south and then west through a low-lying swampy area whose footway has been reinforced with stepping stones. This section is frequently very wet. A blue-blazed alternate route branches right, climbs, traverses, and then descends over semiopen ledges (winter travelers should use caution). The two routes rejoin in about 0.3 mi. The trail then proceeds west up a small ravine, turns sharply left at 0.3 mi. and sharply right at 0.4 mi. (thus avoiding another swamp), then follows the east bank of the stream, terminating at a switchback near the lower end of Tote Rd.

Middle Loop Trail

Distance from Quarry Trail
  to Tote Rd.: 0.5 mi. (25 min.)

Nature Trail

The Nature Trail consists of three short loops and two linking trails. The trails begin at the museum on Smith's Ferry Rd. A printed guide to the flora and geology of the area is available free of charge at the museum and at Stone House. An updated, colorful trail map is sold there as well.

Quarry Trail

This yellow-blazed woods road is the shortest and most convenient route across the range from the reservation center and provides access to several other trails, thus permitting circuits of varying length and difficulty. From the reservation center on Reservation Rd., go southwest 0.1 mi. along Christopher Clark Rd., then turn left uphill onto a paved road, passing the maintenance buildings and a small parking area. Continue through a metal gate and follow an old road about 100 yd. to the beginning of the Quarry Trail, where it crosses the Metacomet–Monadnock Trail.

Almost on the level at its northern end, the trail soon circles around a small pond on the left, gradually bears south, and begins a gentle climb. At 0.3 mi. the D. O'C Trail and the Keystone Trail Extension diverge right and left, respectively. At 0.7 mi., shortly before reaching the height-of-land, the Middle Loop Trail branches right. The descent to the south is noticeably rougher and steeper. At 1 mi. the trail crosses a stream and just beyond the Knox Trail Extension branches left. This is the practical end of the Quarry Trail; while the old road continues for several hundred yards it is barricaded at the end and the Mt. Tom Ski Area, on whose property it lies, has requested users not to attempt access beyond this point.

Quarry Trail

Distances from Metacomet–Monadnock Trail
>   *to* D. O'C. Trail and Keystone Extension Trail: 0.3 mi. (20 min.)
>   *to* Middle Loop Trail: 0.7 mi. (30 min.)
>   *to* Knox Trail Extension: 1 mi. (40 min.)

Tea Bag Trail

This red-blazed trail leaves the north side of Smith's Ferry Rd. at a barway about 0.3 mi. above the Lake Bray parking area. It follows a woods road north a few yards, branches left uphill onto an even older road, and soon branches left to proceed at an easy grade through mature hemlock woods. After crossing and descending from a rocky outcrop at 0.5 mi., the trail resumes its climb, with numerous changes of direction, and soon enters a more open hard-wood forest with luxuriant mountain laurel thickets. Crossing a small divide at 0.9 mi., it bears slightly west and follows another woods road to the trail's end at the Metacomet–Monadnock Trail, a few yards east of the Beau Bridge Trail junction.

Tea Bag Trail

Distance from Smith's Ferry Rd.
>   *to* Metacomet–Monadnock Trail: 1 mi. (50 min.)

HOLYOKE RANGE: WESTERN SECTION

Named after Elizur Holyoke, one of three men appointed by the General Court of the Massachusetts Bay Colony in 1653 to divide lands in this region into plantations for the first settlers, this traprock range extends from the Connecticut River east about 7 mi. in the towns of Hadley, South Hadley, Granby, and Amherst. It includes Mt. Holyoke (878 ft.); Mt. Hitchcock (1002 ft.), named in honor of Edward Hitchcock, a president of Amherst College who did much geological research in the area; Bare Mtn. (1014 ft.); Mt. Norwottuck (1106 ft.), which takes its name from the Norwottuck Indians who lived in the area; and Long Mtn. (920 ft.). The range contains two passes, or notches: Taylor Notch east of Mt. Holyoke, through which runs the automobile road to the summit of Mt. Holyoke (closed in winter), and Amherst Notch (or simply "the Notch") between Bare Mtn. and Mt. Norwottuck, through which runs MA 116. The state-run Notch Visitor Center is located here.

With its open ledges providing extensive views, its lush decidu-ous, hemlock, and pine forests, and the Metacomet–Monadnock Trail along its entire length, the Holyoke Range is attractive to hik-ers, skiers, geologists and naturalists. Much of the land is protect-ed, as part of the Skinner State Park, the Holyoke Range State Park, and adjoining town-conservation lands. Refer to the Mt. Tom/Holyoke map included with this book, and also the USGS Mt. Holyoke and Belchertown quadrangles.

The western part of the range, between MA 47 and MA 116, has three principal summits: Mt. Holyoke, Mt. Hitchcock, and Bare Mtn. Mt. Holyoke is the farthest west and provides impres-sive views of the Connecticut River Valley and of the Mt. Tom range extending southwest on the opposite side of the river. An automobile road (closed in winter) leads to the summit, where the summit house is a popular picnic spot.

Mount Holyoke Summit Trail (Halfway Trail)

This well-graded, unblazed path provides a short but steep route to the summit. It was well-worn in preautomobile days when people used it to reach the hotel on the summit. To find the trailhead, take MA 47 to Mountain Rd. Follow Mountain Rd. to Skinner State Park (signs) and continue up the paved road to the old Halfway House, where parking is available. A sign marks where the trail leaves the road on the right, just below the parking lot. The graded path climbs steeply to a slight col where the white-blazed Meta-comet–Monadnock Trail enters on the right. The Halfway Trail turns left, and the trails coincide the short distance to the summit and the restored hotel.

Mt. Holyoke Summit Trail (Halfway Trail)

Distance from Halfway House parking lot
  to summit of Mt. Holyoke: 0.5 mi. (30 min.)

Dry Brook Trail

This red-blazed trail on the south side of Mt. Holyoke makes a good snowshoe and ski route in the winter and a pleasant hiking route in the spring because of the profusion of wildflowers. The trail leaves the summit road (not open to cars in the winter) at Taylor Notch, where the Metacomet–Monadnock Trail crosses the road heading east and west. Leaving the south side of the summit road, the trail descends gradually along the western edge (right) of a broad, wooded hollow. Bearing more right at the head of a ravine with a small brook, the trail soon becomes a cleared path on the hillside and continues down the ridgeline to join a well-defined woods road. The yellow-blazed Lithia Springs Trail exits left here. The Dry Brook Trail turns right down the road and continues through a splendid forested glen. Beyond a powerline crossing, the trail bears right onto a road just above a deep, rocky ravine and follows it to a small pond on the left. The trail soon turns right onto the cleared strip of an underground telephone line (marked with posts). It continues several yards to its junction with the Metacomet–Monadnock Trail. MA 47 is a few minutes' hike to the left on the white-blazed Metacomet–Monadnock Trail.

Dry Brook Trail

Distances from summit road
  to Lithia Springs Trail: 0.4 mi. (20 min.)
  to Metacomet–Monadnock Trail: 1.7 mi. (1 hr. 15 min.)

Taylor Notch Trail

Starting from the dirt parking area on MA 47 in Hadley, this yellow-blazed trail follows the same route as the blue-blazed Halfway

House Trail for 0.2 mi., where the Halfway House Trail turns right. Taylor Notch Trail goes left a short distance, then turns right and begins a gradual ascent. Soon the trail follows a gully and begins a steeper ascent, terminating at the paved summit access road. The white-blazed Metacomet–Monadnock Trail crosses the summit road just ahead, and the red-blazed Dry Brook Trail descends from Taylor Notch on the south side of the road.

Taylor Notch Trail

Distance from MA 47 parking area
  to summit road: 0.9 mi. (40 min.)

Metacomet–Monadnock Trail

This white-blazed long-distance hiking trail passes through the Holyoke Range and Skinner state parks for about 9 mi. of its total length. It is a scenic hike that never leaves the ridge of the Holyoke Range. For a more complete description, see Metacomet–Monadnock Trail: MA 47 to MA 116.

Halfway House Trail

This blue-blazed trail starts from the same parking area as the Taylor Notch Trail. It follows the yellow-blazed Taylor Notch Trail for 0.2 mi., then turns right where the two trails split. It immediately crosses a wooden footbridge and follows a well-worn woods road across another stream, where the trail begins to climb after turning left. After a series of gentle switchbacks and moderate climbing, the trail terminates at the paved summit access road. (Parking is available here.) To the right and down the paved road a short distance is the unblazed Halfway Trail, which begins on the left and reaches the summit of Mt. Holyoke after a short—but steep—climb.

Halfway House Trail

Distance from MA 47 parking area
  to summit road: 0.8 mi. (35 min.)

Tramway Trail

This red-blazed trail begins in an open field across from Mitch's Marina on MA 47 in Hadley. Marked with orange traffic cones across the hayfield, it soon enters the treeline, where a sign and the red blazes begin. In a short distance it crosses powerlines, and the blue-blazed Devil's Football Trail exits on the right. (The Devil's Football is a large, conglomerate glacial erratic.) The Tramway Trail follows an old cart path past a series of gently climbing switchbacks to the paved summit access road directly across from a parking area. You can return by the Devil's Football Trail, which exits a short distance down the paved road on the right.

Tramway Trail

Distances from Mitch's Marina
 to Devil's Football Trail: 0.4 mi. (20 min.)
 to summit road: 0.8 mi. (40 min.)

HOLYOKE RANGE: EASTERN SECTION

The traprock ridge of the Holyoke Range continues east of the Notch (MA 116), covered with hardwoods and some hemlock stands. The principal summits here are Mt. Norwottuck (1106 ft.) and Long Mtn. (920 ft.). The overhanging ledges on Mt. Norwottuck are the so-called horse caves of revolutionary days, supposed to have been used to shelter the horses of Daniel Shays and his men at the time of Shays' Rebellion. Several cliffs and open ledges afford excellent views. Both mountains are traversed by the Metacomet–Monadnock Trail. For a description, see Metacomet–Monadnock Trail: MA 116 to Harris Rd. Trail information and maps are available in the state park's Notch Visitor Center on MA 116 in Amherst.

Laurel Loop Trail

This short loop trail starts and ends at the Notch Visitor Center. It is marked by blue triangles with green leaves. After descending a hill shaded by large evergreen trees, it takes a sharp left and follows the old trolley bed for 0.3 mi. The trail then exits left from the trolley bed and ascends gradually back to the Notch Visitor Center.

Laurel Loop Trail

Distance from Notch Visitor Center
 to return to visitor center: 0.75 mi. (30 min.)

Brookbank Trail

Follow the Laurel Loop Trail to its exit from the trolley bed, then continue straight on the trolley bed for 50 ft. to the entrance of the Brookbank Trail on the right. The trail is marked by blue triangles with white waves and descends to Sweet Alice Brook. It follows the brook for a while before ascending to the left. Just past a small vehicle barrier, the trail turns sharply left and ascends to the old trolley bed. Take a left at the trolley bed and look for the Laurel Loop Trail on the right. (A right turn at the trolley bed will bring you to the start of the Northside Trail.) A right turn onto the Laurel Loop Trail will return you to the visitor center.

Brookbank Trail

Distances from Laurel Loop Trail
>   *to* Sweet Alice Brook: 0.4 mi. (20 min.)
>   *to* return to Notch Visitor Center via Laurel Loop Trail: 2.4 mi. (1 hr. 20 min.)

Northside Trail

The Northside Trail is marked by blue triangles with white stars and is used primarily as a cross-country ski trail. It connects with the Brookbank Trail at the far northern end of the old trolley bed and winds eastward along a series of old logging roads. The trail exits right from the trolley bed and in 0.1 mi. turns sharply left, then sharply right. After crossing a small brook, it immediately goes left and ascends across a side slope to a large white-pine stand. It turns left onto a logging road and in 100 yd. comes to the corner of an orchard, where it turns right, ascending gradually to a powerline right-of-way. The trail bears right, following the powerline a short distance, then bears left under the line and into the woods. After crossing a brook, the trail turns right onto a logging road and ascends, eventually turning right onto another logging road. It follows this road north for 0.3 mi., then turns sharply left into a hemlock grove. After descending a hill, the trail bears right and then turns sharply right onto a logging road. In 25 yd. it exits left, ascending a steep hill and then turning left onto yet another logging road. The trail leaves this road on the right and continues through the woods until it ends at a yellow-blazed trail in the Town of Amherst's Holyoke Range Conservation Area.

Northside Trail

Distance from Brookbank Trail

   to Holyoke Range Conservation Area: 1.6 mi. (1 hr. 10 min.)

Metacomet–Monadnock Trail

Several miles of a very scenic section of this long-distance hiking trail pass through the eastern section of Holyoke Range State Park. For a complete description, see Metacomet–Monadnock Trail: MA 116 to Harris Rd.

Robert Frost Trail

A section of this 33-mi. orange-blazed hiking trail runs together with the white-blazed Metacomet–Monadnock Trail through the eastern section of Holyoke Range State Park. For a complete description, see Robert Frost Trail: Southern Section.

Amherst Conservation Commission Trails

Much of the land in this part of the range belongs to the Town of Amherst's Conservation Commission, acquired by purchase or gift. A trail guide prepared by the Conservation Commission is available in local bookstores. Conservation area trailheads and access points can be found as follows (all areas have trails unless otherwise noted):

   Eastman Brook: Entrance at a gate on the west side of Leverett Rd. in North Amherst, 0.1 mi. south of the Leverett–Amherst line.

   Podick Sanctuary and Katharine Cole Sanctuary: Entrance and parking area on the west side of MA 116, 0.4 mi. south of the Amherst–Sunderland line.

   Mill River: Entrance from Pine St., State St., Mill St., or MA 63 in North Amherst; handicapped-accessible trail parking is on the south side of State St., 100 yd. east of the main gate and entrance to Puffer's (Factory Hollow) Pond.

   Wildwood: Entrance from the back (east) end of the Village Park Apartments off East Pleasant St., 1.3 mi. north of Amherst center.

Amethyst Brook: Entrance and parking on the north side of Pelham Rd., 0.5 mi. west of the Amherst–Pelham line.

Skillings Path: Trailhead just south of the junior high school on the corner of Chestnut and High streets.

Larch Hill: Parking and environmental education headquarters building (Hitchcock Center for the Environment) on the west side of MA 116 (S. Pleasant St.), 1.1 mi. south of Amherst center.

Larch Hill North: Entrance from Larch Hill (see previous entry) or from the end of Hillcrest Place (west off S. Pleasant St., 1 mi. south of Amherst center).

Upper Fort River: Entrance and parking on S. East St., just north of the bridge over the Fort River, 1.1 mi. south of MA 9.

Lower Fort River: Trailhead on the west side of MA 116, across from the entrance to Crocker Farm School, 2 mi. south of MA 9.

Harkness Brook: Entrance on the west side of Harkness Rd. on the Amherst–Pelham line, 0.6 mi. north of MA 9.

Mt. Castor: Entrance at the end of Valley View Dr., off S. East St., 1.6 mi. south of MA 9.

Hop Brook: Entrance on the east side of S. East St., 2.1 mi. south of MA 9.

Plum Brook: Entrance on the south side of Potwine Lane, 0.5 mi. east of MA 116 in South Amherst and on the north and south sides of Pomeroy Lane, 0.5 mi. east of MA 116.

Mt. Pollux: Entrance at 1403 S. East St. (Take the gravel road uphill through the gate to the parking area.) There is no trail, but you can walk through the orchard to the summit, which affords fine 360-degree views.

Lawrence Swamp: Entrance and parking on Station Rd. at the Central Vermont Railroad crossing, 0.9 mi. east of the South Amherst common; other entrances at 1290 S. East St. (Baby Carriage Trail) and Station Rd., just west of the Hop Brook road crossing.

Elf Meadow: Entrances on Hulst Rd., off Bay Rd., in South Amherst.

Holyoke Range: Take Bay Rd. from MA 116. Entrance and parking via a paved drive off the south side of Bay Rd., just west of the junction of Chapel Rd. and Bay Rd.

Kenneth Cuddeback Trail (7 mi. from Rattlesnake Knob on the Holyoke Range north to MA 9 via the Plum Springs, Plum Brook, Mt. Castor, and Hop Brook conservation areas): Access points on Chapel Rd., 200 ft. north of Bay Rd.; Middle St., 0.25 mi. north of Bay Rd.; Shays St., 0.6 mi. east of MA 116; S. East St., 1.5 mi. south of MA 9; and Old Belchertown Rd., 0.1 mi. south of MA 9.

ARCADIA NATURE CENTER AND WILDLIFE SANCTUARY

Managed by the Massachusetts Audubon Society, the sanctuary is located in Easthampton and Northampton. It comprises approximately 500 acres of floodplain forest, marsh, meadow, and upland forest on an ancient oxbow of the Connecticut River bordering the present famous oxbow. The sanctuary offers several miles of self-guided nature trails (one designed especially for children) and a nature center with a solar greenhouse. It is noted for its exhibitions of food and cover plantings for wildlife and for its observation tower overlooking the marsh. A modest admission fee is charged.

To reach the sanctuary, take I-91 to exit 18 south. Follow MA 5 1.3 mi. to East St., the first right across the oxbow, then follow East St. 1.2 mi. to Fort Hill Rd., the first road on the right. Fort Hill Rd. leads to the sanctuary.

HOLLAND GLEN

The Belchertown Historical Society preserves this steep-sided ravine that has a sparkling stream shaded by a mature hemlock stand. It is located less than 0.3 mi. north of MA 9, 2.8 mi. northwest of the intersection of MA 9 and US 202. The short walk from MA 9 to the glen is well worth taking. The Metacomet– Monadnock Trail also passes through Holland Glen as it proceeds north from the Holyoke Range.

MT. LINCOLN (1240 ft.)

Mt. Lincoln, located in the town of Pelham, has a flat summit that offers extensive views in all directions from the fire tower. The University of Massachusetts Department of Forestry and Wildlife Management owns and manages 1,195 acres as the Cadwell Memorial Forest. Several miles of unmarked woods roads are open to the public for pedestrian use only. A section of the white-blazed Metacomet–Monadnock Trail passes through the forest and over the summit. The summit also has transmission facilities for the five-college radio station. Refer to the USGS Belchertown and Shutesbury quadrangles.

Tower Rd.

A truck road (gravel for the most part) to the summit of Mt. Lincoln is maintained by the University of Massachusetts Department of Forestry and Wildlife Management within the Cadwell Memorial Forest. It leaves Enfield Rd. (old sign says Packardville Rd.) 1.6 mi. south of Pelham–Amherst Rd., passing through an iron gate with a sign for Cemetery Drive. The road bears right where the telephone line appears and continues on to the summit. A footpath follows the telephone line directly to the summit, where it meets the Metacomet–Monadnock Trail.

Tower Rd.

Distance from Enfield Rd.
   to summit of Mt. Lincoln: 0.6 mi. (25 min.)

Metacomet–Monadnock Trail (BCAMC)

Several miles of the 98-mile Metacomet–Monadnock Trail pass through Cadwell Memorial Forest and over the summit of Mt. Lincoln. For a complete description, see Metacomet–Monadnock Trail: MA 9 (Holland Glen) to Mt. Lincoln.

MT. ORIENT (957 ft.)
POVERTY MTN. (916 ft.)

These wooded mountains with rocky ledges are situated in the northwest part of Pelham and together constitute a rugged area about 2 mi. long and 1 mi. wide, divided by Hearthstone Brook and crossed by the white-blazed Metacomet–Monadnock Trail and the orange-blazed Robert Frost Trail. The site of the 80-acre Buffum Falls Conservation Area, Mt. Orient boasts spectacular views of the Holyoke Range and Connecticut River Valley to the south and University of Massachusetts and the town of Amherst to the west, as well as diversified flora, including wild raspberries, low-bush blueberries, and the American hazelnut. Refer to the USGS Shutesbury quadrangle. Maps also are available from the New England Orienteering Club and the Amherst Conservation Commission.

RATTLESNAKE MTN. (1067 ft.)
HERMIT MTN. (1206 ft.)
NORTHFIELD MTN. (1093 ft.)

These mountains in the town of Erving rise steeply on the northwestern side of the narrow valley of the Millers River. (Rattlesnake Mtn. is called Den Mtn. on older USGS maps of the Millers Falls quadrangle.) The first two mountains constitute a rocky ridge with steep eastern cliffs extending southwest to northeast and overlooking the valley. The western side is bordered by the huge dikes and upper reservoir of the Northfield Mtn. pumped-storage hydroelectric complex. Northfield Mtn. is a parallel ridge farther west whose northern end forms one side of the reservoir. The best current access is by taking the Metacomet–Monadnock Trail to Rattlesnake Mtn.

An extensive network of trails has been constructed here and is managed by Northeast Utilities Co. as the Northfield Mtn. Recreation Area. The recreation area includes 25 mi. of hiking and cross-country skiing trails. Few places in Massachusetts provide such a well-groomed, year-round trail system, which offers narrow footpaths on more rugged terrain and wide, grassy roads for easy walking or skiing. While perhaps the most popular cross-country skiing center in the area, the trail system is not used extensively for hiking in the summer. Information is available at the visitor center, reached from MA 63, 2.1 mi. north of MA 2 in Millers Falls.

BRUSH MTN. (1507 ft.)
CRAG MTN. (1503 ft.)

These mountains in the town of Northfield form a 1.5-mi. rocky mass that extends almost north and south. There are extensive views from their bare ledges, which are crossed by the white-blazed Metacomet–Monadnock Trail. For a description of this trail, see Metacomet–Monadnock Trail: MA 2 (Farley) to Crag Mtn.

FIRST BALD HILLS (1276 ft.)
UPPER BALD HILLS (1422 ft.)
STRATTON MTN. (1285 ft.)

These names are given to the rock mass extending about 3.5 mi. north from the Erving town line into Northfield. For a considerable distance this mass parallels Crag Mtn. and Brush Mtn. on its west. Between First Bald Hills on the south and Upper Bald Hills is a notch through which a brook and a road pass. The mountains are wooded, but scenic spots on the open summit of Upper Bald Hills can be reached by the white-blazed Metacomet–Monadnock Trail. For a description, see Metacomet–Monadnock Trail: Farley to Crag Mtn.

MT. GRACE (1617 ft.)

Situated in the town of Warwick, this 1,689-acre state forest includes a wooded summit and a steel fire tower that provides a 360-degree view, including Mt. Monadnock in New Hampshire and the Quabbin Reservoir in Massachusetts. Located on the mountain is an overnight station for hikers using the Metacomet–Monadnock Trail. For a description of the trail, see Metacomet–Monadnock Trail: Crag Mtn. to Mt. Grace and Metacomet–Monadnock Trail: Mt. Grace to MA 32.

Fire Tower Trail

The trail begins on MA 78 opposite the fountain on the common of Warwick village. The trail follows a road that is one house north of the village store (sign: "Northfield 8"). It turns right in 100 yd. onto a dead-end lane beside a barn (where parking is available in the summer), passes through a gate leaving a new house on the right, continues past a barn on the left, and goes through a second gate into the woods. You can find water at the right, just inside this gate. The trail ascends along the road, with a telephone line close by. The Metacomet–Monadnock Trail enters on the left at the foot of the final steep climb to the summit.

Fire Tower Trail

Distances from Warwick village (MA 78)

 to Metacomet–Monadnock Trail: 0.9 mi. (30 min.)
 to summit of Mt. Grace: 1.3 mi. (40 min.)

MT. TOBY (1269 ft.)

This mountain lies partly in Sunderland and partly in Leverett. Its rugged sides are well forested and have numerous brooks. There is a fire tower on the summit affording an excellent view. The Mt. Toby Demonstration Forest, operated by the University of Massachusetts, comprises 755 acres. The trails described here are the usual routes used to climb the mountain, but numerous woods roads also invite exploration. Refer to the USGS Mt. Toby quadrangle.

Woodbury Trail (Middle Mountain Rd.)

This trail is for the most part a logging or jeep road. To reach the trailhead, follow MA 116 1 mi. south of Sunderland (6 mi. north of Amherst), to N. Silver Lane. Turn left (north) onto N. Silver Lane, continue 0.4 mi., then turn right onto Reservoir Rd. Follow this 0.2 mi. to Nebo Rd., turn left, and continue for a short distance to a place where cars can be parked on the left. The trail enters the woods and climbs gradually in a generally northeast direction, following the white blazes at each of several junctions. It passes a deep, forested brook ravine on the right and at 1.5 mi. passes the blue-blazed Link Trail on the left. At about 1.8 mi. the trail passes under a powerline (where a side path leads left to a view from the height-of-land) and becomes less traveled. A short distance beyond, after a moderate climb, the trail emerges in a clearing. (In the 1800s this area was farmed by Irish immigrants and was referred to as the Paddy Farms area.) The trail leads right onto a level grade, following the white blazes over an eroded stream bed. In a short distance the trail joins the orange-blazed Robert Frost Trail, which eventually leads over the summits of Roaring Mtn. and Mt. Toby.

Woodbury Trail (Middle Mountain Rd.)

Distances from Nebo Rd.

> *to* Link Trail: 1.5 mi. (35 min.)
> *to* clearing: 2 mi. (50 min.)
> *to* Robert Frost Trail: 2.2 mi. (1 hr.)

North Mountain Rd.

This red-blazed trail follows a jeep road from MA 116 to the base of the summit and from there follows a cleared and blazed path. To reach the trailhead follow MA 47 north from the center of Sunderland (at the junction of MA 116 and MA 47) for 0.5 mi. to N. Silver Lane. Turn right onto N. Silver Lane and continue 0.2 mi. to Park St. Turn left onto Park St. and continue to the end. Parking is available near the entrance to Sunderland Town Park or at the small pond a short distance down gravel N. Mountain Rd. on the right.

The trail continues straight ahead on the gravel road, which goes uphill past a house on the left and bears left into the woods. The trail passes pudding-stone ledges on the right and soon a small clearing on the left. (Avoid the gravel road that comes in on the left. This road leads to Sunderland–Montague Rd. 1 mi. north of Sunderland.)

The trail follows the red blazes through a red pine plantation and gradually ascends to blue-blazed Gunn Mountain Rd. on the left. Eventually the trail crosses under powerlines and bears left. The blue-blazed Link Trail bears right here to cross a small stream and eventually connect with the white-blazed Middle Mountain Rd. After passing under the powerlines, North Mountain Rd. soon passes the blue-blazed Sugar Farms Trail on the left. It continues uphill past an abandoned sugar shack on the left (last water) and soon leaves the woods road on the right. The trail ascends steeply 0.3 mi. to the summit of Mt. Toby and its junction with the orange-blazed Robert Frost Trail.

North Mountain Rd.

Distances from Park St.

to Gunn Mtn. Rd.: 1 mi. (35 min.)

to Link Trail: 1.3 mi. (50 min.)

to Sugar Farms Trail: 1.4 mi. (55 min.)

to summit of Mt. Toby: 2.1 mi. (1 hr. 25 min.)

Summit Rd.

This white-blazed service road is passable for trucks and jeeps but is not ordinarily open to the public as an automobile road. It provides an easy descent after dark, and unless it is icy, it is suitable for travel on snowshoes and skis in the winter. The road was used to reach the summit with mountain wagons in the late 1800s. At that time there was a passenger stop and picnic area at a railroad station at the foot of the mountain in Leverett. To reach the trail, follow Reservation Rd. to the gate into Mt. Toby Demonstration Forest, where parking is available. (Reservation Rd. runs south of the Sunderland–Montague line between MA 47 and MA 63.) The gate is just west of the white forest headquarters building and shed. The Central Vermont Railroad tracks are a short distance east at Cranberry Pond, and both the tracks and the pond are just off MA 63.

The road, which is well maintained, leads south through conifer plantations, leaving the orange-blazed Robert Frost Trail which it follows for a short distance in the beginning on the right. At 0.2 mi., leave the Robert Frost Trail and follow the white blazes. Soon after the road passes a clearing on the left, the red-blazed Telephone Line Trail exits right from the road. The road continues straight ahead and ascends into the glen of Roaring Brook, passes the blue-blazed Roaring Brook Trail on the left, and swings right and close to the brook. After several brook crossings, the road climbs gently and joins again with the Robert Frost Trail and continues straight ahead. (Do not turn left onto the Robert Frost Trail, which climbs past the Metawampe cabin.) The road soon passes the red-blazed Upper Link Trail on the right, then bears left to reach the junction with the yellow-blazed Robert Frost Bypass Trail. Summit Rd. turns sharply right at the junction with the Robert Frost Bypass Trail and follows the Robert Frost Trail to the summit.

Summit Rd.

Distances from gate to Mt. Toby Demonstration Forest

    to Telephone Line Trail: 0.5 mi. (20 min.)

    to Roaring Brook Trail: 0.8 mi. (30 min.)

    to Robert Frost Trail: 1 mi. (40 min.)

    to Upper Link Trail: 1.2 mi. (50 min.)

    to Robert Frost Bypass Trail: 1.6 mi. (1 hr. 15 min.)

    to summit of Mt. Toby: 3 mi. (1 hr. 45 min.)

Telephone Line Trail

Many hikers use this trail to descend the mountain because it is somewhat steep just below the summit. Combined with Summit Rd., it provides an alternate route on the eastern side of the mountain.

Follow the white-blazed Summit Rd. 0.8 mi. south to the red-blazed Telephone Line Trail, which exits right. The trail soon merges with the orange-blazed Robert Frost Trail, but stays left under the lines as the Robert Frost Trail exits right. The trail continues uphill past the red-blazed Hemlock Hill Loop Trail on the right. At a notch well up on the mountain, it turns right at the junction with the red-blazed Upper Link Trail, which goes left. The trail continues under the telephone lines as it steeply ascends to the summit. (Note: When descending, it is important to turn left at the foot of the steep section below the summit and again left at the junction with white-blazed Summit Rd.) Most of this trail is part of the long-distance Robert Frost Trail and is marked with its orange blazes.

Telephone Line Trail

Distances from Summit Rd.

   to Hemlock Hill Loop Trail: 0.5 mi. (25 min.)

   to Upper Link Trail: 0.9 mi. (45 min.)

   to summit of Mt. Toby: 1.7 mi. (1 hr. 10 min.)

MT. SUGARLOAF RESERVATION (532 acres)

The Mt. Sugarloaf Reservation (532 acres) includes South Sugarloaf Mtn. (652 ft.) and North Sugarloaf Mtn. (791 ft.). South Sugarloaf, commonly called Mt. Sugarloaf, offers an unsurpassed view of the Connecticut River and its fertile valley. A narrow, paved automobile road (not open in the winter) winds up to the summit, where it terminates at an ample paved parking area. The original summit house, built in 1864, burned more than 30 years ago, but a modern replacement has been built and a caretaker is on the premises during the summer. The steep Pocumtuck foot trail at the southern end of the mountain ascends to the summit directly from the parking area at the junction of MA 116 and Summit Rd. Several picnic tables and a small pavilion are located on the summit. The summit road leaves MA 116 about 1 mi. west of its intersection with MA 47 in Sunderland and 1 mi. east of South Deerfield and US 5. Refer to USGS Mt. Toby quadrangle.

Pocumtuck Ridge Trail

The blue-blazed Pocumtuck Ridge Trail begins in a small clearing to the right (east) of the beginning of the summit road. It arrives at the summit between the western end of the wire fence that protects the ledge lookout and the eastern end of a concrete highway fence. The trail follows the paved summit access road briefly to the parking area on the other side of the observation tower. It descends along the fence to the lower parking area to reenter the woods and descend steeply to the hairpin turn in the summit road. It continues on an old woods road that runs east and west through the saddle between South Sugarloaf Mtn. and North Sugarloaf Mtn. where the trail ends.

   Turning right (east) in the saddle leads to the experimental farm of the University of Massachusetts on paved River Rd. at a point opposite Telephone pole 259, 0.7 mi. north of the western end of the Sunderland Bridge and MA 116. Turning left (west) in the saddle leads to the dead end of paved Mountain Rd., 0.5 mi. from MA 116. Turning left onto the red-blazed West Side Trail returns the hiker to the parking area at the junction of MA 116 and the summit road. Plans are in the works to extend the blue-blazed Pocumtuck Ridge Trail north up the steep south slope of North Sugarloaf Mtn. to the summit and then farther north about 5 mi. along the Pocumtuck Ridge.

Pocumtuck Ridge Trail

Distances from parking area at beginning of summit road
>   *to* summit of South Sugarloaf Mtn.: 0.3 mi. (20 min.)
>   *to* lower summit parking area: 0.5 mi. (25 min.)
>   *to* saddle between South Sugarloaf Mtn. and North Sugarloaf Mtn.: 0.8 mi. (40 min.)
>   *to* return to beginning of summit road (via West Side Trail): 1.4 mi. (1 hr. 15 min.)

West Side Trail

This trail begins at the dirt parking area at the junction of MA 116 and the paved summit road. The trail skirts a ball field on the left and follows along a telephone line a short distance into the woods. From here it follows a level grade, then ascends gently to its junction with the blue-blazed Pocumtuck Ridge Trail in the saddle between South Sugarloaf Mtn. and North Sugarloaf Mtn. The Pocumtuck Ridge Trail leads to the summit of South Sugarloaf Mtn.

West Side Trail

Distances from parking area at beginning of summit road
>   *to* Pocumtuck Ridge Trail: 0.6 mi. (35 min.)
>   *to* summit of South Sugarloaf Mtn. (via Pocumtuck Ridge Trail): 1.1 mi. (1 hr. 15 min.)

Hillside Trail

This recently blazed trail is a good access to the summit on the northern side of North Sugarloaf Mtn. from the gate on paved Hillside Rd. in Deerfield. To reach the trailhead, take River Rd. north from its junction with MA 116 next to the Sunderland Bridge over the Connecticut River. Follow River Rd. several miles, past the open fields of the University of Massachusetts experimental farm to its the junction with Hillside Rd. on the left. Proceed up Hillside Rd. a short distance to the gated trail entrance on the left.

The trail goes south on a level grade, then turns right to follow a small stream gully, rather steeply at times, to a lovely swamp on the left. There it joins the blue-blazed Pocumtuck Ridge Trail, which continues to the summit of North Sugarloaf Mtn.

Hillside Trail

Distances from Hillside Rd.
  to Pocumtuck Ridge Trail: 1.1 mi. (1 hr)
  to summit of North Sugarloaf Mtn. (via Pocumtuck Ridge Trail): 1.3 mi. (1 hr. 15 min.)

MOORE'S HILL (1697 ft.)

The fire tower on Moore's Hill in the Daughters of the American Revolution (DAR) State Forest affords a panoramic view of the area and is well worth visiting. This 1,517-acre state forest has more than 14 mi. of hiking, skiing, and snowmobile trails. Most of the skiing is done on the unplowed road system. Hiking trails are marked with blue triangles, and multiuse trails have orange markers. Bridle paths are marked with red triangles and are suitable for hiking, skiing, and snowmobile use. Refer to the USGS Goshen quadrangle.

(*Note:* Several trails in addition to those described below criss-cross the DAR State Forest. Many of these are maintained as bridle paths or snowmobile trails and are marked accordingly.)

Long Trail

To reach the DAR State Forest headquarters and campground, take Goshen–Ashfield Rd. (Cape St.) north from MA 9 in Goshen. Turn right onto a side road to the headquarters and campground. Parking is available here.

The trail starts on the left of the state-forest access road, beyond Camp Howe Rd. (on the right), east of the campground, and at the end (southeast corner) of Highland Lake. The trail follows the upper shore of the lake, then turns sharply right opposite the campground on the northeast shore, soon becoming a woods road. Passing stone walls and several moist hollows, the trail rises to the cellar hole of the old Rice place. Just beyond, it turns right around a stone wall and soon crosses the paved road continuing to the summit and tower.

Long Trail

Distance from campground
    to summit of Moore's Hill: 1.5 mi. (45 min.)

Darling Trail
Marked with blue triangles, this trail climbs east from its junction with the Long Trail along the shore of Upper Highland Lake to the fire tower on the summit of Moore's Hill.

Darling Trail

Distance from Long Trail
    to summit of Moore's Hill: 0.8 mi. (30 min.)

Sunset Trail
Marked with blue, orange, and red triangles, which denote its many uses, the trail leaves from the pavilion in the day-use area of the forest. It climbs gradually to the fire tower on Moore's Hill, following a red-marked horse trail to the summit.

Sunset Trail

Distance from pavilion
    to summit of Moore's Hill: 2.3 mi. (1 hr. 15 min.)

Balancing Rock Trail
Marked with orange and blue triangles, this trail connects Headquarters Rd. to Balancing Rock (a glacial erratic). The trail then loops back to Headquarters Rd.

Balancing Rock Trail

Distance from Headquarters Rd.
    to Balancing Rock: 0.4 mi. (15 min.)

Twinning Brook Trail

This trail is marked with blue triangles and connects the Long Trail to the Twinning Brook group-camping area.

Twinning Brook Trail

Distance from Long Trail

   to Twinning Brook camping area: 0.5 mi. (15 min.)

CONWAY STATE FOREST

An undeveloped facility, Conway State Forest is an underutilized forest where the hiker is assured of solitude. A 7.6-mi. loop trail following along unblazed woods roads offers excellent ski touring. The trail is reached by taking MA 9 to Williamsburg. From the east, turn right over a small bridge where MA 9 bears sharply left. Turn right onto E. Main St., then take the first left onto Nash Hill Rd. After almost 1 mi. bear left, still on Nash Hill Rd. and continue until the pavement ends at 2.2 mi. Follow gravel Depot Rd. 0.8 mi. to a dirt road on the left. A small parking area is located on the left. The USGS Williamsburg quadrangle shows the woods road heading north as the Henhawk Trail. Follow this road past another woods road entering right at 0.2 mi. The trail then begins a long but gradual ascent to a stream and road intersection on the left at 1.1 mi. At 1.4 mi. the trail enters Conway State Forest at a wooden gate. You can take either fork at the intersection, as this is a loop hike that returns you to this gate. To the right is a trail labeled Sinkpot Rd. on the USGS map. To the left an unmarked trail climbs to an improved dirt road past a recent forest harvesting operation and descends to pass around Cricket Hill on its north side. The trail enters private property and passes through a pasture and by a farmhouse on the right. There are nice views of the Connecticut River Valley at this point. The trail reenters the state forest at the gate onto Sinkpot Rd. After crossing Avery Brook and some rock outcrops, the trail completes the circuit at the wooden gate marking the initial entry into the state forest.

DUBUQUE MEMORIAL STATE FOREST

This 7,822-acre forest, situated principally in the town of Hawley but also extending south into the town of Plainfield, is adjacent to the Savoy State Forest and the Mohawk Trail State Forest. It comprises rugged terrain, much of it above 1500 ft. with some points as high as 1800 ft., and includes several ponds and brooks. Many grassy woods roads and old town roads bordered by stone walls crisscross the forest. To follow these roads, refer to USGS map of the Plainfield quadrangle.

The DEM has constructed a trail system in the central part of the forest and has erected four large Adirondack shelters, three of which are accessible by forest-service roads and hiking trails, and the fourth by trail only. The shelters are available on a first-come, first-served basis. Each shelter site has a stone fireplace, a picnic table, a good source of drinking water, and an outhouse. The trails are not uniformly blazed (although there are some paint blazes), but the footway is clear except when obscured by forest litter. There are signs at some intersections.

Approach Roads: The trail system is accessible from the south via Central St., which exits north from MA 116 about 9 mi. west of Ashfield center. The Shaw–Hudson House is located on the northwest corner of MA 116 and Central St. At the junction of Central St. and Union St. (0.5 mi.), continue northeast on Union St. until it makes an abrupt right (east) turn and becomes North St. at 1.3 mi. Proceed straight ahead approximately north on gravel Middle Rd. (not plowed in the winter) to the Hawley–Plainfield line at 2.3 mi. Continue past a path on the right (east) of the road at 3.6 mi. (The path leads into a grove and to a small pond.) At 3.8 mi. turn left (west) onto Moody Spring Rd. (there might not be a sign). (*Note:* When traveling in the reverse direction, be sure to turn right at this intersection. The corner is somewhat confusing because the roads form a small triangle.) Continue on Moody Spring Rd. past a small cemetery on the right at 4.3 mi. At 4.5 mi. you will see a parking area on the right (north). This is Gould Meadow (no sign) and probably the best place to begin a circuit walk on the trails.

Gould Meadow also is accessible from the west via a forest service road (Hallockville Rd.) that exits east from MA 8A (Hawley Rd.) at a point about 1 mi. north of its intersection with MA 116 in Plainfield. Going northeast on the forest service road, avoid a road on the left at 0.9 mi. (King Corner) and a road on the right at 1.3 mi. Pass the Basin Brook Trail on the left at 1.4 mi., the Gould Meadow Trail on the right at 1.5 mi., and Moody Spring Rd. on the left at 1.8 mi. At 1.9 mi. you will see a parking area on the left (north) and the beginning of the Basin Brook Trail on the right (south). This is Gould Meadow (no sign).

A 5.1-mi. continuous walk that begins and ends at Gould Meadow can be made via the Moody Spring Trail, the Hitchcock Meadow Trail, and the Basin Brook Trail (with or without the Ridge Trail as an alternative for part of the Hitchcock Meadow Trail). See the following trail descriptions.

Moody Spring Rd. (DEM)

This forest service road begins near the junction of Middle Rd. and Hunt Rd. and runs west-northwest to Gould Meadow, then southwest to a corner where it turns sharply right (northwest). (The road that goes straight ahead at the corner is the forest service road to MA 8A.) Moody Spring Rd. continues to Moody Spring and the Moody Spring Shelter, built of stone with a dirt floor. Beyond Moody Spring, the road continues northwest to Hitchcock Meadow.

Moody Spring Trail (DEM)

This trail begins at a sign at the northwest corner of the Gould Meadow parking area and runs north. Gould Meadow Shelter, facing an open field with good views east and north, is on the right of the trail a short distance from the parking area. Drinking water is available at a spring about 100 yd. down a little grade to the left (west) of the trail and shelter. The trail runs northwest, bearing left (west), and continuing past a good view south at 0.5 mi. It then starts steeply downhill, crosses a lovely brook at 0.6 mi., and climbs, bearing right and then left, to Moody Spring and the Moody Spring Shelter. Here it joins the Hitchcock Meadow Trail and Moody Spring Rd.

Moody Spring Trail

Distances from Gould Meadow
  to brook: 0.6 mi. (25 min.)
  to Moody Spring: 0.9 mi. (35 min.)

Hitchcock Meadow Trail (DEM)

This trail, which begins at Moody Spring, turns right (northwest) from the Moody Spring Trail, climbs, and then descends. It crosses a brook at 0.1 mi., ascends the hill on the other side with the help of stone steps, and turns sharply left at the top of the rise. The trail passes a good spring and reaches a junction with the Ridge Trail and the Hitchcock Meadow parking area. The trail continues approximately west to another trail junction, where the Ridge Trail enters right (north) and the Basin Brook Trail exits straight ahead.

Hitchcock Meadow Trail

Distances from Moody Spring
  to brook: 0.1 mi. (10 min.)
  to Ridge Trail and Basin Brook Trail: 0.9 mi. (45 min.)

Ridge Trail (DEM)

This trail begins opposite the Hitchcock Meadow parking area, runs behind the shelter, and crosses the Hitchcock Meadow Trail as it heads northwest, ascending and descending but gaining altitude and constantly bearing left (west and then south). Orange blazes are visible on many trees. At a high point on the right (west), the trees have been cleared away to provide fine views from the rocky ledges. The trail continues to a junction with the Hitchcock Meadow Trail and the Basin Brook Trail.

Ridge Trail

Distances from Hitchcock Meadow
  to lookout: 0.6 mi. (20 min.)
  to Hitchcock Meadow Trail and Basin Brook Trail: 0.7 mi. (25 min.)

Basin Brook Trail (DEM)

This trail connects the Hitchcock Meadow Trail and the Ridge Trail with Gould Meadow. It follows a pretty woods road near the rocky gorge of Basin Brook for much of its length. Commencing at its junction with the Hitchcock Meadow Trail and the Ridge Trail, the Basin Brook Trail makes a steep descent, crosses a brook bed, makes a sharp left (southwest) at 0.4 mi., and soon becomes a woods road. When the trail intersects another woods road at 0.9 mi. it again turns sharply left (northeast). (The woods road that goes straight ahead leads to a crossing of King Brook and, in about 5 min., a clearing on the east side of MA 8A, 3 mi. north of MA 116. A state forest sign near the highway indicates that it is an access route to the Hitchcock Meadow Trail as well as to the Basin Brook Trail.)

The Basin Brook Trail soon turns southeast, paralleling Basin Brook on the right, and begins to climb. It passes through a clearing, with the Basin Brook Shelter on the left and Basin Brook on the right. (The general dampness of the area and lack of direct sunlight make the shelter less attractive than it might be otherwise.) Drinking water is available from the feeder stream across Basin Brook about 150 ft. from the shelter. Very soon the trail crosses to the right side of the brook and turns left, ascending. It then crosses diagonally over a stone causeway to the left side of the brook. (*Note:* Watch carefully for this turn, as it is easy to miss.) A considerable section of trail beyond here is through a moist area with swampy land and still water on the right. The trail gradually bears left and emerges on the forest service road, 0.3 mi. southwest of Moody Spring Rd. The trail turns left onto the road and continues to a "Gould Meadow" sign on the right. The trail makes a sharp right off the road and proceeds through the woods. It then makes a sharp left (north) and continues until it emerges on Moody Spring Rd., opposite the Gould Meadow parking area.

Basin Brook Trail

Distances from junction of Hitchcock Meadow Trail and Ridge Trail
    to Basin Brook Shelter: 1.4 mi. (50 min.)
    to Gould Meadow: 3.3 mi. (2 hr.)

Pond Trail (DEM)

This fairly level trail traverses the woods along the shore of Hal-lockville Pond on the west side of MA 8A about 1 mi. north of its junction with MA 116. The buildings and parking area in this part of the forest were formerly used as a boys' camp.

When used as a nature walk, the trail should be followed in a counterclockwise (southerly) direction, commencing at a sign near the western shore at the northern end of the pond beyond the last building. The trail passes a picnic area (with tables) and a primitive camping area (with stone fireplace) on the left, then continues amid large white pines and some signs of former beaver activity. It crosses two brooks at the southwestern end of the pond, one on a rock causeway. Nearby on the higher land are the stone founda-tions of an old dam, spillway, and mill.

After crossing another brook on a plank bridge laid close to the water, the trail turns left and continues northeast on the eastern side of the pond. There are several huge boulders in this area and con-siderable evidence of former beaver activity. Side trails right lead to pump houses and a dwelling. Shortly beyond on the right is a spring with water flowing from a pipe. MA 8A appears through the trees on the right, and a short trail leads to the highway. Pond Trail continues close to the water to its end at the eastern side of the concrete dam on the northern end of the pond. A short trail leads right (east) to MA 8A. To the left (west) of the dam are the build-ings and parking area where the trail begins.

Pond Trail

Distance from sign at Hallockville Pond
  to eastern side of dam (loop): 0.8 mi. (35 min.)

King Corner Rd. (DEM)

This well-maintained dirt-and-gravel road, closed to vehicular traf-fic by locked state forest gates at both ends, leaves the north side of Hallockville Rd (the forest service road that leaves MA 8A opposite what was formerly a boys' camp) 0.9 mi. northeast of MA 8A. (Limited parking is available.) Shown on the Hawley State Forest map as a snowmobile and horseback-riding trail, King Corner Rd. is suitable for hiking, snowshoeing, and cross-country skiing.

Flanked by old stone walls, it travels northwest through an open hardwood forest, climbing steadily to about 1700 ft., then descending. It gradually turns west as the grade becomes steeper. At the low point the road crosses King Brook on a good wooden bridge and soon emerges on MA 8A nearly opposite Stetson Rd., about 2 mi. north of MA 116. This point is designated King's Corner on the USGS Plainfield quadrangle. A large parking area is available on MA 8A.

King Corner Rd.

Distance from Hallockville Rd.
   to King's Corner: 1.8 mi. (35 min.)

MASSAEMETT MTN. (1588 ft.)

Formerly called Bald Mtn. and sometimes called Shelburne Mtn., this long, high ridge in the town of Shelburne, lying just east of the village of Shelburne Falls, must be distinguished from another Shelburne Mtn. (874 ft.)— also in the town of Shelburne but several miles to the east and south. The stone fire tower affords a wide view of west-central New England on a clear day. A fireplace and picnic table, but no water, are located at the summit.

Massaemett Mtn. Trail (Shelburne Mtn. Trail)

This jeep road is used as a ski trail in winter. To reach the trailhead, follow MA 2 west from Shelburne center to Cooper Lane, the second right after Shelburne center. (When traveling east, this is the first good road on the left after passing the Sweetheart Tea Room.) Follow Cooper Lane about 1.5 mi. to Davenport Farm on the eastern side of the mountain. You can park near the equipment shed, with all the other farm buildings to the left. The trail goes into a hollow and through a gate, bears right, then turns left (cottage on left) through another gate. It ascends, passing a radio transmission station, and reaches the summit by an easy grade. An unmaintained trail descends from the summit to the west, reaching

MA 2 west of the Sweetheart Tea Room on the edge of the village of Shelburne Falls.

Massaemett Mtn. Trail (Shelburne Mtn. Trail)

Distance from Davenport Farm

   to summit of Massaemett (Shelburne) Mtn.: 0.5 mi. (1 hr. 30 min.)

PULPIT ROCK

A high point in the town of Rowe, Pulpit Rock affords a fine view of the Deerfield River Gorge. An unmarked path leads from Tunnel Rd. in Rowe (at the Linth place, the first house on Tunnel Rd. south of its intersection with Hazelton Rd.). The path begins to the right of all the buildings as a grassy woods road heading west into the woods. It passes to the left of one sawdust pile and bears slightly to the right in a moist hardwood forest beyond a second sawdust pile. The woods road continues straight ahead to a transmission swath (Bear Swamp). Straight across, an opening in the woods indicates the continuation of the trail, which begins to climb slightly to the ledges, where blueberry plants grow in profusion. Pulpit Rock is at 1 mi. (30 min.) at the outer edge of the ledges. The rough going is less than 100 ft. When returning, be sure to enter the woods to the left of the big boulder and to the right of the sawdust.

MOHAWK TRAIL STATE FOREST

This forest lies in the towns of Charlemont, Florida, Savoy, and Hawley and is accessible from MA 2. (See the USGS Rowe, Massachusetts–Vermont, quadrangle.) It includes 6,457 acres of mountain ridges, deep gorges, and two excellent trout streams, the Cold and Deerfield rivers. Nearby are the 4.5-mi. Hoosac Tunnel and the Rowe Atomic Energy Plant. The forest contains one of the finest natural pine stands in the Northeast. Many trees are more than 100 ft. high, mountain laurel is abundant, and deer, other animals, and birds are numerous. You'll find good views from Clark Mtn. (1920 ft.) and Todd Mtn. (1697 ft.).

Indian Trail from the West (DEM in part)

This trail was the carry used by Indians between the Deerfield and Hoosic river valleys. Outside the state forest, the trail needs some brushing out, but it is easy to follow. Inside the state forest it is well maintained. To reach the beginning of the trail, take MA 2 to S. County Rd., which exits MA 2 beside a house just south of the Drury Post Office. Drive east about 1.5 mi. on S. County Rd. to its end, where there is a house in a clearing that is rapidly becoming overgrown.

The trail starts as a woods road (the entrance is obscured by some birches) and runs southeast from the corner of a field near an old building foundation diagonally opposite the house. There is a good spring directly opposite the house at the edge of the woods, well to the right of the trail entrance. The woods road soon becomes a well-worn but somewhat overgrown path that climbs over Clark Mtn. (wooded) and descends slightly to a junction with the Todd Mtn. Trail (no sign) in a slight col. The Indian Trail descends steeply to a paved forest road and the state-forest campground (with water), turns left onto a forest service road to the forest headquarters, and then turns right over the Cold River to MA 2.

Indian Trail from the West

Distances from S. County Rd.
   to summit of Clark Mtn.: 0.3 mi. (15 min.)
   to MA 2: 2 mi. (2 hr.)

Indian Trail from the East (DEM)

To reach the trail from the east, cross the Cold River at the forest headquarters 1 mi. east of the Berkshire County line on the Mohawk Trail (MA 2). Proceed 0.9 mi. west on the forest service road to the camping area. Turn right at the sign onto the well-worn Indian Trail. The trail ascends through the woods to a saddle between Todd Mtn. and Clark Mtn. It follows the left fork along the ridge to Clark Mtn. (the right fork, the Todd Mtn. Trail, leads to Todd Mtn.).

Indian Trail from the East

Distances from Mohawk Trail State Forest camping area
  to ridge: 0.5 mi. (35 min.)
  to summit of Clark Mtn.: 1.3 mi. (1 hr. 10 min.)

Todd Mtn. Trail (DEM)

This trail exits right (east) from the Indian Trail in a slight col about 0.5 mi. from the state forest campground. It leads to the summit of Todd Mtn. at 0.5 mi.

Todd Mtn. Trail

Distance from Indian Trail
  to summit of Todd Mtn.: 0.5 mi. (25 min.)

Totem Lookout Trail (DEM)

This trail leaves the south side of the Mohawk Trail (MA 2) opposite the state forest picnic area, about 1 mi. west of the state forest campground. (A sign that says "Leaving Pioneer Valley" is located a short distance west on MA 2.) The trail enters the woods on a short woods road leading to a small forest service building and almost immediately turns left (east) at a "Foot Trail" sign. It then starts to ascend the side of the hill, constantly climbing southeast through the woods. "Trail" signs are located at some possibly confusing spots. The trail turns a sharp right (south) just before it emerges on a rocky ledge (1500 ft.), which affords good views to the east and northeast.

Totem Lookout Trail

Distance from Mohawk Trail
  to lookout on ledge: 1.1 mi. (45 min.)

THE FANNIE STEBBINS MEMORIAL WILDLIFE REFUGE

This 320-acre wildlife refuge is maintained by The Fannie Stebbins Memorial Wildlife Refuge, Inc., whose officers and trustees are members of the Allen Bird Club of Springfield, the founding organization. The refuge is located in Longmeadow, on the flood-

plain of the Connecticut River in an area known as the Longmeadow Flats. To reach the refuge, follow US 5 (Longmeadow St.) 2.4
mi. south of the Springfield–Longmeadow line to Bark Haul Rd.
Turn right (west) onto Bark Haul Rd. and continue 0.4 mi. to the
intersection of Pondside Rd. Park there and consult the large map
of the refuge and adjacent town conservation lands, including the
main walking roads and trails. The Fern Trail, Knoll Trail, Perime-
ter Trail, and Cutback Trail go through the swamps and floodplain
forest in the southern part of the refuge. The Sherwood section of
the refuge, with its conifer plantings, the wet meadows beside the
old roads, and the marshes along Pondside Rd. are other favorite
areas among walkers. A small map of the area is available by writing to the refuge in care of the Allen Bird Club, PO Box 1084,
Springfield, MA 01101.

LAUGHING BROOK WILDLIFE SANCTUARY (MAS)

This property of the Massachusetts Audubon Society is located at
789 Main St. in Hampden. It comprises about 259 acres of woodland, fields, and streams, and offers more than 4 mi. of well-maintained and blazed trails. The area includes pleasant woods with wildflowers in season, Laughing Brook, and the Scantic River. Native
animal and bird exhibits are located near the sanctuary's headquarters building, which was built in 1742 and is the former home of the
late writer Thornton Burgess. An environmental center houses an
auditorium, classrooms, a library, and a gift shop. The sanctuary is
easily accessible from MA 21 via Allen St. in Springfield and from
MA 82 via Hampden Rd. in East Longmeadow. Refer to the USGS
Ludlow and Hampden quadrangles.

Ridge Trail

This pleasant forest trail, involving some mild climbing, extends
roughly north and south along a ridge forming the eastern boundary
of the Connecticut River Valley. The trail runs through the towns of
Hampden and Wilbraham and is marked by orange and red blazes.
It is maintained by Boy Scout Troops 171 and 172. The southern
terminus of the trail is located on Main St. in Hampden, opposite

the VFW building, which is about 0.4 mi. east of Wilbraham and about 0.8 mi. west of the Hampden post office. The northern terminus lies at the eastern end of the American Foreign Legion building parking lot, located on US 20 just west of the railroad overpass in North Wilbraham. The intention is eventually to connect this trail with the Shenipsit Trail in Connecticut.

Beginning at the VFW in Hampden, the trail is marked by an orange blaze on a tree high on the hillside above the paved road. It heads north along the edge of the woods and through a clearing atop the first rise, then turns uphill onto a logging road. In 0.1 mi. Goat Rock is located on the left, with fine views to the south and east. The trail follows the logging road on and off for 0.4 mi. and bears right uphill after a grove of hemlocks. It then levels off for 0.2 mi. before it turns sharply left at a spot overlooking Hampden center. The trail soon rejoins the logging road and heads downhill to the northeast. (*Note:* Watch carefully for blazes, as other trails intersect.) In 0.2 mi. the trail turns left (north) at an intersection, and in 0.4 mi. it comes out in an extensively logged area. It continues north and then east on the logging road, crosses a small brook, and bears right off the road at the next rise. It soon passes a small pond on the left and in 0.1 mi. turns north onto another logging road. In 100 ft. it bears right into a wet, logged-over area. It continues 0.1 mi., then turns west paralleling some powerlines. At 2.1 mi. the trail turns left onto Mountain Rd. and then turns right, following the powerlines uphill. At the top of the hill, the trail heads north through a young forest. After crossing a stone wall and a small brook, the trail begins to ascend forested Mt. Vision. It bears right and shortly reaches the summit. In 0.2 mi. the trail joins a private drive to Burleigh Rd. It turns right onto Burleigh Rd., passes the Hampden–Wilbraham town-line marker, and shortly turns northeast onto a logging road. In 0.6 mi. the trail passes a small hill on the right with fine views west. In another 0.6 mi. the logging road becomes paved and intersects Monson Rd. at 4.6 mi. From here to the American Foreign Legion in North Wilbraham (at 9 mi.) the trail is hard to follow and is in the process of being blazed and relocated.

Ridge Trail

Distances from VFW in Hampden

    to Goat Rock: 0.1 mi.(5 min.)

    to Mountain Rd.: 2.1 mi. (1 hr. 20 min.)

    to summit of Mt. Vision: 2.6 mi. (1 hr. 45 min.)

    to Burleigh Rd.: 3.3 mi. (2 hr. 10 min.)

    to Monson Rd.: 4.6 mi. (3 hr. 30 min.)

    to American Foreign Legion: 9 mi. (6 hr. 10 min.)

QUABBIN RESERVOIR AND PARK

Quabbin Reservoir (the name comes from a Nipmuc Indian word meaning "many waters") is an artificial lake with an area of 38.6 sq. mi. It was built between 1927 and 1939 by the erection of two large, earth dams. To create the reservoir, the towns of Enfield, Dana, Greenwich, and Prescott were abolished from corporate existence, a relocation affecting about 2,500 persons. Impounding the runoff from 186 sq. mi. of the Swift River watershed and 98 sq. mi. of the Ware River watershed, the reservoir supplies a major part of the water for Boston and the other cities and towns that comprise the Metropolitan Water District.

Hiking trails crisscross Quabbin Park, the region between MA 9 and the reservoir, an area dominated by Quabbin Hill (1026 ft.). The trails traverse mostly wooded areas, with occasional views from ledges or open spaces. All are suitable for snowshoeing in the winter. In general the trails are short and the gradients easy, and since many of them begin or end either on the main access road or at the summit, it is easy to combine several routes into pleasant circuits of various lengths. All the trails are blazed with yellow paint, but a few are new, and thus it is essential to follow the markings carefully.

Reach Quabbin Park from MA 9 midway between Belchertown and Ware. A paved road branches north 3 mi. east of the junction of MA 9 and US 202 near Belchertown, passes the MDC Quabbin Visitor Center, and crosses Winsor Dam. It then turns sharply left uphill and makes a wide semicircle through the park, returning to MA 9 about 3 mi. east of the first entrance and 4 mi. west of Ware.

Another access road leaves MA 9 midway between the Belcher-town and Ware entrances, meeting Quabbin Rd. just east of Winsor Dam. All three entry gates are closed at sunset. Camping and fires are prohibited in the area, as are alcoholic beverages, dogs, horses, hunting, fishing from the shore (except in designated areas), and wading and swimming. Information is available at the MDC Quabbin Visitor Center in the administration building off MA 9 in Belchertown.

Summit Trail

The Summit Trail connects the lookout on Quabbin Hill to a point near the intersection of the park entrance road and the summit road. It begins just below and south of the summit tower at post 20. Descending through an open area for about 100 yd., it bears right and into the woods in a generally southwesterly direction. A short side trail leads to a vista at 0.3 mi. The trail turns left at the side trail and descends along the former route of the old Martindale Trail, which is now the route of the Summit Trail. At about 1 mi. the trail ends at a dirt road.

Summit Trail

Distance from post 20 on summit of Quabbin Hill
    to dirt road: *est.* 1 mi. (40 min.)

Powers Trail

This is one of two trails that begin on the eastern side of the summit parking area, directly across the lot from the steps leading to the summit tower. (The Woods Trail also begins here.) The Powers Trail bears right and then left around a rocky outcrop, then descends gradually through the woods in a series of broad switch-backs. (*Note:* It is necessary to watch the blazes carefully, as there is seldom any evident footway.) After running almost due north for some distance through an evergreen plantation, the trail turns right and ends on a woods road, which connects the Hanks Place Trail and the Summit Trail.

To return to the summit, go right (south) on the woods road about 0.5 mi. to a clearing, then follow the Summit Trail back to the lookout.

Powers Trail

Distances from summit of Quabbin Hill
   to woods road: 0.8 mi. (20 min.)
   to return to summit (via woods road and Summit Trail): 2.3 mi.
      (1 hr. 10 min.)

Woods Trail

This trail links the summit with the site of the former Woods place to the north. When combined with the Hanks Place Trail, it offers a route from Quabbin Hill to the reservoir. It is blazed only as far as the Woods place, but the route to the Hanks Place Trail is obvious beyond that point.

It begins with the Powers Trail just north of the vista on the eastern side of the summit parking area, directly opposite the path leading to the lookout tower, at post 19. The trail parallels the clearing, then bears left, passes through a stand of birches, and crosses an overgrown clearing. (*Note:* The route is obscure here.) The trail keeps to the upper edge of the field, reenters the woods near a large boulder on the right, then bears right along the north side of a second overgrown clearing and enters the woods again on the left. After passing several large boulders on the left, the trail leads generally northeast, and in about 0.8 mi. it reaches the Woods place, with picnic tables and views to the northeast. Prior to reaching the old camp, the trail is frequently obscure, so blazes should be followed carefully. The unblazed trail continues on to the Hanks Place Trail, then follows it to the reservoir.

Woods Trail

Distances from summit of Quabbin Hill
   to Woods place: 0.8 mi. (20 min.)
   to Hanks Place Trail: 1 mi. (25 min.)
   to Quabbin Reservoir (via Hanks Place Trail): 1.4 mi. (40 min.)

Hanks Place Trail

This is the only trail in the area that leads directly to Quabbin Reservoir. It begins just above Enfield Lookout at post number 6, 0.3 mi. north of the traffic rotary below the summit and directly across from a gravel road leading south to Water Hole 62 (sign). (This road connects with the Woods Trail.) There are very few blazes, but the route is obvious and easy to follow.

The trail begins to the right on an old road (barway) and makes a steady but gradual descent, passing under and north of the lookout and crossing a stone wall and the stream from Water Hole 60. It then continues generally northeast, dropping about 300 ft. in elevation. In 0.5 mi. the trail emerges on the shore of the reservoir, following it to the right for several hundred yards. (There is no set route here; pick the easiest path, which is normally found nearer the water than the trees.) In about 0.3 mi. the trail passes a prominent rocky ledge, where the shore turns left (east). The trail continues along the shore to a low stone wall, which extends about 50 ft. in from the water, immediately west of a small stream. At this point the trail turns right (south) up a faint path, which follows the stream and emerges in a large open field. The path quickly widens into a grassy lane, which continues through the middle of the field, passes through a barway, and bears right along a fence on the western side of the picnic area. The trail reaches the main Quabbin Rd. at 0.3 mi. above the shore. (To return to the starting point from here, go right [northwest] along the road for 0.7 mi.)

(To follow this part of the trail in the reverse direction, descend north from the picnic area and continue along the shore west and then northwest. Just before reaching the northernmost point of land jutting into the reservoir, the trail turns abruptly southwest, ascending the unmarked but obvious old road that leads to Enfield Lookout.)

The trail crosses paved Quabbin Rd., passes through a barway, and continues almost due south on a dirt road. In 0.6 mi. a woods road branches left, and, just beyond, the Powers Trail exits right (cairn). About 0.5 mi. farther along a second woods road branches left. (The woods road continues south about 0.5 mi. to MA 9, about 0.3 mi. east of the middle access road.) About 350 ft. beyond is the old Martindale Farm and the lower end of the Summit Trail. From the Martindale Farm another woods road branches left (west) to the Cove Trail.

To return to the starting point, follow either the Powers Trail or the Summit Trail to Quabbin Hill; there, the Woods Trail and Water Hole 62 lead to Enfield Lookout.

Hanks Place Trail

Distances from Enfield Lookout

to Quabbin Reservoir: 0.5 mi. (10 min.)

to picnic area: 1.3 mi. (35 min.)

to Powers Trail: 1.8 mi. (50 min.)

to Martindale Farm and Summit Trail: 2.3 mi. (1 hr.)

to return to starting point via Powers Trail: 3.5 mi. (1 hr. 45 min.)

to return to starting point via Summit Trail: 4.3 mi. (2 hr. 10 min.)

Peppers Mill Loop Trail

This route circles Peppers Mill Pond, a long, narrow pond between Goodnough Dike and MA 9. There are no blazes, but the footway is obvious throughout, following old roads and a well-worn path. The trail starts just outside the gate on the Ware entrance road (the farthest east of the three access roads) at post 13. Leaving the east side of the road (with barway and sign), it follows the outlet stream and then the northwest shore of the pond, never more than a few feet from the water. In 0.4 mi. a path branches left to the power-line. Almost immediately afterward, the main trail crosses the powerline and soon reaches the beaver dam at the upper end of the pond. Here the Beaver Pond Trail branches left (sign). The Loop Trail crosses the stream on the dam and shortly becomes a dirt road, which leads south around the pond. It bears right at a junction just beyond the dam, crosses the powerline a second time, and continues generally south-southwest for 0.6 mi. The trail ends at a rest area on MA 9, 0.3 mi. southeast of Quabbin Rd.

Peppers Mill Loop Trail

Distances from MA 9 (Ware entrance)

to beaver dam: 0.5 mi. (15 min.)

to MA 9 (loop): 1.1 mi. (30 min.)

Beaver Pond Trail

Follow the Peppers Mill Loop Trail to its junction with the Beaver Pond Trail (sign) at the beaver dam. Take the Beaver Pond Trail north and a little northwest for about 0.1 mi. above and west of the beaver pond. The trail, at first only a narrow path, soon widens into a woods road, somewhat overgrown in places. (Stay on the clearest route, avoiding all fainter paths that branch to the right.) At a fork in the road the trail goes left (right leads about 500 ft. along the pond) and about 500 ft. along goes right at a second fork, continuing uphill. The trail proceeds along the crest of a ridge, gradually bearing southwest and then south, and about 0.5 mi. from the dam it meets a powerline. It turns right (west) and follows the powerline 0.3 mi. to Quabbin Rd. To return to the beginning of the Peppers Mill Loop Trail, turn left onto the road and continue 0.3 mi.

Beaver Pond Trail

Distance from Peppers Mill Loop Trail
  to Quabbin Rd.: 0.8 mi. (25 min.)

GRANVILLE STATE FOREST

Granville State Forest is like a huge, wild garden, where the luxurious laurel growth, cascading Hubbard River, picturesque brooks, and wealth of wildflowers thriving in the shade of a mature growth of evergreens and hardwoods show unspoiled nature at her best. In 1749, Samuel Hubbard, the first white settler in the area, made his home along the banks of the river now bearing his name. The Hubbard River rushes over a series of rapids, dropping 450 ft. in 2.5 mi. The cellar holes of the early settlers are still visible, and many acres along both sides of the Hubbard River have been developed into picnic and camping areas, with fireplaces, tables, and toilet facilities. A swimming pool, bathhouse, and picnic area are located along Halfway Brook near the main forest road.

To reach Granville State Forest, take MA 57 west 0.8 mi. from the church in the village of West Granville (or east 2.8 mi. from Tolland). Coming from West Granville, turn left (south) onto West Hartland Rd. At 0.6 mi. from MA 57 is a sign reading "Entering

Granville State Forest." The abandoned road on the left (east) is
Tom Hayes Rd., which extends along much of the eastern boundary
of the forest. In 0.3 mi. are a gate and road leading to the picnic area
near the Hubbard River. The forest supervisor's office and service
building are located on the right of West Hartland Rd., 1.5 mi. from
MA 57. Refer to the USGS West Granville quadrangle. A map also
is available from the DEM (see "Other Sources of Information").

Hubbard River Loop

This well-worn footpath follows old woods roads. There are no
blazes or signs, and in some sections the brush needs clearing out.
The trail is used principally by fishermen and for fire prevention.
Beginning at the circle terminus of the road serving the Granville
State Forest camping area on the eastern side of Hubbard River
(0.5 mi. from where the road leaves West Hartland Rd.), the trail
follows an old road southeast, roughly parallel to—but out of sight
of—the river. The road soon narrows to a trail and joins a woods
road from the left. The trail continues across a gas pipeline clearing, rejoins the river, and follows it closely through a narrow
scenic gorge with many small waterfalls, pools, and rocky ledges.
As the trail leaves the gorge, it turns slightly more to the east and
continues through open woods, shortly joining the abandoned Tom
Hayes Rd. (unmarked). The trail turns left onto Tom Hayes Rd.
and climbs gradually for nearly 1 mi. This road is badly eroded
near the bottom of the hill, and a more recent, but overgrown, logging road about 100 ft. to the east parallels it, rejoining the Tom
Hayes Rd. shortly. (In most places Tom Hayes Rd. is the eastern
boundary of the state forest).

The trail ascends a hill, with a gully on the left and abandoned
fields on the right, passing a large, dead chestnut tree on the left.
The trail continues on the level between widely spaced stone walls
for about 1 mi. until it again intersects the gas pipeline clearing. It
turns left and follows the pipeline south for slightly more than 0.5
mi., until the pipeline drops off steeply toward the river. At this
point an old woods road crosses the pipeline. The trail turns right
onto the road and descends on it for a short distance until it rejoins

the road from the campground a few hundred feet south of the circle terminus. If the point where the woods road crosses the pipeline is obscure, continue to descend the pipeline until it joins the trail, then turn right to return to the circle terminus.

Hubbard River Loop

Distances from circle terminus
  to Tom Hayes Rd.: 1.5 mi. (45 min.)
  to circle terminus (loop): 4.3 mi. (2 hr. 15 min.)

Valley Brook Loop

This route, which enters the Barkhamsted Reservoir property in Connecticut, can be combined with the Hubbard River Loop to make an interesting walk of about 10 mi. Follow the Hubbard River Loop to Tom Hayes Rd. Turn right (south) onto Tom Hayes Rd. and continue to the junction with Hartland Hollow Rd. Turn right (south) onto Hartland Hollow Rd., crossing a bridge and continuing south to CT 20 at North Hollow. Walk east on CT 20 about 0.5 mi., then north onto the Hartford Water Department service road, which parallels Valley Brook on the east for about 1.5 mi. until it crosses the brook. Turn left (south) and follow the woods road to North Hollow, then retrace your steps on Hartland Hollow Rd. to the junction with Tom Hayes Rd. Follow Tom Hayes Rd. back to the Hubbard River Loop, then follow this to the starting point. Permission to use the Valley Brook Loop must be obtained in advance from the Water Department, Metropolitan District, Hartford County, Hartford, CT 06103.

Valley Brook Loop

Distance from beginning of Hubbard River Loop
  to return to beginning of Hubbard River Loop: 10 mi. (5 hr.)

Halfway Brook Circuit

Beginning on W. Hartland Rd. 2 mi. south of MA 57 at the Halfway Brook Picnic Area (sign) just north of the pond, the trail goes northeast through the picnic and camping areas, keeping to the left of the toilet facilities. It crosses the open field and leaves the southeast corner of the field between campsites 12 and 13. It continues northeast, bearing right opposite campsite 16.

The trail continues to Halfway Brook and follows the brook downstream, past a large boulder in the brook where a path crosses to the south bank. The main trail continues on the north bank and passes another brook crossing on the right. The trail, which is obscure, continues straight ahead, climbing gently to an old road. The trail turns right onto the road (left leads to a camping area and West Hartland Rd.). When the road bears left at the point where the high bank of the ravine has fallen away toward the brook, the trail leaves the road and continues straight ahead through the woods, with the ravine on the right. Again the path is obscure, but the woods are open and the route is easy to follow by keeping the ravine on your right at all times. The trail descends to a gravel parking circle for a picnic area near the brook. (*Note:* Do not follow the "Trail" sign on a tree, which leads right over a bridge to the south side of the brook. Turning left on the gravel road leads to a swimming pool in the Hubbard River with picnic facilities and a bath house, then to West Hartland Rd.)

The main trail continues straight ahead (east) through the woods, past picnic tables, with the brook on the right. It soon reaches the point where Halfway Brook enters Hubbard River. The trail turns right (southeast) here, crosses Halfway Brook, and follows Hubbard River downstream about 100 ft. to a pipeline clearing and trail.

(*Note:* Following the pipeline left across Hubbard River leads to a trail on the east side of the river. Going left [north] on this trail leads to another camping area and W. Hartland Rd. Right [south] leads to a junction with Tom Hayes Rd., which connects with Hartland Hollow Rd. See the description of the Hubbard River Loop.)

The Halfway Brook Circuit turns right (southwest) onto the trail in the pipeline clearing. This trail soon becomes a wide woods road. At a trail junction the trail turns left (southwest), gently ascending. (Right leads about 100 ft. to a bridge over Halfway Brook and the gravel parking area mentioned above.) The trail continues uphill on the south bank of the brook, following it upstream.

Near the top of a rise the trail bears left away from the brook, then soon returns close to the brook. (On the right a path is visible on the north side of the brook.) The trail continues uphill on the south side of the brook and then becomes a narrow path. It passes a large boulder on the right, where another path is visible across the brook on the north bank. The trail continues on the south bank, bearing left uphill and then following the edge of the brook to a pond and picnic area on the right. The trail continues past the pond over a small bridge and gravel path to W. Hartland Rd. opposite a "Beaver Ponds" sign, just south of the "Halfway Brook Picnic Area" sign that marks the beginning of the circuit.

Halfway Brook Circuit

Distances from W. Hartland Rd.

to first brook crossing: 0.2 mi. (5 min.)

to second brook crossing: 0.3 mi. (10 min.)

to parking area and third brook crossing: 0.6 mi. (20 min.)

to Hubbard River: 0.8 mi. (25 min.)

to trail junction: 1 mi. (30 min.)

to W. Hartland Rd. (loop): 1.5 mi. (45 min.)

Hubbard River Swimming Pool

This natural pool in the river below a waterfall, enlarged by a low dam of boulders, provides an idyllic swimming pool in the midst of the forest. Bathhouses for men and women, picnic tables, and a parking area are available. A short trail goes east from the parking area to the waterfall and pool. Crossing the Hubbard River from west to east on the boulders above the pool leads quickly to the Hubbard River Loop.

You can drive to the pool by taking the gravel road that exits left (east) from W. Hartland Rd. 0.9 mi. south of MA 57. You will reach the pool in 0.6 mi. You can also reach the pool on foot from camp-site 22 at the end of the gravel road that exits left (east) from W. Hartland Rd. 2 mi. south of MA 57. Follow the "Trail" sign from the parking space for campsite 22 to an old road not passable by car. (The Halfway Brook Circuit trail joins the road and follows it a short distance until the old road turns left where the bank has fallen into the brook ravine.) The road continues downhill to the junction with the gravel road that exits left to the swimming pool and right to the picnic area adjacent to the bridge over Halfway Brook and the Halfway Brook Circuit. This is 0.5 mi. from campsite 22.

Beaver Ponds Trail

This trail is located on the west (upstream) side of W. Hartland Rd., 2.1 mi. south of MA 57 opposite the pond made by damming Halfway Brook. From a "Beaver Ponds" sign the trail leads west along the south side of a wet area caused by beaver activity. In places the footway is obscured by brush, but farther on are open woods with short side paths to the water.

Trails West of W. Hartland Rd.

This system of trails, marked with white blocks of wood nailed to trees, is located south of Jeffrey Miller Rd., which leaves the west (right) side of W. Hartland Rd. 1.2 mi. south of MA 57. The area is wooded, and the trails follow old woods roads. For description purposes, they are designated here as Trail 1, Trail 2, and Trail 3.

Trail 1 leaves W. Hartland Rd. just north of the parking area opposite the Halfway Brook Picnic Area. Marked with white blocks of wood, it enters the woods on the west side of W. Hartland Rd., crosses a small brook, and ascends a short distance. It then levels off and continues west through the woods. After passing through a pine stand and descending slightly, the trail turns sharply right at the "Trail" sign. The trail follows an obscure footpath through open woods, ascending a slight knoll. It then descends, crosses a small brook, ascends slightly, and ends at a "Trail" sign. To the right (east) is W. Hartland Rd., (about a 3-min. walk) and to the left is Trail 2, leading to Jeffrey Miller Rd.

Trail 2 leaves W. Hartland Rd. at a sign covered with wire mesh and plastic about 150 yd. north of the Halfway Brook Picnic Area. It follows a woods road through hardwoods, passing the "Trail" sign at the end of Trail 1 and continuing straight ahead. The trail turns sharply right (north) at a tall tree stump, then continues through mixed cedar and hardwoods, passing a square hole containing water on the right and soon passing the junction with Trail 3. Trail 2 continues north, passing another water hole, and ends at Jeffrey Miller Rd. about 0.5 mi. west of W. Hartland Rd. (Turn right to reach W. Hartland Rd.)

Trail 3 leaves the west side of W. Hartland Rd. at the "Trail" sign on telephone pole 49. Keeping to the left (south) of a large maple tree and stone wall, the trail crosses an open field to the left (south) of small red-cedar trees and a quaking aspen. Passing through brush, the now-obscure trail crosses a worn stone wall and turns left (west) into low pines. It then ascends northwest, following a slightly worn footpath, and passes through a fine stand of red pine. The trail continues past "Trail" signs, going generally west through a level moist area. It ends at the junction with Trail 2.

COBBLE MTN. (1211 FT.)

This mountain, at the southeast end of Cobble Mtn. Reservoir and about 3.5 mi. south of MA 23 on Cobble Mtn. Rd., is part of the reservoir watershed owned by the city of Springfield in the towns of Blandford and Granville. Cobble Mtn. Rd. leaves MA 23 about 1.5 mi. east of Blandford center and connects with Wildcat Rd., which parallels the south side of Little River Gorge and is reached from Granville Rd. in Westfield. There are good views of the reservoir and Little River Gorge from the ledges and rocky summit of the mountain. A steep, unmarked trail ascends from the east side of Cobble Mtn. Rd., 0.4 mi. south of the dam parking area and abandoned rest rooms. The distance from Cobble Mtn. Rd. to the summit is about 0.3 mi. (10 min.). Refer to the USGS Blanford quadrangle.

CHESTER-BLANDFORD STATE FOREST

Several gravel roads in this forest are passable by car in the summer, but these are also good walking routes, especially in the winter. Refer to the USGS Chester and Blandford quadrangles.

Sanderson Brook in the Chester–Blandford State Forest is worth a visit any time of year, but the coolness of the forest and the gorge through which the brook drops rapidly over a series of high cascades are particularly attractive on a hot summer day. The falls are readily accessible from Sanderson Brook Rd. (gravel) which leaves US 20 in Chester, 4 mi. west of Huntington near a concrete bridge over Sanderson Brook. The road is closed to vehicles at the first concrete bridge. Two parking lots at the bottom provide parking.

On the right (west) side of Sanderson Brook Rd., 1 mi. south of US 20, an unmarked but well-worn path descends from the road (and runs nearly parallel to it) to the brook, bearing west enough to reach the brook at the foot of the falls in about 5 min. The trail continues across the brook to the right of the falls and climbs steeply beside the falls toward the west. At the top of the ridge the trail joins the trail described in the next paragraph, which enters on the left. A right turn here leads to Griffin Brook Rd. (which turns to gravel within a few minutes). There is no sign at the junction of the trails or at Griffin Brook Rd., but this junction is 0.6 mi. (via Griffin Brook Rd.) from the parking area on Sanderson Brook Rd. referred to in the next paragraph.

An unmarked trail begins at the right (west) of a parking area on Sanderson Brook Rd., 1.4 mi. south of US 20 (0.4 mi. beyond the beginning of the trail described above). This trail runs west, continues through an open forest, and descends gradually to the brook. It continues downstream on the right side, then crosses over to the left side, where it climbs at an easy grade, bearing generally to the left. At the height-of-land, the trail described in the preceding paragraph enters on the right, and the two trails go on together to Griffin Brook Rd., which leads back to the parking area.

Another alternative is to continue straight ahead on Sanderson Brook Rd. from the parking area, heading southwest and then south (avoiding the left fork at the parking area, fording the brook, and passing Griffin Brook Rd. on the right). This leads to paved Chester Rd. at 1.7 mi. Turning left (southeast) onto Chester Rd. leads to Blandford and an intersection with MA 23 at about 4.7 mi.

MT. TEKOA (1130 FT.)

This long, steep mountain in the towns of Russell and Montgomery lies just east of the village of Woronoco across the Westfield River and the main line of what was formerly the Boston and Albany Railroad. Although rattlesnakes are occasionally reported here, the southern ridge of the mountain is popular with rock climbers. Its rocky ledges afford panoramic views of the Westfield River Valley and Berkshire Hills.

To reach Mt. Tekoa, follow US 20 west 5.4 mi. from its junction with MA 10 in Westfield. Turn right onto a paved road at the Strathmore Paper Co. sign, and turn right at the bridge over Westfield River in the village of Woronoco. (A number of huge pot holes under this bridge are worth viewing.) Continue through the village 0.25 mi. to a temporary bridge. Bear right at the end of the bridge, and continue past a power plant on the left. Just past the town dump (on the right), park near the powerline that crosses the railroad tracks.

Cross the tracks on foot and on the other side of the tracks turn right (southeast) onto the fire road that parallels the tracks. After walking about 0.1 mi. (8 min.), turn left at a large oak tree standing alone and climb the embankment to a powerline. Follow the powerline southeast to the top of the hill at 0.5 mi. (15 min.). This is where the southern ridge of Mt. Tekoa starts. Heading north up the ridge, you will reach the first knob of Mt. Tekoa after 0.7 mi. (38 min.). Proceeding in a north-northwest direction, follow the bulldozer tracks from a 1970 plane wreck until the grade levels off at 1 mi.(46 min.). Turn left (north-northwest) a short distance to three bench marks. Just beyond is the first outcrop, with a panoramic view of the Berkshires. From here a trail (not maintained) crosses two more outcrops and heads north toward Mt. Shatterack.

SECTION 5
Central Massachusetts

Worcester County is an area of small hills dominated by woodlands, despite the fact that it includes sixty cities and towns and 648,000 residents. The county reaches from Connecticut to New Hampshire in the heart of Massachusetts. Worcester County averages about 800 ft. above sea level, with its highest point at the summit of Wachusett Mtn. (2006 ft.) in the town of Princeton. Except for the Midstate Trail, the hiking trails in the county are scattered rather than being part of one continuous trail system. A small portion of the Bay Circuit Trail crosses through Southborough, the easternmost town of Worcester County. This section of the Bay Circuit Trail is covered in Section 6.

MIDSTATE TRAIL (WCAMC)

The Midstate Trail runs north and south through Worcester County from the Rhode Island to the New Hampshire borders. It provides hikers with access to most of the significant summits and many of the scenic areas of central Massachusetts. Its 92-mile length provides numerous opportunities for overnight treks, and its connection in the north with the Wapack Trail extending into New Hampshire makes it part of one of the longest trail networks in the region.

The Midstate Trail was originally developed in the 1920s, when it ran from Mt. Watatic to Wachusett Mtn. In 1972, plans for the trail's extension to the Rhode Island line were formulated, and the complete trail was dedicated on September 7, 1985. The Midstate Trail Committee of the AMC's Worcester Chapter (tel. 508-797-9744) maintains the trail, and offers a trail guide with maps to the public.

In the trail description below, all mileages are cumulative from the northern terminus of the trail.

Midstate Trail: NH State Line to MA 12

The Midstate Trail begins in Ashburnham, at a monument in a stone wall on the Massachusetts–New Hampshire state line, several hundred feet west of the point where the Wapack Trail crosses the state line. The trail proceeds south, joining a dirt road and passing an intersection with the Wapack Trail on the left at 0.9 mi. At 1.2 mi., the trail crosses MA 119 at a point 1.5 mi. west of its intersection with MA 101. Parking is available here. This is the closest car access to the northern end of the trail.

From the parking area, the Midstate Trail goes south on paved Pierce Rd., turning left off the road at 1.7 mi. to ascend Fisher Hill (1548 ft.). From here, the trail descends through Camp Winnekeag to MA 101 at 3.8 mi., which is followed south for about 0.2 mi. The trail turns left onto Holt Rd. and then right off of Holt Rd. onto a woods trail, which climbs steeply up and around the inconspicuous summit of Mt. Hunger. Descending, the trail crosses Russell Hill Rd. and follows jeep paths and woods paths to its junction with MA 12 in Westminster, about 1.2 mi. east of the Ashburnham Town Hall. Parking is permitted here by courtesy of the abutting land owners; please respect their land.

Midstate Trail: MA 12 to Wyman Brook

The trail proceeds across a field and crosses Phillips Brook on a footbridge, then bears left uphill. It crosses Whitney Hill Rd., passes through a state forest area (no marker), and comes out at Muddy Pond, where the Westminster Conservation Commission has erected a shelter in an attractive setting (no spring). After following a circuitous route around Muddy Pond on an old roadway, the trail turns right into the woods, continues about 1 mi., and comes out on Bragg Hill Rd., where it turns left (south) for 1.2 mi. At a junction of paved roads (Whitmanville) it turns right onto the old Whitmanville Rd., following it 0.5 mi. to the Boston & Maine Railroad underpass. After going through the underpass, it turns left immediately onto a trail, proceeding past stone walls on trails and jeep paths before emerging at the intersection of Town Farm Rd. and North St. in Westminster (14.9 mi.). Reentering the woods just a short distance south and on the same side of Town Farm Rd., the trail heads in a generally south to southeast direction, crossing Howard Rd., MA 2A, and then MA 2 at 17.3 mi. Crossing MA 2 on the Wyman Rd. overpass, the trail follows Wyman Rd. and then Narrows Rd. before joining a path along Wyman Brook at 17.8 mi. This path crosses Wyman Brook before reaching the junction of Narrows Rd. and Stone Hill Rd. at 18.3 mi.

Midstate Trail: Wyman Brook to Redemption Rock (MA 140)

From Wyman Brook, at the junction of Narrows Rd. and Stone Hill Rd., the trail follows Stone Hill Rd. about 400 ft., then turns left into the woods. After 600 ft. it descends along a stone wall, then turns right. After passing through a boulder-strewn area, the trail turns right at an unmarked trail junction. Continuing south, it reaches some stone steps and eventually a fine view at Crow Hills, from which you can see Boston in the distance. (Rock climbers use the cliffs here.) After descending from the outlook, the trail gradually drops to cross a brook and later two stone walls. It reaches a rocky outlook with a view of Wachusett Mtn., then crosses MA 140 about 200 ft. from Redemption Rock, an historic site.

Midstate Trail: Redemption Rock (MA 140) to Wachusett Meadows

The trail leaves Redemption Rock in a southwesterly direction and soon crosses a brook. For the next 1 mi., the trail traverses a City of Fitchburg watershed area. After 0.75 mi. the trail crosses Mountain Rd. (paved) and proceeds into the Wachusett Mtn. ski area and Wachusett Mtn. State Reservation parking area. Information, water, and toilet facilities are available at the state park visitor center, about 1 mi. south on Mountain Rd. The trail continues uphill behind the buildings on a woods road bearing right and passes a glacial boulder called Balance Rock at 23.4 mi. It proceeds up the slope, joining first with the Old Indian Trail and then the Semuhenna Trail, which it follows around the mountain for 1.2 mi. to the Harrington Trail. (The Midstate Trail does not traverse the summit of Wachusett Mtn., 2006 ft., but you can follow the Harrington Trail left to the summit; 0.6 mi. round trip on a steep grade.)

The Midstate Trail turns right onto the Harrington Trail and follows it down the mountain to Westminster Rd. (26.6 mi.), passing a field of windmills. At 27 mi. the trail enters the Mass. Audubon Society's Wachusett Meadows Wildlife Sanctuary, following well-marked trails on relatively level ground through the sanctuary to Goodnow Rd., where the sanctuary's offices are located.

Midstate Trail: Wachusett Meadows to Barre Falls Dam

From Goodnow Rd., the Midstate Trail continues through woodlands and open fields to its intersection with MA 62 in Princeton opposite Ball Hill Rd. The trail here follows several paved roads (Ball Hill Rd., Wheeler Rd., and Bigelow Rd.), the last of which turns into the unpaved Bushy Lane. The trail follows Bushy Lane across three paved roads, the last of which is MA 56. After crossing MA 56, the trail briefly follows a jeep road before joining Davis St. heading into North Rutland. Davis St. ends at MA 68, which is followed left across the Ware River (33.4 mi.). On the far side of the river, the Midstate Trail picks up a woods path on the west bank of the river.

Leaving the river, the trail follows woods paths and roads around a small hill and then crosses the west branch of the Ware River at Brigham Rd. (36.8 mi.). The trail crosses the Barre Falls flood control dam, operated by the Corps of Engineers, 0.9 mi. farther.

Midstate Trail: Barre Falls Dam to MA 122

The head of the Midstate Trail at Barre Falls Dam is accessible by following MA 62 from Princeton or Barre. The road to the dam exits south (marked by a sign) from MA 62. Parking is available at the dam. From the parking area, the trail follows the road east 0.1 mi. There it turns left into the woods and continues to Harding Hill (1031 ft.), where there is no view. After descending 0.5 mi., the trail crosses a dirt road near a small pond. After crossing a field, the trail continues through pines, skirting a swamp for a considerable distance. Just before coming to a dike, the trail turns left onto an old road and continues as far as the Rutland–Oakham town line marker, where it turns left to another dike. After ascending the dike, it goes straight ahead (south) on a ramp road, then passes under a powerline onto a gravel road (closed to vehicles). It continues on this road 1.6 mi. to a junction of roads, where it enters the woods. After 0.6 mi. it comes out on MA 122 (paved) in Rutland at 43.4 mi.

Midstate Trail: MA 122 to MA 31

From MA 122, the Midstate Trail climbs around a hill, first southeast and then south through several stone walls, and continues to Crawford St. at 0.6 mi. It crosses Crawford St. and a small brook, then climbs gradually to a woods road. The trail turns left (south) onto this road and continues through open woods to an access trail on the right. A shelter that can house four or five persons (no water) is located here. The trail proceeds downhill (south) on the woods road to gravel East Hill Rd. After crossing this road, it continues through the Treasure Valley Boy Scout Reservation. After passing under high-tension lines, it crosses diagonally to the right and continues through a deciduous forest. After crossing a stream, it passes an old camp on the right. In 0.5 mi. the trail crosses a cutover area 50 yd. south of East Hill Rd.

The trail continues south through mixed woods to a large glacial erratic called Samson's Pebble. After descending southeast and skirting the edge of a swamp on the left, the trail passes over several stone walls. After a long downgrade it reaches the southern shore of Browning Pond. Browning Pond Rd. is just 100 yd. south. The trail turns left onto Browning Pond Rd. and passes several houses, then turns left onto Boy Scout land. After continuing 0.7 mi. through the woods, the trail again intersects Browning Pond Rd. It turns left onto the road and in 0.2 mi. reaches MA 31 (paved) in North Spencer, across from a sign for Camp Marshall 4-H camp.

Midstate Trail: MA 31 to MA 9

From MA 31 the trail enters the woods, following a path marked "Wildflower Trail." Continuing from the end of this nature walk, the

Midstate Trail ascends Buck Hill (1014 ft.), where there are no views. It then descends southeast past a shelter on the right. At 1.1 mi. the trail crosses a road junction and continues across a concrete bridge over Turkey Hill Brook, where the Spencer State Forest begins. The trail follows a gravel road on a circuitous route 0.8 mi. to a sharp left into evergreen woods, then continues through a cutover area ending at a stone wall. It skirts the edge of a large field to Paxton Rd. (paved). The trail turns right onto Paxton Rd., proceeds 100 ft., then turns left through open woods bordering the Spencer Airport.

The trail now ascends to the top of Moose Hill (1099 ft.), with excellent views. Sugden Reservoir can be seen just below the hill. At the bottom of the hill, parking is available at the gate to the dam (55.9 mi.). From here the trail proceeds south through Spencer on paths and roads, finally reaching its intersection with MA 9 at 57.7 mi.

Midstate Trail: MA 9 to Railroad Bridge (Charlton)

From MA 9 the trail enters a driveway (cars may be parked here) and continues on the driveway along the town line. When the driveway turns right, the trail goes straight along the edge of a field for 0.4 mi. to the Sibley Audubon Reservation. It enters the woods, crosses a brook in 0.2 mi., then ascends a hill for 0.4 mi. to the edge of a field. It skirts the field for 100 yd. to a stone wall, where it turns left and descends to a woods road. The trail turns left onto the road and in 0.1 mi. comes to Greenville St. (paved). It turns left onto Greenville St. and in 0.1 mi. crosses a fence on a stile and enters a pasture. The trail skirts a swamp for 0.6 mi., crosses a powerline, and comes out on Jones Rd. (paved). It turns right onto Jones Rd., then in 150 ft. turns left into the Spencer State Forest.

The trail continues 0.8 mi. to Wilson Rd. (paved), turns right onto Wilson Rd., then turns left onto Charlton Rd. It follows Charlton Rd. 0.8 mi., then turns left onto Clark Rd. In 0.1 mi. the trail turns onto Borkum Rd., follows Borkum Rd. across the Four Chimneys Wildlife Management Area 1.4 mi. to a gas pipeline, then bears left onto the pipeline. It reaches Gould Rd. (paved) in 0.7 mi., turns right onto Gould Rd., and arrives at the railroad bridge in Charlton in 0.1 mi.

Midstate Trail: Railroad Bridge (Charlton) to Cascade Brook

To reach the railroad bridge in Charlton by car, drive north on Northside Rd., which is located on the north side of US 20 opposite the Charlton Motel. (A sign says "Fay Mountain Farm.") Turn left at the Ryder Tavern, then right onto the first street after the tavern, which also has a "Fay Farm" sign. Go past Fay Farm to the railroad bridge.

After crossing the railroad bridge onto a blacktop road, the trail continues south past Wee Laddie Pond on the right. At a road junction, it continues on Cemetery Rd. for 0.5 mi. past a white colonial homestead, which was the home of Dr. William T. Morton, the first doctor to use ether as an anaesthetic. (See the historical marker there.) The trail turns left onto a paved road, then right onto Northside Rd. in 80 yd. The historic Ryder Tavern is at this corner. The trail crosses a bridge over the Massachusetts Turnpike (I-90), then turns left over wire fences into the woods. In 0.4 mi. it turns right onto a gas pipeline and follows it 0.3 mi. to a dirt road. The trail turns left onto the road toward some abandoned buildings and continues 0.3 mi. to paved Carroll Hill Rd. It turns right onto Carroll Hill Rd. and uses a cow tunnel to cross US 20.

Bearing left at the crossing, the trail enters the woods, turns right onto a blacktop road, then turns left onto a woods road. At a horse pasture it crosses a barbed-wire fence on a stile, then passes a small pond on the right and emerges from the woods at a powerline. The trail follows the powerline 0.3 mi. to paved Putnam Hill Rd. It turns right onto Putnam Hill Rd., left onto paved Turner Rd., then continues on Buffum Rd. At the Charlton–Oxford line the road name changes to Old Charlton Rd., and the trail continues to Cascade Brook.

Midstate Trail: Cascade Brook to MA 16 (Douglas)

The trail leaves Old Charlton Rd. in Oxford at the Cascade Brook crossing, bearing right. It follows the left side of this attractive brook, which might be dry in the fall. In 0.5 mi. the trail turns right onto an old railroad bed, turns left in 100 yd., then turns right following high land into the woods. It continues to the Hodges Village

Flood Control Dam, where it crosses on the north side of the dam. It goes east around the pond, then north 0.3 mi. to a dirt road that comes out on paved Rocky Hill Rd. The trail turns right (east) and continues through a residential area. It crosses MA 12 at the traffic light, then proceeds past the Oxford Police Station to paved Dana Rd. and on through the MA 395 underpass. It turns right onto Brown Rd., continues 1.25 mi., then turns left onto Lovett Rd. The trail heads east to the end of Lovett Rd., then bears left onto an unnamed road uphill to Town Farm Rd. (paved). Turning right on Town Farm Rd., the trail passes several nice outlooks over the rural countryside. At Central Turnpike in West Sutton, the trail turns left one block, then right, continuing southerly on Douglas Rd. (paved) past a second Whittier farm, then past the town line, where the road changes its name to Northwest Main St. After another 0.3 mi., the trail turns right onto an old woods road.

The trail now follows paths and old woods roads on a winding, 4.2-mi. route through Douglas State Forest, generally skirting rather than climbing the hills. The trail emerges from the forest just north of its intersection with MA 16 at 86.9 mi.

Midstate Trail: MA 16 (Douglas) to the Rhode Island Line

The final section of the Midstate Trail is in many respects the most remote. The trail meanders for slightly more than 5 mi. through the southern section of Douglas State Forest, following paths and woods roads and crossing several old railroad grades, jeep roads, and a bike path. An open shelter with table and fireplace is located at 91.6 mi. The trail ends 0.5 mi. beyond, at the Rhode Island state line.

Midstate Trail

Distances from New Hampshire state line:

> *to* Wapack Trail: 0.9 mi.
> *to* MA 119: 1.2 mi.
> *to* MA 12: 7.7 mi.
> *to* Muddy Pond Shelter: 10.1 mi.
> *to* MA 2: 17.3 mi.
> *to* Wyman Brook: 20.9 mi.
> *to* Redemption Rock: 21.8 mi.

to Wachusett Mtn. ski area parking lot: 22.9 mi.

to Harrington Tr. junction: 25.6 mi.

to Westminster Rd.: 26.6 mi.

to Wachusett Meadows W.S.: 28.4 mi.

to Barre Falls Dam: 37.7 mi.

to MA 122: 43.4 mi.

to shelter: 45.1 mi.

to MA 31: 50.3 mi.

to MA 9: 57.7 mi.

to railroad bridge (Charlton): 65.9 mi.

to Cascade Brook: 77 mi.

to Northwest Main St.: 82.6 mi.

to MA 16: 86.8 mi.

to shelter: 91.6 mi.

to Rhode Island state line: 92.1 mi.

MT. WATATIC (1832 ft.)

This mountain in Ashburnham is the southern terminus of the Wapack Range, most of which lies in New Hampshire. The trails leading to the summit of Mt. Watatic are surrounded by the 2,000-acre Ashburnham State Forest. The bare summit affords sweeping views in all directions, including Mt. Monadnock in New Hampshire, and Mt. Wachusett in Princeton, MA. On a clear day, you can see the Boston skyline to the east and Mt. Greylock and Vermont's Stratton Mtn. to the west. The fire tower on the summit is a prominent landmark but should not be climbed under any circumstances due to its poor condition. The shelter northwest of the summit has been extensively vandalized and is no longer suitable for use; it may be torn down in the near future. A side trail to East Watatic, the bare lower summit 450 ft. to the southeast, is no longer maintained but can be followed by experienced bushwhackers.

Mt. Watatic is crossed by the Wapack Trail, a long-distance hiking trail which begins at the foot of Mt. Watatic and proceeds north into New Hampshire. The Wapack Trail is maintained by the Friends of the Wapack (P.O. Box 115, West Peterborough, NH

03468), which offers a trail guide and map. This area is also covered in the Midstate Trail Guide, as well as on the USGS Ashburnham and Peterborough quadrangles.

The connection between the Midstate Trail and the Wapack Trail provides long-distance through-hikers with a challenging opportunity to enjoy an extended trip from the Rhode Island line to Greenfield, NH.

Wapack Trail (FOW)

The Wapack Trail, marked with the same yellow triangles used by the Midstate Trail, begins at the small parking lot on MA 119, 1.4 mi. west of MA 101. The first section of the trail coincides with the Midstate Trail. At a trail junction at 0.3 mi., the Midstate Trail continues straight ahead to the state line, while the Wapack Trail turns right to begin its ascent of Mt. Watatic. (*Note:* This new route of the Wapack Trail avoids the old powerline route, which should not be used by hikers.) Slabbing the steep south face of the mountain, with moderate grades alternating with steep pitches, the Wapack reaches the summit at 1.2 mi.

From the summit, the Wapack Trail heads northwest (aim for Monadnock's summit and keep a few feet to the right of the fire tower), following a grassy path downhill about 30 ft. to the trees. Passing abandoned ski lifts and slopes from the Mt. Watatic Ski Area, the trail descends moderately through a state wildlife conservation area, before ascending an open ledgy area known as Nutting Hill at 1.9 mi. Descending from Nutting Hill, the trail widens into an old cart track, passes through an unmarked junction at 2.1 mi., and at 2.4 mi. reaches a stone wall marking the New Hampshire state line. From here, the Wapack Trail continues for another 19 mi. northward into New Hampshire, generally following the ridge of the Wapack Range.

By following the stone wall on the state boundary about 250 ft. to the west, you will reach the Midstate Trail's northern terminus. Following the Midstate Trail to the south (left) will return you to the MA 119 parking area, making possible a circuit over the summit of Mt. Watatic.

Wapack Trail

Distances from MA 119 parking area
  to summit of Mt. Watatic: 1.2 mi. (1 hr.)
  to Massachusetts–New Hampshire line: 2.4 mi. (1 hr. 35 min.)
  to MA 119 parking area (via Midstate Trail): 3.6 mi. (2 hr. 15
    min.)

WACHUSETT MTN. (2006 ft.) AND
WACHUSETT MTN. STATE RESERVATION (DEM)

Wachusett Mtn. in Princeton is the highest point east of the Connecticut River and south of New Hampshire. It is the outstanding
feature of Wachusett Mtn. State Reservation, which now comprises
1,950 acres, partly in Westminster. Panoramic views from its summit stretch to the Boston skyline on a clear day.

The park headquarters and visitor center is located on Mountain
Rd. in Princeton, which is also the starting point for several of the
hiking trails. A paved automobile road to the summit is open to
vehicular traffic from late spring to early fall. Other roads on the
reservation are generally closed to cars at all times. A major ski
area operates on the north slope of the mountain during the winter.
Hikers are not permitted on the alpine ski slopes and trails except
at crossings.

Hiking trails are generally marked with blue triangles. Those
trails which are part of the Midstate Trail system also have yellow
trianges. See the Wachusett map included with this guidebook.

Midstate Trail

The long-distance Midstate Trail, marked by yellow triangles, traverses Wachusett Mtn. From the north, it enters the park at the ski
area parking lot on Mountain Rd. and follows the Balance Rock
Trail, Old Indian Trail, Semuhenna Trail, and Harrington Trail,
exiting on Westminster Rd. From here it follows the Dickens Trail
toward the Wachusett Meadows Wildlife Sanctuary. (See Midstate
Trail: Redemption Rock [MA 140] to Wachusett Meadows in this
book.)

Jack Frost Trail (DEM)

This trail was named for the late Dr. Harold P. Frost, who scouted and cleared most of its length. To reach the foot of the trail, take Mountain Rd. 1.2 mi. north from Princeton center. Turn left (uphill) at a Y-intersection onto Westminster Rd. You can park at the intersection with Administration Rd., which is closed to motor vehicles. An attractive picnic site is located at the right of this intersection, beside a small pool. The water is not potable, and swimming is prohibited. Proceed on foot up Administration Rd. 0.4 mi., where the trail begins on a woods road on the right. The trail crosses a brook and an intersection with the Lower Link Trail and continues east until it crosses a powerline at 0.3 mi. Here it begins to ascend more steeply through hemlocks, passing the High Meadow trail on the right. The trail then travels north on a more-or-less level stretch, ending at the Mountain House Trail about 0.4 mi. below the summit.

Jack Frost Trail

Distances from Administration Rd.

 to Mountain House Trail: 1.5 mi. (45 min.)

 to summit of Wachusett Mtn. (via Mountain House Trail): 1.9
  mi. (1 hr.)

Pine Hill Trail (DEM)

The shortest route to the top of Wachusett Mtn. is via this very steep, old ski trail on the eastern side of the mountain. The trail begins on the west (left) side of Mountain Rd. about 3 mi. north of Princeton center, just before reaching the park visitor center. The upper end of the trail is located at a break in the stone wall about 200 ft. from the end of the "up" road.

Pine Hill Trail

Distance from Mountain Rd.

 to stone wall: 0.5 mi. (25 min.)

Mountain House Trail (DEM)

This trail ascends Wachusett Mtn. from the east. It starts near an old wooden shack on the west side of Mountain Rd., 2.4 mi. north of Princeton center. The trail takes its name from the famous Mountain House, which was formerly located nearby. (The stone-wall cellar holes are still visible.) There are no trail markings, but the trail is broad and easy to follow.

The trail climbs rather steeply up an eroded path through hard-wood forest, passing junctions with the Bicentennial Trail, the Loop Trail, the Jack Frost Trail, and the Link Trail. The trail then turns more to the north, crossing a stone wall and the summit road. From here the trail levels off and parallels the summit road, reaching the summit at 1 mi.

Mountain House Trail

Distance from Mountain Rd.
    to summit of Wachusett Mtn.: 1 mi. (45 min.)

Harrington Trail (DEM)

This trail begins on Westminster Rd., 0.5 mi. west of its junction with Administration Rd. It leaves on the north side of the road opposite the Dickens Trail.

It starts uphill through a field, switching to the northeast and following a stone wall on the left as it enters the woods. Shortly, the trail turns left onto a woods road and continues until it meets the Stagecoach Trail at 0.4 mi. The Harrington Trail soon crosses a stone wall, which marks the boundary of the Wachusett Mtn. State Reservation, then passes through a stand of large hemlocks. Short-ly the trail bears left (north) and crosses a stream bed. It then bears right (northeast) to cross West Rd.

As the trail starts climbing again, painted white blazes are visi-ble, and at 1 mi. the trail crosses Administration Rd. (This point is about 0.8 mi. north of the lower end of Administration Rd.) After crossing three stream beds (dry in the summer), the trail climbs more steeply, levels off, and resumes climbing among rocks. The trail slabs to the right and climbs onto ledges. Facing the ledges, the trail turns sharply left, paralleling the ledges for a short dis-tance, then turns right and climbs steeply over rocks. The Link Trail enters on the right, and the Harrington Trail continues climb-ing steeply over rocks.

Shortly, the trail goes over a stone wall along the side of the summit road, crosses the road, then climbs northeast over less difficult rocks and ledges. The open summit is soon visible, and the trail terminates on the flat rocks southwest of the fire tower.

Harrington Trail

Distances from Westminster Rd.

   to Administration Rd.: 1 mi. (40 min.)

   to summit of Wachusett Mtn.: 1.5 mi. (1 hr. 15 min.)

West Side Trail (DEM)

This trail ascends Wachusett Mtn. from the west side. It begins on W. Princeton Rd. (gravel) in Westminster, 1 mi. north of its junction with Westminster Rd. and 200 yd. north of the intersection of West Rd. The trail terminates at the Old Indian Trail, about 0.6 mi. below the summit. It is difficult to follow in places.

The trail enters the woods on the east side of W. Princeton Rd. (ignore the yellow markings for the cross-country ski trail), passes through a fairly large hemlock stand and over rocks, then swings south to slab up a hillside. The trail crosses more rocks and climbs steeply straight ahead over a cliff.

Above the cliff, the trail levels off into hardwoods, mostly small beeches, and then climbs gradually. It swings left and right and climbs steeply before leveling off again. A short distance along, the trail crosses the summit road and continues southeast to an open spot with large, flat rocks that is surrounded by scrub oak. Nearby, a cairn marks the Princeton–Westminster line.

The trail veers northeast and runs parallel to the road. Here the trail crosses the Semuhenna Trail and passes near a picnic table within sight of the road, then heads back into the woods. It climbs gradually to a junction with the Old Indian Trail.

West Side Trail

Distances from W. Princeton Rd.

   to Old Indian Trail: 1.5 mi. (1 hr. 15 min.)

   to summit of Wachusett Mtn. (via Old Indian Trail): 2.1 mi. (1 hr. 45 min.)

Semuhenna Trail (DEM)

This trail, constructed in 1971 and named after long-time trail volunteer Anne Humes, proceeds essentially north from the ledges on the Harrington Trail to the Old Indian Trail near Balance Rock. It crosses the West Side Trail once and Summit Rd. twice. Through the Link Trail, it also has access to the Jack Frost Trail and the Mountain House Trail, providing opportunities for a variety of loops.

The upper end of this trail starts at the Harrington Trail 0.2 mi. east of Administration Rd., just below the ledges, and about 40 yd. below the western end of the Link Trail. Going downward from the Harrington Trail, it follows a low ridge, crosses a small brook (dry in the summer), rises slightly over two open ledges, and crosses Summit Rd. at a picnic site. Almost immediately it crosses the West Side Trail and enters a stand of large hemlocks. It passes the top of the west T-bar lift (right) and continues on a gentle descent through the hemlock stand to the second crossing of Summit Rd., 60 yd. east of its intersection with North Rd. Beyond this crossing the trail passes through another old hemlock grove, swings gently left to cross a small brook (dry in the summer), then ascends slightly to approach a stone wall. Beyond the wall, the trail passes through a planted grove of white pine, much of which is diseased or dead, and soon intersects the Old Indian Trail 0.2 mi. from Balance Rock.

Semuhenna Trail

Distance from Harrington Trail
   to Old Indian Trail: 1.2 mi. (45 min.)

Old Indian Trail (DEM)

This steep, rocky trail ascends the north slope of Wachusett Mtn. It begins on Balance Rock Rd. (closed to vehicular traffic), opposite the end of the Balance Rock Trail.

The Old Indian Trail leaves the road on the south side and proceeds through mixed hardwoods and pines. The Semuhenna Trail enters right at 0.2 mi. At 0.4 mi. the trail diagonally crosses a ski trail, reenters the woods, and passes under the ski lift at pole 12. The trail crosses the Summit Rd. and then begins to climb gradually. After crossing a brook bed (dry in the summer), the trail climbs steeply to a junction with the West Side Trail. It continues upward over stone steps and zigzags over rocks, crossing a ledge where there is an excellent view of Mt. Monadnock and Mt. Greylock on a clear day. A few hundred feet above this point, the trail levels off and climbs gradually to the summit. It passes close to a high-voltage transformer and ends at the beacon tower on the north side of the summit.

Old Indian Trail
Distances from Semuhenna Trail
   to West Side Trail: 0.6 mi. (30 min.)
   to summit of Wachusett Mtn.: 1.3 mi. (1 hr.)

Balance Rock Trail
This trail begins at the far end of the ski-area parking lot on Mountain Rd., about 1.2 mi. north of the park visitor center. Follow the jeep path for about 0.3 mi. before turning onto a woods path, which soon reaches Balance Rock, a glacial erratic. The path continues a few hundred feet farther to Balance Rock Rd. (closed to vehicles). Across the road, the Old Indian Trail continues toward the summit.

Balance Rock Trail
Distance from ski-area parking lot
   to Balance Rock: 0.4 mi. (20 min.)
   to Balance Rock Rd: 0.4 mi. (20 min.)

Connecting Trails
The following trails, although relatively short, provide useful connections between the major trails described above, permitting a number of interesting loops and circuits.

   Link Trail (0.2 mi.) connects the Mountain House Trail (just above the upper end of the Jack Frost Trail) with the Harrington Trail.

   Lower Link Trail (0.5 mi.) parallels the Administration Rd., connecting the lower end of the Jack Frost Trail with the Harrington Trail.

Loop Trail (0.4 mi.) provides a cut-off between the Bicentennial Trail and the middle part of the Mountain House Trail.

Bicentennial Trail (0.6 mi.) begins at the visitor center and runs south parallel to Mountain Rd., passing the Pine Hill Trail, the Loop Trail, and the Mountain House Trail, before turning steeply upward to end at the Jack Frost Trail.

Stage Coach Trail (0.5 mi.), previously called the Old Logging Rd., runs between the Harrington Trail and Westminster Rd. (near the locked gates at the beginning of Administration Rd.).

WACHUSETT MEADOWS WILDLIFE SANCTUARY (MAS)

This 977-acre bird and wildlife sanctuary is located 1.5 mi. west of Princeton center, and it is owned and maintained by the Massachusetts Audubon Society. Visitors are welcome.

To reach the sanctuary, follow MA 62 0.5 mi. west from Princeton center, then turn right onto Goodnow Rd. (blacktop) at a "Wachusett Meadows Sanctuary" sign. In 1.1 mi. there is a parking area on the left. Four suggested walks are described below. (The long-distance Midstate Trail also passes through the Wachusett Meadows; see Midstate Trail: Wachusett Meadows to Barre Falls Dam.)

Fifth Pasture Loop and Crocker Trail

This pleasant woodland and field trail begins at a sign on Goodnow Rd. about 500 ft. west of the parking area. It proceeds south through open land and woods. Located in the third pasture is a rain shelter. After passing a cairn, the trail (marked by disks) turns left and continues through pines, making a loop. At a junction with the Rock Pasture Trail, it bears left onto the Crocker Trail which leads back to Goodnow Rd. The circuit ends about 200 ft. along the road to the right.

Fifth Pasture Loop and Crocker Trail

Distance from Goodnow Rd.

to Goodnow Rd. (loop): 2 mi. (1 hr.)

BROWN HILL

To reach the summit of Brown Hill, turn right on Goodnow Rd., then bear left across the field to a large maple tree (the Crocker maple, believed to be the fourth-largest sugar maple in the United States). Turn right onto a northerly trail to the shagbark hickory grove, then follow the Chapman Trail to the Glacial Boulder Trail. Turn right onto this trail to view the glacial boulder. Proceed upward, bearing left at a trail junction. Then turn right and continue to the open summit of Brown Hill, where there is a 360-degree view of Wachusett Mtn., Little Wachusett, and the surrounding country. At a trail junction, bear left and continue to the old Bridle Path. Turn right onto the Bridle Path, bear right at two trail junctions, and emerge in a field bordering Goodnow Rd. Traverse the field to your starting point (2 mi., 1 hr.).

Chapman Trail

This trail is named for the late Lawrence B. Chapman, a former MIT professor, amateur ornithologist, and chairman of the Wachusett Meadows Advisory Committee. The trail extends from the glacial boulder to Thompson Rd., where it meets the southern end of the Dickens Trail.

From the headquarters of the Wachusett Meadows Wildlife Sanctuary, the trailhead is accessible by one of two routes. The first route, on the west side of the big meadow, passes the Crocker maple and the hickory grove; the other, on the east side of the big meadow, continues on the east side of a stone wall up a gentle grade through the woods.

The Chapman Trail begins 50 yd. north of and below the glacial boulder, where the Hickory Grove Trail enters from the left. The trail veers slightly right and proceeds northeast through white pine woods. At 180 yd. it passes a walled spring hole (dry in the summer). It crosses a small brook 160 yd. from the spring and another brook 110 yd. farther along; both brooks are dry in the summer. Shortly after the second brook, the trail swings gently right through a brushy area, then turns left again to join the West Border Trail 250 yd. from the second brook. Beyond this junction, the trail turns

90 degrees left, crossing a stone wall, to follow another stone wall, which marks a sanctuary boundary line. About 30 yd. from this turn, the trail veers slightly right and drops gently down to Thompson Rd.

Chapman Trail

Distance from glacial boulder
   to Thompson Rd.: 0.6 mi. (30 min.)

Dickens Trail

This trail connects the Audubon Wachusett Meadows Wildlife Sanctuary trails with the Wachusett Mtn. State Reservation trail system. It starts from Thompson Rd., 2.5 mi. west of Mountain Rd., and continues north to Westminster Rd. opposite the Harrington Trail.

The trail leaves the north side of Thompson Rd. at the western end of a small pond opposite the Chapman Trail. It starts uphill and continues to a logging road, where it turns left onto a road for a short distance and then turns right, leaving the road. It passes a communications tower on the right and then crosses the boundary line of the Wachusett Meadows Wildlife Sanctuary at a break in a stone wall. The trail joins a woods road and continues, crossing the right-of-way for the AT&T continental underground lines just before it terminates on Westminster Rd.

Dickens Trail

Distance from Thompson Rd.
   to Westminster Rd.: 0.8 mi. (30 min.)

LEOMINSTER STATE FOREST (DEM)

This forest, known for its beautiful stands of mountain laurel, comprises more than 4,000 acres and many miles of marked and unmarked trails for excellent hiking and cross-country skiing. The main parking area from which most of the trails lead is on MA 31 on the Princeton–Westminster line about 2 mi. south of the junction of MA 31 and MA 2. A wooden sign in the parking area shows most of the marked trails.

The twin summits of Crow Hills (1234 ft.) are located in Leominster State Forest. The Midstate Trail crosses them. For a description, see Midstate Trail: Wyman Brook to Redemption Rock (MA 40). Two seasonal points of interest in this area are the trailing arbutus in April and the mountain laurel in June.

The shortest way to the top of the Crow Hills and the usual approach to the cliff by rock climbers is from MA 31, starting at a point 100 ft. north of the Princeton–Westminster line. After proceeding about 200 yd. through the woods, the trail comes to a junction of two trails, both of which lead to the Midstate Trail. The trail on the left follows the base of the cliff, and the trail on the right ascends steeply to the northern ridge. Total distance to the top of the ridge by either trail is 0.3 mi. (20 min.).

PURGATORY CHASM (DEM)

Located west of MA 146 in Sutton, Purgatory Chasm State Reservation includes 187 acres of scenic land and odd rock formations. The reservation has picnic facilities, including fireplaces, tables, and spring water. The chasm is a great fissure in solid rock approximately 0.5 mi. long with sheer walls rising 70 ft. A well-marked trail (0.5 mi., 25 min.) leads through the chasm over and under the rocks in a circuitous route.

BLACKSTONE RIVER AND CANAL (DEM)

The Blackstone River and Canal Heritage State Park occupies slightly over 1,000 acres in the towns of Northbridge and Uxbridge. Included within the park are 6 mi. of the Blackstone River and some of the best-preserved sections of the historic Blackstone Canal, built in 1826–1828.

The main trail in the park is the 3.75-mi. Tow Path trail, which runs roughly north and south along a wide, grassy path with gentle grades. Parking is available at both ends of the trail: in the north, at Plummer's Landing on Church St. in Northbridge, just east of MA 122; in the south, at the Stanley Woolen Mill on Cross St., just off MA 16 in Uxbridge. Parking is also available at the Stone Arch

Bridges off Hartford Av. in Uxbridge, which bisects the trail about 2.4 mi. from its northern end.

Parts of the trail follow the original canal tow path. Along its route the trail passes locks, dams, bridge abutments, and other remnants of the early industrial era, as well as scenic outlooks over Rice City Pond and the Blackstone River Valley.

The Goat Hill Trail Loop is a 0.7-mi. side trail to the Tow Path Trail making a circuit to the west over Goat Hill. There are fine views from the top of Goat Hill in fall, winter, and spring, but foliage obscures them in the summer. The southern end of the Goat Hill Trail Loop leaves the Tow Path Trail at the edge of an open field a few hundred feet north of the junction with Hartford Ave. The northern end rejoins the Tow Path Trail near Goat Hill Lock. The climb up Goat Hill is steep in places. From Hartford Ave., the total length of a loop trip over Goat Hill, including return via the Tow Path Trail, is 1.6 mi.

UPTON STATE FOREST (DEM)

This 2,660-acre woodland is located in the northeastern part of Upton, just west of the Hopkinton line. The main entrance (sign) is located at the junction of Spring St. and Westboro Rd. You can reach it by walking west on MA 135 from Hopkinton center, past the Whitehall Reservoir, then turning southwest onto Spring St. and following Spring St. 2 mi. to its end at Westboro Rd. To reach the forest entrance from the west, take MA 140 to Upton center, then turn north onto School St. or N. Main St. (in front of the Congregational Church). Continue 0.4 mi. to Pratt Pond (unmarked), where High St., Hopkinton Rd., and Westboro Rd. meet. Turn north onto Westboro Rd. and go 2.2 mi. to Southboro St. on the right (state forest sign). Refer to the USGS Milford quadrangle.

Whistling Cave Loop (DEM)

This trail has not been reblazed or maintained recently and may be difficult to follow. It begins opposite the parking area at the main entrance east of the gravel road. Follow the white-painted arrows downhill 0.3 mi. to a trail junction, then bear right. The trail soon becomes a road, then turns right off the road as indicated by the arrows. In 0.5 mi. some glacial boulders are piled against each other so that there is a cavelike passage between them known as Whistling Cave. Following the white arrows, the trail passes over a pine-needle carpet and emerges on a road near an intersection of three unmarked roads, where the white arrows stop.

The trail bears left (east) onto the second of these three roads. It bears left at the next road junction and right at the following road junction (unmarked). After about 0.3 mi. it turns left (northwest) off the road onto a path. It continues about 0.2 mi. and emerges from the woods near several woods roads, turning left. Almost immediately the trail turns right (northwest) onto Painted Valley Rd., a rough one-lane dirt road passable by car. After 0.8 mi. the trail makes a sharp left onto a path, continuing to a trail junction. The trail turns right at the junction, following the white arrows uphill to the parking area.

Whistling Cave Loop

Distance from parking area
   to return to parking area: 3.5 mi. (2 hr.)

Dean Pond Loop (DEM)

From the parking lot, walk in the main entrance of Upton State Forest, proceed east on the gravel road, and bear right at the first fork. The road proceeds along the summit of a ridge, then descends. The trail bears left onto Whistling Cave Rd. (unmarked) and continues to the north shore of Dean Pond (1.7 mi.).

The trail continues north along the road, then bears right at the first fork. At the next fork (unmarked) it bears right, following a lane used somewhat as a horse trail. At a gas line (marked by a high stake with orange marks) the trail bears right and follows the gas line path 1 mi. to Gore Rd. The trail turns right and approaches Dean Pond from the south. It goes left around Dean Pond, following the fishermen's paths back to the parking area.

Dean Pond Loop

Distances from parking area
    to Dean Pond: 1.7 mi. (50 min.)
    to return to parking area: 2.5 mi. (1 hr.)

BEARSDEN FOREST

Bearsden Forest is a recreation area under the supervision of the Athol Conservation Commission, off Bearsden Rd., which formerly connected Athol with South Royalston. The bridge over the Millers River was swept away by a flood many years ago and was never replaced. The farms along the northern end of the road have long been abandoned, and the fields and pastures have grown up to woods and bushes. Trails have been laid out and scenic vistas made. A descriptive map flyer is available on request from the Athol Conservation Commission, Town Hall, Athol, MA 01331. Also refer to the USGS Athol quadrangle.

To reach Bearsden Forest, take MA 2A (Main St.) in Athol to Athol Memorial Hospital. Bearsden Rd. is located approximately opposite the hospital and is marked by an Athol Conservation Area sign. Follow Bearsden Rd. to the end of the tar surface, then continue straight ahead on a one-lane gravel road (rough) for 0.4 mi. to a four-car parking area. A posted map nearby shows the trails and roads in the forest.

One suggested walk is as follows: Follow the trail marked with yellow paint blazes through pines to Big Round Top (0.5 mi., 15 min.). At the summit (1278 ft.) there is a picnic table and a 360-degree view of three states, including Mt. Grace, Wachusett Mtn. and Mt. Monadnock. Head northeast along a meandering trail, continuing past another picnic table at Warren Vista, left of the main trail. A short distance beyond, a cairn marks an alternate trail that goes about 100 yd. Bear left at the next signpost, in the direction of the Lawton Barway, leaving the yellow-paint blazes here. Turn sharply right at the next signpost, toward Old Stage Rd. Proceed downhill and cross Buckman Brook. Bear right along the 1799 Old

Stage Rd. and continue 1.1 mi. to Newton Reservoir, a small, attractive woodland pond that serves as a water supply for Athol.

Return via Old Stage Rd. to the trail to the Lawton Barway. Upon reaching the Lawton Barway intersection, turn right onto Old Bearsden Rd. for a 15-min. walk to Sheep Rock, bearing left at By-Pass Rd. and then passing through the rock cut. Bear left at the signpost for Sheep Rock. At Sheep Rock, a 12-ft. viewing tower overlooks the Millers River, B&M Railroad, and adjacent wooded hills. Return via this road and Old Bearsden Rd. to the parking area.

RUTLAND BROOK (MAS)

This wildlife sanctuary in Petersham and Barre consists of 1,480 acres and is maintained by the Massachusetts Audubon Society. It is operated in conjunction with the nearby Cook's Canyon Sanctuary, and some of the latter's summer camp programs are conducted here. To reach the sanctuary, take MA 122 5 mi. north of Barre Common. Just before reaching the bridge near Connor Pond, proceed east on the hardtop for about 100 ft. Bear left at the sanctuary sign, then continue 0.3 mi. to a parking area on the left.

One suggested walk is as follows: After parking, continue on the road past a cottage on the right. About 150 ft. along, turn left onto a trail that leads to a dam and House Pond. Cross the dam and go straight ahead about 200 ft. Turn right onto a path to Beaver Meadow. Turn left onto a path beside Rutland Brook and continue through a forest of big hemlocks. Then turn left onto the road to return to the main gate and parking area. The circuit is 1 mi. (30 min.). A trail map of this area is available from the Massachusetts Audubon Society.

HARVARD FOREST

Harvard Forest, a research and experimental forestry project maintained by Harvard University, is located in the town of Petersham. The headquarters are on the east side of MA 32, approximately 3 mi. north of Petersham center. Located in the forest is the Fisher Museum. The museum contains twenty-three spectacular models

portraying the history of the central New England forests, the silvi-
cultural practices developed at Harvard Forest for application to
local forest conditions, and certain allied functions of modern
forestry. Several trails crisscross the forest, including the Slab City
Loop described below. A map of the forest is available at the headquarters building.

Slab City Loop

This short trail through a portion of the Harvard Forest leaves MA
122 (Barre–Petersham Rd.) 4.5 mi. north of Barre Common. Parking is available on the east side of MA 122 at the "Harvard Forest
Boundary" sign. The trail enters the woods on the west side of MA
122, at first following an old blacktop road, then turning left after
about 350 ft. to follow white paint blazes. The trail turns right at a
cairn near the east branch of the Swift River. (A side trail on the
left leads to a lookout over the river.) The trail proceeds along and
above the river, passes through mature pines, and crosses a small
bridge before returning to MA 122. The parking area is about 800
ft. to the right.

Slab City Loop

Distance from MA 122 (Barre–Petersham Rd.)
    to MA 122 (loop): 1.3 mi. (35 min.)

SECTION 6
North and West of Boston

This section covers most of Essex and Middlesex counties in Massachusetts, stretching from the Atlantic coast north of Boston to the gently rolling terrain northwest and west of the metropolitan area. (Section 7 includes those parts of Middlesex County closest to Boston.) There are no summits of any significance in this area, but it does include parts of the Merrimack River and Charles River watersheds. Much of the region is still covered with woodlands or farmland, but development pressures have been intense as suburbanization extends outward.

BAY CIRCUIT TRAIL

The Bay Circuit Trail is a work in progress. The original concept was proposed by Henry M. Channing and by urban planner Charles Eliot 2d, both of The Trustees of Reservations, in 1929 as an outer "emerald necklace" (to complement Boston's urban "emerald necklace" of parks and open spaces, laid out by Frederich Law Olmsted in the nineteenth century). It would link parks, open spaces, and waterways in a grand arc around the Boston metropolitan area from Plum Island in the north to Kingston Bay in the south. The Massachusetts legislature enacted legislation creating the Bay Circuit Program in 1956. In 1985, the Massachusetts Department of Environmental Management was directed to provide planning and acquisition funds to designated cities and towns in the Bay Circuit corridor. Interested citizens, town officials and representatives of private land-protection organizations attended regional meetings and raised public awareness of the Bay Circuit program. Land acquistion, funded by a bond issue in 1985, included Bay Farm in Kingston and Duxbury, the southern terminus of the Bay Circuit Trail.

The Bay Circuit Alliance (BCA) was founded in 1990 with the

assistance of the National Park Service Conservation Assistance Program. The goal of the BCA is to establish a trail, for passive recreation, connecting green space from the south of Boston in Duxbury and Kingston, to the north of Boston in Newbury and Ipswich. The trail will traverse up to fifty communities in the broad corridor between MA 128 and I-495. It will be between 170 and 200 miles long when it is completed. The trail itself is a new concept that reinforces the original idea of land preservation and connected green space.

The BCA is best described as a partnership of organizations and individuals, public and private. BCA's membership consists of local, regional and statewide member organizations and individuals. The BCA helps local communities establish their portions of the Bay Circuit Trail through planning and technical assistance on route identification, land protection issues, and trail management and construction.

The development of the Bay Circuit Trail is the largest trail project being undertaken today in Massachusetts, and volunteers are needed in all of the Bay Circuit communities to help make it happen. Volunteer activities include trail mapping and description (including history and natural history), trail location, trail clearing, clean-up and maintenance, bridge building, contacting landowners for permission, identifying and aiding in the protection of green space, leading walks and more. At present, 90 miles of trail in sixteen communities have been dedicated, thanks to the efforts of hundreds of volunteers in these towns.

If you are interested in joining this effort, contact the Bay Circuit Alliance at 3 Railroad St., Andover, MA 01810 (tel. 508-470-1982).

THE BAY CIRCUIT ROUTE

In the north, the Bay Circuit Trail starts as two branches: one begins at the Merrimack River in Newbury, and a second starts at Crane Beach in Ipswich. The two branches join to form one trail in the middle of Willowdale State Forest in Ipswich. At present, the dedicated trail for the Newbury branch starts in Rowley, and the dedicated trail for the Crane Beach branch starts in Hamilton.

Newbury

The proposed trail in Newbury starts at the former Sportsman's Lodge, where it joins the Merrimack River Trail. The trail will connect the Spencer-Pierce-Little House (Society For the Preservation of New England Antiquities) and the Old Town Hill Reservation to the proposed trail in Rowley. There are superb views of the salt marsh and surrounding terrain north to Maine from the top of Old Town Hill.

Rowley (0.25 mi. of dedicated trail)

The proposed trail in Rowley begins at the Newbury town line on Old Rowley Road. The trail will connect the extensive salt marsh in this area to the historic district through to Ipswich near Prospect Hill. The summit of Prospect Hill can be reached by a water department right-of-way. It provides views of the town, the Parker River Wildlife Refuge, and the ocean beyond it. At the end of Prospect St., the dedicated trail extends to the Rowley–Ipswich boundary.

Ipswich (4.85 mi. of dedicated trail)

The Newbury branch in Ipswich connects town conservation land to Willowdale State Forest at the Doyon Elementary School on Linebrook Road. In the middle of Willowdale State Forest, this branch will join with the proposed route from Crane Beach. The trail through the state forest provides a long unbroken hike through the woods between Linebrook Road and US 1.

Hamilton (5 mi. of dedicated trail)

The trail now starts at the stone monument in the Appleton Farms Grass Rides. It passes through the Bradford Conservation restriction area, Pingree Farm, and Bradley Palmer State Park. There is a trail guide available from the conservation commission at the town hall.

Willowdale State Forest (5.15 mi. of dedicated trail in Ipswich, Boxford, and Rowley)

The trail connects Bradley Palmer State Park to Willowdale State Forest, where it will join with the Newbury branch of the trail.

After crossing US 1 into the Hood Pond Block of Willowdale State Forest, the trail connects to the Georgetown–Rowley State Forest. (See Willowdale State Forest.)

Rowley (1.1 mi. of dedicated trail)
The trail goes through Georgetown–Rowley State Forest to the Rowley–Georgetown line, where it crosses I-95 on a pedestrian overpass.

Georgetown (1.3 mi. of dedicated trail)
The trail enters Georgetown after crossing I-95, and leaves the state forest at Pingree Farm Rd. It follows Pingree Farm Rd. to MA 97, where it enters Boxford.

Boxford (7.86 mi. of dedicated trail)
The trail passes through the Boxford Historical District, then connects to the Bald Hill Reservation and Boxford State Forest, before entering North Andover at a parking area at the end of Sharpner's Pond Rd. (See Bald Hill Reservation.)

North Andover (4.75 mi. of dedicated trail)
The trail leaves Boxford State Forest, following Sharpner's Pond Road, then crosses Route 114 and connects to Harold Parker State Forest. The trail proceeds through Harold Parker State Forest and enters Andover at Berry Pond Road.

Andover (12.4 mi. of dedicated trail)
After crossing Berry Pond Rd. the trail connects many of the extensive parcels of the Andover Village Improvement Society and town conservation land in Andover. It links the Skug River Reservation to the Hammond Reservation, and then to the Charles W. Ward Reservation. Holt Hill in the Ward Reservation provides excellent views as far as the Boston skyline. The trail crosses MA 125 and enters onto Phillips Academy land, and then to the Purdon Reservation. The trail connects to the Indian Ridge Reservation, West Parish Reservation, and the Doyle Link, and then crosses over I-93 and I-495. It then enters the Harold R. Rafton Reserva-

tion, and connects by way of a water department right-of-way to the Deer Jump Reservation, which parallels the Merrimack River. The Bay Circuit Trail joins the Merrimack River Trail here, and proceeds to the Andover–Tewksbury line, where it branches again into two separate routes. (See Andover Village Improvement Society: Indian Ridge, Harold Rafton, and Deer Jump Reservations; Charles W. Ward Reservation.)

Tewksbury, Lowell, Chelmsford, Westford, Carlisle, Acton

The Lowell branch passes through Tewksbury along the Merrimack River to the Lowell Heritage State Park and Lowell National Historic Park, then on city roads to the former Wang Building (now Cross Point Towers) where it passes under MA 3 and I-495 on the abandoned Lowell Secondary railroad line. The route then proceeds through Chelmsford, Westford, and Carlisle via the proposed Bruce Freeman multi-use bike/pedestrian trail, and leaves the abandoned rail line about 200 yd. inside Acton (where active railroad service exists). The route continues through Acton conservation lands and country roads to the Concord–Acton border. Community groups in Concord have considered several different ways to connect Acton to dedicated trail in Lincoln and Bedford, but this important connection is still conceptual.

Tewksbury, Billerica, Bedford

The Billerica branch would enter Tewksbury from Andover and pass through Tewksbury and Billerica on a combination of country roads, abandoned railroad lines, town water department, and state-hospital lands. In Bedford the route follows some existing trails before entering Concord, where it meets the Lowell branch.

Concord

The proposed trail would enter Concord from Carlisle and Bedford near the Great Meadows National Wildlife Refuge. It would link the refuge with federal, state and town conservation lands and parks, and then enter Lincoln at Walden Pond State Park.

Lincoln (3.2 mi. of dedicated trail)

The trail enters Lincoln from Walden Pond State Park in Concord. It proceeds, mostly by trail, through conservation land at Adams Woods and Mt. Misery, past the Sudbury River to Wayland at the Great Meadows National Wildlife Refuge. There is also a 2.3-mi. bicycle path that parallels the trail on Route 126.

Wayland, Sudbury, Framingham, Marlborough

The proposed route traverses a portion of Wayland via roads, farms, and various parcels of private and public open space, crosses the Sudbury River into Sudbury, and connects to Callahan State Park in Sudbury and Framingham through an abandoned railway line and various parcels of private and public protected land. The route then proceeds via Marlborough municipal lands to a junction with MDC Sudbury Reservoir property in the vicinity of Parmenter Rd. and Pine Hill Rd. on the Southborough border.

Southborough

The proposed route follows the Sudbury Reservoir and a series of major and minor roads to the eastern border of Southborough, where it crosses the Mass. Pike into Ashland on Oak St.

Ashland (9 mi. of dedicated trail)

A major portion of the trail traverses the Ashland Town Forest to Ashland center. From here it continues via road, cemetery land, and a trail along the Sudbury River to a point near the eastern border with Sherborn, where it utilizes a dike to cross wetlands into Sherborn.

Sherborn (10.6 mi. of dedicated trail)

Sherborn's section of the Bay Circuit Trail runs through the town in a crescent-shaped arc. The character of the trail varies from scenic overlooks of the Charles River to heavily wooded forest. It follows the edge of the railroad yard from the Sherborn–Ashland town line. The trail links the Barber Reservation to the Rocky Narrows Reservation by way a powerline right-of-way, roads, trails, and a pipeline right-of-way. It enters Medfield on Route 27 as it crosses the Charles River. For a comprehensive description and detailed trail maps of all the public land walks in Sherborn, the book *Sherborn Walks* is published by the Sherborn Forest and Trail Association and is available at the Town Hall.

For a description of the Bay Circuit route from Medfield to its southern end on the coast in Duxbury and Kingston, see Section 8.

Two detailed trail guides have been published which cover a 35-mi. stretch of the Bay Circuit from the Ipswich River in Willowdale State Forest, through Boxford, North Andover, and Andover, to the Merrimack River. These are *The Bay Circuit and AVIS Guide to Walks in Andover,* published by the Andover Trails Committee and the Andover Village Improvement Society, and *The Bay Circuit Guide to Walks in and Around Boxford,* published by the Boxford Bay Circuit Program Committee. They can be purchased at the AMC headquarters in Boston and at other retail outlets. As the trail develops, more detailed trail descriptions will be prepared for other areas and will also be included in future editions of this guidebook.

Some of the more popular sections of the trail are also described in greater detail later in this section, in conjunction with the parks and reservations through which the trail passes.

The standard trail marking adopted for the Bay Circuit is a white, vertical blaze the size of a dollar bill. Four-inch square Bay Circuit emblems will be placed at road crossings and trailheads. Where the trail is well trod and obvious, there are fewer blazes. Hikers should expect to find sections which have not yet been blazed to this standard.

DOGTOWN

The Dogtown area of Cape Ann, which occupies approximately 3 sq. mi. of undeveloped land between Gloucester and Rockport, was the site of an early village. In the 1600s it was "common land" where each settler in the village at the southern end of the Cape had rights for cutting wood and pasturing; thus it was known as the

Commons. When a village started to grow here in 1719, it was known as the Commons Settlement. About twenty-five houses were built here in the 1700s, but after the American Revolution the more prosperous families began moving to the coast, where opportunities for trade were better. For a time the houses were occupied by various poorer people, including widows of seamen, who kept large dogs for protection. After the last occupant was taken to the poorhouse in 1830, these dogs ran wild, hence the name Dogtown. The houses are long gone, but the cellar holes and wells are still visible along the Dogtown Circuit Trail, which follows the main roads of the settlement. The cellars are designated by numbers carved on nearby rocks.

The city of Gloucester owns much of the Dogtown area; some is privately owned. It is undeveloped, and the trails are mostly unmarked, but it is an interesting area for those who wish to hike on trails that have not changed much since the Colonial days. The lack of trash barrels makes it imperative that picnickers take their trash with them when they leave.

There is much in Dogtown to interest the naturalist as well as the historian and hiker. Most of Dogtown sits on a high, rocky moor, which includes a large terminal moraine as well as many isolated boulders (some of these have been carved with mottoes extolling various virtues). The area supports an abundance of birds, blueberry and bayberry bushes, red cedar, and many other varieties of plants and animals. For those who wish to know more about the history and natural history of Dogtown, *The Saga of Cape Ann,* by Elliot C. Rogers and Melvin Thomas Copeland, has an informative chapter on the subject.

To reach Dogtown and the beginning of the Dogtown Circuit Trail, take MA 128 to the rotary in Gloucester (exit 11). Turn left onto MA 127 toward Annisquam and continue 1 mi. to Reynard St. on the right, just after crossing the Mill River. Take Reynard St. until it ends at Cherry St. Turn left onto Cherry St. and drive for about 0.15 mi. until you reach the Dogtown Rd. turn-off (first right off Cherry St.), where a sign—"Welcome to Historic Dogtown"— marks the entrance to Dogtown Rd. Park where Dogtown Rd. forks and two gates bar cars, taking care not to block the gates. The left gate is the continuation of Dogtown Rd.; the right gate is the entrance to the Cape Ann Outdoor Range (gunshots are often audible). Refer to the Dogtown map included with this book. Hikers should be aware that development on surrounding properties and lack of routine trail maintenance in this area makes trail navigation a challenge.

Dogtown Circuit Trail

The Dogtown Circuit Trail provides a tour of the old Commons Settlement, passing most of the old cellar holes. It follows three of the original roads (Dogtown Rd., Wharf Rd., and Commons Rd.) of the quadrangle that made up Dogtown, then cuts back to Dogtown Rd. via a blacktop road along the reservoir, footpaths, and a short bushwhack of 100 ft. through thick brush. The fourth road of the original quadrangle, Back Rd. (now Cherry St.), has been almost obliterated by housing developments and a new reservoir.

From the parking area on Dogtown Rd., continue along the graveled, sometimes paved, road. As it emerges from the woods, with a large cleared area on the right, a gate straight ahead marks the end of the gravel. The road continues beyond the gate on a narrower track. (*Note:* There are large arranged rocks to the left of the gate; the bushwhack at the end of the circuit brings you to the clearing behind them.)

At 1 mi. (measured from the beginning of Dogtown Rd. at Cherry St.), the Cross-Dogtown Trail leaves to the left just before cellar hole 18, and shortly thereafter Granny Day Swamp is visible on the left. At 1.2 mi. the trail reaches Dogtown Square, where a low rock on the right is marked "D.T. SQ." Here the Beaver Dam Trail and the Tent Rock Trail turn right and the Dogtown Circuit Trail turns left onto Wharf Rd., a footpath. The circuit trail soon passes an old well on the right, and proceeds through close woods to a junction at 1.4 mi. Taking the right fork, the trail immediately passes cellar hole 24 on the right, and at 1.6 mi. it turns left onto Commons Rd. (To the right on Commons Rd. is the Whale's Jaw Trail, leading to Whale's Jaw and Briar Swamp). Running between two stone walls (the one on the right being more visible), the trail reaches cellar hole 36 on the left at 1.8 mi. The trail continues past cellar hole 34 on the right, a pine forest on the left, and a road that leaves to the left (leading to the Cross-Dogtown Trail). The Circuit Trail continues on Commons Rd. to its end at a blacktop road (for maintenance vehicles only) that circles the Goose Cove Reservoir (completed in 1963).

The trail turns left onto this road and follows it past gravel pits and over a hill. While descending the hill, the road flattens out twice for short stretches. The trail leaves the blacktop road to the left after the second flat section. The turn is marked with white letters on the pavement; a swampy pond is immediately visible on the right and on the left the ground is much higher than the path.

Keeping a concrete stream barrier on the right, the trail crosses laid-out flat stones and climbs the opposite bank, curving around to the right, where it shortly passes on the left a small cave formed by a car-sized rock perched on several smaller rocks. Running a few feet from a stone wall on the left, the path crosses this wall at a break where another stone wall comes in from the right, perpendicular to the wall on the left. The path swings downhill briefly before turning back to the right towards the wall it just crossed, which is now on the right. The path ends abruptly where the stone wall meets a wet area. By crossing the wet area on the stone wall and then bushwhacking 100 ft. at a slight angle to the left of the stone wall, you emerge into the clearing behind the row of arranged rocks, on the other side of which is Dogtown Rd. A right brings you back to the parking area and Cherry St.

Dogtown Circuit Trail

Distances from junction of Cherry St. and Dogtown Rd.

   to Dogtown Square: 1.2 mi. (50 min.)

   to Commons Rd.: 1.6 mi. (1 hr.)

   to Goose Cove Reservoir: 2.2 mi. (1 hr. 10 min.)

   to Dogtown Rd.: 3 mi. (1 hr. 30 min.)

   to Cherry St. (loop): 3.2 mi. (1 hr. 40 min.)

Cross-Dogtown Trail

This short, but pleasant trail crosses Dogtown Commons diagonally from Dogtown Square to Commons Rd., near the reservoir. In conjunction with the Dogtown Circuit Trail, it provides a scenic loop through the Commons Settlement area while allowing hikers to avoid the bushwhack at the end of the Circuit Trail.

The trail goes left off Dogtown Rd. just after cellar hole 17, which though not signed, is visible on the left. (Cellar hole 18 is very visible on the left side of Dogtown Rd., thirty paces beyond the Cross-Dogtown Trail junction.) The trail immediately crosses the remains of a stone wall, where a rock on the left is marked with a white blaze and a rock on the right bears traces of both blue and white blazes. The narrow—but definite—footpath rambles up and down over open, rocky terrain, reaching a stone wall at 0.16 mi. and continuing generally west until it goes downhill to an open field with a pine grove on the left. Keeping straight along the edge of the grove, the trail turns right across the field (where the trail from the blacktop reservoir road enters left from the pine grove) and bears left, reentering the woods. The trail follows a grassy road, passing through larch and pine woods on either side, and then bears right onto a woods road, continuing on to Commons Rd.

Cross-Dogtown Trail

Distance from Dogtown Rd.

   to Commons Rd.: 0.4 mi. (15 min.)

Whale's Jaw Trail

This trail leads from the Dogtown Circuit Trail to Whale's Jaw, an interesting (if somewhat hard to find) rock formation. Parts of the trail are obscure and may be difficult to follow; novice hikers might prefer the Pool Hill Circuit as an alternative route to Whale's Jaw.

The trail begins on the Dogtown Circuit Trail at the junction of Wharf Rd. and Commons Rd., 1.6 mi. from Cherry St. Where the Dogtown Circuit Trail turns left onto Commons Rd., the Whale's Jaw Trail goes right (east) and then north, continuing up and down over fairly open land and past Peter's Pulpit, a large rock formation. At 0.5 mi. it follows a sign (painted on a large rock) pointing to Whale's Jaw. (*Note:* This rock might be obscured by foliage in the summer.) The trail continues through the woods until it comes out in the open just before reaching Whale's Jaw.

Whale's Jaw Trail

Distance from junction of Wharf Rd. and Commons Rd.
   to Whale's Jaw: 0.8 mi. (20 min.)

Beaver Dam Trail

The starting point of this trail is the Babson Museum, a restoration of an early cooper's shop which is open only in the summer. To reach the Babson Museum, take MA 128 to the traffic light at exit 10 in Gloucester. Turn left onto MA 127 and drive 1.7 mi. to the Babson Museum on the left, 0.3 mi. beyond the Rockport town line. Parking is available here.

The Beaver Dam Trail, marked with red blazes, begins behind the museum. Branching to the right from the dirt road leading to the museum's parking area, it crosses the railroad track. (*Caution:* a bend in the track limits visibility to the right.) It then enters the woods and crosses a brook on stone slabs. Turning left onto a dirt road, the trail runs parallel to the railroad for 300 yd. before again crossing the brook. The trail turns right and follows the brook upstream. The path rapidly becomes smaller and can be hard to follow, but red blazes on trees are frequent. The path crosses the stream twice on its way uphill, and then leaves it to cut diagonally left across the hillside, reaching the top about 0.3 mi. after leaving the dirt road. At the crest is an open rock slab with three large boulders. The trail continues through undulating scrub forest, turning right at an intersection with a larger trail marked with faint blue blazes. This becomes a dirt road, leading to the Beaver Dam Trail's end at Dogtown Square.

An interesting circuit from the Babson Museum of about 3.6 mi. combines the Beaver Dam Trail with the Tent Rock Trail and the Old Rockport Rd. (below). The recommended direction is counter-clockwise, as the Tent Rock Trail is easier to follow leaving Dogtown Square than the Beaver Dam Trail.

Beaver Dam Trail

Distance from Babson Museum
   to Dogtown Square: 1.4 mi. (45 min.)

Tent Rock Trail

The Tent Rock Trail is noted for the many boulders on which mottoes extolling various virtues were carved in the 1920s. For lack of any other trail markers, these rocks serve as landmarks. If you are arriving on Dogtown Rd. from the southwest, locate Granny Day's Swamp, around which the road makes a sharp left-hand bend. Just before this point, a rocky dirt road lined with ruined stone walls branches off to the right. Follow this road 0.1 mi., to where the Tent Rock Trail bears right and the Beaver Dam Trail leaves to the left. (*Note:* If you arrive via the Beaver Dam Trail, the Tent Rock Trail will branch from the left side.) The Tent Rock Trail is wide at this point, and a large rock engraved with "STUDY" can just be seen about 100 ft. to the south. If you are in doubt, explore turnoffs until this landmark is found. Once past "STUDY" ("BE ON TIME" is on the rear of the same rock) the trail becomes a definite footpath over flat terrain strewn with many large boulders—one particularly large boulder requires a short side trip to view its message of "SPIRITUAL POWER." After "INDUSTRY" and "INTEGRITY" the woods begin to close in and the trail descends past "KINDNESS". After crossing a couple of small undulations, and passing "LOYALTY," "COURAGE," and "WORK," the trail descends to "TRUTH" and enters a former sandpit on the shore of the Babson Reservoir.

Here the trail passes around the tip of the reservoir to the railroad track. Part of the reservoir is located on the far side of the track and this section of the water forms an obstacle to a direct crossing. Turn right and follow the railroad track past the end of the reservoir on the left. (*Caution:* This track carries commuter trains between Rockport and Boston. Service is frequent in both directions, even on weekends.) After another 50 ft., a gravelly path rises up and forward on the left. Follow this path into the woods, passing numerous branchings and Tent Rock itself ("SAVE," along with "GET A JOB" and

"HELP MOTHER"). If you take a generally uphill route, you will have little difficulty in reaching the trail's end at the Blackburn Industrial Park. The radio mast on the hilltop at the industrial park can be seen from open areas and helps in navigation.

To reach the trailhead at this end, enter the industrial park off MA 128, and at the end of the entrance road, take an immediate left. The first few yards of the trail follow an old dirt road which leads around the side of the radio tower enclosure, before beginning the descent to the railroad and the reservoir.

Tent Rock Trail

Distances from Dogtown Square
  to Babson Reservoir: 1 mi. (30 min.)
  to Blackburn Industrial Park: 1.4 mi. (45 min.)

Old Rockport Road

The Old Rockport Road is an overgrown woods road running generally northeast from the vicinity of the Blackburn Industrial Park to MA 127 south of the Babson Museum. Most hikers will be hiking this route as part of a circuit with the Tent Rock and Beaver Dam Trails.

The route begins on the Tent Rock Trail where the railroad track is followed in a southwesterly direction across the end of Babson Reservoir. As soon as you reach the end of the water, turn left to reenter the woods on a woods road, walking about 0.2 mi. to the Old Rockport Road proper. Turn left onto the road, which takes an attractive and mostly level route through the woods, with occasional swampy areas. Two turnoffs to the right lead up Railcut Hill, but these are not recommended, as the old bird sanctuary has been replaced by a quarry. At about 1 mi. the woods road ends at a gate just off MA 127. From here, a trail runs parallel to MA 127 about 100 yd. from the road, ending at 1.2 mi. at the Babson Museum parking area.

Old Rockport Road

Distances from Tent Rock Trail (Babson Reservoir)
  to Old Rockport Road proper: 0.2 mi. (10 min.)
  to MA 127: 1 mi. (40 min.)
  to Babson Museum: 1.2 mi. (50 min.)

Pool Hill Circuit

This loop trail allows the closest approach to Whale's Jaw by car. It also goes over one of the highest hills on Cape Ann and skirts the edge of Briar Swamp. To reach the starting point of this circuit, take MA 127 past the Babson Museum into Rockport. Just after MA 127 makes a sharp turn left, it passes the railroad station. The second left after the station is Squam Rd. Follow Squam Rd. uphill, bearing left at the fork. After the pavement ends, the road makes a sharp left. Straight ahead is a barrier. Park along the road. The trail starts beyond the barrier.

The trail begins as a woods road, reaching a junction with the Quarry St. Circuit at 0.3 mi. It turns left at the junction and following double dot blazes, reaches Whale's Jaw at 0.8 mi. Here the Quarry St. Circuit leaves to the right, while the Pool Hill Circuit continues south. At 1 mi. it turns left at a trail junction toward Briar Swamp; the Whale's Jaw Trail leaves to the right at this junction heading toward Dogtown. The trail passes a path on the left at 1.2 mi. and turns right (southeast), proceeding through birch and beech woods and over a cement dam. After the dam, the trail turns left and is marked by single orange dots. This portion of the trail skirts the southern end of Briar Swamp, reaching a fork at 1.8 mi. The trail bears left at the fork and, now marked by orange and blue dots, leads across a stone wall at 1.9 mi. and becomes a woods road which comes to an intersection with another road at 2 mi. The trail turns left (east) onto this road and follows it to another road. The trail turns left onto this road and proceeds up Pool Hill (227 ft.). The trail then descends very steeply past huge boulders to Squam Rd. Turn left on Squam Rd. to return to the original starting point.

Pool Hill Circuit

Distances from Squam Rd.

    to Whale's Jaw: 0.8 mi. (20 min.)

    to Pool Hill summit: 2.3 mi. (1 hr.)

    to Squam Rd.: 2.5 mi. (1 hr. 10 min.)

    to return to beginning (loop): 2.7 mi. (1 hr. 20 min.)

Quarry Street Circuit

This trail begins on Quarry St. in Bay View, on the western side of Cape Ann. You can make a circuit from Quarry St. to Whale's Jaw and back or to Squam Rd. in Rockport, using this trail in conjunction with the Pool Hill Circuit. This trail intersects many other trails and woods roads, so follow the description very carefully. A compass is helpful if you make a wrong turn.

To reach Quarry St., take MA 128 to exit 11, then take MA 127 toward Annisquam from the rotary. Follow MA 127 (Washington St.) past Annisquam to Bay View, where Quarry St. exits right just past the fire station (3.7 mi. from MA 128). Follow Quarry St. 0.6 mi., going straight ahead at the fork where the pavement ends. The trail starts on the right of this road 0.1 mi. after the pavement ends.

The trail starts as a faint path but becomes more distinct as it enters the woods and turns left in front of a large rock. It continues uphill and downhill, passing a stream at 0.3 mi. The trail keeps heading south, past woods roads on both sides, reaching a gate to private land at 0.5 mi., where a stone farmhouse is visible to the right. Here the trail turns sharply left and at 1 mi. comes to a fork branching left (east) and right (south). The trail bears left onto a woods road and proceeds past an overgrown trail on the right. The trail heads generally northeast, up and down, past a path on the right and a trail on the left.

After passing the top of a knoll with many large boulders and small pine trees, the trail bears left (east) at another fork at 1.4 mi. In about 50 ft. the trail turns right (southeast), bears left at the next fork, then turns right at another fork at 1.8 mi. (Left leads to a quarry.) Almost immediately the trail meets the Pool Hill Circuit just after a boundary stone marking the Rockport line. (Straight ahead, the Pool Hill Circuit leads to Squam Rd in Rockport.) The Quarry St. Circuit turns right here and continues on to Whale's Jaw in tandem with the Pool Hill Circuit.

At Whale's Jaw, the trail leaves the right (west) side of the rock formation, heading north through pretty woods of pine, oak, and birch. It descends to a brook where there are many large ferns and a huge beech tree, goes uphill, then descends to a woods road at

2.5 mi. The trail turns left onto the road, passes a wide trail on the left at 2.5 mi., and continues straight ahead on a wide but rocky path. It passes through a stone wall at 2.6 mi., keeping left where a faint trail bears right at 2.7 mi., and in about 150 ft. reaches a wider road running northwest to southeast. The trail turns left onto the road, descends steeply, and reaches the edge of the farmland with the stone farmhouse straight ahead (2.8 mi.). The trail turns right (east) here, in about 100 ft. bears left at a fork, and returns to the starting point on Quarry St. (*Note:* It is not recommended that this trail be followed in the reverse direction because it is difficult to find the trail to Whale's Jaw when going in reverse.)

Quarry Street Circuit

Distances from Quarry St.
> *to* Whale's Jaw: 2.1 mi. (1 hr. 10 min.)
> *to* return to beginning (loop): 3.3 mi. (1 hr. 40 min.)

RAVENSWOOD PARK (TR)

This 300-acre wooded reservation, located in the Magnolia section of Gloucester, was founded by Samuel Sawyer in 1889—one of the very first examples of private land conservation in America. Now a property of The Trustees of Reservations, it includes rocky hills and swampland covered with a mature open forest of birch, beech, oak, hemlock, and swamp maple. The park is located on MA 127 in Gloucester. From MA 128, take exit 14; follow MA 133 east for 3 mi. to MA 127. Go south on MA 127 for 2 mi.; the entrance and parking are located on the right.

A broad carriage road (closed to vehicles) enters the park from the main entrance and is intersected by an extensive network of narrow woodland paths. New trail markers are now in place.

Valley Rd.

Also known as the Gravel Rd., this broad carriage road runs north from the main entrance. It soon passes the southern end of the Ledge Hill Trail on the right. Shortly thereafter, the Swamp Path leaves to the left and a cut-off to the Ledge Hill Trail leaves right. At 0.3 mi.

another broad carriage road, the Ridge Rd., leaves right. At 0.5 mi. the Valley Rd. ends at an intersection with the Old Salem Rd.

Valley Rd.

Distance from entrance
   to Old Salem Rd.: 0.5 mi. (30 min.)

Old Salem Rd.

This trail begins on MA 127, about 0.3 mi. west of the main entrance. As there is no parking here, most hikers approach this trail via the Valley Rd.

The trail enters the woods north of MA 127 as a narrow footpath, and soon crosses the Swamp Trail (to the left on the Swamp Trail is the swamp, and to the right is the Valley Rd.). Shortly an unmarked link to the Swamp Trail is passed on the left. At 0.6 mi., the trail meets the Valley Rd. and continues straight (northeast) on the carriage road. To the right on the carriage road, the Valley Rd. trail leads back to the main entrance. Also at this junction is another link to the Swamp Trail, leaving east past an old cellar hole.

The Old Salem Rd. continues on the carriage road, past a trail junction where the northern end of the Swamp Trail leaves left and an unmarked link to Ridge Rd. leaves right. At 1 mi., another carriage road, the Evergreen Rd., leaves on the right, followed shortly by an unmarked link to the Evergreen Rd., also on the right.

At 1.6 mi., a stone with a plaque marks the former location of the old Hermit Shelter. At this point, the carriage road turns to the right and becomes the north end of the Evergreen Rd. The Old Salem Rd. reverts to a narrow path and continues straight. The Ledge Hill Trail departs to the right just before the Ravenswood property boundary. The Old Salem Rd. continues off the property and ends at MA 127 a short distance north of Hough Ave.

Old Salem Rd.

Distances from MA 127 (Western Ave.)
   to Valley Rd.: 0.6 mi. (20 min.)
   to southern end of Evergreen Rd.: 1 mi. (30 min.)
   to northern end of Evergreen Rd.: 1.6 mi. (50 min.)
   to MA 127 (Western Ave.): 1.8 mi. (1 hr.)

Other Trails

Several other, smaller trails bear off from the Old Salem Rd.

The Spring Trail leaves the Old Salem Rd. to the right almost immediately after the trailhead. It leads past a spring to the Ledge Trail (0.8 mi.).

The Swamp Trail leaves on the left between two boulders, 0.2 mi. from the trailhead. After traversing huge flat ledges, it descends the western side of the moraine to a large swamp filled with ferns in the spring and scarlet swamp maples in the fall. After crossing the swamp, the trail veers north for 0.5 mi. before rejoining the Old Salem Rd. by an old cellar hole (1.5 mi.). The swamp can be impassable in the spring but you can avoid it by taking a shorter trail which runs north along the western side of the moraine before rejoining the Old Salem Rd. by the cellar hole (0.8 mi.).

The Ledge Trail leaves the Old Salem Rd. directly opposite the south junction with the Swamp Trail. It winds its way northeast past Otter Pond, around boulders covered with evergreen ferns, between tall hemlocks and oaks, and past views over a quarry and Buswell Pond. It ends at the north end of the Old Salem Rd. (2 mi.).

Further up the Old Salem Rd. is the forked entrance to Ridge Rd., which leads northeast to connect with the Evergreen Rd.

HALIBUT POINT (DEM and TR)

Halibut Point in Rockport is Cape Ann's northernmost headland, originally called "Haul-about Point" by mariners heading to and from Annisquam to the southwest. The protected land on the point includes a 54-acre state park (DEM) and an adjoining 12-acre property of The Trustees of Reservations, and features a stretch of rock-bound coastline similar to that found farther north in Maine.

From the intersection of MA 128 and MA 127 in Gloucester, follow MA 127 north for 5.4 mi. and turn right onto Gott Ave., which leads to the public parking lot.

The state park is dominated by a large, abandoned quarry. In the early 1900s, stone blocks of up to 40 tons were moved from here with the aid of steam drills, four hoisting derricks, and a railroad system. The Great Depression, along with the shift in construction from cut stone to concrete, led to the end of quarrying in 1929. The main quarry is now flooded and the deep green water appears to invite swimming, but this is strictly forbidden due to the danger of submerged rocks and equipment. Another feature of the site is a concrete observation tower, which was part of Boston's defense system during World War II. A small museum is located in the park headquarters next to the tower.

Halibut Point offers some easy and well-marked walking trails leading to the rocky coast overlooking the Atlantic Ocean. Below the high-tide level, many tidal pools lie among the granite boulders; use caution as the rocks can be slippery. A consistent ocean breeze blows over the point, and from the top of the "grout pile" (waste stone heap), you can enjoy a view extending to Maine on a clear day.

MAUDSLAY STATE PARK (DEM)

This 450-acre state park is located on the Merrimack River in Newburyport. Formerly the Moseley estate, it includes woodlands and wetlands as well as landscaped areas, and is a popular spot for cross-country skiing in winter.

From I-95, take exit 57 (West Newbury, Newburyport) and follow MA 113 east for 0.5 mi. Turn left on Noble St. (at a cemetery), and then left at the end of Noble St. onto Ferry St. Bear left at a fork and follow Ferry St. for about 1 mi. to the park entrance on the left.

Two attractive walks are the Castle Hill trail, which leads to the highest point on the property and takes about an hour, and the Merrimack River Trail, which takes about one-and-a-half hours.

PARKER RIVER NATIONAL WILDLIFE REFUGE

The Parker River National Wildlife Refuge on Plum Island, in Newbury, Rowley, and Ipswich, is operated by the U.S. Department of the Interior's Fish and Wildlife Service. It includes a 7-mi. barrier beach and extensive salt marshes. The bird life, especially shore birds, is outstanding. The area is managed primarily as wildlife habitat; recreational use is limited accordingly.

To reach the refuge from the traffic light on MA 1A just south of the center of Newbury, turn right (northeast) onto the Plum Island Turnpike, continue 0.5 mi., and turn right (east) again. Proceed 2.3 mi. (passing the airport on the right) to a paved road on the right (south). Turn onto the paved road and enter the refuge in 0.5 mi.

The number of visitors is strictly limited; on busy days the entrance gate may close as early as 9 am. (*Note:* The gate closing applies to cyclists as well as those arriving by car.)

A road, part paved and part gravel, runs the length of the refuge. Various small parking lots provide access to boardwalks to the beach. The salt pans, just after lot 2, attract numerous and varied shore birds. At lot 4, the Hellcat Swamp nature trail traverses a series of boardwalks over the marsh, passing a bird blind and an observation tower. Other short trails are located at lots 5 and 6. The road ends at Sandy Point State Park, which includes more beach and a wooded hill.

The beach provides habitat for the piping plover and the least tern, highly endangered species whose vulnerability arises from nesting on the open sands. The beach is therefore closed during nesting season, from April 1 through about the third week in August. Current information about closings can be obtained from the Fish and Wildlife Service (tel. 508-465-5753).

Public access in the refuge is limited to the road, the beach, and the marked trails. Areas that are off-limits are clearly indicated by blue and white signs.

CRANE RESERVATION AND WILDLIFE REFUGE (TR)

The Richard T. Crane, Jr., Memorial Reservation and the Cornelius and Mine S. Crane Wildlife Refuge are properties of The Trustees of Reservations located in Ipswich and Essex. The properties include the Great House and landscaped grounds of Castle Hill, a 4-mi. barrier beach, extensive sand dunes and salt marshes, several islands, and the protected waters of the Castle Neck River and other streams that meander through the marshes. The area is known for its birdwatching and fall foliage.

From exit 20N off MA 128, take MA 1A north 8.3 mi. through Wenham and Hamilton, past the MA 133 intersection. Just before the right turn around the green in Ipswich center, turn right on Argilla Rd. and follow the signs to Crane Beach.

During peak season (Memorial Day to Labor Day), Crane Beach is a popular albeit expensive swimming beach. (Admission fees are lower for cyclists.) Summer weekends can be particularly crowded.

Two trails start from the right side of the beach parking lot: a short, well-marked nature trail, and a longer, less well-defined "low-impact" trail marked by posts in the dunes. You can make a pleasant round trip of about 5 mi. by following the posts up and down the dunes until you emerge on the bank of the Castle Neck River. (Exact location of the posts may change occasionally to minimize the impact of foot traffic.) At the river, turn left and follow the riverbank around the point to the barrier beach, and then follow the beach back to the parking lot.

(*Note:* This area is ecologically fragile. The dunes, which prevent the land from being engulfed by the sea, are held together by the long, connected roots of plants. Stay on the marked trail and do not walk along the crests of the dunes, slide down the dunes, or step on the vegetation.)

As in all coastal areas, hikers must be also aware of the dangers of Lyme disease (see Section 1 of this book).

BRADLEY W. PALMER STATE PARK (DEM)

This park, located in the towns of Hamilton and Topsfield, comprises 721 acres of old farmland and pastureland, now mostly wooded, extending south from the Ipswich River. Unmarked trails of various lengths total more than 20 mi. Horseback riders use them extensively as bridle paths as well as cross-country skiers and snowshoers. Willowdale Hill (196 ft.), known locally as "Moon Hill," provides a good view north from its grassy top.

To reach the main entrance and park headquarters, follow Ipswich Rd. in Topsfield 1.25 mi. east from US 1 (state park sign), and turn right on Asbury St. The park entrance is a short distance on the left. The eastern entrance off Highland St. in Hamilton is no longer open to cars.

Grassland Trail (DEM)

This trail begins on the paved road (closed to vehicles) leading northwest through a gate opposite the parking area. At 0.3 mi. the road curves left (heading toward the Ipswich River and the River Trail), while the Grassland Trail continues as a dirt road straight ahead. At a trail junction at 0.5 mi., the Willowdale Trail goes left (north) to a junction with the River Trail and the Fisherman's Trail at a footbridge over the Ipswich River, while the Bittersweet Trail goes right (south) toward Blueberry Hill. Shortly thereafter the Grassland Trail turns sharply right; the Winthrop Trail leads straight ahead from this junction 0.3 mi. to the Ipswich River, near Willowdale Dam and the remains of an old grist mill. (From the end of the Winthrop Trail, a return loop can be made via the Fisherman's Trail and the River Trail.

Heading south, the Grassland Trail passes a short side trail to the right leading to the open field atop Willowdale Hill. Passing several other trail junctions but continuing straight, it ends near the recreation area at the eastern end of the park.

Grassland Trail

Distances from park headquarters
  to Willowdale Trail: 0.5 mi. (15 min.)
  to Winthrop Trail: 0.6 mi. (20 min.)
  to recreation area: 1.4 mi. (40 min.)

WILLOWDALE STATE FOREST (DEM)

This 2,060-acre forest in Ipswich is composed of three separate areas, each of which consists of mixed conifer and hardwood growth scattered amid swamps and meadows. The smaller areas have no trails, but the large main area is traversed by a number of

easily followed, but unmarked, woods roads on high ground bordering and separating the eastern and western sections of Willowdale
Swamp, which occupies most of the central section of the area.

All the areas border on Linebrook Rd. in Ipswich, which crosses US 1 at a point 3.6 mi. north of the junction of US 1 and MA 97
in Topsfield. The small areas are on the right (north) and left
(south) of Linebrook Rd., 1.5 mi. and 2 mi., respectively, west of
its junction with US 1. The main entrance to the forest is through a
gate on the right (south) side of Linebrook Rd., 0.8 mi. east of US
1 and 100 yd. west of Howe St. A woods road goes right (south)
from the gate, reaches a fork at 150 yd., goes left, and continues to
a second fork, where the Willowdale Circuit Walk begins. (A right
turn at the first fork, continuing south at all intersections, leads to a
point on Gravelly Brook Rd. a few hundred yards north of where
Gravelly Brook Rd. joins Ipswich Rd. opposite the western
entrance to Bradley W. Palmer State Park.) Refer to the USGS
Georgetown quadrangle.

Willowdale Circuit Walk (DEM)

This walk begins 300 yd. south of the entrance to the forest at the
second fork in the woods road leading from the entrance. It turns
left (east) along a woods road, passes a woods road on the left
leading to Linebrook Rd., and, near a grove of red pines, turns
right (south) along another woods road that follows along a glacial
esker just north of Willowdale Swamp. The trail turns right (south)
along a dirt road, continues through a cornfield, and crosses a
causeway over a narrow neck of the swamp and Bull Brook, the
northeast outlet of the swamp. It continues east to a fork (dirt surface ends here) and follows a woods road right (south). (Going left
at the fork skirts the northern base of steep, twin-summited
Bartholomew Hill [184 ft.] and ends at Pine Swamp Rd., the eastern boundary of the forest.)

The trail continues south on the woods road and in 0.3 mi.
descends a bluff to a woods road on the right. (This 0.4-mi. road
connects the eastern and western parts of the circuit and can be
used to shorten the walk by 1.5 mi.). The trail continues south from

this junction, then turns right at a crossroads. (The woods road traveling northeast from here passes between the northern and southern summits of Bartholomew Hill. The woods road traveling southeast skirts the base of the southern summit. Both roads end at Pine Swamp Rd., 0.1 mi. apart.) The trail bears sharply right (west) along a 160-yd. causeway that crosses a narrow strip of swamp including Gravelly Brook (the south outlet of Willowdale Swamp), which between this point and the Ipswich River forms the eastern boundary of the forest.

The trail proceeds right at a fork to a grassy triangle, makes a sharp right turn (northwest), and soon bears right (north) at a wide triangle. (A left turn leads south to Gravelly Brook Rd., which in turn goes south to Bradley W. Palmer State Park.) The trail follows the woods road north between the eastern and western sections of the swamp, crosses the narrow northwestern end of Gravelly Brook, passes through a gravel pit, and reaches the western end of the shortcut. The trail then crosses an unnamed stream via a bridge and slightly more than 0.3 mi. farther north returns to the beginning.

Willowdale Circuit Walk

Distance from second fork in woods road
  to return to beginning (loop): 3.5 mi. (2 hr. 30 min.)

Bay Circuit Trail

The Bay Circuit Trail enters the Pine Swamp section of Willowdale State Forest on Topsfield Rd. in Ipswich, at the pedestrian bridge over the Ipswich River which connects the State Forest with Bradley Palmer State Park. The trail heads north, then northwest, then west, reaching Old Right Rd. at 1.5 mi. Turning left on Old Right Rd., the trail crosses US 1 and proceeds another 0.7 mi. on the road, at which point it turns right at a gate into the woods, entering the Hood Pond section of the state forest.

The trail heads west through the woods, reaching Rowley Rd. at 3.1 mi. Go right on Rowley Rd. for 0.2 mi., then turn left onto Linebrook Rd. for 0.25 mi. Here the trail turns right onto the Esker Ridge Trail, following a woods road northeast past a shrub swamp. The trail then climbs steeply to the top of an esker, and follows the ridge of the esker northeast to Boxford Rd. From here the Bay Circuit Trail goes right on Boxford Rd. for 0.1 mi. and turns left into Georgetown–Rowley State Forest.

Bay Circuit Trail

Distances from Topsfield Rd.

    to Old Right Rd.: 1.5 mi. (45 min.)
    to trail into Hood Pond Section: 2.5 mi. (1 hr. 15 min.)
    to Rowley Rd.: 3.1 mi. (1 hr. 35 min.)
    to Esker Ridge Trail: 3.6 mi. (1 hr. 50 min.)
    to Boxford Rd.: 4.8 mi. (2 hr. 50 min.)

IPSWICH RIVER WILDLIFE SANCTUARY (MAS)

This sanctuary, consisting of 2,300 acres of unspoiled woodland and marsh, is located in Topsfield and is owned and operated by the Massachusetts Audubon Society as a wildlife refuge and conservation education center.

From the intersection of US 1 and MA 97 in Topsfield, go east on MA 97 and turn left at the first street (Perkins Row). The sanctuary is located about 1 mi. on the right.

Trails are well-marked by numbered posts at junctions, keyed to a trail map available at the registration desk.

Swamp Marsh Edge

This circuit route combines parts of several different trails to provide an interesting and varied walk.

Proceed south from the sanctuary headquarters to post 6 and follow the Bunker Meadows Trail for 0.4 mi. along a stone wall, crossing Drumlin Trail at post 7. To the right is a wooden observation tower that offers a nice view of Bunker Meadows marshes, notable for its magnificent expanse of water lilies in the summer. Bunker Meadows Trail turns east to the Ipswich River. At post 10, continue northeast, picking up the South Esker Trail, which offers a resting bench with a view of Wenham Swamp and Fowler's Island. The South Esker Trail turns north through higher ground and ends at a wooden bridge (post 29). A few yards north a larger stone bridge with views of Mile Brook and Waterfowl Pond, often offers sightings of painted turtles and colorful dragonflies.

At post 30, follow the signs to Averill's Island. The Averill's Island Trail splits at post 32 and comes together again at post 34, with both branches heading north. At post 38, stay left to pick up the White Pine Trail, and follow this trail west to the Mile Brook Trail. Turn left (south) on the Mile Brook Trail, following the edge of a privately owned swamp (*Note:* The Mile Brook Trail may be very wet. Several paths to the right lead to the higher North Esker Trail, which can be used as an alternate route.) Both Mile Brook and North Esker Trails go south through forest to reach the stone bridge.

Cross the stone bridge and turn right at post 28 onto the Innermost Trail, a boardwalk through marshy woods that leads to a wide grass path back to the sanctuary headquarters.

PHILLIPS ACADEMY BIRD SANCTUARY

This sanctuary in Andover is especially beautiful in May and early June when the azaleas and rhododendrons are in bloom. Wild ducks and Canadian geese often land on the artificial ponds, and many birds inhabit the woods. The trails are well-maintained gravel roads. The sanctuary closes at 6 pm.

Circuit Trail

This trail begins in Andover at the end of Chapel Ave., just beyond the Andover Inn at the parking area beyond George Washington Hall. The trail leads straight ahead on a continuation of Chapel Ave. past Phillips Academy dormitories on the left and George Washington Hall on the right. The trail passes Stimson House on the right (sign) and enters the Moncrief Cochran ornamental memorial gate. Soon after passing through this gate, the trail leads through the right-hand door in the metal sanctuary fence. (*Note:* Be sure that the gate is securely latched after you enter. Dogs are not allowed in the sanctuary.) The trail proceeds up a path among rhododendron bushes. At the crest of a rise, it bears right at the fork.

A road soon enters left. This is the western end of a loop around two artificial ponds. The Circuit Trail continues straight ahead, crossing a bridge over a small brook in a short distance. It ascends a slight rise and passes the eastern loop road on the left. The trail continues straight ahead and soon reaches a log cabin at the crest of a hill. The trail continues on the road, which bears a sharp left downhill. It turns left at a fork at the foot of the first short descent, passes a trail on the right (a shortcut), and continues straight ahead. The eastern loop around the pond soon enters left. The trail then crosses a bridge over a pond outlet. Near the top of a steep rise, the western loop enters left. The trail bears right uphill and soon swings left, leading back to the crest of the rise.

PROPERTIES OF ANDOVER VILLAGE IMPROVEMENT SOCIETY (AVIS)

AVIS is an open-membership, private society that acquires and holds land in Andover for conservation and recreational purposes. All its lands are kept in a natural state and are open to the public under suitable regulations. Total holdings are about 1,000 acres, divided into twenty-two sections, nine of which are described in this guide. For information about the other sections and trails not mentioned here, contact the Andover Conservation Commission, 36 Bartlett St., Andover, MA 01810 (tel. 508-470-3800), or the Andover Village Improvement Society, P.O. Box 5097, Andover, MA 01810. AVIS maps are on sale at the town library and at many local stores. (*Note:* In the descriptions that follow, the I-93 exits cited are for travel heading north.)

ROCKY HILL RESERVATION (33.4 acres)

Part of the eastern section of this reservation is wetland, and the rest is hilly with rock outcrops. To reach the reservation, take I-93 to exit 41, then follow MA 125 east 2.9 mi. Just past the police barracks on the right, turn left and park west of MA 125 at the intersection with Gould Rd. Rocky Hill Rd. (unpaved) runs off of Gould Rd. diagonally across the reservation from southeast to northwest.

Two places in the reservation are especially worth visiting: some rocky cliffs and an interesting view of a deep valley. To reach the cliffs, follow Rocky Hill Rd. north for 750 ft., turn right onto a woods road for about 500 ft., then turn left up a short, steep slope, following the white blazes, to the upper part of Rocky Hill Rd. From here the trail gradually descends to a rocky knob with a good view into a deep ravine, and then continues on to complete the loop at the Gould Rd. parking lot. (Loop distance: 1 mi.).

VALE RESERVATION (46 acres)

Located between the commuter rail tracks and the Shawsheen River, this reservation consists of hillocks and wetlands. To reach it, follow I-93 to exit 42, then take Dascomb Rd. east. Turn right onto Clark Rd. and continue 0.5 mi. Turn right onto Andover St., cross the railroad tracks, turn sharp left onto Dale St., and continue to the end of the dirt right-of-way (no sign) where the reservation begins. You can park here.

The marked trail begins on the right (east) and continues to the Shawsheen River. After about 0.25 mi. the trail crosses over an elevated platform and splits. The right fork follows the west side of the river downstream and then rejoins the left fork. (The right fork may be impassable during wet weather.) The left fork heads north through woods and open fields into the Shawsheen River Reservation. (Loop distance: 2 mi.).

SHAWSHEEN RIVER RESERVATION (27 acres)

This reservation extends 0.5 mi. between the Shawsheen River and the railroad tracks. It is mostly woodland, with some grassy fields and some wetlands along the river. Take I-93 to exit 43, go east on Dascomb Rd. 1.3 mi., turn left on Andover St., and go 0.7 mi. to the Horn Bridge. Park just beyond the bridge in an open space on the right.

Walk under the bridge onto Central St. and enter the reservation on the right. The trail leads across a meadow. In 0.1 mi. a marshy brook traverses the field. Cross the small bridge near the railroad tracks, then follow the river past some large granite blocks. At 0.5 mi. a path diverges across the meadow (possible short loop) and the trail continues south to the Vale Reservation.

INDIAN RIDGE RESERVATION (33 acres)

This reservation includes open pine woods, an esker, a swampy wooded area, and an open field. It lies between Reservation Rd. on the west and Red Spring Rd. on the east, with signs at the entrances on both roads. Both roads start at the intersection directly opposite the Horn Bridge (see Shawsheen River Reservation), with Reservation Rd. running northwest and Red Spring Rd. running north. The entrance on each road is 0.1 mi. from the Horn Bridge. Several unmarked woods roads crisscross the reservation. About 800 ft. along the ridge near the reservation entrance is a plaque mounted on a large rock commemorating Alice Buck, whose efforts more than 70 years ago helped preserve these woods.

Bay Circuit Trail

The Bay Circuit Trail follows the Esker Trail across the reservation for a distance of about 1 mi. Beginning at the entrance on Reservation Rd. the trail goes northwest 0.3 mi. to ascend the esker. Continuing northeast about 400 ft., the trail reaches the end of AVIS property. It continues along the esker about 0.4 mi. on town property to a red paint mark on a tree beyond the last house on the left. The trail turns left, entering AVIS land abutting the housing development known as Colony East, descends a steep slope, crosses the marsh on an elevated platform behind the houses, and follows the eastern edge of an open field. It then enters another marsh, crosses over another elevated platform, and emerges on Reservation Rd. across from the entrance to Baker's Meadow Reservation. Turn right to stay with the Bay Circuit Trail; turn left to return to the Horn Bridge.

BAKER'S MEADOW RESERVATION (55.4 acres)

This bird sanctuary is remarkable for its migratory waterfowl. It consists of a marsh and a pond (good skating in the winter) along with a bordering strip of higher ground. The entrance is located on Reservation Rd., 0.8 mi. northwest of the Horn Bridge (where parking is available), opposite the exit from the Indian Ridge Reservation and the Esker Trail. The marked, 1.3-mi. trail begins at a sign for Baker's Meadow. It passes through hilly woods and then skirts the edge of a pond. At 0.7 mi. a marked spur trail on the right leads 0.3 mi. to Argilla Rd. The main trail, bearing left around the pond, crosses a dam and continues around the pond for 0.2 mi. It then leaves the pond, running 0.1 mi. northeast to Reservation Rd. It continues 0.3 mi. northwest on the road to the beginning. (*Note:* Heavy beaver activity in this area may cause sections of the trail to become flooded.)

Four Reservations Trail

This trail traverses the Vale, Indian Ridge, Baker's Meadow, and Shawsheen River reservations. Begin at the southern end of the Vale Reservation (see the description of the Vale Reservation for directions). The trail proceeds north along the Shawsheen River, leaves the Vale Reservation at the Horn Bridge, turns left under the bridge, then proceeds northwest on Reservation Rd. to the entrance to the Indian Ridge Reservation. It continues through this reservation on the Esker Trail, emerging on Reservation Rd. The trail crosses the road to the entrance to the Baker's Meadow Reservation and continues through the reservation to Reservation Rd. Crossing the road, the trail follows the Indian Ridge trail to the top of the slope. The trail then turns right and proceeds southeast to the entrance to the Indian Ridge Reservation. It turns left onto Reservation Rd. and continues southeast to the Horn Bridge. After passing under the bridge, it turns right into and through the Shawsheen River Reservation and crosses town land into the Vale Reservation. It continues across an open field and along the base of the railroad embankment to the beginning. The circuit is 6.3 mi. (4 hr. 30 min.)

HAROLD R. RAFTON RESERVATION (226 acres)

This reservation is bordered by High Plain Rd. on the west, I-93 on the east, and I-495 on the south and is bisected by a powerline right-of-way that runs from west to east. Most of the terrain is rocky woodlands. The western section is high and hilly, while the eastern section is low, including a marsh through which Fish Brook passes, from south to north. To reach the reservation, take I-93 to exit 44, then take Lowell St. east 0.3 mi. Turn left onto Greenwood Rd. and in 0.9 mi. turn left onto High Plain Rd. Cross over I-93 and I-495 and continue to the top of the hill. About 400 ft. beyond the top of the hill, an AVIS sign is mounted high on a tree on the right. Parking is allowed on the roadside.

Bay Circuit Trail

The Bay Circuit Trail follows a well-trodden path for 1.9 mi. through the reservation. It heads into the woods a few feet beyond the sign. At 0.2 mi. the trail turns parallel to a powerline, continues through a stone wall, and divides. The left branch passes under the powerline, enters the woods, and continues on fairly level ground. At 0.3 mi. it turns left, then descends about 1200 ft. to a wide water-line right-of-way running north and south. Cross Fish Brook on a bridge to the west of the right-of-way and continue 0.9 mi. to a field. Cross the field to the intersection of Chandler Rd. and River Rd. (To return by road to the starting point, turn left on River Rd., left on Forest Hill Dr., left on Cross St., and left on High Plain Rd.)

DEER JUMP RESERVATION (130 acres)

This reservation lies between River Rd. and the Merrimack River in West Andover. It contains two large wooded areas, each with a 0.3-mi. frontage on the river, connected by a relatively narrow strip of shore varying from about 60 to 400 ft. wide and 2.3 mi. long. Some of the terrain is hilly, with several small gullies and brooks.

To reach the reservation, take I-93 to exit 45, then follow River Rd. west 1 mi. Turn right onto Launching Rd. and park in the small parking area just past the second cul-de-sac on the left.

Bay Circuit Trail

The Bay Circuit Trail follows Launching Rd. from River Rd. and enters the woods through a stone wall opposite the parking area. It

follows the stone wall to the left, recrosses the stone wall, and proceeds down a gentle slope to the river's edge. Here it intersects with
the Merrimack River Trail at a small bridge crossing a tributary
stream. (A short distance to the right on the Merrimack River Trail
is the pond and pumping station at the outflow of Fish Brook. Eventually this trail will continue to Heritage State Park in Lawrence.)

The Bay Circuit Trail turns left onto the Merrimack River Trail,
which follows the river's edge upstream (south), crossing over four
more bridges. It then bears left up the side of a steep bluff and,
bearing right, continues on high ground. The slope at the right falls
off sharply to the river's edge. Continuing along the bluff, the trail
passes through a stand of hemlocks and birches and then passes
under a powerline, where there are good views across the river.
Shortly thereafter the trail reaches the end of the Deer Jump Reservation and traverses the St. Francis Seminary before reaching the
publicly owned Spaulding Reservation at the Andover–Tewksbury
town line. (*Note:* Through-hikers should request permission before
crossing seminary property.)

Bay Circuit Trail

Distance from Launching Rd.
>   *to* overlook at powerlines: 2.1 mi. (1 hr. 10 min.)
>   *to* Tewksbury town line: 2.7 mi. (1 hr. 25 min.)

THE GOLDSMITH WOODLANDS (131 acres)

This lovely tract bordering Foster's Pond is accessible directly from
MA 28, 0.1 mi. north of its intersection with MA 125. The major
trail, a former dirt road for summer campers, runs the length of the
reservation, with side trails to high points and views. Foster's Pond
lies north of the main trail. Just inside the reservation, there is a
posted map of all the trails, nearly 4 mi. of which are maintained.

CHARLES W. WARD RESERVATION (TR)

This reservation in Andover and North Andover is owned and
administered by The Trustees of Reservations. It includes Holt Hill

(420 ft.), the highest point in Essex County, and Boston Hill (385 ft.), separated by Cat Swamp. The reservation is an excellent place to see club mosses, ferns, and other flora. For the most part, the reservation paths pass through wooded areas, but the hilltops have some viewpoints of Mt. Monadnock and the Temple Hills to the west, southern Kearsarge to the northwest, and Boston and Great Blue Hill to the south.

Two reservoirs and a fire tower are located on the summit of Holt Hill. Also notice the solstice stones located in the northeast and northwest quadrants of the summit. These indicate the location of the sunrise and sunset on the horizon during the summer solstice. Likewise the stones in the southeast and southwest quadrants mark the location of the sunrise and sunset during the winter solstice.

To reach the reservation from I-93, take exit 41, go north on MA 125 for 5 mi., then turn right onto Prospect Rd. Trail information and maps are available at the parking area.

Bay Circuit Trail

This section of the Bay Circuit Trail begins on the north side of Prospect Rd., 0.2 mi. below the parking area. The trail heads northeast through wetlands. At 0.3 mi., it turns right at a trail junction. (Straight ahead leads directly through Cat Swamp.) The trail proceeds uphill for another 0.3 mi., reaching Prospect Rd. just below the summit of Holt Hill. Turn left and follow the paved road to the summit.

From the summit, the trail descends a winding path to the south, then turns east to intersect with Tucker Rd. Turn left briefly on Tucker Rd., then turn right to cross Conservation Commission property en route to the Hammond Reservation.

Bay Circuit Trail

Distance from Prospect Rd.
   to Holt Hill summit: 0.8 mi. (35 min.)
   to Tucker Rd.: 1.2 mi. (50 min.)

BALD HILL RESERVATION

Located in the towns of Boxford, North Andover, and Middleton, the Bald Hill Reservation is comprised of three adjacent, protected properties: Boxford State Forest, John Phillips Wildlife Sanctuary, and property owned by the Essex County Greenbelt Association.

To reach the forest, take I-95 to the Topsfield Rd. interchange. Follow Topsfield Rd. 1.3 mi. west to Boxford center and turn left onto Main St. Follow Main St. 0.3 mi. to Middleton Rd. Turn left onto Middleton Rd. and proceed 1.7 mi. to the Bald Hill Rd. entrance to the reservation.

A trail map is posted, and is also available from the Essex County Greenbelt Association, 82 Eastern Ave., Essex, MA 01929 (tel. 508-768-7241). Trail junctions are numbered and are keyed to the trail map. A volunteer group, Friends of Bald Hill Reservation, has been organized to assist with trail maintenance and land-use planning, and can be reached through the Greenbelt Association.

Bay Circuit Trail

The Bay Circuit Trail enters the reservation at the Bald Hill Road parking area on Middleton Rd. The trail follows the Bald Hill Road, a well-worn wagon road, for its entire route through the reservation.

Heading west through a locked gate at the parking area, the trail heads west past Crooked Pond, a popular birding area. It then turns south through some wetlands and circles the southern end of Bald Hill, a 247-ft. drumlin. (A side loop over the top of Bald Hill leaves right at junction 12 and rejoins the main trail at junction 10. At junction 11, the Sawyer Trail leaves to the left [south]).

From Bald Hill the trail heads generally northwest through some more wetlands and forest. After junction 8 it begins winding back and forth, finally passing an area cleared in the late 1960s for a proposed—but never built—anti-ballistic missile site. This section of the trail ends at a small parking area at the end of Sharpner's Pond Rd. in North Andover. From here the Bay Circuit Trail follows Sharpner's Pond Rd. southwest toward Harold Parker State Forest.

Bay Circuit Trail

Distance from Middleton Rd.
    to Sharpner's Pond Rd.: 3.5 mi. (1 hr. 55 min.)

Sawyer Trail

This trail begins at trail junction 11 on the Bald Hill Road and proceeds generally south along a wood road to Peabody St. in Middleton. This wood road is referred to as Thomas Rd. on most maps
and is a private drive into the Wissa Farm (formerly the Sawyer
Farm) at the Peabody St. end. The trail is not marked but is very
obvious for its entire length. Those wishing to use the trail at the
extreme southern end should request permission at the farm.

After leaving the Bald Hill Road, the trail passes a small burial
plot on the left at 0.25 mi., passes a narrow trail left at 0.35 mi.,
and then continues through fairly dense woodland to a junction
with a wood road on the right (dead end) at 1 mi. The trail continues straight ahead at this junction and passes another trail junction
on the left at 1.3 mi. After passing through some partially cleared
land, the trail reaches the Wissa Farmhouse and Peabody St., just
west of the Ipswich River.

Sawyer Trail

Distance from Bald Hill Road
    to Wissa Farm (Peabody St.): 1.6 mi. (50 min.)

WEIR HILL RESERVATION (TR)

This 192-acre property in North Andover, belonging to The
Trustees of Reservations, is bounded by Lake Cochichewick and
Stevens Pond. It includes 1 mi. of lakeshore frontage and 4 mi. of
woodland trails. The property is an ideal spot for hiking, cross-
country skiing, nature study, picnicking, and photography.

From exit 41 of I-91, travel north on MA 125 7 mi. to North
Andover. Continue on MA 125 through two traffic lights, then turn
right at the third light on Andover St. Go 0.7 mi., bearing right at
the fork, and continue one block past the Common to the old center
of North Andover. Go straight on Great Pond Rd. one block, pass

the white church on the left, then turn left on Stevens St. Continue
0.8 mi. on Stevens St. to the reservation entrance.

A detailed trail map is posted at the Stevens St. entrance as well
as at many of the trail junctions.

HAROLD PARKER STATE FOREST (DEM)

This 3,000-acre forest located in Andover and North Andover is
open for swimming, fishing, and hiking. Hardwoods abound, with
occasional patches of white and red pine. The waterways amid the
wooded terrain, and the abundance of birds and wildflowers, make
for scenic hikes. Most of the forest ponds are the result of dams
built in the 1930s.

The state forest is accessible from a number of roads, including
Middleton Rd. (where the forest headquarters is located); the eastern section of Harold Parker Rd. (which runs south from MA 114
in North Andover); and the western section of Harold Parker Rd.
(which runs east from MA 125 in Andover).

Stearns Pond Trail (DEM)

The Stearns Pond Trail is reached from a short trail that begins on
the east side of the eastern section of Harold Parker Rd., 0.3 mi.
from MA 114 or 0.8 mi. from Middleton Rd. Limited parking is
available at this end of the trail; no on-street parking is available at
the other trailhead on Marblehead St.

The trail begins as a gravel road (closed to vehicles) that enters
the woods, and leads to a footpath that follows the bank of a pond,
and then crosses a brook below a spillway dam. Shortly thereafter,
a second trail diverges left to a second dam.

The trail runs into a paved road, from which other roads lead to
a large parking lot, a swimming beach, and park headquarters. The
trail soon passes through another gate and reaches Middleton Rd.
Turning left on Middleton Rd., the trail re-enters the woods in
about 25 yd. (marked by a sign, "Upper Salem Pond Rd."). The
trail winds around, climbing slightly, until it reaches Salem Pond
and crosses a small footbridge over a narrow channel between
parts of the pond.

The trail now continues past another section of the pond on the left to a fork, where it bears left. In about 0.3 mi., the Salem Pond Rd. (also known as the Sudden Pond Trail) diverges left. The Stearns Pond Trail continues straight past this junction, winds and climbs for a short distance, then descends straight past Bradford Pond on the right, to its end at Marblehead St. A side trail that circles Bradford Pond diverges from the Stearns Pond Trail just before Marblehead St.

Stearns Pond Trail

Distances from Harold Parker Rd.

    to Middleton Rd.: 1.2 mi. (45 min.)
    to Sudden Pond Trail: 2.5 mi. (1 hr. 15 min.)
    to Marblehead St.: 3.5 mi. (1 hr. 45 min.)

Sudden Pond Trail (DEM)

This trail begins at the last fork in the Stearns Pond Trail, turning left at a sign marked "Salem Pond Rd." The trail soon skirts the southern end of Salem Pond, crosses a bridge over the pond outlet, and bears sharp right. Shortly after crossing the pond outlet the trail bends left and almost immediately forks, with both forks leading quickly to Middleton Rd. The trail turns right onto Middleton Rd. and continues past the North Andover–North Reading boundary sign and the Forest Riding Academy (both on the left). It proceeds southeast on Middleton Rd. and turns left onto paved Sudden Pond Rd. just past the riding academy. This point is located about 1 mi. southeast of the forest headquarters.

The trail follows Sudden Pond Rd. briefly, then turns right off the paved road where the road turns sharply left. The trail follows a woods road leading north and soon crosses the pond outlet. It continues along the shore and soon branches right and then turns sharply left. Soon it turns left onto a woods road, then left again at a large rock. It follows this side path back to Sudden Pond Rd. (*Note:* If you miss this path, just follow the shore of the pond and rejoin the trail on Sudden Pond Rd.) Continuing west, the trail passes a path on the right and almost immediately passes between two posts and emerges on Middleton Rd. at a point a short distance southeast of where the Stearns Pond Trail crosses Middleton Rd.

Sudden Pond Trail

Distance from fork
   to Middleton Rd.: 2.8 mi. (1 hr. 15 min.)

Brackett Pond Trail

The Brackett Pond Trail begins at the main parking lot on the western section of Harold Parker Rd., 0.3 mi. east of MA 125.

From the parking lot, walk east along Harold Parker Rd.; Collins Pond will soon appear on your left, and Field Pond on the other side of the road. Fifty yards after passing the partially submerged fish-stocking structure below the Collins Pond dam, turn left into a smaller parking lot and through the gate. This woods road brings you along the eastern shore of Collins Pond and then Brackett Pond. About 200 yd. along this road a trail leaves to the left, crossing between the two ponds on a scenic route that leads almost directly back to the starting point.

For a longer hike, continue north on the road along the eastern shore of Brackett Pond. Bear right at a fork leading away from the pond north on a woods road (Walker Rd.). (A left at this fork leads around Brackett Pond back to Harold Parker Rd.). You will soon reach a second fork; a left turn leads to another pond, while a right turn leads another 0.5 mi. to the trail's end at the forest boundary.

Brackett Pond Trail

Distance from parking lot
   to forest boundary: 1.4 mi. (45 min.)

NORTH ANDOVER TOWN FARM

The North Andover Town Farm, managed by the town's Conservation Commission, is located on either side of Dale St. between Appleton St. and Bradford St. Today it consists primarily of gently rolling woods with some wetlands, and is sometimes referred to as the town forest. The old stone walls running through the property are a reminder of the time when farmers attempted to scratch out an existence in the hardscrabble New England soil.

Two trails, each about 1 mi. long, extend east and west from Dale St. The Town Farm–Forest Trail begins at the large white barn with green doors on the south side of Dale St. Walk past the barn to an open baseball field, and follow the well-worn, grassy path into the woods. At about 0.75 mi. the trail passes a ropes course on the left. It ends on S. Bradford St., a dirt road extension of Bradford St.

The Purgatory Lane Trail begins on the north side of Dale St., at a fence about 0.25 mi. east of the white barn. It winds along scenic wetlands and swamps (although the trail itself is generally dry) and through woods. It ends a driveway (public way) leading to Carriage Chase, a small road off of Casstlemere. Part of this trail runs across private property and may be rerouted if the town is unable to purchase the land.

READING TOWN FOREST

The Reading Town Forest and Well Fields comprises 276 acres and is under the supervision of the Reading Town Forest Committee. One-hundred thousand red and white pines as well as some spruce, balsam, and scotch pines were planted by Boy Scouts and other townspeople beginning in 1930. The area includes several examples of hard woods and many fine eskers, and the proximity of the Ipswich River makes it a good place for bird watching. The forest is home for some great horned owls and numerous red fox and boasts many varieties of wildflowers, particularly the pink lady's slipper. In the winter, cross-country skiing and snowshoeing are excellent. There are several forest roads and short trails that lead off these roads. Most are easy to follow, and many are paint blazed.

To reach the forest, take MA 129 (Lowell St.) 1 mi. from Reading Square toward Wilmington to a traffic light. Turn right on Grove St. and continue 1.3 mi. (past the golf course) to Strout Ave. on the right. Follow Strout Ave. to the gate at the water plant. Parking is available on either side of Strout Ave. or, if the gate to the avenue is closed, you may park on the side of Grove St. Walk inside the gate at the water plant, turn right, and walk past the plant, taking the road to the right to a sign marked "Big Pine Trail." To get a trail map, send a self-addressed, stamped envelope to: Town of Reading Conservation Commission, 6 Lowell St., Reading, MA 01867.

Big Pine Trail

This trail uses unpaved roads and short trails marked with bright yellow blocks and arrows. It begins immediately behind the trail sign and follows the path along the ridge of an esker to an overlook of the Point One parking area (the Ipswich River is on your left). Here the trail doubles back (south) along a smaller esker (a road runs parallel below). After a short distance the trail drops to the road, crosses it, and continues south along an esker until it is intersected by a road. The trail drops down right to the road junction, then goes left (northeast) along the well-traveled dirt road. It continues past the "Old Council Ring" on the right and a pump-house on the left, emerging from the pines as the road descends to a fork.

On the right, the road continues to Scrub Oak Hill; ahead on the left is the Ipswich River and the site of an old swimming hole. However, the trail immediately cuts back into the pine woods to the southeast along a well-worn path. (Look carefully on your right for the two yellow arrows and the continuation of yellow markings.) After about 200 yd., just before reaching a woods path, the trail follows the Garden Club Trail left (east). It continues 30 ft., crossing a damp area, then goes right (southwest) at a fork on an esker until reaching its end (watch along the left of the esker for a wide variety of spring wildflowers and dogwood.)

From the esker the trail continues to be marked with yellow blazes. It goes through a wet area, then up another esker, following it until arriving at the top of a cliff overlooking the junction of the well-traveled road. The trail drops down to the road, turns right at the fork, and then turns immediately left at the next fork in the road. After about 0.1 mi. the road arrives back at the Big Pine Trail sign.

Big Pine Trail

Distances from Big Pine Trail sign
   to Garden Club Trail: 1.1 mi. (45 min.)
   to return to Big Pine Trail sign: 1.6 mi. (1 hr.)

WILLARD BROOK STATE FOREST (DEM)

Located in Ashby and Townsend, this 2,380-acre forest is hilly and rocky, with many large areas of mountain laurel. It is a scenic area, especially in the vicinity of Willard Brook. Trap Falls Brook, Trap Falls, and Pearl Hill Brook are other attractive features.

The trail network can be reached from the Damon Pond recreation area or the Pearl Hill Brook Pond recreation area. To reach Damon Pond from the junction of MA 119 and MA 124 in West Townsend, go 3.1 miles west on MA 119 and turn left onto Hosmer Rd. To reach Pearl Hill, follow MA 119 west from West Townsend. Almost immediately after passing MA 123, turn left on New Fitchburg Rd. and follow it 1.8 mi. to the recreation area. Parking, trail information, camping, swimming, and picnicking are available at both recreation areas; a parking fee is charged in season. Parking along the sides of the roads within the state forest is prohibited.

From Damon Pond, two main hiking trails are maintained by DEM which can be combined into an interesting 3-mi. loop. The shorter trail leaves Damon Pond and follows the south side of Willard Brook through hemlock forests. Leaving the brook, it climbs briefly, crosses two wet areas, and at 1.2 mi. reaches the Trap Falls Brook area and the forest headquarters on MA 119.

The longer trail leaves from the southeast corner of the Damon Pond picnic area (reached by a dirt road across from the Hosmer Rd. parking area), and begins to rise. The trail crosses some ledges, then bears left (northeast) through dense laurel. Lady's slippers and American chestnut shoots are visible here. At 0.8 mi., the trail turns left along a dirt road, passes a small pond on the left, and continues 0.4 mi. to a fork. The trail then turns left, proceeds 0.3 mi. to another fork, turns left again, and passes an abandoned dump on the left. At 1.8 mi. the trail reaches Willard Brook and MA 119 opposite the forest headquarters.

To return via the brook trail, turn west off the dirt road 0.1 mi. from MA 119. Distance around loop from Damon Pond: 3 mi. (1 hr. 40 min.).

The dirt road loop is also accessible from the Pearl Hill Pond area by following a woods road and a trail from Vinton Pond Rd., which intersects New Fitchburg Rd. 0.3 mi. north of the parking area. Follow Vinton Pond Rd. west (the trail is shortly joined by a second trail from Vinton Pond Rd. that is white blazed). The trail turns left (west) at a fork (right leads north to MA 119, approximately 0.5 mi. east of the forest headquarters) and continues to a water hole (the white blazes stop here). It continues northwest, bears left at the next trail intersection, and proceeds to a dirt road. The trail turns right (north) onto the road and continues to the forest headquarters for a circuit of 2 mi.

GULF BROOK AND HEALD'S POND

This is the most scenic area of Pepperell, lying in the western part of town and crisscrossed by a series of blue-blazed connecting trails. Refer to the USGS Townsend quadrangle.

Blood's Ravine Trail

This trail runs from Jewett St. to Shag Rock on the west shore of Heald's Pond over Pepperell Conservation Commission land. To reach the trailhead, take MA 113 northeast from its intersection with MA 119 near Pepperell. In 0.25 mi. turn left onto Shattuck St. and continue past Harbour St. to its end on Jewett St. Turn left (west) onto Jewett St. and follow it 0.6 mi. to a small pond or swamp on the left draining through a culvert into Blood's Brook on the right.

The trail begins 200 ft. east of the culvert at a sign marking the Blood Brook Ravine Conservation Area. Watch carefully for the yellow blazes that mark the trail, as the footpath is not well worn. Most of the trail is clearly blazed with yellow triangles, except for a section along the shore of Heald's Pond, which is marked with a few faded blue blazes.

The trail passes the foot of the highest rock face in Pepperell and meets Heald's Pond at the mouth of Blood's Brook. Here the trail turns left (north) and steeply upward to the face of Shag Rock, which slopes steeply down into the pond. Once over Shag Rock, the trail skirts the pond to its northern end on Heald St. (behind the Community Church on MA 113 in Pepperell center). Distance from Jewett St. to Heald St.: 1 mi. (est.), (30 min.).

Gulf Brook Trail

This trail leads through a gulf or gorge following the brook from Heald St. to Chestnut St. Although scenic, the hiking is difficult because you must make your own path along the brook by scrambling over rocks or fallen trees. Marked by occasional single blue blazes, the trail begins at Heald St. across from the end of the Blood's Ravine Trail. The trail follows a well-travelled cart path along the left (west) bank of the stream, which is littered with rocks and forest debris. The cart path ends after several hundred yards, passing on the left the almost-closed entrance to a pre-Revolutionary silver mine blasted out of solid rock. Several hundred yards farther on are the remains of a mill and dam in the middle of the gorge. The trail now crosses land owned by the Belmont Springs Water Company, and the walking becomes a little easier as it reaches its end at Chestnut St. Distance from Heald St. to Chestnut St.: 1 mi. (est.), (40 min.).

(*Note:* To the left on Chestnut St. is the start of the Jeff Smith Connector trail, which in turn leads to the Jeff Smith trail to Hollis, NH. The latter trail's crossing of the Nisitissit River may be difficult at most times of the year. The Jeff Smith trail is not described here as it is primarily a New Hampshire trail.)

GROTON TOWN FOREST

This area is in the southwestern part of Groton, generally northwest of Ayer. It includes Dead River, an old channel of the Nashua River through which the flow supposedly was from north to south during the glacial period. The forest includes numerous woods roads, which are good for hiking. Refer to the USGS Ayer quadrangle.

Nashua River Walk

To reach the trailhead, follow MA 2A for 1.1 mi. northwest of its junction with MA 111 in Ayer. Turn right (east) at an unmarked road just before the Nashua River. Continue about 200 yd. to a railroad crossing just before the state-owned Ayer Pheasant Farm. Park on the road. The trail follows the tracks to the left (northwest) under a powerline and across the river. (*Caution:* Watch your step as you cross the bridge. The crossing may be uncomfortable for people with a fear of heights.)

About 75 yd. after crossing the river, the trail turns right (northeast) and joins a woods road near the tracks. The trail follows the road on a winding but generally northerly course. The lower end of the trail affords views of the Nashua River on the right. (*Note:* Avoid taking any of the intersecting trails; follow the main trail, which is the widest.)

Continuing north, the trail passes an intersection marked by a utility sign. In a short distance is a bluff, with a view to the right of the old Dead River bed. The trail continues to an intersection marked with a Groton Town Forest memorial plaque to veterans of the "Great War." Here the trail turns into Town Forest Rd. and continues north to MA 225 (called W. Main St. or W. Groton Rd.). The trail turns right onto W. Main St., crosses the Nashua River, and turns right at a large brick gateway entrance to the private Groton School. Walk behind the gate and continue past a stone memorial to the Groton Hunt. The trail then bears right and follows a path along the river, heading south with the river on your right. At junctions stay to the right along the river. The trail ends at Richard's Boat House (owned by the Groton School). Distance from railroad crossing to Richard's Boat House: 3.3 mi. (1 hr. 40 min.).

WALKS IN THE VICINITY OF AYER

Walks may be started at Woodford of Ayer, the former Ayer Hospital on Winthrop Ave. (a brick building on top of the hill east of the village). To reach Woodford of Ayer from Main St. (MA 111), go north on Washington St., then east on Highland Ave. to its end.

Proceed south on Winthrop Ave. Woodford of Ayer is on the left. These walks visit Chapel Hill, Pingrey Hill, Snake Hill, and Tophet Swamp, the last being a deep gorge presumed to have been formed during the glacial period. They do not follow marked trails, so you must follow the directions carefully. Interesting variations of the walks described are possible with the aid of the USGS Ayer quadrangle. Take care when crossing private property.

Chapel Hill Walk

This walk begins in front of the Woodford of Ayer Nursing Home on Winthrop Ave. and ends at the corner of Old Ayer Rd. and Indian Hills Rd. in Groton. It goes north on Winthrop Ave. and continues generally north and uphill for 0.3 mi. through the woods to the Ayer water towers. The trail crosses the Ayer School grounds to the east, keeping right of all the buildings and left of the athletic field, then descends to Groton–Harvard Rd. The trail turns left onto Groton–Harvard Rd. (downgrade) and continues 0.3 mi. to the second powerline. On the right an obscure path ascends the ledges on the left side of the powerline. The trail follows this path about 500 ft., then goes left (leaving the powerline) on a good path to a big hay field with extensive views. (*Note:* Do not cross the hay field.) The trail goes northeast along the edge of the field next to the woods, then turns left onto Snake Hill Rd. and right onto Old Ayer Rd. It continues to the foot of the hill, turns right at the Chapel Hill sign, and continues 0.5 mi. to the top of the hill (view in all directions). The trail descends (no path) northeast to Indian Hills Rd. It turns left onto Indian Hills Rd. and continues a short distance to the junction with Old Ayer Rd. Distance from Woodford of Ayer Nursing Home to junction of Indian Hills Rd. and Old Ayer Rd.: 3.5 mi. (2 hr. 45 min.).

Snake Hill Walk

Follow the directions for the Chapel Hill Walk to Snake Hill Rd. This trail turns right onto Snake Hill Rd. then descends under a powerline to the telephone company's underground cable. It turns a sharp left and continues to the top of Snake Hill (view west). The trail follows the cable line 1 mi. to a woods road, turns right onto the road, and proceeds 50 yd. to Wright Rd. It turns right onto Wright Rd., and continues 0.5 mi. past several driveways on the left leading to cottages on Sandy Pond. At the end of Wright Rd. the trail turns right onto Snake Hill Rd., passes the Ayer Gun Club on the right, and continues to the powerline. After crossing a powerline, the trail immediately turns left onto a path and recrosses the powerline. Following the path blazed with metal triangles through the woods, the trail continues 0.5 mi. to a brook, crosses on a broken-down dam, then bears left along a meadow, proceeding uphill past Balance Rock. It turns left onto a woods road, which leads to Groton–Harvard Rd. The trail turns left onto Groton–Harvard Rd., proceeds to the first house, then turns right onto a winding woods road. Ascending, the trail makes a sharp left to avoid another woods road on the right. Near the top of the hill, this trail merges with the beginning of the Chapel Hill Walk. It passes a small swamp and turns right, then left onto Winthrop Ave., where the walk began. Distance from Woodford of Ayer Nursing Home to return (circuit): 3 mi. (1 hr. 30 min.).

TOWNSEND STATE FOREST (DEM)

This 2,713-acre forest lying generally north of MA 119 in Townsend has no developed recreational facilities, but abandoned roads and forest service roads offer good walking. Access to two of the trails described is from Dudley Rd. (formerly Old Back Rd.), which runs west from MA 13 (Brookline Rd.), 0.8 mi. north of Townsend center. Access to the other two trails described is from MA 12. Refer to the USGS Townsend and Massachusetts– New Hampshire quadrangles.

Barker Hill Trail

This unmarked trail in West Townsend (which should not be confused with Barker Hill Rd. shown on the USGS Ayer quadrangle) begins as a dirt road running west from MA 13 to Canal St. and crosses Old Turnpike Rd. 1.9 mi. west of MA 13. You can reach the junction by driving west on Dudley Rd. from MA 13 or by going north on Mason Rd. from MA 119 in West Townsend to Dudley Rd., turning left (east) onto Dudley Rd. and continuing across the railroad tracks.

From its head the trail goes west nearly to the railroad tracks and before reaching them turns right (northwest). After a short distance it turns right again (north) along a logging road maintained for about 1 mi. by state forest personnel. (A brook parallels the trail a few hundred yards to the west.) At the end of the logging road the trail becomes a path and climbs gradually through mixed hardwoods, rhododendrons, and high-bush blueberries until it peters out on high ground on the western side of Barker Hill, about 0.3 mi. west of the summit (752 ft.).

Barker Hill Trail

Distances from junction of Dudley Rd. and Old Turnpike Rd.
to logging road: 0.6 mi. (25 min.)
to western side of Barker Hill: 2.1 mi. (1 hr.)

Jeep Trail

This unmarked trail follows a former jeep road from the north side of Dudley Rd., 0.4 mi. west of MA 13. It climbs steadily northeast through birches and other hardwoods, crosses several plateaus, and eventually reaches an altitude of 600 ft. before ending at the New Hampshire line. For the first mile or more, the trail parallels a brook on the right (east), then crosses the brook as it turns toward the northwest. It is possible to reach the Foundation Trail from the brook crossing by bushwhacking east 0.5 mi.

Jeep Trail

Distance from Dudley Rd.
to New Hampshire line: 3 mi. (1 hr. 30 min.)

Fessenden Hill Trail

This unmarked trail follows an abandoned dirt road from the west side of MA 13, 1.3 mi. north of Townsend center. It runs north, passing an old CCC camp on the left (west) (where the Foundation Trail begins) and continuing parallel to the east side of a brook for several hundred yards before climbing to a new housing development on the western side of Fessenden Hill (650 ft.). The trail passes the New Hampshire line and continues north.

Fessenden Hill Trail

Distances from MA 13

   to old foundation and Foundation Trail: 1 mi. (30 min.)

   to New Hampshire line: 2 mi. (1 hr.)

Foundation Trail

This unmarked trail goes west from the Fessenden Hill Trail at an old foundation 1 mi. from MA 13. It can be reached by taking Dudley St. west off MA 13 for about 1 mi. The trailhead is on the north side of the street, opposite a nursing home, and is marked by three large yellow barrels. Parking is available on the north side of the street.

After a few hundred yards, the trail crosses a path heading southwest. The Foundation Trail continues north, passing a picturesque swamp with ferns and pine trees. After about 40 yd. the trail crosses two brooks. Another trail enters from the right and circles the swamp. The Foundation Trail heads north and uphill to an open summit about 500 ft. in elevation. It is possible to reach the Jeep Trail from this point by bushwhacking west 0.5 mi.

Foundation Trail

Distances from Fessenden Hill Trail

   to summit: 1.8 mi. (1 hr.)

ASHLAND TOWN FOREST

This town-maintained forest occupies a 2-sq.-mi. section of northeastern Ashland. It is bounded on the west by Oak St., on the north by Oregon Rd. and Salem End Rd. (the latter in Framingham), on the east by Myrtle St. and Badger Rd., and on the south by Winter St., on which the main forest entrance is located. To reach the entrance, start from the intersection of MA 135 and Main St. in Ashland. Go north on Main St. for about 0.5 mi. and bear right onto Myrtle St. After about 100 yd., turn left onto Pine Hill Rd. At the road's end, turn left onto Winter St. In about 200 yd. on the right is a sign marked "Ashland Town Forest." There is parking for about five cars at this entrance.

The main trail from this entrance is smooth and well maintained, having once been a fire road. It bisects the town forest for 1.5 mi. from Winter St. to Oregon Rd. (also a trailhead, but no parking available). The trail has many turns on slightly rolling terrain, rising gradually for the first two-thirds of the trail, and then descending gradually to Oregon Rd. It crosses three very small brooks. Eight unmarked side trails leave from the main trail to surrounding roads. At these trail junctions the main trail is marked by white blazes. The side trails are maintained, but they are rockier with steeper sections, so caution should be used. Side trails branching west from the main trail are generally less strenuous, although some are steep in places. Some of the trails branching east pass interesting rock formations and converge on top of Wildcat Hill (436 ft.). Refer to the USGS Framingham quadrangle. The main trail is excellent for cross-country skiing.

ASHLAND STATE PARK (DEM)

The chief attraction of this state park is the Ashland Reservoir. A trail skirts its wooded shore, offering interesting views of the water and shore as well as distant views of Ashland and the surrounding hills. The entrance to the state park is located on the south side of MA 135, 5.5 mi. southwest of the Ashland–Framingham line. During the winter the park gate is closed, but the reservoir dam is accessible via Metropolitan Ave. (the first left after the Main St. traffic light when traveling west on MA 135 in Ashland). Refer to the USGS Holliston quadrangle. Maps also are available from the DEM (see appendix).

Ashland Reservoir Trail (DEM)

White circles mark most sections of this trail, but all of it is well worn and easy to follow. The trail begins right of the park bathing beach, follows the shore south for a short distance, then cuts through a wooded area to the Ashland Girl Scout Camp. It crosses the camp area to the left of the main camp building and continues south close to the shore until it reaches a dirt road at the southern end of the reservoir. The trail then follows the dirt road left (east) across a bridge over an inlet to a boat-launching area, passes to the right of a small bathing beach, and continues north beside an old wire fence to within sight of the reservoir dam. The trail goes west across the top of the dam, turns left, and follows the shore south to the starting point at the beach.

Ashland Reservoir Trail

Distances from park bathing beach
    to Girl Scout camp: 0.5 mi. (20 min.)
    to inlet bridge: 1.2 mi. (35 min.)
    to dam: 2.5 mi. (1 hr. 20 min.)
    to return to beach: 3.2 mi. (1 hr. 45 min.)

SECTION 7
Boston and Vicinity

This section covers hiking areas in the immediate vicinity of the city of Boston.

BLUE HILLS RESERVATION (MDC)

The Blue Hills Reservation is located less than 10 mi. south of downtown Boston in the communities of Milton, Canton, Randolph, Braintree, Dedham, and Quincy. This mostly wooded, 7,000-acre reservation—under the jurisdiction of the Metropolitan District Commission—is the largest open space located within the inner metropolitan area. I-93 (MA 128) bisects the reservation. The larger, northern section includes a stretch of the Neponset River and the adjoining wetlands of Fowl Meadow; a series of wooded summits, the largest of which are Great Blue Hill (635 ft.) and Chickatawbut Hill (517 ft.); Houghtons Pond and several smaller ponds; and the Quincy Quarries historic site, now a popular rock-climbing locale. Ponkapoag Pond, the largest body of water in the reservationis the principal attraction south of the highway.

The reservation offers many outdoor activities in addition to hiking. Picnicking, fishing, boating, horseback riding, swimming, mountain biking, and rock climbing are all permitted in various parts of the park. In the winter, there is alpine skiing at the Blue Hill Ski Area on the western side of Great Blue Hill, ice skating at several ponds and artificial rinks, and cross-country skiing on many of the reservation trails and across the neighboring Ponkapoag golf course.

The Mass. Audubon Society operates two educational facilities within the reservation. The Trailside Museum on Blue Hill Ave. (MA 138), 0.5 mi. north of MA 128, is open to the public Wednesday through Sunday (tel. 617-333-0690). The Chickatawbut Hill Education Center offers workshops and programs for organized groups by reservation only.

The AMC's Ponkapoag Camp, on the east shore of Ponkapoag Pond, has cabins available for rent. Reservations are required; contact the AMC's Joy St. headquarters for information.

For the hiker, the reservation offers miles of trails, woods roads, and old carriage roads that can be combined into trips of varying lengths. Trail difficulty generally ranges from easy to moderate. A large network of trails has been re-marked in recent years. The new blazing system uses circles to indicate a loop trail, with the color of the blaze—yellow, green, or red—indicating easier, moderate, or more strenuous terrain. Rectangular blazes indicate one of the two major trails that traverse the park: the 9-mile Skyline Trail (blue blazes) and the 6-mile Massachuseuck Trail (orange blazes). Trail intersections have been marked with 4-digit numbers keyed to the MDC's Blue Hills Reservation map, which is posted at many trailheads. Blue diamonds denote trails recommended for cross-country skiing.

In addition to the marked trails, many older, unmarked paths beckon the adventurous. Although it is hard to become truly lost in the Blue Hills due to the proximity of roads and other major landmarks throughout the park, hikers on these paths will find a map and compass useful.

Trail information and maps are available at the Trailside Museum (see above) and at the reservation headquarters on Hillside St., behind the state police station. Also refer to the Blue Hills map included with this book.

Great Blue Hill Red Loop Trail (MDC)

This 1.2-mi. loop trail (red circles) is the most popular route for climbing Great Blue Hill. It begins at the bulletin board behind the Trailside Museum and heads generally east and then southeast. After crossing the paved Summit Rd., it becomes somewhat steeper and rockier. At the summit, the Eliot Tower offers views of the Boston skyline and the surrounding area. Descending, the trail heads northeast from the summit, takes a sharp left at marker 1082, and follows a pleasant woods path back to the museum.

Great Blue Hill Green Loop Trail (MDC)

This 2.8-mi. loop meanders through the Great Blue Hill section of the reservation. It generally follows the cols between the hills, never ascending to any of the summits.

It begins at the north parking lot at the Trailside Museum. Heading northeast, it soon reaches the paved Summit Rd., where it turns right and immediately bears left onto a dirt road, which heads east through a stand of tall white pines. At marker 1085, the loop proper begins, with the return trail coming in from the right. Continue straight on the road for a few hundred feet to marker 1100, where the trail turns left and runs northeast along the edge of some wetlands.

At marker 1135 the trail turns right and heads southeast through the col between Wolcott Hill on the right and Hemenway Hill on the left. At marker 1141, it crosses a dirt road and the Skyline Trail. Continuing southward, the trail circles Wolcott Hill and turns north through Wildcat Notch, which separates Wolcott Hill from Great Blue Hill. It passes two small swamps, and just after the second, the trail turns left and heads northwest to the dirt road where the loop began. Turn left onto the dirt road to return to the parking lot.

Houghtons Pond Yellow Loop Trail (MDC)

This easy, 1-mi. trail is a popular walk for families with small children. The trailhead is at the main parking lot for the Houghtons Pond swimming area. Take exit 3 north from I-93 (MA 128), turn right onto Hillside St., and turn right into the parking lot in 0.3 mi. There is supervised swimming here in the summer.

The trail proceeds to the left (east) past the beach, bearing right just after the bathhouse. It joins a dirt road for a short distance around the east end of the pond, and then turns right off the road just before reaching a playground. The trail continues along the southern edge of the pond, crosses the pond's outlet at the western end, and heads north past a field and playground. The trail then travels through a small swamp and bears left (east) up a hill past a pavillion to the starting point.

Houghtons Pond Green Loop Trail (MDC)

This 2.8-mi. trail begins at Houghtons Pond and circles (but does not ascend) Tucker Hill to the northeast of the pond. It begins at the Houghtons Pond beach parking lot, and follows the yellow loop trail along the north shore of the pond. After passing the bathhouse, the green loop bears left from the yellow loop, crosses the Massachuseuck Trail, then turns left and heads due north on an old paved carriage road. At marker 2070, the loop proper begins. Traveling clockwise, the trail leaves the paved road and continues north, crossing the Massachuseuck Trail again and then the Skyline Trail (which leads right up to the summit of Tucker Hill).

Circling around the north end of Tucker Hill, the trail approaches (but does not meet) Chickatawbut Rd., then heads south through Dark Hollow, recrossing the Skyline Trail and then the Massachuseuck Trail again. At marker 2096 it turns right onto a dirt road and heads generally west back to the starting point of the loop. Turn left at this intersection to return to the trailhead.

Ponkapoag Green Loop Trail (MDC)

This 3.9-mi. trail starts at the small parking area just south of exit 3 on I-93 (MA 128). It heads south for 0.3 mi. to a fire gate on the left, where the green loop trail splits, heading either east or west and returning to the same point. Traveling west (right), it follows a woods road for 0.4 mi. to the YMCA camp, where a mapboard and trail marker on the left indicate the entrance to the Ponkapoag Bog boardwalk. (Ponkapoag Pond is slowly drying up, and the bog represents the first stage in the pond's transition to what will eventually be dry land.)

From the YMCA camp, heading left (south), the trail proceeds along the eastern edge of the Ponkapoag golf course for 0.6 mi. to the fire gate at the end of the paved road leading from Blue Hill Ave. Turning left, the trail follows the south shore of the pond for 0.8 mi. to Fisherman's Beach, on the left, where there is a scenic view of Great Blue Hill. Continuing east through wetlands and then turning north, the trail passes the AMC's Ponkapoag Camp (reservations required). At marker 5365 it meets the

Massachuseuck Trail and follows it to the left for a short distance. At marker 5343 the Massachuseuck Trail bears right, while the Ponkapoag loop continues west on a bluff above the pond back to the starting point of the loop.

Skyline Trail (MDC)

This trail, marked by blue rectangular blazes, is the longest in the Blue Hills Reservation, extending from Fowl Meadow in Canton east to Wampatuck Rd. in West Quincy. You can access the trail from any one of four major streets: Blue Hill Ave. (MA 138), at a parking lot on the west side about 0.5 mi. south of the Trailside Museum; Hillside St., at the reservation headquarters; Randolph Ave. (MA 28), where the closest parking is about 0.25 mi. south of the trail crossing; and Wampatuck Rd., where the trail ends at a parking area opposite St. Moritz Pond.

Skyline Trail: Little Blue Hill section (MDC)

This section of the Skyline Trail was established in 1979. From the parking lot on Blue Hill Ave., the trail runs west through open woods along the south face of Little Blue Hill for 1 mi., to Green St. The Skyline Trail officially ends in this area. However, it is possible (with some difficulty) to continue on various paths in a generally northwest direction, skirting an abandoned highway interchange to reach Burma Rd. This 2 mi.-long dirt road runs north through the Fowl Meadow wetlands bordering the Neponset River, eventually reaching a parking area at the intersection of Brush Hill Rd. and Neponset Valley Pkwy.

Skyline Trail: Blue Hill Ave. to Hillside St. (MDC)

From the parking area on Blue Hill Ave., the trail leads 0.5 mi. steeply up the southwest side of Great Blue Hill to the circular road and bridle path at the summit.

From the top of Great Blue Hill, two routes, the North Skyline Trail and the South Skyline Trail, lead east, joining at the reservation headquarters on Hillside St. The longer, northern branch crosses Wolcott, Hemenway, and Hancock Hills, while the southern branch crosses Houghton Hill. Blue blazes mark both.

The North Skyline Trail begins at marker 1163, to the east of the stone tower on the summit of Great Blue Hill, at the north end of the stone bridge. It descends steeply to Wildcat Notch and the junction with the Great Blue Hill green loop at marker 1092. It follows the green loop left about 50 ft., then turns right across low ground and ascends the ridge of Wolcott Hill (470 ft.). It continues over the summit and down to a hollow, where it bears right for 50 ft., then left up a rise to the top of the ridge. The trail continues down the ridge to the Five Corners trail junction (marker 1141) in the Wolcott–Hemenway col, where it crosses the other side of the Great Blue Hill green loop. The trail goes straight across the junction and ascends, first gently and then steeply, to the ridge of Hemenway Hill. At 1.8 mi. the trail forks right over ledges with good views ranging from southeast to northwest. At 1.9 mi., the trail bears left across some ledges, then in 225 ft. it turns sharp right around a large boulder. It descends left to a small col, crosses an unmarked path, and ascends a rocky grade to the ridge of Hancock Hill (510 ft.). After crossing an old bridle path, the trail climbs a short rise to the summit of Hancock Hill. From the top, the trail descends more gradually near a ledge on the left (with good views) to meet a woods road, which it follows left to a gate. Turn right on a gravel path to the MDC stables. With the stables on the left, it continues on a paved driveway to Hillside St. and the junction with the South Skyline Trail.

At the summit of Great Blue Hill, the South Skyline Trail leaves east from the circular summit drive at marker 1066, about 200 yd. south of the stone bridge. The well-defined trail passes over ledges, with good views east and south. It descends Shadow Cliff via a steep, rocky path and continues on the right side of a wet-weather brook to a brook crossing on large stones. Continuing on the left side of the brook, it soon passes between large boulders. Leaving the brook, it crosses several unmarked trails and then ascends the slope of Houghton Hill. Crossing just south of the summit, the trail then turns right and descends steeply to Hillside St. Follow Hillside St. left (north) 200 ft. to meet the northern branch.

Skyline Trail: Blue Hill Ave. to Hillside St.

Distances from Blue Hill Ave.

    to summit of Great Blue Hill: 0.5 mi. (30 min.)

    to summit of Hancock Hill (via northern branch): 2.2 mi. (1 hr. 20 min.)

    to Hillside St. (via northern branch): 2.5 mi. (1 hr. 30 min.)

    to Hillside St. (via southern branch): 1.9 mi. (1 hr. 15 min.)

Skyline Trail: Hillside St. to Randolph Ave. (MDC)

This section of the trail starts at the junction of the North and South Skyline trails at the marker on Hillside St. across from the MDC stables. It bears right onto a well-worn woods road for about 400 ft., then turns left into the woods at marker 2054. It bears right up a slope, crosses several unmarked paths, and continues to the west ridge of Tucker Hill (499 ft.), where it turns left at marker 2097 and then turns right and proceeds through scattered pine trees (care needed here) to a ledge with fine views to the west and south. It continues along ledges and down a steep, rocky trail to the bottom of Dark Hollow. Next it bears left, then right; it crosses low ground and climbs gradually on a rocky trail, passing through a wooded section over the north ridge of Boyce Hill (404 ft.). Continuing eastward, the trail ascends a steep, rocky grade to the ridge of Buck Hill (496 ft.). From the summit, the trail plunges down a steep, rocky slope.

At marker 2210, the Massachuseuck Trail enters from the right, and together the two trails continue down the hillside to Randolph Ave. (MA 28).

Skyline Trail: Hillside St. to Randolph Ave.

Distances from Hillside St.

    to summit of Buck Hill: 1.9 mi. (1 hr.)

    to Randolph Ave. (MA 28): 2.2 mi. (1 hr. 10 min.)

Skyline Trail: Randolph Ave. to Wampatuck Rd.

After crossing Randolph Ave., the Skyline Trail quickly reaches a pipeline right-of-way, where the Massachuseuck Trail turns left. The Skyline Trail follows an easy route to a hemlock grove, where it turns right onto a bridle path. It continues through the grove about 100 ft. to marker 3042, where it turns left and proceeds up Chickatawbut Hill (517 ft.) on a steep, rocky path. It bears right at the top of the ridge and turns left into the woods within 100 ft. Soon ascending another steep ledge, the trail bears right uphill. At the top of the ledge, the trail ascends gradually into the woods and over more ledges, passing a large puddingstone boulder on the left. The trail skirts the summit of Chickatawbut Hill, then descends into Slide Notch Path, climbs back up over Kitchamakin Hill, then down again over stone steps to Sassaman Notch. (Local rock climbers call the large boulder here the Grepon.)

From Sassaman Notch, the Skyline Trail turns right for 50 yd., then turns left and follows the blue blazes up some stone steps. At the top of the steps the trail turns right, away from an intersecting trail, and ascends steeply to the ridge of Nahanton Hill, following ledges to the summit (480 ft.), where there are good views north and south. The trail bears right through scrub oak and over open ledges, some of which offer views of South Shore Plaza. The trail descends gradually through the Broken Hills and across several cols with short steep descents and ascents until it reaches a fence around the Blue Hills Reservoir.

The trail follows the fence to the right some distance, then proceeds over more ledges to Chickatawbut Rd. It crosses the road at a trail marker post, and at the Wampatuck Hill marker post it goes right up the slope and over the ledges of Wampatuck Hill (353 ft.), providing views of Boston and the bay. The trail turns right along ledges south of the summit (an unmaintained trail to the left leads to the summit) and continues along the rim of a cliff with views of South Shore Plaza and Braintree Great Pond. The trail descends into scrub oak at the end of the ledges and soon crosses an MDC pipeline.

After crossing the pipeline, the trail descends and bears to the left. After 40 yd., it turns right up a steep, rocky trail to Rattlesnake Rock. Bear left to skirt a smooth ledge near the top of Rattlesnake Rock. At the top, the trail turns right and crosses a trail to the right that leads to the top of Rattlesnake Rock and many views. The

Skyline Trail descends rock steps, crosses an old trail, climbs briefly, and continues over a ledge and boulders to an old quarry. It continues around the quarry to a gravel path, which it follows to the right for about 140 yd., then forks left. It soon forks left again into pines and oaks, and after some distance reaches an old woods road, which it follows to the right a short distance to Wampatuck Rd.

Skyline Trail: Randolph Ave. to Wampatuck Rd.

Distances from Randolph Ave.

  to summit of Chickatawbut Hill: 0.7 mi. (20 min.)
  to summit of Nahanton Hill: 1.3 mi. (35 min.)
  to Chickatawbut Rd.: 2.1 mi. (1 hr.)
  to Wampatuck Rd.: 3.3 mi. (1 hr. 35 min.)

Massachuseuck Trail

This 6-mi. trail extends from Chickatawbut Rd. in Milton, on the reservation's northern boundary, to Reed St. in Randolph, on the southern boundary. Although the name and routing are new, for the most part it follows sections of trails which have long existed under a variety of other names. It is much less strenuous than the Skyline Trail, tending to skirt rather than climb the hilltops. It passes through a wide variety of habitats, with much of interest to the observer of natural history.

Orange rectangles blaze the Massachuseuck Trail. It follows part of the route of the old Great Dome Trail, which is no longer maintained under that name.

The northern trailhead is at a parking area on Chickatawbut Rd., just east of its intersection with Randolph Ave. (MA 28). The Massachuseuck Trail heads south on a woods road in concert with a red loop trail. After a few hundred yards, the Massachuseuck Trail bears right off the road onto a pipeline right-of-way, while the red loop trail continues on the road circling around Chickatawbut Hill. The pipeline heads due south through a marshy area for about 0.5 mi., reaching an intersection with the Skyline Trail. At this intersection the Massachuseuck Trail turns right and runs in concert with the Skyline Trail a short distance to Randolph Ave.

Continuing west, the Massachuseuck Trail diverges left from the Skyline Trail about 500 ft. from Randolph Ave. Heading southwest, the trail slabs around the south side of Buck Hill and then descends to the west into Doe Hollow. At the bottom of the hollow it turns left onto a woods road, and then turns right off the road at marker 2137.

Heading west, the trail climbs through the col between Boyce Hill and Burnt Hill, then descends into Dark Hollow, where it crosses the Houghtons Pond green loop at marker 2094. The trail now climbs over Breeze Hill (295 ft.). (An unmarked trail near the summit leads north to the summit of Tucker Hill.) From the top of Breeze Hill the trail descends steeply to a second crossing of the Houghtons Pond green loop. Here the Massachuseuck Trail turns south and continues to descend toward Houghtons Pond, crossing the green loop for a third time just before reaching the playground at the western end of Houghtons Pond.

At the playground, the Massachuseuck Trail joins with the Houghtons Pond yellow loop, following it south and then west along the pond's shores. The Massachuseuck Trail then bears left away from the yellow loop and in a short distance reaches a paved road (the old MA 128, now a park access road). Turning right on this road, the trail reaches Blue Hill River Rd., which it follows to the left across an overpass over I-93 (MA 128).

On the south side of the overpass, the trail passes the parking lot at the trailhead for the Ponkapoag green loop. The two trails run together for a short distance, then the Massachuseuck Trail bears left and heads southeast, rejoining the Ponkapoag loop just above the north shore of the pond. The two trails again run together for a short distance. At marker 5365, the Massachuseuck Trail bears left, while the green loop bears right toward the AMC Ponkapoag Camp. The Massachuseuck Trail runs east over level terrain to MA 24, which it crosses via a horse bridge. Shortly thereafter it turns south and follows a woods road, emerging at the parking lot of the Margaret J. Donovan School on Reed St. in Randolph.

Massachuseuck Trail

Distances from Chickatawbut Rd.
  to Randolph Ave.: 0.6 mi. (20 min.)
  to MA 128, exit 3: 3.1 mi. (1 hr. 40 min.)
  to Donovan School: 5.1 mi. (2 hr. 40 min.)

Quarries Footpath (MDC)

This 1.5-mi. trail in the northeastern corner of the reservation leads to the abandoned granite quarries in the Quincy Quarries Historic Site. It begins at the small parking area on Wampatuck Rd. opposite St. Moritz pond, which is also the eastern trailhead of the Skyline Trail. The Quarries Footpath traverses varied and at times rugged terrain. It passes over private as well as public land, so stay on the marked path which is blazed with white rectangles.

Heading northwest into the woods from Wampatuck Rd., at 120 yd. the trail takes a sharp left (northwest). (Note the house with a stone foundation above.) The trail goes gently up a slope through mature woods for 0.25 mi. At this point the trail bears right (north) and gets steeper. (Note old stone foundations on both sides of the trail left over from quarrying days.) The trail then takes a sharp left (northwest) up onto exposed ledge (some scrambling will be involved).

At the top of the hill is a trail intersection, 0.44 mi. from Wampatuck Rd. This intersection is at the top of Bunker Hill Quarry. There are many scenic vistas in this area, and there is much archaelogical evidence of the old granite industry. Views to the west are of the Blue Hills, to the south Quincy Shipyard, and to the east Boston Harbor.

The trail proceeds to the right (east) over rough, rocky terrain. At 100 yd., at the top of the ledge portion of Bunker Hill Quarry, are the best views south and east. The trail continues downhill, then to the left (north) for a short distance, then up over an old road bed. This is at the top of the timber run of the old Granite Railway terminus. (Note the wall of abandoned Berry's Quarry in the distance to the northeast.)

The trail now takes a sharp right (northeast) across a construction area for 0.25 mi. until it meets Ricciuti Drive. Swingle's Quarry lies directly across the street behind a chain link fence. Two points of interest along this part are a spur trail on the right at 0.1 mi., which goes to the Granite Railway terminus, and Berry's Quarry at 0.15 mi. on the left.

The trail follows Ricciuti Drive to the left (west) for 0.2 mi. to the Quincy Quarries Historic Site sign. The trail now takes a right (northeast) into the woods and proceeds 0.1 mi., up a grout pile to a Granite Railway Quarry overlook, with stunning views into the quarry. The ledges up to the left (northwest) afford spectacular views of Boston Harbor and the Boston skyline. Many remains of the granite industry are visible in this area.

Backtrack the trail for a few yards, then take a right fork and walk 50 yd. to stone steps on the right. Go down the steps (north) to water level. Follow the trail around the left (west) side of the quarry. On the left (west) 0.1 mi. from the Granite Railway Quarry overlook is Little Granite Railway Quarry, which is popular with rock climbers. Continue straight on the trail, until it starts heading down a slope (north). At 25 yd. from that point the Quarries Greenbelt Trail branches off to the left (west); it goes to Lyons Turning Mill past numerous other abandoned quarries. The Rim Trail to the top of little Granite Railway Quarry is also down this path.

Keep heading straight down the hill for 120 yd. until you reach the top of the Granite Railway Incline, which offers more views of the Boston skyline. Walk to the bottom of the incline for historical information on this site.

STONY BROOK RESERVATION (MDC)

The MDC's 400-acre Stony Brook Reservation is located between the West Roxbury and Hyde Park sections of Boston, crisscrossed by a network of easy—although generally unmarked—hiking paths. Although none of these paths can be considered major hiking trails, what makes Stony Brook notable is that it is probably the largest publicly owned, undeveloped forest preserve within the city limits. As such, it provides Bostonians with the chance to do some easy forest walking without traveling farther. Despite its location,

Stony Brook is relatively unknown. Visitors are unlikely to encounter the crowds normally found at other urban parks.

Stony Brook Reservation is located on both sides of the Enneking Parkway (formerly the Turtle Pond Parkway). The section to the east of the parkway is the larger of the two, and includes such points of interest as Stony Brook itself, Turtle Pond, and some excellent examples of glacial drumlins. On the east side of the reservation is Bald Knob, a rock outcrop with good views of Hyde Park and the Blue Hills. At the northeast tip of the reservation, at the corner of Washington St. and the West Roxbury Pkwy., is Bellevue Hill, the highest point in Boston. At one time this summit afforded an excellent panoramic view, but in recent years the view has become all but obliterated by trees.

There is some limited parking along Enneking Parkway, although the parking areas may be closed at times due to MDC budget cutbacks. There is always parking available at the recreation complex at the very south end of the parkway, although this requires a short walk to reach the undeveloped part of the reservation.

BOSTON HARBOR ISLANDS STATE PARK

The Boston Harbor Islands State Park encompasses an area of 50 square miles in and around Boston harbor, including 180 miles of shoreline and 30 islands with an area of over 1,200 acres. The area is comprised of the inner harbor, into which the Charles River, the Mystic River, and Chelsea Creek empty; and the outer harbor, which includes Hingham Bay, Quincy Bay, and Dorchester Bay. The Neponset River, the region's other major waterway, drains into Hingham Bay.

The harbor islands have experienced many commercial and public uses over the past 350 years, including forts, prisons, hospitals, lighthouses, sewage plants, a firing range, an airport, and even a glue factory. As some of these older uses faded, efforts began to convert some of the islands to recreational uses, which in turn led to the establishment of the state park.

Boston Harbor Islands State Park is managed jointly by the state's Department of Environmental Management (DEM) and the Metropolitan District Commission (MDC). As of this writing, the islands are being considered for inclusion in the national park system. Information is available from the rangers on Georges Island and from the DEM and MDC. Another excellent resource is the nonprofit Friends of the Boston Harbor Islands (tel. 617-523-8386), which has played an important role in promoting the preservation and recreational use of the harbor islands.

Just a few years ago, the harbor islands were virtually unknown to most of the general public. But as more attention has been paid to all of our long-neglected waterfront and harbor resources, the harbor islands have been rapidly growing in popularity. Today, some of the more accessible islands can attract significant crowds on warm summer weekends. To avoid the crowds, visit at other times or seek out some of the lesser-known islands.

Most of the islands have easily-followed walking paths, and many have interesting abandoned fortifications and historical ruins. Care should be taken, as these ruins, as well as the rubble left from other past uses, can create some hazards for walkers.

Most of the islands can only be reached by boat. Private ferry service is available in season to Georges Island from downtown Boston and other locations. Free water taxi service is available from Georges to several other islands.

Among the islands currently open for public recreation are:

Great Brewster Island (23 acres). Has one of the highest and most weathered hills in the harbor islands. Storm damage to the pier limits access by boat. Camping is permitted with DEM permit.

Middle and Outer Brewster Islands (12 and 17.5 acres, respectively). Originally used for agriculture, but because of impressive sea cliffs, often used for defense. No marked trails; bushwhacking is common. Access by private boat only.

Lovells, Gallops, and Georges Island (62, 16, and 28 acres). These islands have piers, picnic areas, guided walks, restrooms, and refreshments. All are accessible by ferry and water taxi. Georges Island has access for physically challenged visitors.

Rainsford Island (11 acres). Located in Quincy Bay between Long Island and Peddock's Island. As there is no pier, access is only available at a small cobblestone beach. Trails are grass-covered paths.

Peddock's Island (113 acres). Formed by five glacial drumlins. Includes old military fortifications, privately owned cottages, plus a nesting area for black-crowned night herons. Trails include old military roads plus newer trails cut during the past decade.

Raccoon Island (3 acres). A small, poison ivy-infested knoll close to Hough's Neck in Quincy, just off Rock Island Head. It can be accessed on foot at low tide or by private boat.

Sheep Island (2 acres). A small bar located between Peddocks and Grape Island in Hingham Bay.

Grape, Slate, and Bumpkin Islands (50, 12.4, and 35 acres). Reachable by private boat. Grape and Bumpkin have camping areas; reservations required.

WHITNEY AND THAYER WOODS RESERVATION (TR)

This property of The Trustees of Reservations in Hingham and Cohasset comprises 817 acres of gently rolling glacial woodland with some marshy areas, brooks, and huge glacial boulders (erratics). More than 12 miles of cart paths and foot trails weave through a hemlock-pine-hardwood forest with scattered American holly trees. Clusters of azalea and rhododendron bushes bloom in the spring next to wildflowers and ferns. Stone walls running throughout the woods mark much of the land as having once been farms and pasture. The property contains a stretch of Brass Kettle Brook and a portion of Great Swamp. Turkey Hill, a 187-ft. high glacial drumlin, offers a view of Cohasset Harbor. The trails are open for hiking, cross-country skiing, and snowshoeing. The property abuts the 3,500-acre Wompatuck State Park.

The entrance to the reservation is on MA 3A opposite Sohier St. in Cohasset, 2 mi. south of the junction of MA 228 and MA 3A. Numbers in the descriptions below refer to numbered trail junctions. Detailed trail maps can be purchased at the service station across from the entrance on MA 3A.

Howe's Rd. (TR)

This dirt road forms the base of the trail system on the south side of the reservation. It starts at the north side of the parking lot and goes southwest, ending at a wire fence that marks the boundary of Wompatuck State Park. At 0.3 mi. there is a private home on the left. (*Caution:* Beware of the dogs, which are chained.) Distance from parking lot to wire fence: 1.3 mi. (40 min.).

Whitney Rd. (TR)

This road exits right at 22 (generally north and northwest) from Howe's Rd., 0.5 mi. from the beginning of the latter. It passes several roads and trails, all of which are marked. The road ends at 15, Side Hill Rd., which continues out to MA 3A. Distance from Howe's Rd. to 15: 1.1 mi. (45 min.)

Bancroft Trail (TR)

This white-blazed trail begins at the Nature Trail sign in the grassy field near the entrance on MA 3A. It travels south across the reservation, passing along ledges and intersecting Howe's Rd. at 2. It then proceeds west to 3 at Bigelow Boulder, a 200-ton glacial granite boulder with a nearby smaller boulder. Turning south and crossing Whitney Rd. at 4, the trail climbs steeply through giant hemlock and white pine woods, crossing Howe's Rd. at 21. Rooster Rock, a glacial boulder supported on one side by a small stone, is on the left. The trail descends through hemlock woods to Ode's Den (where Theodore Pritchard once lived under a large fragment of the granite rocks). Swinging north, the trail crosses Howe's Rd. at 20, Whitney Rd. at 5, and Boulder Lane at 6, then circles eastward, ending at Bigelow Boulder. Distance from Nature Trail sign to Bigelow Boulder: 1.8 mi. (1 hr.).

Boulder Lane (TR)

This road leaves Howe's Rd. at 1, 0.3 mi. from the parking area, and goes right (northwest) past Bigelow Boulder, ending at Whitney Rd. (7). Distance from Howe's Rd. to Whitney Rd.: 0.8 mi. (25 min.)

Milliken Memorial Path (TR)

This path, a continuation of Howe's Rd., begins at 19, 1.1 mi. from the parking lot. It continues to the junction of James Hill Lane and Ayer Lane at 18. Heavily used as a bridle path, it is popular because of its rhododendrons, azaleas, and other plants not commonly found in the area. Distance from Howe's Rd. to junction of James Hill Lane and Ayer Lane: 0.8 mi. (25 min.)

James Hill Lane (TR)

This trail exits left (west) at 18 from the Milliken Memorial Path and continues 1 mi. to Leavitt St. in Hingham.
Distance from Milliken Memorial Path to Leavitt St. (Hingham): 1 mi. (30 min.).

Ayer Lane (TR)

Ayer Lane is a connecting link from the Milliken Memorial Path (18) to Whitney Rd. (10), and is often used as a bridle path. Distance from Milliken Memorial Path to Whitney Rd.: 0.4 mi. (15 min.).

Thayer Trail (TR)

One of the main east-west trails, the Thayer Trail begins on Whitney Rd. at 8 and circles east, passing an abandoned well and turning west after Adelaide Rd. (12). Continuing west, the trail turns right at 14, crosses an abandoned railroad bed, and winds through a magnificent holly grove. The trail then crosses One Way Lane at 16 and ends at Turkey Hill Lane.

Turkey Hill Trail (TR)

Starting at the intersection of One Way Lane and the Thayer Trail (16), the Turkey Hill Trail climbs north on One Way Lane to

Turkey Hill Lane (paved). The trail turns right and continues a short distance to pastureland on the left, from which there are views over Cohasset Harbor. Return via the same route, as the old Turkey Hill loop trail has been abandoned. Distance from 16 to pasture: 0.3 mi. (15 min.).

WORLD'S END PENINSULA (TR)

This 250-acre peninsula owned by The Trustees of Reservations is located in Hingham. Originally laid out by Frederick Law Olmsted, the peninsula includes an interesting drumlin and beach. The drumlin is shaped like a figure eight, the upper and lower parts of which are connected by a narrow neck about 500 ft. wide. The surface is mainly grassy, but there are some granite outcrops. An unnamed, unmarked trail about 4 mi. long makes a complete circuit of the peninsula. The upper section of the drumlin has a 0.4 mi. loop trail, and the lower section has a cross trail of about 500 yd. There are also a number of old carriage roads (closed to vehicular traffic) that can be followed.

To reach the peninsula, take MA 3A east from MA 3 in Quincy, following it around Hingham harbor to East Hingham. At the traffic circle where MA 3A goes right, continue straight ahead on a four-lane highway 0.5 mi. to Four Corners. Turn left at Four Corners onto Martin's Lane and continue 0.8 mi. to the reservation parking lot. Parking is limited and often fills up, particularly on pleasant spring or fall weekends. The circuit trail starts from the gate.

CUTLER PARK (MDC)

This park on the Charles River, maintained by the MDC, covers 800 acres of marsh and woods in the towns of Dedham, Needham, and Newton. The park has a surprising variety of plant and animal life, considering its proximity to an urban area. Refer to the USGS Boston South quadrangle.

From I-95, take the Highland Ave. (Needham) exit, and turn left at the first light on Highland Ave. onto Hunting Rd., which parallels I-95. In about half a mile, turn left onto Kendrick St., which immediately crosses the highway. The Cutler Park parking area shares a driveway with a Polaroid building at 140 Kendrick St.

Cutler Park Loop

An interesting path through the park circles around Kendrick Pond to the south of the parking area, and an extension from the most southerly part of this loop leads to Powells Island. The path begins at the parking area and bears to the left of the pond, going east to south through marshland. At 0.3 mi. it enters the woods and continues south, passing the pond (out of view) and following the Charles River. At 0.5 mi. there is an open view of the opposite bank and a distant view of the Blue Hills. Also in view are some abandoned concrete bunkers, originally used by the MDC for water control operations.

At 0.65 mi. the main path turns right and heads back toward Kendrick St., while a smaller path continues straight ahead to Powells Island (see below). Quite soon a spur on the left leads to a view of a small kettle hole, and at 0.8 mi. another fork appears and two paths diverge to the left. The far left path deadends at I-95, while the center path ascends an esker for about 0.5 mi. This side trail passes through a mature oak forest, where lady slipper orchids are abundant in early June. It then descends the esker and rejoins the main path at a point where the pond is visible. The path soon comes to another open view of the pond, including the Wells Industrial Park and the gothic tower of the Gosman Jewish Community Center in Newton. The path finally ends back at the parking lot, having made a circuit of about 1.6 mi.

To reach Powells Island, leave the main loop trail at 0.65 mi. and head southeast. The path descends into a boggy area and at 0.25 mi. from the main trail crosses a stream bed and ascends to an oak forest that extends southeast in a strip about 350 yd. wide between the wetlands and I-95. At 0.7 mi. the path crosses a short stretch of marsh to Powells Island, which still shows the scarred trunks and standing deadwood left from a forest fire in the late 1980s. (Powells Island is actually what southerners would call a hammock, surrounded on three sides by the Charles River and sep-

arated from the mainland by about 100 yd. of marsh.) At 0.9 mi.
there is a meadow and at the far end a path begins which circles
around the island. Turn left at the first fork, and for 0.3 mi. the path
runs along the embankment above the river, dropping down twice
for boat landings. The reviving forest is an ideal bird habitat and a
bench along the path is a good place to watch and listen. At the
next fork, a triple masted radio tower to the NW serves as a landmark, and the righthand path will return to the meadow in 0.1 mi.
From there retrace the path to the main trail.

Cutler Park Loop

Distance from parking lot

   to Powells Island cut-off: 0.65 mi. (20 min.)

   to marsh crossing: 1.5 mi. (45 min.)

   to island circuit and return to mainland: 2.25 mi. (1 hr. 5 min.)

   to return to main loop: 3 mi. (1 hr. 30 min.)

   to return to parking lot: 4 mi. (2 hr.)

WEBSTER CONSERVATION AREA

This 113-acre wooded area in the Newton Centre and Chestnut Hill
sections of Newton is owned and maintained by the city of Newton.
Adjoining the Webster Conservation Area west of Hammond Pond
Pkwy. is the 14-acre woodland owned by Temple Mishkan Tefila
and the 38-acre MDC Hammond Pond Reservation. (The reservation includes an easement granted by the MDC to the Mall at Chestnut Hill and the Chestnut Hill Towers condominium for vehicular
access to these two establishments and to the reservation.)

The trails through the Webster Conservation Area are short and
easy to follow, but it is helpful to consult the map available from the
Newton Conservation Commission. Deer Park is a popular spot in
the area. To reach Deer Park, park at the end of Suffolk Rd. (off
Hammond St.) and walk along Lowell Lane to the Deer Park gate,
where the deer shelter, feeding station, and watering trough are
located.

Blue Trail

The Blue Trail follows a path that meanders through the Hammond Pond Reservation from the parking area at Hammond Pond, just behind the Mall at Chestnut Hill on MA 9. The trailhead is unmarked, but the Blue Trail is the largest trail leading from the parking lot. The blue dots and directional triangles begin about 200 yd. up the trail, although they are at times difficult to follow.

At Hemlock Vale the trail continues across the culvert over Tarn Pond Brook, takes a sharp left just before the MBTA Green Line, and crosses Hammond Pond Pkwy. to the parking lot of the Temple Mishkan Tefila, where it follows the Temple Path. On the north side of the temple the trail turns right into the Webster Conservation Area woods, passes Cake Rock, and comes to Gooch's Caves, located on a high rock ledge. The trail then returns to Hammond Pond Pkwy., turns right along the fence (unmarked), and uses the same crossing and trail back to the parking lot.

Green Trail

To reach the Green Trail, park in the gravel parking lot west of Temple Mishkan Tefila, then follow the Temple Path to the Green Trail on the right. When the Green Trail reaches Gooch's Caves, it turns left and continues to the Elgin Path. At the intersection with the Elgin Path, the Green Trail turns sharp left and continues 150 yd., then turns to the right for 200 yd. to the fence at the MBTA tracks. At the fence, the trail turns sharply left and goes a short distance past a spur on the right. The spur leads to a sign identifying the undeveloped Webster Playground land, near the intersection of Warren and Elgin Streets. The main trail continues another 200 yd. and turns left onto the Temple Trail, which returns to the temple parking lot.

Orange Trail

The Orange Trail follows the Temple Path from the north side of the temple, passes the Green Trail on the right, then exits right into the woods. At a bend the Orange Trail turns right onto the Green Trail and both continue to Gooch's Caves. At the caves, the Orange Trail follows the Blue Trail back to the temple.

Yellow Trail

The Yellow Trail meanders around the Houghton Garden section of the Webster Conservation Area near Lowell Crossing. Parking is available along the garden's Suffolk Rd. frontage.

Temple Path

The Temple Path starts at Hammond Pond Pkwy., passes the north side of the temple, and continues west to its junction with the Carlisle Path (left) and the Elgin Path (right) in the Charles Cohen Conservation Area (also known as Webster Vale). Many small paths bear right to large rock formations, including Gooch's Caves and Cake Rock.

Carlisle Path

The Carlisle Path is accessible from the westbound lane of Boylston St. (MA 9) by turning right onto Langley Rd. then right again onto Madoc St. to the gate. From the gate take the Madoc Path to its junction with the Carlisle Path. Turn left onto the Carlisle Path, which continues between the Charles Cohen Conservation Area (Webster Vale), the Hammond Pond Reservation, and the Temple Mishkan Tefila woods to the junction with the Temple Path (right). A short distance north of this junction, the Carlisle Path becomes the unmarked Elgin Path, which ends at the fenced Green Line right-of-way over which there is no legal access. At this point you can take the Green Trail (right) to Gooch's Caves and back to the Temple Path or switch to the Orange Trail or the Blue Trail at Gooch's Caves and follow either of these to the Temple Path. Alternatively, you can take the Blue Trail to Hammond Pond Pkwy. and pick up any of the trails on the east side of the parkway.

Elgin Path

The Elgin Path enters the Webster Conservation Area from Hammond Pond Pkwy. (*Note:* In the section north of the Green Line and west of the parkway, the MDC does not permit parking on the parkway berms or on the road. Parking is available along the Houghton Garden frontage at the end of Suffolk Rd. Follow Suffolk Rd. one block to the intersection of Old England Rd. and

Clovelly Rd., where a path enters the woods. Follow this along the north fence of Deer Park to Hammond Pond Pkwy. Cross the parkway and turn right to reach the Elgin Path.) The Elgin Path joins the Ledge Path (right), which skirts the base of some magnificent sandstone ledges and an old quarry area. The trail continues on log steps up to the ledges, runs along the rim of the ledges, then returns to the parkway.

HEMLOCK GORGE (MDC)

Hemlock Gorge, owned and maintained by the MDC, is visible from MA 9 where the Charles River flows under the highway near the point where Newton, Wellesley, and Needham meet. Here the river wore through cliffs of Roxbury puddingstone and attracted early settlers to a water power site they named Newton Upper Falls. The old mill building, now a restaurant, and many eighteenth-and nineteenth-century homes remain on the Newton side. The reservation is bounded on the north by the MA 9 off ramp; on the east by Ellis St., Newton, and the river; on the south in part by River Ave., where there are two MDC signs and an entrance; and on the west by homes in Needham. Parking is available for about three cars near the old stone building on the MA 9 off ramp.

There are a few trails along the steep Needham side of the gorge and in the woods on the Newton side where the grades are gentler. The most conspicuous landmark in the gorge is Echo Bridge, a high stone bridge built in 1875 that carries the Sudbury Aqueduct. Views up and down the river from the walkway on the bridge are impressive, and you can hear a nice echo if you walk underneath. The dam and waterfall upstream of the bridge are also worth visiting.

ROCKY WOODS RESERVATION (TR)

This tract of land, which lies mainly in Medfield and partly in Dover, comprises more than 491 acres with beautiful woods, lovely ponds, excellent views, and hiking and cross-country ski trails. The Trustees of Reservations maintain it.

To reach the reservation, take US 1 south from Boston to Dedham. Take MA 109 from Dedham to its junction with Hartford St. in Medfield, 5.6 mi. south of MA 128 (I-95). Follow Hartford St. right (east) 0.6 mi. to the main entrance to the reservation on the left (marked by a sign). An automobile road runs to the visitor center on the shore of Chickering Lake.

The reservation has a network of about 12 mi. of trails, leading to features such as Whale Rock, Hemlock Gorge, Echo Lake Bridge, and Cedar Hill. All trails are level or have a moderate grade, except the Ridge Trail, which is steep in places.

The starting point for most of the trails is the visitor center, above the parking area. Trail maps are available at the visitor center.

ROCKY NARROWS RESERVATION (TR)

This property of The Trustees of Reservations is situated in the southeastern part of Sherborn. It consists of 126 acres of rocky woodland on the west bank of the Charles River, lying about 1 mi. upstream from the Farm Street Bridge between Dover and Sherborn. It is most accessible by canoe, but it can also be reached on foot from the adjoining Sherborn Town Forest via the Town Forest Trail. To reach the closest trailhead for this trail, go north on MA 27 for 0.5 mi. from its junction with MA 115 and turn right onto Snow St. Follow Snow St. to Forest St. and turn right onto Forest St., which leads to the Sherborn Town Forest parking lot on the left just before the railroad tracks. (*Note:* Hikers are requested to not use the former Rocky Narrows Trail, which is on private land.)

Town Forest Trail: Town Forest entrance to Rocky Narrows

From the Sherborn Town Forest parking lot, cross the railroad tracks and walk a short distance to the Sherborn Town Forest entrance, which is blocked by a chain. The trail begins here on a woods road that leads into the forest. The Town Forest Trail passes two side trails on the left (marked by red blazes), continues through a wet area, then passes another trail on the right. The trail forks at a very steep hill, where a side trail to the right ends at the railroad track, while the main trail continues up the hill. Passing the top of the hill, the trail descends to a junction from which the railroad tracks (and possibly the river, depending on foliage) are visible. The trail turns left at the junction, ascending another steep hill into the woods. After passing three more side trails, the Town Forest Trail leaves the main path to the right on a narrow trail marked by a small cairn. This route goes east over a rock outcrop overlooking the Charles River, turns north through a stone wall, and then rejoins the wider path.

Reaching a bend, the trail passes another trail entering left. Just before starting downhill, it turns left at a yellow blaze. Descending across the hill, the Charles River is visible in the distance on the right. White blazes mark the trail here.

The trail continues straight ahead to Rocky Narrows Reservation, passing more lookouts over the river and descending past a stone wall to a wide woods road. Turning right into the reservation, it passes a red and green blazed trail on the left and a narrow trail a short distance beyond on the right. The trail then reaches a four-way intersection, where it turns right (southeast) to a pine grove and picnic area on the river.

Town Forest Trail: Town Forest entrance to Rocky Narrows
Distance from Town Forest entrance
   to pine grove and picnic area: 1.8 mi. (50 min.)

SHERBORN TOWN FOREST

This forest occupies several irregular contiguous and nearly contiguous tracts in the eastern and northern parts of Sherborn. It is mildly hilly and is bordered on the west by higher hills. The section of the forest just north of the junction of Goulding, Lake, Forest, and Snow streets (a triangle with a small house in the middle) has many trails of various lengths and conditions, but these trails, with the exception of the Town Forest Trail, leave the forest and traverse the surrounding area, including Mt. Misery and the woodlands west of the forest. Refer to the USGS Natick and Medfield quadrangles.

Town Forest Trail: Pine Street School to Lake Street

This easy hike passes near two wooded summits with limited views. The trailhead is located at the Pine St. School in Sherborn, just off MA 16 (Eliot St.) near the intersection with MA 27. Parking is allowed in marked spaces in the school lot from dawn to dusk on non-school days, but is not allowed on Lake St. The trail leaves the parking lot by the rear of the jungle gyms and is marked with single white blazes. Double blazes mark the frequent turns.

The trail turns left in about 0.1 mi. and climbs quickly to the summit of Pine Hill, keeping to the right at a fork just before the summit. At about 0.2 mi. the trail bears right at a second fork, passing a horse-jumping field on the right. Turning right again, the trail follows a pipeline right-of-way down to Farm Rd.

The white blazes continue on the south side of Farm Rd., as the Town Forest Trail joins the Bay Circuit Trail. The trail bears left and returns to the pipeline track in about 0.1 mi., follows the pipeline for about 0.2 mi., and enters the woods to the right. When the Town Forest Trail bears left in about 100 yd., a short side trail to the right leads to the summit of Mt. Misery (279 ft.). The remainder of the trail winds through the woods down to Lake St., just north of the intersection of Lake, Goulding, Forest, and Snow Streets. A green metal gate marks this end of the trail.

Town Forest Trail: Pine Street School to Lake Street

Distance from Pine Street School
  to Lake Street: 2 mi. (1 hr.)

Girl Scout East–West Trail

This trail is one of two trails on Brush Hill (396 ft.) marked by the Girl Scouts, using painted can tops attached to trees.The east-west trail begins as a narrow, grassy path leading west off MA 27, 0.3 mi. north of its junction with MA 16. The road soon crosses a railroad track at 0.2 mi., passes through a clump of red pines, and reaches a former Girl Scout camp. From the camp, the wooded path continues southwest, then west, rising sharply to the height-of-land, where it crosses the north-south trail. From this intersection, unmarked but well-traveled trails lead 0.3 mi. north to Prospect St. and 0.3 mi. south and west to Hunting Lane. This trail is part of the Bay Circuit.

Girl Scout East–West Trail

Distance from MA 27

   to intersection with north-south trail: 1 mi. (30 min.)

BROADMOOR WILDLIFE SANCTUARY (MAS)

This Massachusetts Audubon Society sanctuary comprises about 600 acres off Eliot St. (MA 16) and South St. in South Natick and Sherborn and borders the Charles River. The area around Little Pond in Sherborn (262 acres) was given to the Audubon Society in 1962 by Henry M. Channing in memory of Katherine Minot Channing. Broadmoor in South Natick and Sherborn was donated by Dr. and Mrs. Carl Stillman in 1968.

The entrance to the sanctuary is at 280 Eliot St. (MA 16), 1.8 mi. southwest from South Natick. Trail maps are available at the nature center, a 1911 horse barn renovated in 1983. The center is solar heated and has composting toilets.

A number of well-marked trails leave from the parking area. Trail information and maps are available at the information center.

WALDEN POND STATE RESERVATION (DEM)

Walden Pond and its surrounding woodlands, the site of Henry David Thoreau's retreat, were given to the state in 1922 with the provision that the public be allowed to swim, canoe, hike, and picnic there. During the summer Walden Pond is a popular swimming and picnic spot. In the off-season visitors find the pond and its environs a tranquil escape. Maps of the extensive trail system are available at the park office or at the parking entrance. Trails include the 1.8-mi. Pond Path circuit; two trails to the site of Thoreau's cabin; loop trails west of the railroad tracks around the "Andromeda" ponds; and trails that connect to adjacent conservation land in Lincoln and Concord. (A detailed map of the Lincoln conservation land trails is available for $1 at the Lincoln Town Hall, located at the intersection of Trapelo Rd. and Bedford Rd. No map is currently available for the Concord conservation area.)

Near the pond hikers are asked to stay on marked trails and off the steep slopes, where bank erosion has been a problem in recent years. Park staff conduct year-round programs about Thoreau's life and his stay at Walden. A small bookstore is located adjacent to the parking lot.

The reservation is located in Concord at the intersection of MA 126 (Walden St.) and MA 2. There is a parking fee from May through October (space for 350 cars). The lot may fill up on summer weekends due to the popularity of the pond's beach. Cars parked on the state highway will be towed. Dogs and mountain biking are not permitted. For more information, contact the park supervisor (508-369-3254).

GREAT MEADOWS NATIONAL WILDLIFE REFUGE

Incorporating inland wetlands that are prime birding areas in the state, this refuge is located 20 mi. west of Boston and encompasses 12 mi. of the Concord and Sudbury rivers. This freshwater marsh area is divided into two large units that provide a habitat for a great diversity of migrating and nesting birds, including waterfowl, shorebirds, and songbirds. Great Meadows offers opportunities for wildlife observation, hiking, photography, and nature study.

The Dike Trail (1.7 mi.), Black Duck Creek Trail (about 1 mi.), and Timber Trail (0.5 mi.) are located in the Concord (northern) unit of the refuge. To reach this unit, follow MA 62 (Bedford Rd.) 1.4 mi. northeast of Concord center toward Bedford. After about 1 mi., turn left onto Monsen Rd. (refuge sign), then continue to the refuge entrance at a dirt road on the left. Turn left onto Monsen Rd.; then turn left farther down the road onto a dirt road marked with a refuge sign. Parking, photo blinds, and a seasonal comfort station are provided.

The Weir Hill visitor center–headquarters complex is located in the Sudbury (south) unit of the refuge. A three-story building houses exhibits, the refuge headquarters, and facilities for seasonal interpretive programming. The visitor center is open weekdays year-round; closed holidays and weekends except during May and October. A 1-mi. loop trail traverses the river edge, upland woodland, and a red maple swamp. Parking, a trail shelter, and restrooms are provided. Follow Concord–Sudbury Rd. about 1.7 mi. north from Sudbury center; turn right onto Lincoln Rd. (high school on corner); proceed about 1.4 mi. and turn left onto Weir Hill Rd. (refuge sign); follow signs to visitor center. The Wood Duck Hollow Trail (0.5 mi.) is also located in the Sudbury unit. Follow MA 20 west through Wayland and turn left onto Pelham Island Rd. Continue to a parking lot on the right side of the road, across from Heard Pond. Parking is provided.

The U.S. Fish and Wildlife Service headquarters address is: Great Meadows NWR, Weir Hill Rd., Sudbury, MA 01776 (tel. 508-443-4661).

MIDDLESEX FELLS RESERVATION (MDC)

This reservation, lying in Stoneham, Medford, Winchester, Melrose, and Malden, is maintained by the MDC. It contains 3.2 sq. mi. of rough woodland and granite outcrop traversed by woods roads, bridle paths, and footpaths. Stone towers on Pine Hill and Bear Hill, as well as numerous outlooks, offer good views. The reservation also contains a number of scenic ponds and brooks. The reservation is heavily used, and parts of it have suffered somewhat from overuse and lack of adequate maintenance.

To reach the southern section of the Fells, take exit 33 off I-93; to reach the northern section, take exit 34 (northbound only) or exit 35 (southbound only) off I-93. Alternatively, take MA 28 (Fellsway West) to the Fells. Intertwining, I-93 and MA 28 divide the reservation into eastern and western sections. Several MBTA bus lines and its Orange Rapid Transit Line (Oak Grove Station) provide access to various sections of the Fells.

Cross Fells Trail (MOC)

The blue-blazed Cross Fells Trail is a good connecting trail between the eastern and western sections of the Middlesex Fells Reservation, because it touches every major trail in the Fells. This trail uses sections of the Rock Circuit Trail, the Mini Rock Circuit Trail, the Virginia Woods Trail, the Skyline Trail, and the Spot Pond Trail. The eastern end of this trail is 0.6 mi. north of the Oak Grove terminal of the MBTA Orange Rapid Transit Line. To reach the trailhead in the eastern section of the Fells, follow Washington St. north to Goodyear Ave., then follow Goodyear Ave. west (left) to the trailhead in Melrose, near the Melrose–Malden line.

The trail climbs west along easy wooded grades to a high rocky ridge. Here it turns left (south) with the Rock Circuit Trail (white-blazed) and the Mini Rock Circuit Trail (orange-blazed) to Black Rock. The Cross Fells Trail continues some distance with the Rock Circuit Trail (but not with the Mini Rock Circuit Trail) before exiting right (west) to cross Black Rock Path (a bridle trail) and Fellsway East (paved). It continues west, skirting the south side of the high reservoir and picking up the Mini Rock Circuit Trail. Shortly, the two trails come to the Virginia Woods Trail (red-blazed). The Mini Rock Circuit Trail exits right (north) with the Virginia Woods Trail, and the Cross Fells Trail continues west.

The trail crosses several bridle paths before passing south of Shiner Pool. After this pool, it rejoins the Rock Circuit Trail in crossing a swampy section. It leaves this trail and crosses Woodland Rd. (paved) just north of the hockey arena. It then joins the Virginia Woods Trail, passing the southern end of Quarter Mile Pond and heading west over the hills. In 0.3 mi. the Virginia Woods Trail exits left (south) to Wright's Pond, while the Cross Fells Trail continues west to Fellsway West (MA 28). The trail follows Fellsway West and the Spot Pond Trail (yellow-blazed) a short distance to an underpass of I-93, then crosses Fellsway West.

The trail follows Brooks Rd. (dirt) to a junction with the Skyline Trail (white-blazed). Here the Cross Fells Trail turns left (south) to go partway up a short hill with the Skyline Trail. Soon the Cross Fells Trail turns right (west) to follow a ridge above

Brooks Rd. The trail bends left (south) and picks up a series of bridle paths before turning left (east) into the woods to rejoin the Skyline Trail on the summit of Wenepoykin Hill. The two trails then head south together to East Dam Rd. (dirt). Here the Cross Fells Trail continues south downhill to a brook and on to rejoin another section of the Skyline Trail. The two trails continue west until the Cross Fells Trail turns left (southwest) to pick up a group of bridle paths. After crossing S. Border Rd. (paved), the trail climbs a hill to the site of the former Lawrence Observation Tower. Descending the hill, the trail follows bridle paths to the Whitmore Brook Entrance to the Fells on Winthrop St. in Medford, across from Playstead Rd. (the end of the MBTA Sullivan Square–West Medford bus line).

Cross Fells Trail
Distance from Goodyear Ave. (Melrose)
 to Whitmore Brook Entrance to the Fells: 4.3 mi. (2 hr. 30 min.)

Rock Circuit Trail (MDC)
This white-blazed trail affords the best views in the Middlesex Fells. Living up to its name, it is very rocky and offers rewarding but rugged hiking. A convenient approach to this trail is from Woodland St. in Medford, opposite the northern end of the parking lot for the hockey arena (south of New England Memorial Hospital in Stoneham). Follow a woods road east for a short distance to the crest of a hill, where you can pick up the Rock Circuit Trail.

Turning right (south), the trail climbs a nearby ridge overlooking sections of Medford. Here it joins the Virginia Woods Trail (red-blazed) for a few feet, then goes south along the ridge before turning left (east) to another ridge, where it goes north before turning sharp right (east) to drop into a valley, crossing a bridle path and a brook.

At the brook, the trail turns left (north) and soon rejoins the Virginia Woods Trail, again only for a few feet. The Rock Circuit Trail crosses a bridle path and climbs southeast up a ridge. In 0.1 mi. the trail turns right (south) and drops into a valley. The trail then makes a long, gentle climb southeast to Boojum Rock, where it picks up the Mini Rock Circuit Trail (orange-blazed) for 0.1 mi. Leaving fine views of the Boston area, the trail drops sharply and heads east to cross a bridle path and then Fellsway East (paved). It rejoins the Mini Rock Circuit Trail and climbs Pinnacle Rock, from which there are fine views. At Pinnacle Rock both trails turn north, almost doubling back on themselves, and pass a television tower enclosure, where the Mini Rock Circuit Trail exits.

The Rock Circuit Trail then follows a rough ridge north to Black Rock. At Black Rock, this trail combines first with the Cross Fells Trail (blue-blazed) and then with the Mini Rock Circuit Trail to mount a fine viewpoint. The three trails continue north a short distance before the Cross Fells Trail turns sharply right (east) downhill to exit the Fells. The two Rock Circuit Trails continue north along the top of the ridge to White Rock and Melrose Rock with many fine views.

At Melrose Rock the two trails separate, with the Rock Circuit Trail turning left (west) through the woods to recross Fellsway East (paved) and to skirt the eastern end of the high reservoir. The trail crosses Wyoming Path to enter some young tree growth and soon rejoins the Virginia Woods Trail and then the Mini Rock Circuit Trail. It ascends a ridge behind (east of) New England Memorial Hospital, from which there is a fine view north. The Virginia Woods Trail separates here, with the two Rock Circuit Trails turning left from the ridge. Soon the Mini Rock Circuit Trail exits left (south), and the Rock Circuit Trail goes right (west) through a fine pine grove to join the yellow-blazed Spot Pond Trail for 0.2 mi. while passing south of New England Memorial Hospital. After leaving the Spot Pond Trail and crossing several bridle paths, the Rock Circuit Trail passes the northwest shore of Shiner Pool and soon joins the Cross Fells Trail to cross a swampy area. It then leaves the Cross Fells Trail, turning left (south) along a ridge adjacent to Woodland Rd., and then completes the circuit.

Rock Circuit Trail

Distance from trailhead
  to return to trailhead: 4 mi. (3 hr. 30 min.)

Mini Rock Circuit Trail (MDC)

The Mini Rock Circuit Trail is a shorter and smoother variation of the Rock Circuit Trail. This orange-blazed trail takes in the best high points of the Rock Circuit Trail and some fine sections of other trails but avoids many rough sections. On a clear day this trail affords spectacular views. The Mini Rock Circuit Trail is accessible from any of the other trails in the eastern section of the Fells or from either of its two crossings of Fellsway East. For this approach, follow the Cross Fells Trail (blue-blazed) from its eastern end on Goodyear Ave. in Melrose. The Mini Rock Circuit Trail turns right (north) from the Cross Fells Trail 0.1 mi. from Goodyear Ave.

The Mini Rock Circuit Trail goes along a ridge with the Rock Circuit Trail (white-blazed) over White Rock and Melrose Rock. The trails then turn left (west) and separate, with the Mini Rock Circuit Trail following a bridle path to Fellsway East (paved). After crossing Fellsway East, the trail winds gently west and ascends to a high rock behind (east of) New England Memorial Hospital, where it joins the Rock Circuit Trail and the Virginia Woods Trail (red-blazed). The latter separates almost immediately at a fine viewpoint. The other two trails descend and separate shortly, with the Mini Rock Circuit Trail going left (south) through the woods to rejoin another section of the Virginia Woods Trail.

These two trails soon come to Bent Rd. (dirt), which they follow right (west) until the fence on the left (south) turns left around the high reservoir. The trails also turn left, and in 0.1 mi. they leave the fence, heading right (southwest) to meet the Cross Fells Trail. Here the Mini Rock Circuit Trail leaves the Virginia Woods Trail and turns left (southeast) to join the Cross Fells Trail. The two trails work back to the high reservoir fence and continue down a ridge before separating. The Mini Rock Circuit Trail continues southeast a short distance along a fire road before turning right (southwest) to zigzag up a hill to rejoin the Rock Circuit Trail on Boojum Rock.

The Mini Rock Circuit Trail turns left (southeast), and the two trails soon reach an excellent viewpoint of Boston, its harbor, and the surrounding land. At the viewpoint, the trails separate, and both head for Pinnacle Rock. The Mini Rock Circuit Trail bears left (northeast), crossing two bridle paths and Fellsway East (paved). The two trails remerge for a short distance at Pinnacle Rock and then almost double back. They go north, separating after passing a television tower enclosure. The Mini Rock Circuit Trail follows bridle paths north to Black Rock, where it joins the Rock Circuit Trail and the Cross Fells Trail at another fine viewing location. The three trails continue north a short distance to complete the loop for the Mini Rock Circuit Trail.

Mini Rock Circuit Trail

Distance from trailhead
  to return to trailhead: 2.8 mi. (2 hr.)

Skyline Trail (MDC)

This trail is located in the western section of the Fells. Marked with white blazes, it circles the Winchester Reservoirs as it travels through Medford, Stoneham, and Winchester. A popular starting point is Bellevue Pond, off S. Border Rd. in Medford, a short distance west of I-93 (exit 33) and MA 28. Quarry Rd. (dirt) goes east (right) of Bellevue Pond. The Skyline Trail follows Quarry Rd. to the first blaze near the northern end of Bellevue Pond.

The trail turns right up Pine Hill, at the top of which is Wright's Tower with commanding views of Boston, its harbor, and the Blue Hills. The trail continues north along a rocky ridge before turning west to drop into a valley. It mounts the ridge to the west and on top of the second ridge turns north for 0.3 mi., dipping once to cross a notch with a spur of Quarry Rd. (bridle path). At the northern end of the ridge is a good view north over I-93.

The trail descends northwest, passing the northern end of the next ridge before turning more west and dropping into a valley. It continues west, descending a hill. Near the summit, the trail turns right (north) and joins the Cross Fells Trail (blue-blazed) for a short distance to the summit. The Skyline Trail follows high land north over several hills, including Silver Mine Hill. Soon after Silver Mine Hill, the Skyline Trail rejoins the Cross Fells Trail for a short distance as it descends to Brooks Rd. (dirt). The Skyline Trail continues north over Gerry Hill and on to Chandler Rd. (dirt) along the Winchester Reservoir fence, which detours the Skyline Trail with the Reservoir Trail (orange-blazed) to the right (east) a short distance and then left (north).

Very shortly the Reservoir Trail exits left (northwest), while the Skyline Trail goes uphill to the Sheepfold Picnic Area. The trail passes the eastern end of the parking lot, skirts the east side of the picnic area, then crosses a former soapbox derby track on the way north to Winthrop Hill, where there is a fine view of the Winchester North Reservoir. From here it continues along a ridge toward Bear Hill. About 0.2 mi. north of Winthrop Hill the Skyline Trail turns sharply left (west) downhill at a trail junction. (*Note:* Straight ahead—north—uphill is the short Bear Hill Connector Trail, which connects with the Spot Pond Trail at the Bear Hill observation tower.)

The Skyline Trail crosses Dike Rd. (dirt), where it joins the Reservoir Trail to cross a brook and continue through a former meadow and a pine grove to another dirt road. Here the Reservoir Trail exits left (southwest) on the dirt road, while the Skyline Trail continues straight over Money Hill. On the west slope of Money Hill the two trails remerge and descend, crossing N. Border Rd. (dirt), into a ravine north of the Winchester North Reservoir dam. The trails cross a brook (leakage from the reservoir), then soon bend left (south) a short distance before zigzagging up the west slope of the ravine to pass north of the old firehouse. They continue to paved Alben St., on to Reservoir St., and finally on to Hillcrest Pkwy., where there is parking and access to the trail. Both trails very shortly leave the paved roads and go south via West Dam Path. After crossing a dirt service road, they soon separate. The Reservoir Trail exits right, while the Skyline Trail continues straight over a couple of minor hills. The Skyline Trail crosses the Reservoir Trail and soon climbs steeply up Nanapashemet Hill, where there are limited views.

The Skyline Trail continues south over numerous hills to merge with the Reservoir Trail at the Winchester South Reservoir standpipe. The two trails continue south, then east around waterland property at the west reservoir dam. The trails almost reach S. Border Rd. before passing over a hill to the Middle Road Path. A dirt road on the right leads shortly to a parking area off S. Border Rd. and an access to the two trails. The trails soon bend left (north) to pick up the East Dam Path. They soon separate, with the Reservoir Trail going straight (north) and the Skyline Trail turning right uphill. At the top of the hill the trail bends right along a ridge before turning left to cross Middle Rd. (dirt) and soon joins the Cross Fells Trail for a short distance. The Skyline Trail turns right to head for Panther Cave, passing almost directly over the cave before dropping to cross the Red Cross Path and Straight Gully Brook. It then climbs Little Pine Hill on its way to Bellevue Pond, where it completes its circuit.

Skyline Trail

Distance from Bellevue Pond
  to return to Bellevue Pond: 6.8 mi. (5 hr.)

Reservoir Trail (MDC)

This orange-blazed trail is a very pleasant circuit around the three Winchester reservoirs. Individuals using the trail should be aware that the adjacent waterlands are not for general public access and that the nearby "No Trespassing" signs should be observed. This trail avoids major hills and rocky terrain. The trail was designed to be a possible ski touring trail when snow is sufficient. It has many fine vistas.

You can pick up the Reservoir Trail from several locations. It will be described here starting from the Sheepfold and going counterclockwise. The trail follows close to the fence on the southern and western boundaries of the Sheepfold picnic area. It leaves the fence, crosses the former soapbox derby track, and enters the woods on an old bridle path. Soon it leaves the path and winds under Winthrop Hill along gentle slopes to keep between the hill and waterlands property. North of the municipal waterlands property the trail drops down to Dike Rd. (dirt). It follows this road north to meet the Skyline Trail (white blazes) coming down from the side of Bear Hill. Here the Reservoir Trail turns left (west) with the Skyline Trail, goes to Dike Brook, then goes straight ahead through a former meadow and a pine grove to a dirt road. Here the Skyline Trail goes over Money Hill while the Reservoir Trail leaves left (southwest) down the road and then climbs to skirt Money Hill to rejoin the Skyline Trail. The two trails descend together to cross N. Border Rd. (dirt) and enter a ravine north of the North Dam. The trails cross a brook formed by leakage from the reservoir. Shortly the trails bend left (south) a short distance before zigzagging up the west slope of the ravine to pass north of the old firehouse (which has water pumps in the basement) out onto Alben St. (paved) to Reservoir St.–Hillcrest Pkwy. There is parking and access here for the two trails. The two trails very shortly leave the paved roads and go south via the West Dam Path. They cross a dirt service road and soon separate. The Skyline Trail goes ahead (south) while the Reservoir Trail goes right (southwest) to skirt a couple of marshes, crosses a brook, and then crosses the Skyline Trail before joining a dirt road southeasterly toward the Middle and South reservoirs. At the end of the road, the trail enters a bluff with fine views of the Middle and South reservoirs with a causeway between them. The trail bends back and drops into a ravine. It crosses a brook and goes over one small hill and then over the shoulder of another hill to a dirt road. From here the trail goes south for nearly a mile crossing Molly Spring Rd. (dirt), two brooks, and several stone walls and eventually rejoining the Skyline Trail adjacent to the South Reservoir standpipe. The two trails go south, then east around the waterlands property near the reservoir's West Dam. The trails almost reach S. Border Rd. before going over a hill to the Middle Road Path. (The dirt road to the right leads shortly to parking off S. Border Rd.—an access spot for the two trails.) The two trails go straight, then bend left (north) to pick up the East Dam Path, where they separate. The Skyline Trail turns right (east) up a hill while the Reservoir Trail goes ahead (north). As the Reservoir Trail approaches the South Reservoir it leaves the road and heads northeast, not far from East Dam Rd. (dirt). Adjacent to the small East Dam, the trail descends into a ravine, then ascends it and continues parallel to the patrol road going north. After going over Silver Mine Hill, the trail passes close to the sealed shaft of a silver mine. (Note the concrete posts of a former fence around the mine shaft.) The trail continues north with more views of the reservoirs, not far from the patrol road, until it reaches Chandler Rd. (dirt) with a fence on its north side. The trail goes right (east) along Chandler Rd., joins the Skyline Trail, and heads for the Sheepfold to complete its circuit.

Reservoir Trail

Distance from the Sheepfold
  to return to the Sheepfold: 5.5 mi. (3 hr.)

BREAKHEART RESERVATION (MDC)

The MDC's Breakheart Reservation, in Saugus and Wakefield, covers more than 600 acres of oak-hemlock-pine forest, with numerous hills and two freshwater lakes. A network of blacktop roads serves all areas of the reservation, although only Pine Tops Rd. is open to vehicular traffic. Pine Tops is a loop road that heads north from the reservation headquarters to the south side of Pearce Lake, where swimming is allowed only when lifeguards are on duty. The road then parallels the shore of Pearce Lake and later the shore of Silver Lake before returning to the reservation headquarters. Pine Tops is a one-way counterclockwise loop. The other paved roads are Elm Rd. and Hemlock Rd., which connect to form another loop from Pine Tops Rd. near the Pearce Lake swimming area, around the west side of the lakes, and back to Pine Tops Rd., about 200 yd. before the exit at the headquarters. Elm Rd. and Hemlock Rd. meet at the Wakefield Vocational High School gate, where parking is allowed. Vehicular access to the reservation is prohibited here. Finally, unpaved Flume Rd. runs between Pearce and Silver lakes, connecting Hemlock Rd. to Pine Tops Rd. in the middle of the reservation.

In addition to the roads, an extensive series of hiking trails crisscrosses the Breakheart Reservation. Fox Run, Breakheart, Saugus, and Lodge trails are all marked with yellow blazes as well as wooden trailhead posts.

Take the Lynn Fells Pkwy. exit off US 1, then continue south-west 0.4 mi. to Forest St. on the right. Follow Forest St. to the parking area at the reservation headquarters. Trail information is available at the headquarters building.

Fox Run Trail (MDC)

This trail begins about 75 yd. from the front gate after the entrance onto Pine Tops Rd. and after a wooden fence on the left. A gate and a wooden post mark the trailhead. It climbs steeply for a short dis-tance, bears right at a fork (where the Breakheart Hill Trail goes left), and runs parallel to Pine Tops Rd. The trail then turns sharply left at the junction with the Saugus River Trail, and 100 yd. farther turns right toward an exposed rock ledge. Once above and behind the ledge, the trail bears right at a T-intersection, and then traverses a series of small hills and valleys. It crosses a large rocky plateau overlooking Pearce Lake, and then descends steeply to the Pearce Lake swimming area. Distance from gate to Pearce Lake swim-ming area: 1 mi. (30 min.).

Breakheart Hill Trail (MDC)

This trail branches left off the Fox Run Trail at the first fork. At the top of the hill, the trail passes a short spur on the left leading to expansive views of Boston, Lynn, and Saugus. The trail continues downhill and ends at the Silver Lake parking area. Distance from Fox Run Trail to Silver Lake parking area: 0.2 mi. (10 min.).

Saugus River Trail (MDC)

This trail begins at the first gate on the right after entering the reservation on Pine Tops Rd. It heads east toward the river and connects with a spur on the right, which leads to the somewhat buried remains of a stone dam built in the early 1800s. (*Note:* If you take the spur, stay to the right after a large opening before a small picnic area; otherwise you will just get to a small stream.) The main trail stays to the left and follows the river, eventually turning west and crossing Pine Tops Rd. The trail reenters the woods about 50 yd. to the right on Pine Tops Rd. Shortly after this point, the trail bears left at a fork, continues straight, and intersects with the Fox Run Trail. Distance from gate to Fox Run Trail: 0.8 mi. (25 min.).

Lodge Trail (MDC)

The reservation map does not show the Lodge Trail, but it is well-marked by a wooded trailhead marker. It exits left from the Saugus River Trail a short distance from its trailhead, and passes a rhododendron grove and then the scant remains of an 1800s hunting lodge built by the founder of the reservation. The trail continues on to Pine Tops Rd., 0.25 mi. from the reservation headquarters building. Distance from Saugus River Trail to Pine Tops Rd.: 0.3 mi. (10 min.).

Beach Trail (MDC)

This trail starts at the Pine Tops parking lot, 0.8 mi. from the reservation headquarters. The path runs through the Pine Tops picnic area and ends at the Pearce Lake parking area adjacent to the beach. Distance from Pine Tops parking lot to Pearce Lake parking area: 0.2 mi. (10 min.).

Pearce Lake Trail (MDC)

This trail starts at the swimming area and circles Pearce Lake, hugging the shore line, which varies from sandy beach to rocky outcroppings to dense hemlock groves. It is a well-traveled path marked with blue blazes, and passes the Flume Trail, which leads to the Silver Lake Trail. Distance from Pearce Lake beach to return (loop): 1.3 mi. (45 min.).

Silver Lake Trail (MDC)

This trail starts at the Silver Lake parking area and follows the shore of Silver Lake. It continues past the Flume Trail, a short spur that connects the Silver Lake Trail to the Pearce Lake Trail. The trail then returns to the beginning. Distance from Silver Lake parking area to return (loop): 0.9 mi. (30 min.)

Ridge Trail (MDC)

This trail, clearly marked with white blazes, begins just before the Pine Tops Rd. exit gate to the left of the headquarters building. It heads in a northwesterly direction, crossing Ash Path twice, and follows a series of ridges and valleys. A spur trail on the left leads to the top of Castle Rock (good views). The Ridge Trail continues north and connects with Hemlock Rd. 1 mi. from where Hemlock Rd. intersects Pine Tops Rd. near the reservation headquarters. Distance from trailhead to Hemlock Rd.: 1.7 mi. (50 min.).

Ash Path (MDC)

This path starts on Hemlock Rd., approximately 200 yd. before its intersection with Pine Tops Rd. near the reservation headquarters building. It loops around Ash Hill and ends back on Hemlock Rd. a short distance from the starting point. Distance from Hemlock Rd. to return (loop): 1 mi. (30 min.)

LYNN WOODS

These 2,000 acres of woodlands, located northwest of Lynn, are separated into northern and southern sections by Walden Pond (not to be confused with Thoreau's Walden Pond in Concord). About one quarter of the park (the wilder part) lies north of the pond, and the remainder lies south. It is said that before the American Revolution, Lynn Woods was a favorite hiding place for pirates who came up the Saugus River in small boats. (A free copy of the pirate legend is available from the Lynn Historical Society, tel. 617-592-2465.) No automobiles are allowed in the area, but picnicking is permitted, and fireplaces are provided. The trails are principally narrow dirt roads or woods roads with several connecting paths. For the most part they are unmarked, and can be difficult to follow in places.

There are two main entrances to the reservation: Penny Brook Rd. and Great Woods Rd., which is also the entrance to the Happy Valley Golf Club. Maps can be purchased from the DPW Engineering Dept. at Lynn City Hall, or refer to the USGS Lynn quadrangle.

Penny Brook Rd.

This city road exits left (north) from Walnut St. 2 mi. east of the Walnut St. exit of US 1. It continues into the reservation through a gate and there becomes a reservation road with the same name. Park in the area immediately inside the gate.

From the parking area the Jackson Path leads right to a picnic area with fireplaces and then to Lantern Rock, named for its reputed use as a signaling point by pirates. Penny Brook Rd. (closed to cars) continues through another gate past the maintenance buildings, then passes Waycross Rd. on the right and soon is joined by the Great Woods Rd. on the right. Penny Brook Rd. continues north, paralleling Penny Brook and a portion of Walden Pond, crosses the western border of the reservation, and continues as a city road named Walden Pond Rd. to Walnut St. at a point only a short distance from the US 1 Walnut St. overpass.

Great Woods Rd.

This city road exits west from MA 129 (Lynnfield St.) about 3 mi. east of its junction with US 1. It continues into the reservation through a gate and becomes a reservation road with the same name. Immediately inside this gate, a paved road exits sharply left uphill to the Happy Valley Golf Club. Great Woods Rd. continues straight ahead to a parking lot with an athletic field on the right.

This road (closed to automobiles) continues through a stone gateway at the far left corner of the parking lot and runs parallel to and some distance from the south shore of Walden Pond. Cooke Rd. enters left, and soon the Mt. Gilead Loop and Dungeon Rock Rd. enter left. Farther along a picnic area with fireplaces is located on the right. Great Woods Rd. continues along the south and east shores of Walden Pond, parallels and then crosses Penny Brook, and ends at Penny Brook Rd.

Mt. Gilead Loop

This wide footpath exits left (south) with Dungeon Rock Rd. from Great Woods Rd., 0.5 mi. from the stone gate at the Great Woods parking lot. It leads to the summit of Mt. Gilead (273 ft.), where there is a steel observation tower (closed to the public). It then descends Mt. Gilead to rejoin Dungeon Rock Rd. about 1000 ft. from its beginning.

Dungeon Rock Rd.

Dungeon Rock Rd. exits left (south) from Great Woods Rd. with the Mt. Gilead Loop, 0.5 mi. from the stone gate at the Great Woods parking lot. It continues past the junction with the return of the Mt. Gilead Loop, winding along past Burrill Hill Rd. on the left to Dungeon Rock. At Dungeon Rock, a footpath leads right to the entrance of a dungeon, which is closed by an unlocked iron grill. Beyond this grill a narrow tunnel was drilled into the rock in search of a cave, rendered inaccessible by an earthquake in 1658, where pirates are thought to have hidden their loot. You can make a fascinating descent into the cave with care and a flashlight.

The trail goes steeply downhill from Dungeon Rock on over-grown steps. (Footing may be better on an unmarked path about 15 ft. to the left.) At the base of the hill, near Breed's Pond, the trail turns sharply right, with the Cornell Path entering left. It parallels Breed's Pond for a short distance and then diverges from the pond as Jackson Path from Lantern Rock enters left. (Jackson Path continues on the other side of the trail, climbing steeply by some stone steps to Dungeon Rock.) Dungeon Rock Rd. continues to its terminus on Penny Brook Rd.

Burrill Hill Rd.

Burrill Hill Rd. exits left (south) from Great Woods Rd. a few hundred yards from the stone gate at the Great Woods parking area. It ascends Burrill Hill (284 ft.) to a stone observation tower (closed to the public) and continues along a ridge to Dungeon Rock Rd.

Ox Pasture Road

This trail is the feeder for the trails in the northern section of the reservation. A former jeep road closed to vehicular traffic, it leaves the far right (northwest) corner of the Great Woods parking area, to the right of the pumping station, and slabs the base of Mt. Spickett close to the north shore of Walden Pond for about 0.5 mi. At this point the Overlook Trail exits left (white blazes), and Ox Pasture Rd. turns inland, continuing through the draw between Bow Ridge and the Weetamoo Cliffs. About 1 mi. from the fork it passes the Valley Trail entering right and a short trail to the Wolf Pits, also on the right. The Overlook Trail enters left shortly thereafter, and the trail continues on to US 1. The principal high points on Bow Ridge are Mt. Hermon (282 ft.), Mt. Spickett (261 ft.), and the Elephant Rocks.

Overlook Trail

The Overlook Trail is the most scenic trail in the reservation. It exits left (west) from Ox Pasture Rd. at the point where the road turns inland. The Overlook Trail is white-blazed and easy to follow. It follows closely along the north shore of Walden Pond, climbing to two contiguous rock outcrops, then turns sharply inland to the Great Frog Boulder and the Weetamoo Cliffs. From here the trail passes the Balanced Boulder, loops around through the woods, and rejoins Ox Pasture Rd. a short distance west of the Wolf Pits.

Valley Path

The Valley Path exits right from Ox Pasture Rd. near the Wolf Pits and crosses Bow Ridge to the powerlines in the vicinity of Nell's Pond. From here a footpath more or less follows the powerlines to Lynnfield St.

SECTION 8
Southeast Massachusetts

This section includes the part of Massachusetts that is located to the south and southeast of the Boston metropolitan area. It extends from the Warner Trail corridor in the west to Cape Cod in the east. It comprises much level land, some rolling country, and the major portion of the Massachusetts seacoast. There are no mountains of any significance, although there are a few scattered ridges and smaller hills in the western portion. Along the coast, pine woods, sand dunes, freshwater ponds, and many miles of shoreline, including the Cape Cod National Seashore, are the natural attractions.

Hikers in the coastal areas should be particularly alert to the dangers of Lyme disease; see Section 1 of this book. Poison ivy is also abundant in many of these areas.

WARNER TRAIL (AMC)

The Warner Trail offers delightful and varied outdoor experiences as it stretches more than 30 mi. from Canton, MA, to Diamond Hill State Park in Rhode Island. The possibility of establishing a woodland trail connecting the south fringe of the Boston area with the trail system in Rhode Island was first envisioned by AMC members Charles H. Warner and John Hudson prior to World War II. With the energetic assistance of Ron Gower and a number of other AMC members, the trail was slowly put together, one section at a time, starting at the AMC Ponkapoag Camp. By 1947 it extended south to High Rock in the Gilbert Hills State Forest. By the early 1950s the trail had reached Diamond Hill, RI, but development soon resulted in the loss of the stretch from the Ponkapoag Camp to the Canton Junction Rail Station. Thus, the trail now begins at the rail station in Canton.

The basic philosophy in the development of the trail was to maximize the challenges while at the same time providing the greatest amount of enjoyment. As a result, the trail wanders considerably from elevated viewpoints to swamp crossings, brooks, and reservoirs. It connects a number of state and town forests, Audubon Society land, conservation land, and other public land.

The trail is maintained by AMC volunteers from the Boston, Narragansett, and Southeast Massachusetts chapters. These individuals take care of blowdowns, marking, and relocations. If you would like to get involved in the stewardship of this trail, contact the Friends of the Warner Trail, 30 Water St., Foxboro, MA 02035 (tel. 508-543-2633).

This trail can be enjoyed as a series of day hikes, or sections of it can be used for snowshoeing or as scenic paths to several lunch spots. Users are asked to respect the property of private landowners who have generously granted permission for the trail to cross their land. Please leave nothing behind but footprints.

The trail is marked by white plastic triangles and white or stainless steel disks on trees and telephone poles, and a few white paint marks on rocks or pavement where trees are missing.

You can obtain information on the trail from the Moose Hill Audubon Sanctuary, the offices for the Gilbert Hills and Wrentham state forests, AMC headquarters in Boston, or the Friends of the Warner Trail. A detailed trail guide with maps is available from the Friends of the Warner Trail (send SASE with two stamps).

Warner Trail: Canton Junction Rail Station to Moose Hill

To reach the northern end of the Warner Trail, leave US 1 south of Boston near the Norwood Memorial Airport or take I-95. Take Neponset St. east into Canton, then turn left (north) onto Chapman St., following it to the railroad tracks. The rail station is a short distance to the right, where the Warner Trail begins.

The trail follows Wattles St. west a short block, turns left onto Jackson St., follows Jackson St. to its end, turns left onto Neponset St., then curves right onto Walpole St. (*Note:* Do not walk under the viaduct.) The trail follows Walpole St. up a long rise, then down a short slope. Just before Walpole St. makes a long bend to the right, the trail turns left through brush and into the woods, continuing to an old woods road, onto which it turns right. The trail follows the road uphill through pleasant woods to the Knollwood Memorial Park Cemetery. The trail winds southwest across the cemetery on paved roads, passing a small Iwo Jima memorial statue and farther along a large, white statue of Christ. (Follow the white paint marks on the pavement). The trail follows the right edge of the cemetery and turns onto a short, gated road into the Sharon Memorial Park Cemetery.

The trail continues on paved roads southwest toward a prominent high ledge on the southwest side of Dedham St., passing around the western end of a hedge along Dedham St. After crossing Dedham St. (parking for three or four cars), the trail winds through woodlands over a small hill, generally heading to the southwest, until it reaches a powerline clearing. The trail turns right onto the powerline service road and then almost immediately left through a metal gate onto Mt. Fern St. This gravel road becomes paved and continues to Bullard St. (*Note:* No parking allowed at the end of Mt. Fern St.)

Turning right on Bullard St., the trail crosses Norwood St. (MA 27) into the woods, where it turns right onto a narrow horse path through stunted growth to a powerline right-of-way. Here the trail turns right for a short distance and then left onto Everett St. (a wide gravel road).

The trail follows Everett St. south as it becomes a woods road, going between two large open fields and passing a large outcrop on the left. Turning right onto another woods road, the trail climbs slowly and then levels, passing a woods road entering from the right rear and another entering directly from the right. In another 500 ft. the trail turns right onto a path, goes down a slope, and turns left onto a mowed path which it follows to Moose Hill Pkwy., just west of its junction with Upland Rd. Jogging to the right a few feet, the trail enters the Moose Hill Audubon Sanctuary, going south on a path that turns right onto the Forbush Trail. The Warner Trail follows the Forbush Trail generally west almost to Moose Hill St., then turns right onto a path to the sanctuary parking lot.

Warner Trail: Moose Hill Audubon Sanctuary to Gilbert Hills State Forest

The trail (also marked with the letter "A" within the sanctuary) turns left through the parking lot gate and jogs slightly to the right to a gravel road passing between two stone posts. In about 50 yd. the trail turns right onto the Summit Trail, which it follows to the fire tower on the top of Moose Hill. Proceeding southwest from the fire tower, the trail comes out on a rocky knoll and drops down fairly steeply through the woods to a woods road, which it follows to the right. The trail later turns right, then turns right (southwest) onto another woods road and continues to a fork on the north slope of Bluff Head. Here the trail turns left (south), briefly following the Bluff Head Trail, then bears right at the next junction, continuing to Bluff Head, an ideal lunch spot with a wonderful view south. The trail travels southwest, slabbing across and down several rocky ledges and making one brief sharp climb. It then turns left onto a woods road, which descends to a fork near the bottom of the slope. The trail forks right, then goes left uphill to Walpole St. in Sharon, 0.8 mi. southeast of the intersection of Walpole St. and US 1.

The trail crosses Walpole St., turns left for about 50 ft., then turns right (west) into the woods and climbs to the top of Pierce Hill (350 ft.), where there is a good view south and west. The trail drops rapidly and steadily until it intersects the Old Post Road (once a main thoroughfare but now a woods road), which it follows south 0.3 mi. The trail then turns right onto a path that develops into a driveway (for an underground house) to Pine St. The trail turns left onto Pine St., then continues to S. Walpole St. It turns right (southwest) onto S. Walpole St., going over the northbound and under the southbound lanes of I-95, and continues to the first bend, where it turns left off the street onto an overgrown dirt road (Dudley Hill Rd.). (*Note:* No parking here.)

Taking care to go around the end of a blocking fence without damaging the bushes (intended to discourage all but pedestrians), and keeping right at the first fork, the trail follows a mostly straight woods road through swampy areas. Near the back of several new houses, the trail bears right, crosses a gas line easement, and winds through a swamp, with a stone wall on the left at times. As it approaches some lawns, the trail goes through a gap in a snow fence and then directly toward Beach St. It turns right onto Beach St., continues for 50 yd., then turns left (south) onto a right-of-way just beyond a large pin oak and a wooden fence. It continues through a row of large rocks and past two lonesome pin oaks, then turns left onto an old gravel road, which it follows a short distance to Edwards St.

The trail turns right on Edwards St. and in 0.6 mi. turns left up a bank. Proceeding through some woods, it follows the gravel Camp Rd. into the Whispering Pines development. Traveling on paved roads (McKenzie Ln. and Munroe St.) through the development, it reaches a cul-de-sac and reenters the woods onto Foxboro Conservation Commission land.

Heading to the south through open woods, the trail passes Neponset Reservoir on the left and the dam at the outlet of the reservoir. Just before reaching some railroad tracks, the trail turns left and parallels the tracks on several bog bridges (constructed by the Boy Scouts) leading to Chestnut St. Going to the right on Chestnut St., the trail crosses Main St. at a pedestrian light (look for a Dairy Queen and donut shop), turns left for a few yd., and then turns right into the Foxboro Conservation parking lot.

From the back of the parking lot, the trail follows a lane to the west, turning right at a trail junction. As it approaches Lakeview Rd., it turns right onto a somewhat obscure path to a Heritage Estates cul-de-sac, where it follows paved streets out to Lakeview Rd. The trail turns left and crosses the dam for Lakeview Lake. It then turns right along the side of the lake and continues west until it comes to Upper Dam Pond, where it crosses the dam and swings southeast around the pond to the gravel Messenger Rd.

The trail turns right onto the road and begins a long climb toward High Rock in Gilbert Hills State Forest. As the road nears the top, the trail forks right onto an old woods road and climbs almost to a fenced-in old radar test station. Here the trail turns left at the foot of a large boulder (High Rock itself) and follows a short path over the rise to the gravel clearing at the foot of a large microwave relay tower and base building. A paved road, maintained by the telephone company, leads to US 1, 0.5 mi. south of its intersection with US 1 and MA 140.

Warner Trail: Gilbert Hills State Forest to Wampum Corner

To reach the northern end of this section of the Warner Trail follow US 1 0.5 mi. south of its junction with MA 140 to the paved road (High Rock Rd.) on the left. Park only on the gravel area; do not park on the AT&T paved parking area, and do not block the fire-lane gate.

The trail leaves the eastern end of the gravel clearing near the foot of the microwave tower, just west of the barrier gate. In 150 yd. it turns left and follows a winding path, dropping down and passing under an overhanging cliff (Goat Rock—look for the tree growing out of the rock). Swinging to the right over a number of large rocks, the trail reaches the foot of a climb using a series of rock steps built by the CCC. The trail turns left, proceeds over the top, and passes a junction with the Acorn Trail, a rugged path leading 1.7 mi. to the state forest headquarters on Mill St. in Foxboro.

From here the trail goes south a short distance to the top of a large rock slab (excellent view west). The trail descends southwest to the base of the slab, and after a short distance turns right (north-northwest) on a woods road. In 0.4 mi. the trail turns left onto a path, continues 0.4 mi., then turns left onto a woods road, which leads a short distance to US 1. The trail crosses US 1 and proceeds on Myrtle St. in Wrentham. It follows Myrtle St. a few yards, then turns left into the woods just before a dirt road forks left and Myrtle St. veers right.

Following a path that parallels US 1 for a short distance, the trail jogs right and then left on a telephone-company cleared way and into pine woods, where it skirts a swamp and crosses over an extended bog bridge, eventually emerging on the cul-de-sac at the end of Davis Ave. The trail follows Davis Ave. one block to its end on Ames Ave., turns right onto Ames Ave. for one block, then turns left onto Dunn Ave. After one block the trail turns right onto Thurston St. and continues briefly to Warner Trail Rd., onto which it turns left. The trail follows Warner Trail Rd. 0.3 mi. to a cul-de-sac, continues straight on a conservation easement (10 ft. wide), then bears left, circling around through a notch to the remains of the sealed-over Wrentham landfill and through the gate to Madison St.

The trail continues into the woods directly across from the gate, turns sharp left, and, after a short flat stretch, circles to the right and steadily climbs to the first of several peaks, with some views north to Boston. The trail descends to a woods road, where it turns right. After a long descent, it veers left on a flat stretch and forks right (southeast) to descend another long slope. The trail then turns left (east) over rocky but fairly level terrain, ascends a short slope, and turns right for a few yards. It then turns left and continues over the top of an outcrop. Descending slowly, the trail crosses several trail-bike trails, passes through a couple of stone walls, and turns right (southwest) at a large boulder on the right. It then proceeds through woods and a short bramble patch, turning right (west) onto a woods road. The trail follows this road 0.2 mi., then turns left onto one woods road, left onto another, and sharp left (east) onto a third.

Following this road, the trail turns right (south) onto a newer path that swings left to skirt the right side of a stone wall (forest boundary). In 0.5 mi. the trail turns right (south), goes through a swampy area, and, after passing a small outcrop, continues almost due west, where it crosses Minnehaha Brook and then another small swamp. After a few yards the trail turns left (south) on a recently cut path, continuing 100 yd. to a rocky knoll called Outlook Rock. It leaves the knoll on the left (east), descending a slope and across a trail bike trail. The trail turns right (south), crosses a swampy area, and ascends to the top of a cliff overlooking Minnehaha Pond and the remains of an impressive dam on the right. It follows the east side of Minnehaha Brook 50 yd. to a woods road (the Red Fox Path), onto which it turns right (southwest). (A short bushwhack south about 100 yd. leads to the rapids named Minnehaha Falls.)

The Warner Trail and the Red Fox Path follow the woods road 0.6 mi. The Red Fox Path then forks left, and the Warner Trail continues northwest, following woods roads, trail-bike trails, and paths for another 0.5 mi. It then turns left onto a winding path, continues about 200 ft. to Taunton St., and turns right (north) onto the street. After 0.1 mi. the trail turns left (west) into handsome pine woods, where it turns right and almost parallels the street, crossing the Wrentham Water Works road (paved) at the fork (0.8 mi. south of MA 140 in Wrentham center). The trail continues almost due north 0.5 mi. to the bottom of an abandoned ski lift, where it turns left almost 180 degrees and ascends the steep slope to the summit of Knuckup Hill (extensive view north, including the Boston skyline).

The trail continues, following the gravel road left and down the hill, branching right on a path that avoids the brick building. At the paved road the trail turns right and then forks left down a slope and goes right on a narrow path along the south side of an attractive pond. The trail follows the gravel road past another pond on the left and out to Beech St. (at a point 0.5 mi. southeast of MA 1A). The trail goes southeast on Beach St., forking right onto Bear Swamp Rd. (a private woods road—please respect it), which enters the Wrentham State Forest and almost reaches I-495. Here the trail turns right, approaching I-495 twice more before curving to the right and going north, climbing slowly. The trail turns left and, after a long descent, a short sharp climb, and a drop through an area of abandoned autos and trucks, comes to MA 1A. To the right is Wampum Corner, the junction of MA 1A and MA 121.

Warner Trail: Wampum Corner to Hancock St. (Wrentham)

The trail leaves Wampum Corner on MA 121. In a few yards the trail turns left up a steep bank onto an abandoned railroad bed. The trail passes under I-495 on the railroad bed and immediately turns right, paralleling the highway for 0.2 mi. It then turns left, ascending to the top of an outcrop, where there is a view of the Boston skyline. The trail turns right (south) and follows the ridge, crossing a trail-bike trail. After more wandering, it turns left, crosses more ledge, and drops down across a well-worn path. The trail then climbs a rise to the top of another outcrop.

Continuing along the ridge, the trail turns left (southeast) and then southwest and comes to a powerline, where it bears left across the clearing and past a small illegal dump to a large tree with a white-plastic trail marker. Following southwest, the trail crosses rocky ledges, goes along a ridge, drops down, and turns left. In a few yards it comes to a new road and turns right to emerge on Green St. The trail turns right onto Green St. and follows it to a gravel and sand road. The trail turns left onto this road and continues approximately 1 mi. as the road deteriorates into an old woods road. The trail turns right onto an old trail and continues to the top of a ledge. The trail climbs 0.1 mi. to another outcrop, which affords limited views of Providence to the south and the High Rock microwave tower to the north.

The trail continues a few yards to a powerline, where it jogs right 20 yd., then turns left into the woods. It proceeds to Red Brush Hill and Sunset Rock, with excellent views west and southwest toward Diamond Hill in Rhode Island. Continuing southwest, the trail descends the ledge through the woods and soon emerges on Hancock St. at a point 0.8 mi. east of MA 121 in Sheldonville (a part of Wrentham).

Warner Trail: Hancock St. (Wrentham) to Diamond Hill

Turning left onto Hancock St., the trail turns right in about 0.4 mi. onto a lane to a Christmas tree farm (Hancock Crafts). (*Note:* No parking is permitted at the farm entrance or on Hancock St.). Follow the lane through the lot and down a slope for about 275 yd. to a small brook, where the trail turns left over a crude bridge and proceeds through a young-tree lot. (*Note:* Use care in crossing the tree lots, and watch for blue flags denoting seedlings.)

The trail now travels southeast to southwest across a large swampy area, mostly on the Wentworth Civil Engineering Campus, turns right across a concrete slab bridge, and follows a woods road until it turns out to an open field. The trail does not follow the road into the field but continues in the woods to the right of the field, then crosses a field to emerge on Rhodes St. in Plainville. The trail follows the street right across the Massachusetts–Rhode Island line and continues to Burnt Swamp Rd. in Cumberland. It turns right (northwest) onto this road and proceeds 0.5 mi. to Tingley Rd., where it turns sharply left.

The trail passes Ker-Anna, a summer camp, and turns right onto a driveway leading to a dam for the small lake. After crossing the dam, the trail follows a woods road west and southwest to a small triangle formed by paths. Here it turns right (north) to circle around the Diamond Hill Reservoir on a woods road, a brief cut-off to the left, and another woods road. The trail continues generally west to a small brook, where it turns left (south) and goes through a swampy area and then along the side of the reservoir, sometimes coming within a yard of the water. Climbing up to the right, the trail then slabs along the side of a hill for about 0.5 mi. It then climbs west to a rocky ledge with an open crest and views of the Diamond Hill Reservoir.

The trail goes generally south along a down-sloping ridge, proceeds onto a woods road, and, just before the road goes underwater, turns right onto a path that leads up and over a rise. In 0.1 mi. the trail turns left (southwest) through some heavy brush, crosses a small stream, and climbs up a sharp rise. Descending the other side, the trail bears left (south) onto a woods road. It then bears right onto a path through many muddy, narrow spots along the side of the reservoir until it comes to Fisher Rd. (stone cairn) and turns sharp right up the remains of the old road. The road becomes paved in the middle of a condominium project and the trail continues on the paved road for about 200 yd., where it turns left onto a well-worn path up a slope. The trail turns left on the first woods road and zig-zags to the summit of Diamond Hill (481 ft.), where you can see indistinct remains of the old ski operations. On the east side, below the summit, the Boston and Providence skylines are visible in good weather. A sheer 150-ft. cliff on the south side is often used by rock climbers for practicing rope techniques.

From here the trail passes a large water tank and wanders south along the ridge, emerging at the edge of several sheer drops, and finally comes to a steep drop-off on the right. At this point the trail descends to RI 114 in Cumberland. This is an abandoned quarry, at the bottom of which the trail turns right to parallel a gas-line easement that is blocked by a cable. Eventually the trail goes over to the easement and crosses a brook on the exposed 18-in. gas pipes. The trail then continues to the Diamond Hill parking lot.

(*Note:* During periods following heavy rains or snow, the Wentworth swamp may be impassable except with rubber boots. An alternate route starts with a right turn on Hancock St. after coming down from Sunset Rock. Walk about 0.1 mi. and keep left at the fork (following Hancock St.), going another 0.4 mi. to Burnt Swamp Rd. Follow this road to the left for 1.5 mi., where it meets the main trail at the intersection with Tingley Rd.

Warner Trail

Distances from Canton Rail Station:

    to Moose Hill Audubon Sanctuary: 7.3 mi.
    to High Rock: 17.3 mi.
    to Wampum Corner: 25.8 mi.
    to Hancock St.: 28.9 mi.
    to Diamond Hill summit: 33.4 mi.
    to Diamond Hill parking lot: 34.5 mi.

BAY CIRCUIT TRAIL

The Bay Circuit Trail, the region's newest long-distance hiking trail, is still under development. When completed, it will stretch for almost 200 mi. in a great arc around the entire Boston metropolitan area, connecting now-isolated parks and reservations into a continuous greenbelt. For a complete description of this project, see Section 6 of this book. Described below is the status of the Bay Circuit Trail in the various towns it will traverse in the southern part of the route. See Section 6 for a description of the northern and western parts of the route.

A vertical white rectangle will be the standard blaze for the Bay Circuit Trail, although the hiker should expect to find sections which have not yet been blazed to this standard.

Medfield, Walpole, Sharon, Easton

The proposed route passes through Medfield on a variety of open and cemetery land but primarily on country roads until it reaches the Noon Hill Reservation. From there it proceeds via subdivision and country roads to the Walpole border where it connects to Walpole town-forest land via a powerline right-of-way. Walpole's major tracts of conserved town-forest land provide a trail corridor through Walpole Center and over I-95 to Moose Hill Wildlife Sanctuary in Sharon. Here, it intersects with the Warner Trail. After Moose Hill the proposed route connects to Borderlands State Park in Easton, primarily via secondary roads. It then continues through the center of Easton on country roads and conservation lands until it reaches an abandoned railway line, which it follows to the border between Easton and West Bridgewater, near the Hockomock Swamp Wildlife Management Area.

West Bridgewater, East Bridgewater, Hanson

As yet there is no clear off-road route leading from the Hockomock Swamp area in West Bridgewater through East Bridgewater and Hanson to Pembroke. Country roads and an abandoned railway line offer some possibilities, and considerable open space exists to the south of MA 106 along rivers and in wetlands, as well as north of MA 106. A more definitive route awaits the ingenuity and enthusiasm of local community organizations.

Pembroke (1 mile of dedicated trail)

Pemboke's dedicated trail is located in central Pembroke near the Hobomock School on town conservation land. A local alliance is working on a proposed trail network that will enter Pembroke from Hanson, link with the dedicated trail, and branch to meet both the Duxbury dedicated trail and a proposed Kingston connection.

Kingston

The proposed route in Kingston would enter from Pembroke near Silver Lake, follow the Jones River, and end at the Bay Farm on Kingston Bay.

Duxbury (7 miles of dedicated trail)

Red blazes mark the trail in Duxbury, which includes views of Kingston Bay, old cranberry bogs, and forests. It enters from Pembroke at Valley Street by Upper Chandler Pond. The trail connects via paths on private and town land, and some paved roads, to the southern terminus of the Bay Circuit Trail at the Bay Farm on Kingston Meadow.

To reach this end of the trail, take exit 10 off MA 3. Continue east on MA 3A about 0.5 mi., then turn right onto Parks St. At a Y-intersection, bear left on Loring St. There is parking on the left soon after a stop sign.

MOOSE HILL AUDUBON SANCTUARY (MAS)

The 227-acre Moose Hill Wildlife Sanctuary is the oldest sanctuary operated by the Massachusetts Audubon Society. Located 25 mi. from Boston, it includes mixed woods, open fields, and wetlands. The terrain, vegetation, and geology of the sanctuary are diverse for this region.

From the intersection of US 1 and MA 27 in Walpole, go 0.2 mi. east on MA 27 and turn right onto Moose Hill St. The sanctuary is 1.5 mi. on the right.

Highlights include the summit of Moose Hill (534 ft.), with a panoramic view from its firetower; Bluff Hill and Bluff Head (450 ft.), a hill that rises steeply on its west, south, and east sides with precipitous granite ledges and spectacular views to the south and west; and geology, including drumlins, a kettle hole, a bog, and granite ledges and outcrops.

A network of trails and woods roads of varying length and challenge make much of the property accessible. The Warner Trail (marked by white markers) passes through the sanctuary and over the summits of Moose Hill and Bluff Hill. See the description of the Warner Trail earlier in this section. It is also part of the planned route of the Bay Circuit Trail. Trail maps are available at the information shelter at the sanctuary parking lot or at the sanctuary office.

Summit Trail (MAS)

This trail travels north from the sanctuary headquarters, crosses a gravel road (Billings Way) in about 100 yd., then turns northwest and follows a fairly straight course. After crossing an old woods road, it continues to the summit of Moose Hill, where there is a fire tower with views in all directions. For most of its distance it coincides with the long-distance Warner Trail, and is marked with the Warner Trail's white blazes plus the letter "A".

Summit Trail

Distance from parking lot
    to summit of Moose Hill: 0.5 mi. (20 min.)

Bluff Hill (MAS)

This route, which is actually a combination of parts of three separate trails, provides the most direct access to Bluff Hill from the sanctuary parking lot.

From the parking lot, start on the "B" (Billings/Boardwalk) trail, and then bear right onto the "C" (Cistern) trail. This leads through pine woods, past a wall of rocks on the right, to a junction with the Warner ("A") Trail in the col between Moose Hill and Bluff Hill. Turn left on the Warner Trail, heading uphill past an old water cistern and a couple of small ponds to the summit of Bluff Hill.

Bluff Hill

Distance from parking lot via "B", "C", and "A" trails:
    to Bluff Hill summit: 1.5 mi. (45 min.)

BRISTOL BLAKE STATE PARK (DEM) AND STONY BROOK WILDLIFE SANCTUARY (MAS)

This 300-acre reservation in Norfolk is comprised of both state (DEM) and Massachusetts Audubon property, and is managed by the Audubon Society. The terrain includes open fields and woods, Stony Brook, three interconnected ponds known collectively as Stony Brook Pond, adjoining marshes, and a narrow, wooded isthmus centrally located amid the three ponds. The northernmost and largest pond is called Kingfisher Pond.

The Stony Brook Nature Center, which includes the park's office, is located a short distance south of the junction of North, Pond, and Needham streets in Norfolk. From Norfolk center follow MA 115 for 1 mi. south to North St. Turn right onto North St. to the sanctuary entrance on the right. Maps are available at the nature center.

Stony Brook Nature Trail (MAS)

This loop trail starts from the rear of the nature-center building. It is marked by numbered stakes and identifying labels and is described in detail in a booklet available at the center. It leads between stone walls, passes through woods, and crosses a brook connecting Teal Marsh (where muskrat houses are visible in the distance) with Stony Brook Pond. The trail then climbs a forested glacial knoll and leads to a boardwalk over the marsh, counter-clockwise around an island, and back over the boardwalk, passing Lookout Point, a boulder-strewn area overlooking Kingfisher Pond. It goes on past a large, fallen (and now mostly decomposed) red maple, traverses a forest of white birch and mixed species, and threads its way through flowering dogwood to Stony Brook. Near-by are part of an old mill foundation and mill race. The trail then crosses an open meadow to the starting point.

Stony Brook Nature Trail

Distance from Stony Brook Nature Center
   to return to Stony Brook Nature Center: 1 mi. (30 min.)

BORDERLAND STATE PARK (DEM)

This state park was purchased in 1971 from the estate of Blanche Ames. The name, given to the property by the Ameses, refers to the Easton–Sharon border on which the park lies. Wooded hills, ponds, and open fields are included in this 1,600-acre reservation.

To reach the park from Sharon center (MA 27 at N. Main St. and Depot St.), go south via Pond St. and Massapoag Ave., passing Lake Massapoag, for 4.4 mi. From the east, south, or west, use MA 106 or MA 123, which cross in this part of Easton. Opposite the

Belcher Malleable Iron Co., turn north onto Poquanticut Ave. Follow this 1.5 mi. to the second left, then turn northwest onto Massapoag Ave. and continue 2 mi.

Interesting features of the landscape include the many dams constructed in an attempt to transform swampland into ponds. The Ameses created a forest and wildlife preserve on the majority of the estate, while developing the land's potential for outdoor recreational activities such as hiking, canoeing, skating, and skiing.

The park contains a number of hiking trails, most of which are easy to follow and suitable for hikers of all abilities. There is a lovely trail over the Long Dam which separates Lower and Upper Leach ponds. Farther to the east lie more ponds and the site of the historic Colonel Israel Tisdale House, which was destroyed by fire in 1983.

The more difficult trails are the Lower Granite Hill Loop and Upper Granite Hill Loop, both of which lie to the north of Upper Leach Pond. These interconnecting trails (a total of 3 mi.) wend their way through oak forests and large granite outcrops. The latter can be difficult for skiers.

The ponds are great for fishing and nonmotorized boating and are most easily reached via the park road that leads in from the Bay Rd. entrance on the east side of the park. No open fires are allowed, and a strict no-alcohol policy is enforced. A map is available from DEM; also refer to the USGS Mansfield quadrangle.

MYLES STANDISH STATE FOREST (DEM)

Myles Standish State Forest in Carver is one of the largest reservations in the Massachusetts state park and forest system. In addition to hiking, the forest offers camping, bicycling, canoeing, and swimming.

Park headquarters is located on Cranberry Rd. From the west, follow MA 58 into the town of Carver (Tremont Rd.). Where MA 58 turns left off Tremont St., continue straight ahead on Tremont Rd. for a little less than a mile. Cranberry Rd. will be on the right. (From the other direction, turn left off MA 58 where it turns right onto Tremont Rd.).

Easthead Trail (DEM)

The original Easthead Trail is a 3-mi. loop circling Easthead Reservoir. In 1991, the 4.5-mi. Bentley loop was added at the northern end of the original loop. Both the original trail and the Bentley loop are blazed with blue trail markers or blue paint slashes.

The trail begins on the north side of Cranberry Rd., about 150 yd. east of park headquarters. A sign indicates the entrance to the Easthead Nature Trail. Entering the woods, the trail proceeds north, roughly following the east side of the reservoir. In about 1.4 mi., the trail turns left onto a well-used bridle path, which is also a powerline. In a short distance, the trail reaches two marked junctions. At the first, the original loop turns left to return to the starting point via the west side of the reservoir.

To continue on to the Bentley loop, walk a few yards farther to the second junction, where the trail turns right onto a paved road. It follows the paved road a short distance to the first dirt road on the left (with a metal gate numbered 75). The trail follows this dirt road a short distance and then turns right onto a woods road. At the end of this road, just before a meadow, is a trail junction, with the Bentley loop heading both left and right.

Turn left at the junction and follow the blue markers onto the Bentley loop. (*Note:* Use care, as the loop is well marked but crosses many other paths worn by hunters and hikers. If no trail marker is seen after a short distance, retrace your steps to the last intersection.) The trail skirts the edge of New Long Pond, bears right, then left, and passes Three Cornered Pond on the left. Soon the trail reaches the first of several meadows. It proceeds almost straight across this meadow (there is a 5-ft. post in the middle of the meadow) and then enters the woods again. The trail turns left just before another meadow and moves northerly toward College Pond.

At another meadow, the trail turns left and continues along the left edge of this meadow until it turns left into the woods at another marker. Soon it reaches its northernmost point at a trail junction, where a path leads north to the College Pond parking area. The Bentley loop turns right at the junction and proceeds south, following a well-worn bicycle path.

After about 50 yds., the trail turns left off the bicycle path, continues down a hill, and then turns sharply right. Soon the trail comes to another meadow (the first since turning south), where it proceeds down the center of the meadow, exiting to the left at the far end. Soon College Pond Rd. is visible on the left. The trail skirts the edge of a parking lot, then turns right into the woods.

Another meadow is reached, which is also followed down the center to its end. Here the trail plunges into the woods, turns to the right, and goes straight across one more meadow at the bottom of a hill. After another turn, the trail arrives at the starting point of the Bentley loop.

To return to the lower loop, walk down the woods road, turning left at the dirt road and proceeding to the gate at the paved road. Turn right on the paved road, follow it to the bridle path, turn left on the bridle path, and then make a quick right to continue on the second half of the Easthead loop. This is followed for about 1.5 mi. around the reservoir back to the starting point.

Easthead Trail

Distances from Cranberry Rd.
   to northern end of lower loop: 1.5 mi. (45 min.)
   to return to lower loop via Bentley loop: 6 mi. (3 hr.)
   to return to Cranberry Rd.: 7.5 mi. (3 hr. 45 min.)

STONY BROOK VALLEY (CAPE COD)

A small, but interesting network of trails is located in the town of Brewster, on property belonging both to the town and to the Cape Cod Museum of Natural History. These trails are in the valley of Stony Brook, which flows down from a series of freshwater ponds, becomes a tidal estuary merging with a salt marsh, and has its outlet in Cape Cod Bay. The town of Brewster owns Wing's Island on the north side of the shore road, an area comprising some 33 acres of upland plus 90 acres of salt marsh and beach. The Cape Cod Museum of Natural History owns 5 acres adjoining the road, plus 48 acres of marshland and beech woods to the south.

The trails traverse salt marsh, sandy scrub, and woodland, with views over Cape Cod Bay. All of the trails are well-marked and easy to hike. Park at the museum parking lot on MA 6A (1.7 mi. west of the junction of MA 6A and MA 137, and a short distance west of Paine's Creek Rd.). Maps are available at the museum.

NICKERSON STATE PARK (DEM)

This 1,779-acre state park contains 7.7 mi. of bicycle paths and more than 15 mi. of excellent hiking trails. Although the trails are not blazed, they are easy to follow as they wind through the scrub pine around the various lakes and ponds. The Southeast Chapter of the AMC maintains the trails in this park.

The park entrance is located on the south side of MA 6A in Brewster, about 1.5 mi. west of exit 12 on the Mid-Cape Highway (MA 6). The main parking lot is on the right just inside the entrance to the park. An easy access to some of the trails is at the end of Flax Pond Rd., which is the first road on the left after entering the park. Follow it to a parking area between Big Cliff Lake and Little Cliff Pond, where there is a boat ramp. Park maps are available at the entrance gate; also refer to the USGS Harwich and Orleans quadrangles.

CAPE COD NATIONAL SEASHORE

Established in 1961, the Cape Cod National Seashore is maintained by the U.S. Department of the Interior's National Parks Service. The seashore includes six beaches—Coast Guard Beach and Nauset Light Beach in Eastham, Marconi Beach in South Wellfleet, Head of the Meadows Beach in Truro, and Race Point Beach and Herring Cove Beach in Provincetown—plus extensive inland areas of scrub pine, salt marsh, and swampland.

There are two visitor centers—Salt Pond Visitor Center in Eastham and Province Lands Visitor Center in Provincetown. The Salt Pond Visitor Center, the starting point for a number of interesting walks, is located on the right side of MA 6, 4 mi. north of the

Orleans rotary. Maps, nature guides, and other publications are available at both visitor centers. Also refer to the USGS Orleans, Wellfleet, North Truro, and Provincetown quadrangles.

There are a large number of hiking paths and nature trails in the National Seashore. Most are well marked and relatively easy to hike.

Great Island Trail

Great Island is open only to hikers and boaters; no vehicles are permitted. To reach the beginning of the Great Island Trail from the town pier in Wellfleet, turn right onto Kendrick Rd., then left onto Chequesset Neck Rd. The trail begins at a parking lot at the end of the road. Great Island Trail is a scenic but somewhat strenuous loop through woods, dunes, and swamps. (*Note:* Along the marshes the trail might be wet during high tide, especially during the fall and winter.)

From the parking lot the trail winds through a pitch pine forest and proceeds across the marshy neck of land which connects Great Island to the mainland. The actual loop begins on this neck of land. On reaching the island, the trail turns left and proceeds in an east to southeast direction, skirting the marshes and dunes along the northern edge of Great Island. Just before reaching the cliffs on the northeastern corner of the island, the trail turns sharply right. A side trail continues ahead to the edge of the cliffs, with scenic views across Wellfleet Bay.

The trail now winds through the woodlands covering the interior of Great Island, heading generally west and south. As the terrain turns more to marshland, the trail heads to the south, crossing over Great Beach Hill. At the southern end of Great Island is a trail junction, where a spur trail leads south along a sand spit toward Jeremy Point. Due to encroachment by the sea, it is no longer possible to walk all the way to Jeremy Point.

From the trail junction the Great Island loop returns to the north, following the beaches along the western edge of the island. Ascending over some dunes via stairs and a boardwalk, the trail reaches the neck of land between Great Island and the mainland, where the loop ends. From here, turn left to return to the parking lot.

Great Island Trail

Distance from parking lot
  to return to parking lot: 7.5 mi. (3 hr. 45 min.)

MARTHA'S VINEYARD

This triangular island off the south shore of Cape Cod, measuring approximately 25 mi. from east to west and 10 mi. from north to south, has a number of towns and settlements, including Edgartown, Vineyard Haven, Oak Bluffs, Gay Head, and Menemsha. The island abounds in freshwater ponds, lakes, coves, and beaches. Many dirt roads bordered by wildflowers offer excellent bicycling and walking. A combination of beaches, cliffs, ponds, and woods makes the south shore the best recreational section of the island, although the north shore offers the best woods walking. Refer to the USGS Vineyard Haven, Edgartown, Squibnocket, Tisbury Great Pond, and Naushon Island quadrangles.

Year-round car and passenger ferry service is operated by the Steamship Authority from Woods Hole in Falmouth (tel. 508-548-3788 for schedules and fares).

Among the protected open spaces on the Vineyard offering hiking opportunities are Martha's Vineyard State Forest (DEM), Felix Neck Wildlife Sanctuary (MAS), Long Point Wildlife Refuge (TR), Menemsha Hills Reservation (TR), and Cedar Tree Neck Wildlife Sanctuary. There are also scenic beach walks at Wasque Reservation (TR) and Cape Poge Wildlife Refuge (TR) on neighboring Chappaquiddick Island, reached via a short ferry ride from Edgartown.

SECTION 9
Rhode Island

Despite its small size and lack of any significant summits (its highest point is only 812 feet above sea level), Rhode Island offers many points of interest and opportunities for outdoor recreation. In particular, the state parks and forest-management areas along the western edge of the state offer a number of excellent hiking trails.

Rhode Island state maps, which list the locations of state parks and management areas, saltwater and freshwater beaches, stocked trout ponds, streams, and other points of interest, are available free from the Rhode Island Tourism Division, 7 Jackson Walkway, Providence, RI 02903 (tel. 800-556-2484).

Any outing in a state-owned area involving ten or more participants requires a permit that can be obtained from the appropriate park or management area headquarters.

Caution is urged when using trails in state-owned areas, particularly during the deer shotgun season in December, as most areas are open to hunting.

ARCADIA MANAGEMENT AREA

The state's most extensive hiking-trail network extends over a large forested area just 35 miles southwest of Providence. Public properties in this area include the Arcadia Management Area, Arcadia State Park, Beach Pond State Park, and Pachaug State Forest just across the state line in Connecticut. The trails in this area are maintained by the Narragansett Chapter of the AMC (NCAMC), with assistance from the Rhode Island Department of Environmental Management (RIDEM), Division of Forest Environment. There are also fireplaces, picnic tables, and toilet facilities at the picnic areas, two ponds with beaches for swimming, and two overnight shelters.

For further information, contact the park headquarters at Division of Forest Environment, 260 Arcadia Road, Hope Valley, RI 02832 (tel. 401-539-2356).

Several of the trails described below cross RI 165 between RI 3 and the Connecticut state line. To reach RI 165 from I-95, take exit 5A at the RI 102 interchange and follow RI 102 east to RI 3. Turn right (south) onto RI 3 and continue 1.3 mi. to RI 165 on the right (west).

Refer to the Rhode Island—Arcadia Management Area trail map included with this book.

Arcadia Trail (NCAMC)

This trail, marked with plastic yellow blazes, starts at the Division of Forest Environment headquarters on Arcadia Rd. To reach this location, follow RI 165 from its beginning (see previous description) 1.5 mi. to Arcadia Rd. on the left. Take Arcadia Rd. 3.2 mi. south through Arcadia village to the headquarters on the right. Parking facilities are available here. The Arcadia Trail (sign) begins on the left (east) side of the road.

Signs and blazes mark this trail clearly. (*Note:* There are a few wet places in very wet seasons.) Most brook crossings are by bridges, and the trail generally consists of modest grades with good footing, except in the two boulder-strewn areas, which can be bypassed by using a white-blazed cutoff trail.

From Arcadia Rd. the trail winds 0.8 mi. to a crossing of K–G Ranch Rd. The trail goes over a brook on a 10-ft. bridge about 0.2 mi. from the road. In a short distance the Arcadia Trail takes a sharp right, while a white-blazed trail continues straight ahead on an old road with easy grades. This cutoff rejoins the main trail in 0.9 mi. at a point 3.3 mi. from the trailhead.

The main trail winds a long distance through moderate hills and two short sections requiring very rough scrambling over interesting boulder fields, before connecting with the white-blazed cutoff trail. The trail then continues to a dirt road (Tefft Hill Trail), turning right (east) a few feet to a junction with another trail blazed with white plastic rectangles and blue paint marks. This side trail leads through a closed campground, with the white blazes continuing 0.6 mi. to RI 3 at the inactive Dawley Memorial Park, and the blue blazes continuing 0.5 mi. along a path straight to RI 3. The blue-blazed trail is part of the new North–South Trail (N–S Trail) that is planned to extend the length of the state.

The Arcadia Trail turns left at the junction, dips down to and crosses Spring Brook and soon Roaring Brook, then turns sharp right (north) at a trail junction. Here another side trail, marked with both white plastic rectangles and the N–S Trail's blue paint blazes, leads 0.3 mi. to Arcadia Rd. near Arcadia Pond (Browning Mill Pond on the USGS quadrangle) and the Browning Mill Recreation Area. There is a beach, picnic area, and parking facilities at the recreation area.

From the junction the Arcadia Trail and the N–S Trail continue together, first north and then westerly across Arcadia Rd. They enter the woods and soon reach Bates Schoolhouse Rd. Turning right, the trails join a gravel road that bears left and is barricaded to vehicles. Both trails follow this road west. Just beyond a water hole on the left, the N–S Trail continues on the road while the Arcadia Trail turns right into the woods. It continues northwest, slabbing on a hillside, and comes to a junction with the end of the Mount Tom Trail on the left. Crossing a wet area (poison sumac in the area), the Arcardia Trail reaches its terminus at Appie Crossing on RI 165.

There is a small parking area on the south side of RI 165 and another on the John B. Hudson Trail, about 200 ft. north of the trail sign on RI 165.

Arcadia Trail

Distances from forestry headquarters

    to K–G Ranch Rd.: 0.8 mi. (25 min.)

    to start of white cutoff trail: 1 mi. (30 min.)

    to end of white cutoff trail: 3.3 mi. (2 hr. 10 min.)

    to Tefft Hill Trail: 3.6 mi. (2 hr. 20 min.)

    to Appie Crossing (RI 165): 6.7 mi. (4 hr. 10 min.)

    (*Note:* White cutoff trail shortens the distance to Tefft Hill Trail and Appie Crossing by 1.4 mi. [1 hr. 15 min.])

John B. Hudson Trail (NCAMC)

This trail, formerly part of the Breakheart Trail, runs north from
Appie Crossing to Fish Ladder Dam on Breakheart Pond. The trail
is named after John B. Hudson of Coventry, a member of the first
NCAMC trail committee who devoted much time and energy to
maintaining the trails for the use and enjoyment of others. The trail
begins on RI 165, 2.5 mi. west of RI 3. A large sign with map, trail
descriptions, regulations, and bulletins for the Arcadia Management Area is located in the parking area just off RI 165.

Marked with yellow blazes, the trail travels north on an old logging road, passing through a heavily cut area of oak, which is now
overgrown with pine. An observation tower constructed by the
Youth Conservation Corps in 1976 is located just to the left of the
trail in this section.

Very soon the trail narrows and dips left, descends a slight
slope, then bears right. Just before the trail crosses the Tripp Trail
(a forestry road), a sign on the right points out an old cemetery. At
0.8 mi. the white-blazed Shelter Trail (sign) leads left (west) to
Frosty Hollow Rd. and eventually to a junction with the Breakheart
Trail near Penny Hill. (A shelter is located on the Shelter Trail 0.6
mi. from the John B. Hudson Trail. Reservations to use the shelter
must be made with the Division of Forest Environment; see beginning of this section for address and phone).

At the start of the Shelter Trail, the John B. Hudson Trail forks,
following either the yellow primary blazes or the white secondary
blazes. The white trail drops down a feeder brook to Breakheart
Brook (where the mountain laurel is pretty in mid-June), then turns
right and goes upstream along Breakheart Brook to Austin Pond
Rd. at the Fish Ladder Dam of Breakheart Pond. (*Note:* Heavy use
of the white-blazed trail has changed areas of sphagnum moss,
kept wet by springs, to muddy footing for most of the year.) The
yellow-blazed trail that turns sharp right at the fork is only 0.1 mi.
longer than the white trail and offers dry, easy walking over high
ground to Breakheart Pond at the Fish Ladder Dam.

Parking for many cars is available at the fisherman's access to
the dam and in a parking area up the hill. Side trails, with white

paint marks, provide for several short, interconnecting walks from the dam.

John B. Hudson Trail

Distances from RI 165
>   *to* Shelter Trail: 0.8 mi. (25 min.)
>   *to* Fish Ladder Dam on Breakheart Pond
>   *via* white trail: 1.6 mi. (45 min.)
>   *via* yellow trail: 1.7 mi. (50 min.)

Breakheart Trail (NCAMC)

Marked with yellow paint, this trail follows Austin Farm Rd. a short distance east from the bridge below Fish Ladder Dam on Breakheart Pond. As it turns left onto an old logging road, a sign shows the distance to various landmarks along the trail. The trail turns left again at 0.8 mi., crosses Breakheart Brook north of the pond, then abruptly turns right (north). (At this point a side trail with white paint connects to short interconnecting trails, to a walk circling back to Fish Ladder Dam, or to the midpoint of the Shelter Trail. On the latter, notice "No Trespassing" signs around Camp E-HUNT-EE, a camp operated by the Eckerd Foundation for clients of the Department of Children and Families and located in part of an area formerly known as Beach Pond Camps.)

As the Breakheart Trail turns north, it parallels the brook, then winds west, goes through two lovely pine groves, and crosses Acid Factory Brook. In 0.5 mi. it crosses Phillips Brook, follows an old woods road a short distance, then skirts a swampy, brushy area. After passing this area, the trail turns right off the road, while the white-blazed Shelter Trail continues on the road through the abandoned section of Beach Pond Camps and to the shelter near Breakheart Brook.

The Breakheart Trail gradually ascends a shoulder of Penny Hill through the woods, and in 0.5 mi. passes a short connecting link to the Shelter Trail (sign). The trail reaches the summit of Penny Hill (370 ft.) in another 0.5 mi. This rocky shoulder affords a fine view of the surrounding country. Descending to the west, the trail crosses Austin Farm Rd. (gravel) and proceeds with a northwest jog at a fire lane and another at a muddy area to Falls River Bridge and a junction with the Ben Utter Trail and the Escoheag Trail. Parking for several cars is available near the bridge and just up the hill on an old gravel bank. (*Note:* The trail is marked by posts at 1, 2, 3, and 4 mi.)

Breakheart Trail

Distances from bridge on Breakheart Pond
>   *to* Acid Factory Brook: 2.4 mi. (1 hr. 15 min.)
>   *to* Phillips Brook: 2.9 mi. (1 hr. 30 min.)
>   *to* summit of Penny Hill: 4.1 mi. (2 hr.)
>   *to* Falls River Bridge (Ben Utter Trail and Escoheag Trail): 4.9 mi. (2 hr. 30 min.)

Mt. Tom Trail (NCAMC)

This white-blazed trail begins at Appie Crossing on RI 165 at the junction of the Arcadia Trail and the John B. Hudson Trail, 2.5 mi. west of RI 3. The trail follows the Arcadia Trail 0.1 mi. south, then turns right (west) through a wooded area, crossing two dirt roads and coming to a parking area on the Wood River, just south of RI 165. (Parts of this trail have suffered badly from heavy use.) From the parking area the trail crosses the Wood River Bridge west on RI 165, but almost immediately departs left from the highway into an open space with a Quonset hut on the left and a good parking lot. This is the checking station for hunters. The trail then leads generally south through young pines, emerging on a dirt road (the Blitzkrieg Trail).

The trail turns left for a few hundred yards on the road, then abruptly turns right at the bridge over Parris Brook. It follows the north side of the brook to the paved Mt. Tom Rd. at another bridge. Immediately before crossing this bridge, the trail turns right (north) and ascends Mt. Tom along the edge of a steep cliff to the Mt. Tom Cliffs, which afford a fine view. The trail continues north over rocky ledges and crosses RI 165 4.3 mi. west of RI 3. Across the highway the trail continues north to a junction with the Escoheag Trail, which leads left (west) to the Ledges overlook and parking area and right (east) to the Ben Utter Trail and the Breakheart Trail.

Mt. Tom Trail

Distances from Appie Crossing
   to Wood River: 0.9 mi. (30 min.)
   to Mt. Tom Cliffs: 2.3 mi. (1 hr. 10 min.)
   to RI 165: 2.8 mi. (1 hr. 25 min.)
   to Escoheag Trail: 3.9 mi. (2 hr.)

Escoheag Trail (NCAMC)

To reach the start of this trail by car, take Escoheag Hill Rd. north 0.9 mi. from RI 165. Turn right onto the first gravel road (Austin Farm Rd.), then right onto another gravel road (marked with white plastic blazes) that leads to the Ledges parking area. The Escoheag Trail starts at the southern end of the parking area. At 0.1 mi. a short trail leads to an open shelter, constructed in the 1930s by the CCC, with obstructed views. The main trail continues east through a forest with interesting ledges, crosses two valleys, and meets the northern end of the Mt. Tom Trail at a gravel road (the Barber Trail) at 0.8 mi. The Escoheag Trail crosses the road and proceeds north through an area of second growth and open country to an intersection with a part of the North–South Trail. Turning left, the Escoheag Trail joins the N–S Trail and both continue about 1200 ft. to Austin Farm Rd. Here the Escoheag Trail turns right and quickly reaches its terminus at a junction with the Ben Utter and Breakheart Trails at the Falls River Bridge. Parking is available near the bridge on both sides of the river.

Escoheag Trail

Distance from Ledges parking area
   to Falls River Bridge: 2 mi. (1 hr.)

Ben Utter Trail (NCAMC)

This trail is dedicated to the memory of George Benjamin Utter, long active in the promotion of hiking in Rhode Island. Ben Utter was a member of the original trail committee of the NCAMC. Trail blazing and maintenance were his principal hobbies, but he was also a leader in organizing Rhode Island Camps, Inc. (Beach Pond Camps) for underprivileged children. Part of the original camping area is now operated by the Eckerd Foundation as Camp E-HUNT-EE for clients of the Department of Children and Families.

Marked with yellow plastic blazes, the Ben Utter Trail starts at the Falls River Bridge on Austin Farm Rd., at a junction with the Breakheart and Escoheag trails. The trailhead is reached from RI 165 by going about 0.9 mi. north on Escoheag Hill Rd. and then 1.8 mi. east on Austin Farm Rd., which is the gravel road to the management area. Austin Farm Rd. is barricaded near Escoheag Hill Rd. during the winter months.

The Ben Utter Trail follows the west side of the Falls River for 0.5 mi., then bears northwest. The foundation of an old gristmill and a vertical sawmill may be seen close to the trail. Shortly before reaching the Stepstone Falls camping area, a white-blazed side trail leads right along the river to the Stepstone Falls. The main trail continues to the camping area, where there are fireplaces and a shelter, but no water or tables. (Reservations to use the area must be made in advance through the Division of Forest Environment.) The Ben Utter Trail now joins with the Tippecansett Trail and both continue 0.3 mi. to Stepstone Falls and Falls River Rd.

Ben Utter Trail

Distances from Falls River Bridge (Austin Farm Rd.)
   to Stepstone Falls camping area: 1.4 mi. (40 min.)
   to Stepstone Falls and Falls River Rd.: 1.7 mi. (50 min.)

Tippecansett Trail (NCAMC)

Although this is the longest trail in the area, the Tippecansett Trail is broken into three nearly equal sections by two highways. Marked with yellow plastic blazes, it starts at Stepstone Falls on Falls River Rd. This is a dirt road turning off Escoheag Hill Rd. about 3 mi. from RI 165.

From the small parking area at Stepstone Falls the Tippecansett Trail, together with the Ben Utter Trail, runs uphill about 0.3 mi. to the Stepstone Falls camping area. (For information see the Ben Utter Trail.) Leaving the Ben Utter Trail at this point, the Tippecansett Trail proceeds to the north end of the paved area and then through the woods to a town road (Falls River Rd.), where it turns left uphill to Escoheag Hill Rd. The trail turns right (north), continuing to a cemetery on the east side of the road. At the cemetery the trail turns left (west) at a junction with the white-blazed Canonicus Trail that connects with the Pachaug Trail in Connecticut. For a description of these trails, see *Connecticut Walks Book*. Entering the woods, the Tippecansett Trail passes a fire tower and goes south, then southwest, descending gradually through mixed woods with areas of ferns, partially covered boulders, and laurel. The trail crosses Parris Brook, then swings right for a short distance. Tippecansett Pond is visible through the trees to the right. Off the trail 100 yd. north is an old cellar hole and other interesting foundations. (*Note:* Part of this section passes through South County Rod and Gun Club property and is closed to all except members during deer hunting season.)

The trail then turns left (southwest) through a cutover forest and at 2.3 mi. reaches an abandoned road (Old Voluntown Rd.) now used as a fire trail. The trail turns left (south) onto this road, and in about 750 ft. a white-blazed side trail leads right 0.1 mi. to Wildcat Spring. Continuing south, the main trail reaches a trail junction at 2.8 mi. Here the Deep Pond Trail begins and follows the road to the left, while the Tippecansett Trail turns right along an eroded road, soon passing a barricade. About 500 ft. past the barricade a blue-blazed side trail leads right to the Pachaug Trail. In another 0.5 mi. the Pachaug Trail (see *Connecticut Walks Book*) enters from the right. Here the two trails cross a dirt road and continue another 0.5 mi. following both yellow and blue blazes to Beach Pond on RI 165.

The Pachaug Trail leaves right (west) onto RI 165 and the Tippecansett Trail crosses RI 165 (south) and proceeds along the east shore of the pond. About 0.7 mi. from RI 165 a short white-blazed side trail on the left leads 200 ft. to the top of Hemlock Ledge. From the Ledge there is a fine view back to Beach Pond. At this junction another white-blazed trail leads ahead to Deep Pond. Turning sharp right (west), the Tippecansett Trail leads through hemlock and then oak woods to the Connecticut line. Turning left (south) the trail continues on abandoned town roads.

About 2.6 mi. from RI 165, the blue-blazed Dye Hill Trail leads off to the left, while the Tippecansett Trail continues ahead another 0.4 mi. to RI 138.

Crossing RI 138, the trail travels south on an old road, then makes a sharp right. (*Note:* From here the trail will run through private property owned by the Narragansett Council of the Boy Scouts of America.) The trail proceeds through open woods, thick laurel, and second growth to Dinosaur Rock. At this point the trail formerly turned left onto a section now closed at the request of the Boy Scouts. The new route bears right, drops to a bog bridge, and ascends a steep ledge to the Rhode Island–Connecticut line. It then continues south to open ledges and a junction with the Narragansett Trail. The blue-blazed Narragansett Trail and the yellow-blazed Tippecansett Trail run together for 0.5 mi. to Yawgoog Rd., where the Tippecansett Trail ends and the Narragansett Trail switches to yellow blazes and continues back into Rhode Island.

Tippecansett Trail

Distances from Stepstone Falls

to shelter: 0.3 mi. (10 min.)
to fire tower: 1.2 mi. (40 min.)
to Old Voluntown Rd.: 2.3 mi. (1 hr. 10 min.)
to Deep Pond Trail: 2.8 mi. (1 hr. 25 min.)
to side trail to Pachaug Trail: 3 mi. (1 hr. 30 min.)
to Pachaug Trail: 3.5 mi. (1 hr. 45 min.)
to Beach Pond (RI 165): 4 mi. (2 hr.)
to Hemlock Ledge: 4.7 mi. (2 hr. 25 min.)
to Dye Hill Trail: 6.6 mi. (3 hr. 20 min.)
to RI 138: 7 mi. (3 hr. 30 min.)
to Narragansett Trail: 8.4 mi. (4 hr. 15 min.)
to Yawgoog Rd.: 8.9 mi. (4 hr. 30 min.)

Deep Pond Trail (NCAMC)

The Deep Pond Trail, marked with white plastic blazes, starts at the southern junction of the Tippecansett Trail and the abandoned Old Voluntown Rd. It follows the road east 0.3 mi. to a junction with a dirt road, which it follows south 0.7 mi. to RI 165. Crossing RI 165, the trail enters a dirt road at the Roscoe M. Dexter Memorial Management Area sign. The trail follows the dirt road for 0.5 mi. and turns left into the woods. (The road, marked with white blazes, leads 0.5 mi. to a junction with the Tippecansett Trail near Hemlock Ledge.) The Deep Pond Trail proceeds through wooded areas and over some rock outcroppings for 0.8 mi. to a junction with the Dye Hill Trail, and then ends at Deep Pond 0.1 mi. beyond.

Deep Pond Trail (NCAMC)

Distances from Tippecansett Trail:

to RI 165 (Roscoe Dexter): 1 mi. (30 min.)

to turnoff from dirt road into woods: 1.5 mi. (45 min.)

to Dye Hill Trail: 2.3 mi. (1 hr. 10 min.)

to Deep Pond: 2.4 mi. (1 hr. 15 min.)

to Hemlock Ledge: via dirt road 2 mi. (1 hr.)

Dye Hill Trail (NCAMC)

The Dye Hill Trail, marked with blue blazes, starts at a junction with the Tippecansett Trail 0.4 mi. north of RI 138. The trail follows a dirt road 0.6 mi. and turns left into the woods. (This point is 0.2 mi. from the end of Kenny Hill Rd., the closest road access to the trail. See below for directions). From the dirt road the trail continues east 0.3 mi. to a junction where it joins the Brushy Brook loop. The Brushy Brook Trail goes straight ahead and to the left, with the Dye Hill Trail following the branch to the left. The two trails slab the side of Dye Hill for about 0.2 mi., then drop downhill to a flat area and then to a boulder field, in the middle of which is the rather small Brushy Brook. After the boulder field the trails make a sharp left turn and go through a flat area, then climb steeply to a junction where the Brushy Brook Trail leaves to the right. The Dye Hill Trail continues 0.1 mi. to its end at a junction with the Deep Pond Trail.

To reach the Dye Hill Trail from Kenny Hill Rd. (formerly Dye Hill Rd.), follow RI 138 south from the Tippecansett Trail crossing for about 0.7 mi., then turn left onto Grassy Pond Rd. Kenny Hill Rd. is reached in 0.4 mi. Cars can drive 0.4 mi. up the road, at which point it becomes private; limited parking is available here.

Follow the road on foot for another 0.2 mi. to a junction with the Dye Hill Trail, which continues straight ahead on the road toward the Tippecansett Trail or to the right into the woods, heading toward the Brushy Brook Trail and Deep Pond.

Dye Hill Trail

Distances from the Tippecansett Trail:
>   *to* turnoff into woods: 0.6 mi. (20 min.)
>   *to* first junction with Brushy Brook Trail: 0.9 mi. (30 min.)
>   *to* Brushy Brook: 1.2 mi. (40 min.)
>   *to* second junction with Brushy Brook Trail: 1.5 mi. (50 min.)
>   *to* Deep Pond Trail: 1.6 mi. (55 min.)

Brushy Brook Trail (NCAMC)

The Brushy Brook Trail is a loop trail with no direct road access. It can only be reached via the Deep Pond Trail or the Dye Hill Trail. The shortest approach is 0.5 mi. via Kenny Hill Rd. and the Dye Hill Trail. Leaving the Dye Hill Trail, the white-blazed Brushy Brook Trail goes straight ahead and soon reaches a group of stone walls and a spring, marking the site of the old Simon Palmer farm. At 0.2 mi. from the junction, the trail makes a sharp left turn and reaches Brushy Brook a few hundred feet beyond. (*Note:* This flat area is typically very wet in the spring.)

Leaving the brook, the trail goes straight for a couple of hundred feet and then turns left. It continues through an overgrown meadow and then along an up-and-down ridge, reaching the other junction with the Dye Hill Trail at 1 mi. The Brushy Brook Trail follows the Dye Hill Trail to the left, with both white and blue blazes. (To the right, the Dye Hill Trail reaches the Deep Pond Trail in 0.2 mi.) The two trails drop down steeply, run along a ridge, and descend again to a flat area at 1.3 mi. After a short distance the trails turn sharp right, climb over a low hill, and reach a boulder field and a diminished Brushy Brook at 1.4 mi. After crossing the boulders the trails bear left, travel uphill, and then slab Dye Hill before reaching the starting point. From here, turn right to return to Kenny Hill Rd.

Brushy Brook Trail

Distances from Dye Hill Trail junction:
 to Simon Palmer farm: 0.2 mi. (10 min.)
 to Brushy Brook, first crossing: 0.3 mi. (15 min.)
 to Dye Hill/Brushy Brook junction: 1 mi. (40 min.)
 to Brushy Brook, second crossing: 1.4 mi. (50 min.)
 to Dye Hill Trail junction: 1.7 mi. (1 hr.)

Narragansett Trail (NCAMC)

This blue-blazed trail begins in Connecticut (for a description, see *Connecticut Walk Book*) and follows the Connecticut–Rhode Island line south 0.5 mi. to Yawgoog Rd. (This section of the trail coincides with the yellow-blazed Tippecansett Trail described above.) The Narragansett Trail, now marked with yellow blazes, follows Yawgoog Rd. left (east) 0.2 mi., then turns right into the woods. The trail follows the west shore of Yawgoog Pond, ascends to a junction with Boy Scout trails, bears right (south) through native rhododendron thickets, and turns left onto Hopkinton–Rockville Rd. (also called Long Bridge Rd.). The trail exits right from the road in 0.3 mi. onto land owned and managed jointly by the RIDEM, the Audubon Society of Rhode Island, and the Nature Conservancy. (*Note:* This area is designated a National Ecological Area. Please give it due respect.)

 As the trail turns right off the road, there is parking for three cars and a large sign describing the terrain, management, and use. The trail ascends gradually, but ruggedly, over rock ledges, and through rhododendrons and mountain laurel to a high point with pines and blueberry bushes (views right of Ell Pond). Here an unmarked side trail leads right (west) to Ell Pond. Descending abruptly, the trail passes through a cleft in the rock formation, crosses a wet area on a log bridge, and climbs up then down, passing huge hemlocks in a rough rock ledge terrain. The trail then ascends again to a prominent view of Long Pond.

 About 0.5 mi. beyond this lookout, at a point close to and within sight of Canonchet Rd. (Long Pond Fishing Area parking lot), the trail turns right onto an old woods road, continues a few yards, then turns left into the woods and a swampy area where laurel grows profusely. At the western end of Ashville Pond, at the Hopkinton Town Recreation Area (picnicking and swimming in season), the trail ends at a parking area for several cars. (*Note:* The trail formerly continued left 0.5 mi. on Stub Town Rd. to Canonchet Rd., where more parking is available a few hundred yards on the left, close to the eastern end of Ashville Pond. Canonchet Rd. leads north 2.5 mi. to RI 138 and south 1.3 mi. to RI 3.)

Narragansett Trail

Distances from Yawgoog Rd.

to Hopkinton–Rockville Rd. (Long Bridge Rd.): 2.3 mi. (1 hr. 10 min.)

to side path to Ell Pond: 2.8 mi. (1 hr. 30 min.)

to Hopkinton Town Recreation Area: 4.5 mi. (2 hr. 45 min.)

GEORGE WASHINGTON MANAGEMENT AREA

Located in the northwest corner of Rhode Island is the George Washington Management Area, which includes the George Washington Memorial State Forest and the Casimir Pulaski Memorial State Park (contiguous state properties in the towns of Burrillville and Glocester). Several hiking trails are being developed in this "wild country." The Walkabout Trail and its several side trails are already completed. Both state properties offer other attractive opportunities for recreation, including camping at the George Washington Memorial State Forest and cross-country skiing at Pulaski State Park.

Camping permits are issued at the State Forest headquarters, RFD 2, Box 2185, Chepachet, RI 02814 (tel. 401-568-2013).

Refer to the Rhode Island—George Washington Management Area trail map included with this book.

Walkabout Trail (RIDEM)

This loop trail was designed by members of the Rhode Island Department of Natural Resources (now the RIDEM) and marked with white-painted rings. It was originally cut and blazed by a group of Australian sailors in the summer of 1965 while they were waiting for work to be completed on their ship, HMAS Perth (see *Appalachia*, June 1966, pp. 178–179). Since that time the RIDEM has improved the trail and has cleared and marked several side trails.

The usual starting point of the circuit is the George Washington Memorial State Forest picnic area. The entrance to the State Forest is on the north side of US 44, about 22 mi. west of Providence and about 2 mi. east of the Connecticut–Rhode Island line. Upon entering the park at a sign for camping, bear left at the second fork to parking and picnic tables by the reservoir (no fires allowed). The Walkabout Trail starts and ends here.

The main trail is 8 mi. long and is well marked with orange blazes. Two cut-off trails, the first blazed turquoise and the second red, can be used to create shorter circuits of either 2 mi. or 6 mi., respectively.

The Walkabout Trail can also be reached from Pulaski Memorial State Park via the Peck Pond Spur Trail. Follow a road leading about 1 mi. north from US 44 (near the Connecticut– Rhode Island line) to Peck Pond bathing beach and picnic area. (Peck Pond is called Keach Pond on the USGS Thompson, CT quadrangle.) Follow the path right along the edge of the pond past picnic tables and watch for the red-blazed Peck Pond Spur Trail, which leads 0.5 mi. to the Walkabout Trail.

Walkabout Trail

Distance from George Washington Memorial State Forest picnic area to return to picnic area: 8 mi. (4 hr.)

BURLINGAME STATE PARK

Burlingame State Park is located in southwestern Rhode Island near Charlestown. To reach the trailhead, take US 1 west about 1.5 mi. from its junction with RI 2 in Charlestown. Turn right onto Prosser Trail. The entrance to the parking area and picnic area is on the left, about 0.5 mi. north on Prosser Trail.

Vin Gormley Trail (RIDEM)

The Vin Gormley Trail is a scenic 8.5 mi. loop around Watchaug Pond. It is named after John Vincent Gormley in recognition of his many years of work in maintaining this and other trails in the state.

The trail, marked with yellow plastic blazes, starts at the entrance to the parking lot and runs easterly on the park access road 0.1 mi. to Prosser Trail. It turns left onto Prosser Trail and in 0.3 mi. turns left onto Kings Factory Rd. In another 0.2 mi. it turns left off the road into the woods. It soon crosses a blacktop road and continues for 0.8 mi., where an overgrown dirt road leaves on the right. In another 0.2 mi. a second abandoned road goes right. The trail turns left, crosses two small streams on bridges, and crosses a wide dirt road about 2 mi. from the start. (The road runs left to a dead end at Watchaug Pond and right to a barricade at Kings Factory Rd.)

Here the trail dips down to a series of bog bridges (built single-handedly by Vin Gormley) in an area that is very muddy in wet seasons. Climbing a short slope and then turning left and down, the trail makes a long curve toward the right, reaching Buckeye Brook Rd. about 3 mi. from the start. Turning left, the trail follows the road west for about 0.2 mi., crossing Buckeye Brook and then turning left off the road back into the woods. About 1.2 mi. from Buckeye Brook Rd., the trail makes a sharp right turn at a sign warning of an abandoned bridge. In another 0.2 mi. the trail runs very close to Klondike Rd., then curving left, it crosses more bog bridges to Perry Healy Brook.

Crossing the brook and then more bog bridges, the trail curves to the east and comes to another warning sign for the abandoned bridge. Here the trail turns right, crosses some more bog bridges, and reaches the state park camping area. The trail follows the paved camp roads straight ahead toward the camp store. Going around the left side of the store, the trail leaves the state park and traverses the adjoining Kimball Bird Sanctuary. After leaving the sanctuary, the trail continues along a paved road back to its start at the parking area.

Vin Gormley Trail

Distance from parking area
   to return to parking area (loop): 8.5 mi. (4 hr.)

About the Appalachian Mountain Club

The Appalachian Mountain Club pursues an active conservation agenda while encouraging responsible recreation. Our philosophy is that successful, long-term conservation depends on firsthand experience of the natural environment. AMC's 64,000 members pursue interests in hiking, canoeing, skiing, walking, rock climbing, bicycling, camping, kayaking, and backpacking, and—at the same time—help safeguard the environment.

Founded in 1876, the club has been at the forefront of the environmental protection movement. As cofounder of several leading New England environmental organizations, and as an active member working in coalition with these and many other groups, the AMC has successfully influenced legislation and public opinion.

Conservation
The most recent efforts in the AMC conservation program include river protection, Northern Forest Lands policy, Sterling Forest (NY) preservation, and support for the Clean Air Act. The AMC depends upon its active members and grassroots supporters to promote this conservation agenda.

Education
The AMC's education department offers members and the general public a wide range of workshops, from introductory camping to intensive Mountain Leadership School taught on the trails of the White Mountains. In addition, volunteers in each chapter lead hundreds of outdoor activities and excursions and offer introductory instruction in backcountry sports.

Research
The AMC's research department focuses on the forces affecting the ecosystem, including ozone levels, acid rain and fog, climate change, rare flora and habitat protection, and air quality and visibility.

Trails Program
Another facet of the AMC is the trails program, which maintains more than 1,400 miles of trail (including 350 miles of the Appalachian Trail)

and more than 50 shelters in the Northeast. Through a coordinated effort of volunteers, seasonal crews, and program staff, the AMC contributes more than 10,000 hours of public service work each summer in the area from Washington, D.C. to Maine.

In addition to supporting our work by becoming an AMC member, hikers can donate time as volunteers. The club offers four unique weekly volunteer base camps in New Hampshire, Maine, Massachusetts, and New York. We also sponsor ten-day service projects throughout the United States, Adopt-a-Trail programs, trails day events, trail skills workshops, and chapter and camp volunteer projects.

The AMC has a longstanding connection to Acadia National Park. Working in cooperation with the National Park Service and Friends of Acadia, the AMC Trails Program provides many opportunities to preserve the park's resources. These include half-day volunteer projects for guests at AMC's Echo Lake Camp, ten-day service projects, week-long volunteer crews in the fall, and trails day events. For more information on these public service volunteer opportunities, contact the AMC Trails Program, Pinkham Notch Visitor Center, P.O. Box 298, Gorham NH 03581; 603-466-2721.

Alpine Huts

The club operates eight alpine huts in the White Mountains that provide shelter, bunks and blankets, and hearty meals for hikers. Pinkham Notch Visitor Center, at the foot of Mt. Washington, is base camp to the adventurous and the ideal location for individuals and families new to outdoor recreation. Comfortable bunkrooms, mountain hospitality, and home-cooked, family-style meals make Pinkham Notch Visitor Center a fun and affordable choice for lodging. For reservations, call 603-466-2727.

Publications

At the AMC main office in Boston and at Pinkham Notch Visitor Center in New Hampshire, the bookstore and information center stock the entire line of AMC publications, as well as other trail and river guides, maps, reference materials, and the latest articles on conservation issues. Guidebooks and other AMC gifts are available by mail order 1-800-262-4455, or by writing AMC, P.O. Box 298, Gorham NH 03581. Also available from the bookstore or by subscription is *Appalachia,* the country's oldest mountaineering and conservation journal.

Sources of Information

ORGANIZATIONS

Listed below are various organizations that maintain open space and hiking trails in this region, or can provide information about hiking and recreational activities. Many of the publications and maps produced by these organizations are also available at outdoor recreation suppliers and bookstores, as well as at the AMC's Joy St. headquarters.

The Appalachian Trail Conference

The Appalachian Trail Conference (ATC) was organized in 1925 for the purpose of establishing and maintaining the Appalachian Trail as a continuous, marked footpath through the mountains and woods of the eastern United States. It is comprised of the various clubs maintaining sections of the AT, as well as other clubs and organizations interested in the AT and individual dues-paying members. The ATC holds general meetings every other year.

Various periodicals and books about the Appalachian Trail are available from the ATC. Among these is a series of ten guidebooks, with maps, covering the entire length of the trail. Volume 3 of the series covers the AT in Massachusetts and Connecticut.

For information about ATC publications or membership, contact: Appalachian Trail Conference; PO Box 236; Harpers Ferry, WV 25425.

Audubon Society of Rhode Island

The Audubon Society of Rhode Island was founded in 1897 to further proper utilization of natural resources and to carry out a broad conservation education program. Its headquarters at the Powder Mill Ledges Wildlife Refuge houses several collections and an outstanding natural history library. The Society maintains a number of wildlife refuges in the Rhode Island area. Written permission is needed to visit any of the refuges except Powder Mill Ledges. For information on membership and on specific properties, contact: Audubon Society of RI; 12 Sanderson Rd.; Smithfield, RI 02917 (tel. 401-231-6444).

Massachusetts Audubon Society

The Massachusetts Audubon Society is one of the oldest conservation organizations in the world and the largest in New England. Dedicated to conservation, education, and research, its program embraces many services and activities. The Society maintains sixty-six sanctuaries totaling more than 15,461 acres in Massachusetts. Some of these sanctuaries are staffed to provide public-education programs. The Society invites the public to use the trails from sunrise to sunset, seven days a week, throughout the year. A few of the properties have a modest admission charge.

For membership information, or information and maps relating to specific sanctuaries, contact: Mass. Audubon Society; South Great Rd.; Lincoln, MA 01773.

Massachusetts Department of Environmental Management

The Massachusetts Department of Environmental Management's Division of Forests and Parks operates the nation's sixth-largest system of state parks and forests, encompassing more than 250,000 acres. Many of the parks and forests have extensive recreational facilities, and admission fees are generally charged in season. Virtually all of the properties have extensive hiking opportunities, although the condition of individual trails may vary widely.

For general information, contact DEM's Boston headquarters: Division of Forests and Parks; 100 Cambridge Street; Boston, MA 02202 (tel. 617-727-3180). The best source of up-to-date trail information and maps are the individual park offices or DEM's regional offices: Berkshires (413-442-8928); Connecticut River Valley (413-549-1461); Worcester County (508-368-0126); Northeast (508-369-3350); and Southeast (508-866-2580).

Massachusetts Division of Fish and Wildlife

The Massachusetts Division of Fish and Wildlife maintains a series of wildlife management areas for hunting, fishing, and other recreational uses. Hikers using these areas should be aware of open hunting seasons and take appropriate precautions. For information and maps, contact: Massachusetts Division of Fish and Wildlife; Field Headquarters; Westborough, MA 01581 (tel. 508-792-7270).

Metropolitan District Commission

The MDC is a Massachusetts state agency that maintains parkland and recreational facilities in the metropolitan Boston area. It also manages the recreational uses of the Quabbin Reservoir watershed in central Massachusetts. For information about MDC properties, contact: MDC; 20 Somerset St.; Boston, MA 02108 (tel. 617-727-5250).

New England Cartographics

This private company publishes a series of excellent, full-color trail maps covering the major hiking areas of central and western Massachusetts, including Mt. Greylock, the Holyoke Range, Mt. Tom, Mt. Toby, the Quabbin Reservoir, and Wachusett Mtn. For information, contact: New England Cartographics; PO Box 369; Amherst, MA 01004.

New York/New Jersey Trail Conference

This organization, a federation of seventy-five hiking and environmental organizations in the New York/New Jersey area, publishes an excellent waterproof, tear-resistant map covering the trails in the South Taconic region of Connecticut, Massachusetts, and New York. For ordering information, contact: NY/NJ Trail Conference; GPO Box 2250; New York, NY 10116 (tel. 212-685-9699).

Rhode Island Department of Environmental Management

The Division of Forest Environment of the Rhode Island Department of Environmental Management is responsible for all state parks, forests, and outdoor management areas. Many of these properties include developed recreational areas, with camping, picnicking, boating, and other resources. For information and maps, contact: RIDEM, Division of Forest Environment, 260 Arcadia Rd., Hope Valley, RI 02832 (tel. 401-539-2356).

Town Conservation Commissions

This guidebook covers only a few of the many open space properties maintained by local city and town conservation commissions. Most of these properties have walking paths and hiking trails. For further information, contact the local conservation commission, in care of the appropriate city or town hall. Many of these commissions also provide maps of their properties, either free or at a minimal charge.

The Trustees of Reservations

The Trustees of Reservations, a private, nonprofit land conservation organization, was created in 1891 to preserve for public use places of natural beauty and historic interest within the Commonwealth of Massachusetts. Its headquarters are at 572 Essex St., Beverly, MA 01915 (tel. 508-921-1944). Today, The Trustees are custodians of more than 75 open space and historic areas from the Berkshires to Cape Cod, totaling more than 19,500 acres of seashore and woodland, rivers and streams, wetlands, marshes, and wildlife refuges.

It is the policy of The Trustees to acquire and maintain reservations of distinctive character that will satisfy a wide range of public interests. They range from a magnificent summer mansion of the 1890s with formal gardens, to acres of wild beach and salt marsh, to wooded hillsides and quiet riverbanks within minutes of downtown Boston. For the most part the houses are museums, architectural examples of their time. Among these are three National Historic Landmarks. Open space properties are generally managed as natural areas, to be enjoyed for their plants and flowers, topography, wildlife, and scenic beauty. Many of these reservations have unique botanical, geological, and ornithological features. Certain properties are subject to admission fees and time schedules.

Membership in The Trustees of Reservations is open to the public. Members receive a 100-page guidebook to the reservations and free admission to all properties, while helping to support The Trustees' land conservation efforts. For membership information, please send a self-addressed, stamped envelope to the Beverly headquarters. Detailed maps of many Trustee properties are also available for a nominal charge. Contact the Beverly headquarters for additional information.

U.S. Department of the Interior

The U.S. Department of the Interior's Geological Survey (USGS) is a principal source of maps for hiking and outdoor activities. The most commonly used USGS maps are the 7.5-minute quadrangle series, which are available for all of Massachusetts and Rhode Island. These maps have a scale of 1:25,000, meaning that 1 in. on the map equals about 2000 ft. on the ground. They are generally very accurate with respect to terrain and natural features, but trail locations (where shown) may not be up-to-date.

USGS maps are available at most camping and outdoor equipment stores and at some bookstores. They can also be ordered by mail from: Distribution Branch; U.S. Geological Survey; P.O. Box 25286; Denver, CO 80225. Map indexes for each state, and an informative pamphlet entitled "Topographic Maps," are available free of charge.

BOOKS ON NATURAL HISTORY

Listed below are a few of the many excellent books available on the natural history of New England:

Berrill, Michael and Deborah Berrill. *The Sierra Club Naturalist's Guide To The North Atlantic Coast.* San Francisco: Sierra Club Books, 1981. 464 pp.

Connor, Sheila. *New England Natives: A Celebration of People and Trees.* Cambridge, MA: Harvard University Press, 1994. 274 pp.

Jorgensen, Neil. *A Guide to New England's Landscape.* Old Saybrook, CT: The Globe Pequot Press, 1977. 256 pp.

Jorgensen, Neil. *The Sierra Club Naturalist's Guide To Southern New England.* San Francisco: Sierra Club Books, 1978. 417 pp.

Raymo, Chet and Maureen Raymo. *Written In Stone: A Geological History of the Northeastern United States.* Old Saybrook, CT: The Globe Pequot Press, 1989. 163 pp.

Skehan S. J., and James W. *Puddingstone, Drumlins, and Ancient Volcanoes—A Geologic Field Guide Along Historic Trails of Greater Boston.* Weston, MA: Westone Press, Boston College, 1979. 63 pp.

Sutton, Ann and Myron Sutton. *Eastern Forests: An Audubon Society Nature Guide.* New York: Alfred A. Knopf, Inc., 1985. 638 pp.

Index

To Massachusetts and Rhode Island
Forests, Parks, and Preserves

(*Note:* this index locates forests, parks, and preserves on the statewide sheet map folded into the back-cover pocket of this guide. Please refer to that map when using this index.)

Index